THEATERS of TRANSLATION

STRODE STUDIES IN EARLY MODERN LITERATURE AND CULTURE

Michelle M. Dowd, series editor

THEATERS of TRANSLATION

COSMOPOLITAN VERNACULARS IN SHAKESPEARE'S ENGLAND

ANDREW S. KEENER

THE UNIVERSITY OF ALABAMA PRESS
Tuscaloosa

The University of Alabama Press
Tuscaloosa, Alabama 35487-0380
uapress.ua.edu

Typeface: Plantin

Cover image: Detail from Noël de Berlaimont, *Colloquia et dictionariolum octo linguarum*, 1631; 418 B514; courtesy of the Charles Deering McCormick Library of Special Collections and University Archives, Northwestern University.
Cover design: Lori Lynch

Cataloging-in-Publication data is available from the Library of Congress.
ISBN: 978-0-8173-2232-8 (cloth)
ISBN: 978-0-8173-6204-1 (paper)
E-ISBN: 978-0-8173-9567-4

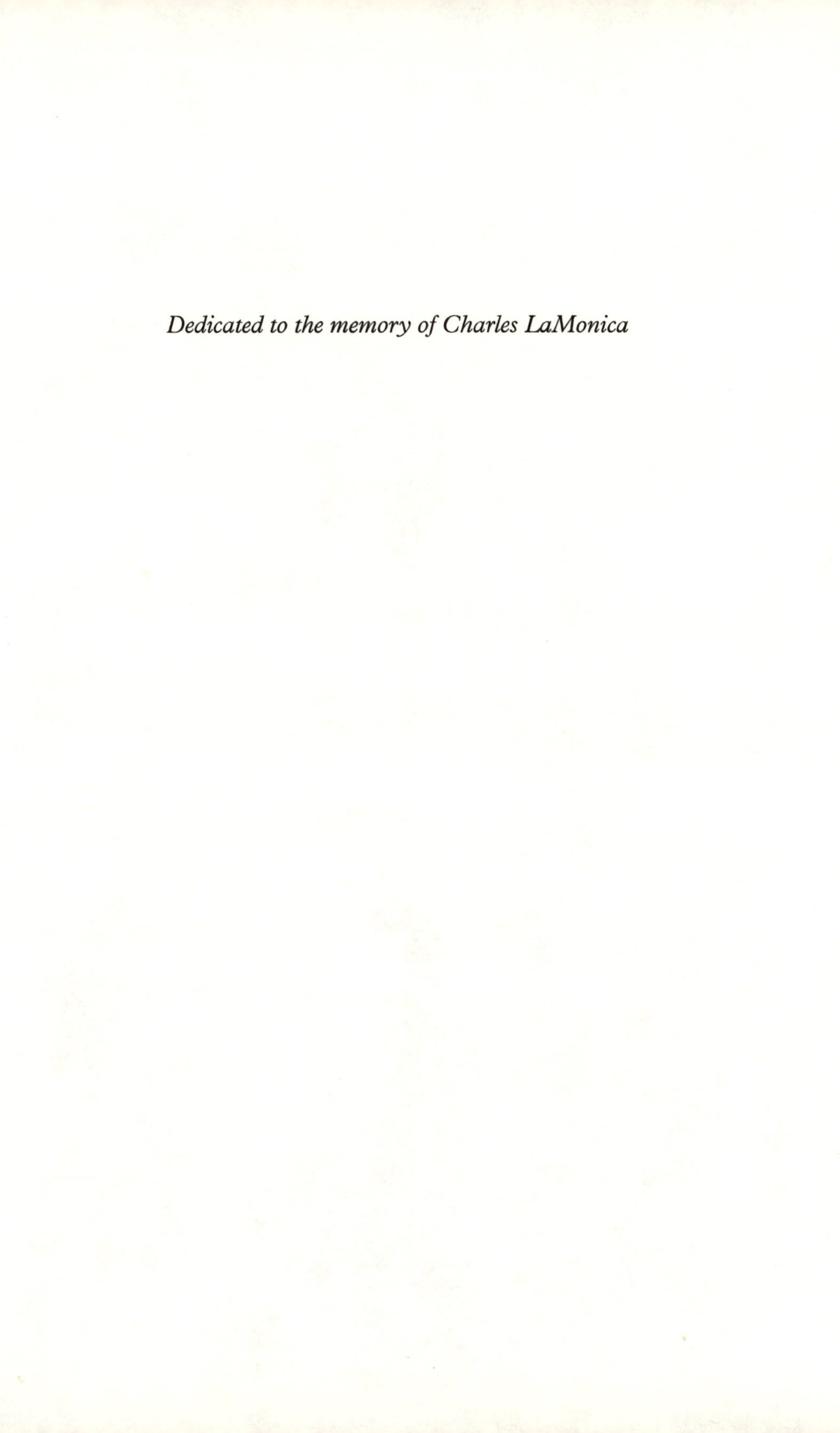

Dedicated to the memory of Charles LaMonica

Contents

List of Figures | ix

A Note on Transcription and Citation of Sources | xi

Acknowledgments | xiii

1. Shakespeare's "World of Words" in Renaissance England | 1

2. "For the Easier Understanding": Language Instruction in Thomas Kyd's *Spanish Tragedy* | 36

3. Mary Sidney Herbert's "Fatall Change": *The Tragedy of Antony* and the Countess of Pembroke's Religious Translation | 69

4. "O, the Generation of Languages": Exchanges and Interchangeabilities in William Haughton's *Englishmen for My Money* | 99

5. "All Translations Are Reputed Femalls": The Propagation of Women's Speech in Ben Jonson's *Epicene* | 132

Coda: Toward a "New World of Words," from John Florio to Samuel Johnson | 161

Notes | 167

Bibliography | 213

Index | 237

Figures

1.1 German annotations in Shakespeare's Second Folio of 1632, Venice, Italy | 2

1.2 "Associatio Linguarum" frontispiece for James Howell, *Lexicon Tetraglotton* | 15

1.3 Noël de Berlaimont, *Colloquia et Dictionariolum octo Linguarum* | 19

1.4 Janus-Mercury-Mars head from the 1662 frontispiece for Berlaimont's *Colloquia* | 24

2.1 Beehive frontispiece for John Baret, *An Alvearie or Quadruple Dictionarie* | 41

2.2 Gabriel Harvey's annotated copy of *An Italian Grammer*, title page | 46

2.3 Gabriel Harvey's inscriptions at the end of his copy of *An Italian Grammer* | 49

2.4 Italian annotations in a copy of Thomas Kyd's *The Spanish Tragedy* | 53

2.5 Woodcut illustration for Thomas Kyd's *The Spanish Tragedy* | 60

3.1 Petrarch verses inscribed in an Italian grammar owned by the Sidney family | 79

3.2 Henry Sidney and Mary Dudley Sidney annotations, in multiple languages | 81

3.3 An early reader's annotations in the Sidney family's Italian grammar | 82

3.4 Engraved portrait of Mary Sidney Herbert, Countess of Pembroke | 85

4.1 Frontispiece for the 1631 edition of Berlaimont's *Colloquia et Dictionariolum* | 104

4.2 Frontispiece for the 1662 edition of Berlaimont's *Dictionariolum et Colloquia* | 104

4.3 "Acquaintance" section in frontispiece for Richard Brathwait, *The English Gentleman* | 106

4.4 Typographic variety in Berlaimont, *Colloquia et Dictionariolum* | 110

4.5 Handwritten annotations in a copy of Berlaimont's *Colloquia et Dictionariolum* | 111

4.6 Financial inscriptions in a copy of Berlaimont's *Colloquia et Dictionariolum* | 112

5.1 An early reader's English annotations in Pietro Aretino, *I Ragionamenti* | 149

5.2 An edition of Aretino's *I Ragionamenti* with the imprint "Cosmopoli" | 150

5.3 Ben Jonson's inscribed copy of Aretino's *I Ragionamenti* | 152

5.4 An early reader's classically oriented annotations in the text of Ben Jonson's *Epicene* | 158

C.1 Owner's inscriptions in William Thomas, *Principal Rules of the Italian Grammer* | 162

A Note on Transcription and Citation of Sources

When quoting directly from early modern textual sources, I have retained original spelling and punctuation, including i/j and u/v, although I change the "long s" (ſ) to short (s), for legibility; I have additionally made "vv" to appear as "w." Original italics are also retained.

When referring to early modern titles, I use shortened titles in my discussion but employ longer versions in the notes and bibliography, which use original spelling but are regularized for i/j, u/v, the "long s," and vv/w. STC and Wing numbers appear in the bibliography for readers wishing to locate a particular edition I am citing.

Acknowledgments

The appearance of this book in the world would not be possible without many people, and I feel fortunate to be able to make my gratitude known here. My first words of thanks go to the three scholars who, about a decade ago, helped me bring the seeds of this project into being in Northwestern University's Department of English. I owe a great deal to Jeffrey Masten, who provided countless insights and generous support as I conducted the research on which this book is based. Susan Phillips and William N. West helped me see what this project could become and offered robust support for its attention to multilingual language manuals and for the element of theatrical performance. In ways big and small, this project also grew through my conversations with Northwestern's spectacular community of early modernists: Kasey Evans, Martin Mueller, Cynthia Nazarian, Regina Schwartz, Laurie Shannon, and Wendy Wall. Additionally, without the support of library staff at Northwestern University. This work would be far less concrete. I owe thanks to Scott Krafft, Nick Munagian, Jason Nargis, and Sigrid Perry; I also am grateful to Josh Honn.

I am very grateful to fellow early modernists whose conversation about Renaissance literature and culture, language learning, and book history and bibliography gave me particularly valuable insights for this project as it has developed over the years. Some of these discussions have been more writerly in nature, and for those I am especially thankful. A doctoral research seminar at the Newberry Library led by Lisa Freeman and Mary Beth Rose provided critical guiding support for this project's origins, and I owe Brad Hunt for other opportunities to share my work there. Seminars at the Shakespeare Association of America convened by Alan Stewart, Lehua Yim, Karen Newman, Bernadette Andrea, and Abdulhamit Arvas—and one that I co-convened with Claire Bourne—have strengthened my approach to the sources and methods in this book, while also helping me better understand my own motivations and goals as a researcher. I would also like to thank Laetitia Sansonetti and Sophie Lemercier-Goddard for allowing me the chance to share my work with the Université de Paris-Nanterre and at the Ecole Normale Supérieur de Lyon. Additionally, I offer specific and abundant thanks to Chris Albi, Katie Blankenau, Anne Boemler, Claire Bourne, Casey Caldwell, Meghan Costa, Rebecca Fall, Aaron Greenberg, Megan Heffernan, Lee Huttner, Joseph Mansky, Harris Mercer, Simon Nyi, Stephanie Pentz, Will Pierce, Raashi Rastogi, Sheryl Reiss, Elizabeth Rodriguez, Marjorie Rubright, Kathryn Vomero Santos, Whitney Sperrazza, Seth Swanner, Whitney Taylor, Mara Wade, Simone Waller, Sarah Wilson, Emily Wood, Amanda Zoch, Adam Zucker, and Michael Zampelli, SJ, for reading and commenting on prior versions of the arguments that appear in these pages and some that do not, and for offering helpful comments and suggestions on those words. Like many people, I wish that the pandemic had not hobbled or foiled other scholarly conversations that pertained to this work, since it is not just the written exchanges but also the in-person conversation that, for me, make scholarship such a joyful endeavor and something intrinsically worth the doing.

I owe my thanks to a host of other conversations with brilliant early modernists, many of which took place at universities, libraries, and conferences, and all of which have strengthened my thinking and fortified me in times of doubt: Anston Bosman, Daniel Blank, Liza Blake, Meaghan Brown, Josh Calhoun, A. E. B. Coldiron, Megan Cook, Heidi Craig, Loren Cressler, Chris Crosbie, Andy Crow, Margreta de Grazia, Carla Della Gatta, Laura Estill, Alan Farmer, Will Fisher, Heather Froehlich, John Gallagher, Joey Gamble, John Garrison, Christine Griffiths, Stephen Guy-Bray, Matthew Harrison, Adam Hooks, Jonathan Hope, Michel Jourde, Jessica Keene, Andy Kesson, András Kiséry, Jonathan Lamb, Kathleen Lynch, Tara Lyons, Ellen McKay, Dianne Mitchell, Jorge Mojarro, Marissa Nicosia, Hillary Nunn, Alexander Paulssen-Lash, Aysha Pollnitz, Vim Pasupathi, Jason Rosenholtz-Witt, Christopher Shirley, Simran Thadani, Jacob Tootalian, Whitney Trettien, Susan Valladares, Katherine Walker, Sarah Werner, Michael Witmore, Jessica Wolfe, and Julian Yates. It gives me pleasure to thank each of you, along with all others whose insights and suggestions have fed into this work.

The research that resulted in this book had the great privilege of funding support through fellowship programs and grants offered by the following organizations and institutions: the Bibliographical Society of America, Columbia University Libraries, the Folger Shakespeare Library, the

Graduate School at Northwestern University, the Harry Ransom Center at the University of Texas at Austin, the Houghton Library at Harvard University, the Huntington Library, the Literary Encyclopedia, the Newberry Library, Princeton University Library, Rare Book School at the University of Virginia, and the Society for the History of Authorship, Reading, and Publishing. I am deeply grateful for this generous financial support, as well as for the expertise, labor, and hours of the library and research staff I met among these centers of research and learning. There are far too many names for me to list here, but I would like to offer special thank-yous to Jill Gage, Juan Gomez, Karen Christianson, Aaron Pratt, Stephen Tabor, David Whitesell, Owen Williams, and Heather Wolfe, without whom I cannot imagine this work's ultimate outcomes.

I would also like to make known my thanks to colleagues at Santa Clara University who, during the years I worked there, helped me move my writing and thinking forward. Particular thanks go to Julie Chang, who organized a chance for me to share my work with the English Department, as well as to Eileen Elrod and Amy Lueck for their welcome insistence on the importance of structured writing time, which I absolutely benefited from. Evelyn Ferraro, Matt Gomes, and Heather Turner provided writerly camaraderie; for their conversation and scholarly kindness, I also thank John Hawley and Andy Garavel, SJ. Michelle Burnham, Kirstyn Leuner, Nadia Nasr, and Kelci Baughman McDowell helped me keep my bibliographical skills sharp in ways that have greatly benefited this project's later stages, and Danielle Morgan and Aparajita Nanda helped me think through my plans for this book's development. I owe Jackie Hendricks, Phyllis Brown, and Aldo Billingslea for sustained conversation on premodern and theater-related things, and Kurt Schab and Sarah Banducci for their friendship and support. I'm also grateful to Patricia Parker, Ivan Lupić, Roland Greene, John Mustain, Nick Fenech, and the community of early modern scholars, graduate students, and librarians at Stanford University who extended welcome to me on several occasions and gave me opportunities to share my work and engage in rewarding discussion.

On more than one occasion, I set this work aside, in the midst of moving, marriage, and a new employment path. Sometimes, I felt that the book's chances were "over." Yet I returned to it eventually with new energy, steadily on weekends and evenings, no small thanks to Michelle Dowd at the University of Alabama's Hudson Strode Program in Renaissance Studies and Dan Waterman at the University of Alabama Press. Both have been unfailingly supportive since they have known about this project. And I must make known my abundant thanks to the anonymous readers who saw value in the arguments and offered welcome suggestions. Thanks also to Bonny McLaughlin for her indexing work. Any remaining errors in the text are my own.

The discussion of *The Merry Wives of Windsor* in chapter 1 appeared originally in a much-abbreviated form as "Cosmopolitan Windsor: Seduction and Translation in Shakespeare's 'English' Comedy," *Shakespeare Studies* 48 (2020): 139–45, and a slightly longer version of the same argument appeared as "Windsor's World of Words: Multilingualism in *The Merry Wives of Windsor*," *English Literary Renaissance* 51, no. 3 (2021): 409–41. A version of the treatment of *Epicene* in chapter 5, meanwhile, first appeared as "Jonson's 'Italian Riddle': *Epicene* and the Translation of Female Speech," *Shakespeare Quarterly* 65, no. 2 (2014): 120–39. I am grateful for the permission to reprint this material.

My family has been there for me from the beginning with steady encouragement, love, and financial support for my education, all of which underpin the hours and interests that culminated in this book. I am so grateful for Charlé LaMonica, Stephen Keener, Tonya Keener, Margaret Keener, and Roberto Quercia, for Stephanie, Max and Emily Learner, and all the extended network of Chavis, Keener, and LaMonica family and cousins: I love you. I feel so fortunate for the boundless friendship and intellectual and emotional support of Conor Schlick and Santosh Chittegoppe, among many other friends from Chestnut Hill to Rogers Park to Santa Clara, and in North Carolina, too. I especially wish three people were here to see this work come into being: Robert Keener, Jo Anne Keener, and Kristen Keener. My greatest thanks go to a fellow reader and a huge supporter of this project and of me as a person, whom I was lucky to meet at the Folger Shakespeare Library on February 4, 2011—a day that changed my life forever in the best possible way. My thanks and my love to you, Mary Learner, and to our little C. as well.

THEATERS of TRANSLATION

| *Chapter One* |

Shakespeare's "World of Words" in Renaissance England

The fourth act of *The Merry Wives of Windsor* (ca. 1597–1598), a play traditionally known as "Shakespeare's English comedy," begins—in the folio text, at least—with a lesson in translation.[1] Here, the Welsh parson and schoolmaster Sir Hugh Evans quizzes young William Page on Latin terminology as his mother looks on. As many critics have noticed, this episode draws on the widely circulated text of William Lilly and John Colet's *Short Introduction of Grammar*, a Latin language manual one might expect to see in Shakespeare's time. However, the lesson has another rather unexpected participant: the French Doctor Caius's housekeeper, Mistress Quickly, whose interjections, as Patricia Parker and Elizabeth Pittenger have noted, expose the links in this play between language learning, translation, and reproductive and erotic vocabularies.[2] Her remarks punctuate the schooling session:

EVANS. What is your genitive case plural, William?
WILLIAM. Genitive case?
EVANS. Ay.
WILLIAM. *Genitivo horum, harum, horum.*
QUICKLY. 'Vengeance of Jenny's case, fie on her! Never name her, child, if she be a whore.[3]

Here, "case" points in both genitive and genital directions. In this scene and others, critics have named Mistress Quickly a source of unschooled malapropism, a "loose" challenger of masculinist pedagogy, even an emblem of incipient English national dominance.[4] Yet, alternatively, one might perceive in this episode instead a dramatization of the importance of education to the capital of copious linguistic "store."[5] Quickly's Latin here may be less than perfect, and she does seem to mock Doctor Caius's accented

English in her first onstage appearance. But if one broadens Evans's lesson to include her as another student rather than a surplus character or interjector, if one lingers on the multilingual elements that her language introduces into the comedy and keeps in focus her mobile status as a "go-between," a different and more cosmopolitan figure comes into view.

As if to further underscore the cosmopolitan dimensions of this chambermaid character, and in a manner that extends beyond Latin to include Europe's variety of vernacular languages, one seventeenth-century reader of *Merry Wives* redesignated Mistress Quickly in a Second Folio's margin as a German woman: "Enter *Frau Schnellfuss*" (figure 1.1).[6] Complementing not only the play's mysterious, offstage "cozen Germans," but also the translingual manner in which Caius hails his housemaid in the play's folio text with "*de-peech quickly*" (sig. D3v), one sees in this particular copy a Germanized quick-foot, "Schnellfuss."[7] Strikingly, this macaronic inscription occurs right at the moment when Quickly is named a "messenger to this paltry knight" (i.e., Sir John Falstaff) (2.1.143–44), fusing the notions of message carrying and linguistic conversion in relation to her character's function—and, in an early modern hand. These bilingual markings appear amid an array of other annotations throughout the play's text and the volume; for instance, a note in what seems to be a different, secretary hand reads, "in prag" (Prague) (in *King Lear*, sig. 2t1r), and dozens of underlined words and "N.B." marks surface in the text of *Hamlet*. Did this German-marked Second Folio pass through what is now Czechia while en

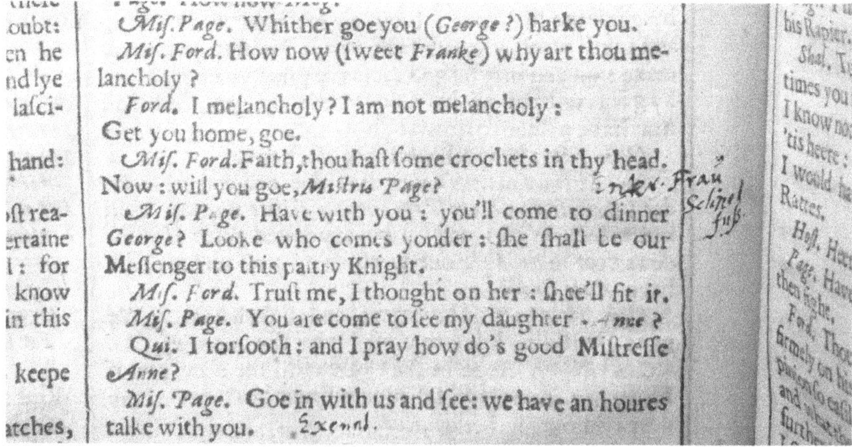

FIGURE 1.1 William Shakespeare, *Mr. William Shakespeares Comedies, Histories, and Tragedies*, 1632, sig. D4v. Rari 0139. Photograph by the author, and reproduced with permission of the Biblioteca Nazionale Marciana, Venice, Italy.

route to its current home in Venice, Italy? Did an owner, or some combination of owners, treat it as a kind of lexicon of English "hard words," as one Continental reader of Christopher Marlowe's *Edward II* seems to have done?[8] It seems that this volume's annotations, indicating entrances and exits, may be witnesses to the phenomenon Anston Bosman has termed "Renaissance intertheater," a theater of the in-between, both "international and multilingual."[9] After all, this Second Folio's annotations evoke, even amplify, Mistress Quickly's tendency to cross boundaries and mix languages—an exclamation of "whore" indexing translingual "store"—and for an early modern reader, as well. Here, an English "messenger" character based on the Italian theater's *mezzana* archetype (in-*mezzo*, in-the-middle) is rechristened as a German *Frau*, during the early modern era, and quite possibly on the European Continent, too.[10] Occupying a playful position in a language lesson and serving as a "go-between" among the characters of *Merry Wives*, Mistress Quickly also goes between languages, nations, and literary traditions in the pages of this striking Second Folio.

Connected Theaters, Connected Language-Learning Books

Taking up border-crossing examples such as this one, *Theaters of Translation* demonstrates connections between multilingual manuals, grammars, and dictionaries for nonclassical, vernacular languages and works of drama, both on the page and on the stage. Europe's polyglot language-learning publications can be understood as a cohesive group of materials, and they have been examined recently in studies by John Considine and John Gallagher.[11] While acknowledging the distinctive, genre-specific qualities of these multilingual, pedagogically purposed books, I exhibit in this study a variety of features these publications share with plays, drawing on striking evidence across these texts' typography, marginalia, and binding arrangements, as well as in their formal and thematic elements. In analyzing these connections, though scholarship on early modern England's literature traditionally champions "the triumph of the English language" and its progress toward today's more standardized forms, *Theaters of Translation* investigates the interval between the Latin lingua franca and the consolidation of a more modern-looking English.[12]

This was a tidal moment of linguistic diversity for authors, playgoers, and readers. Adopting the complexities of the schoolroom-to-playhouse paradigm (chiefly Latin-focused) proposed by Lynn Enterline, my study explores both the vernacular territory of Renaissance education and the consequences of dramatists studying, copying out, and imitating or adapting literature in foreign vernaculars.[13] It also, however, considers the possibilities language manuals and dictionaries held out to "new audiences in new spaces," to use Gallagher's phrase, including for women and men in less educationally privileged circumstances.[14] In this sense, my investigation captures as well both the radically egalitarian "intelligence of the book" and the emancipation of the spectator (through the idiom of translation) as discussed by theorist Jacques Rancière.[15] Adopting these terms circumvents the usual tendency to split readers or theater audiences into "educated" and "ignorant" segments, those who got the joke and those who did not. Instead, I highlight the ways a play itself, through its linguistic substance in the text and through performance, constituted the moment of learning in the first place—potentially opening audiences to multiple languages.

Indeed, *Theaters of Translation* analyzes instances of linguistic multiplicity around and within the English language to shed light on the texts and embodied exchanges associated with the vernacular schoolroom and the playhouse. Within this crucial historical moment I am investigating, Carla Mazzio perceives "a range of distinctly *English* concerns about linguistic incoherence" signaling to her "a profound ambivalence about an increasingly alienated and scattered tongue."[16] While concurring with Mazzio's emphasis on the diversity within English at this moment, a view shared by many critics, my approach focuses on the period's more permissive and cosmopolitan attitudes toward diverse vernacular languages, both in print and in performance. In this way, my analysis builds on the recent investigations of Margaret Tudeau-Clayton, who perceives in the early modern era a "discursive struggle" between the translingual *copia* exemplified by the works of figures such as the translator and lexicographer John Florio and, on the other hand, a plainspoken, reformation-powered approach to language contesting and curtailing it.[17] Similarly, I am interested not only in eloquence but in a variety of intersecting competences with a number of vernacular languages, including English (or perhaps, to use Tudeau-Clayton's wording, "Englishes"). In proffering this picture of multiplicities, *Theaters of Translation* uncovers both the constructive influence of vernacular polyglossia on drama in Renaissance England—and, occasionally, beyond—and the implications of such translinguistic productions toward a broader understanding of early modern translation.

In restoring attention to this period of linguistic diversity and its intercourse with printed and staged drama, *Theaters of Translation* also aims to alter prevailing narratives of English national consolidation and, in doing so, to bridge them to research on the transnational dimensions of England and its emergent imperial character. In the past three decades, scholarship has furnished a compelling and mostly cohesive story: that the sixteenth century witnessed not only the consolidation of the English language but also the incipient stages of English nationhood.[18] This picture structures current research in substantive ways; for instance, the field has witnessed hundreds of monographs studying a particular topic "in Early Modern England." However, other critics attentive to Europe's early modern travelers and emergent colonial and racial discourses have begun to address the transnational and transatlantic scope of early modern English thought as well, along with the implications of these discourses on both human subjectivities and (proto)national formations in relation to literary and theatrical forms.[19] Aligning particularly with a subset of scholars focused on language, translation, and lexicography within the European context, and assuming a place within the broader array of multimethod and multidisciplinary attempts to analyze the "transnational," "global," or "cosmopolitan" Renaissance, I elucidate the ways that multiple printed vernaculars circulating within Renaissance England overlapped, intersected, and constituted conceptions of language that were more expansive than what critics have traditionally assumed.[20] Not only did these "worlds of words," to borrow John Florio's phrase, bring foreign tongues in print to readers and writers in England; they also contributed to, conditioned, and shaped the period's drama at the hands of playwrights including Thomas Kyd, Mary Sidney Herbert, William Haughton, and Ben Jonson, as well as those playwrights' printers, booksellers, theatrical audiences, and readers.

In focusing on connections between multilingual language publications and Renaissance drama, *Theaters of Translation* also builds on recent contributions to theater studies, particularly those employing transnational approaches. Anston Bosman has already advocated for connecting the disparate national histories of early modern drama through his useful term "Renaissance intertheater." "Against the isolated theaters of *or*," he states, polyglot nomadic players throughout Europe "counterposed an intertheater of *and*."[21] Mapping the transnational European picture in Bosman's work back onto England itself, I aim to complicate current theater studies of Renaissance cosmopolitanism in London. Indeed, these studies often assimilate or reify the insular generic terms of "city comedy" or "London comedy," terms that I will question in the course of this study.[22] Seeking the worlds of words in but pointing beyond England, my analysis considers the in-betweens, border crossings, and mobilities of the period's drama. *Theaters of Translation*, that is, examines the intertheater within. I employ Bosman's term alongside the influential work of Louise George Clubb, who offers in her scholarship a useful approach to transnationally circulating "theatergrams": units, figures, actions, topoi, and framing patterns that could be combined and reassembled for particular dramatic effects across today's taken-for-granted national boundaries; I adapt this concept to analyze what I call "theatergrammatical elements" including but not limited to drama.[23] Finally, though I conduct this research with a focus on England, and specifically London, I am alert to the relevant ways England's polyglot and translated drama came to be legible, transportable, and vendible in Continental Europe as well (as the Venice Second Folio suggests). After all, Shakespeare's First Folio was advertised for sale in a German bookfair catalog months before its printing was completed in England.[24] I am arguing that there is much more to be made out of details such as these, details that have been obscured or ignored because they do not always accord with prevailing, nationally focused pictures of Renaissance literature in England.

To this end, in *Theaters of Translation* I employ a bibliographical approach attentive to physical evidence linking early modern multilingual dictionaries, grammars, and dialogue books with printed drama. In this way, I build on the pioneering early modern book history scholarship of William H. Sherman and Jeffrey Todd Knight, who show how "used books" and *Sammelbände* of the period retain signs of "material intertextuality," suggestive evidence for Renaissance researchers of today.[25] My method therefore involves some of what Stephen Best and Sharon Marcus would term "surface reading," though in a manner attentive to the various "depths," historical and material, of handpress-era books: the thicknesses of inks on paper, the depressions made by pieces of new and worn type, the sewing or pasting of paper onto other paper or boards, leather, or cardstock, all across the long histories of these objects' lifetimes.[26]

Indeed, from my examination of over 1,500 printed volumes and manuscript materials at nearly fifty libraries in Europe and North America, I have found substantial proof of overlooked connections between language-learning publications and playbooks. In particular, I study the ways that the elements of typography, handwriting, and binding bring together these textual genres, which otherwise might be considered on separate terms. Attending not only to the dramatic and linguistic texts at the center of this study, then, but also the production, circulation, and use of the *books* in which they appeared, I show how vernacular languages and performance intersected in conspicuous but previously unnoticed ways. In the remainder of this chapter and the chapters that follow, I use this evidence to substantiate my claims for a more cosmopolitan English Renaissance theater than is commonly understood, and along translingual lines perceptible in textual and performative contexts.

Engaging in detail with the actual material objects of early modern language learning and translation has resulted in some remarkable finds and new connections.[27] In chapter 2, I discuss how the sixteenth-century scholar Gabriel Harvey bound together and annotated an Italian grammar and Continental playbooks. Although they have since been separated and acquired by three different research libraries, the segments of this *Sammelband* can be imaginatively reunited to reflect on the ways Harvey used language-learning books and plays together. In chapter 3, I analyze a bilingual Italian-English dictionary the provenance of which was previously unknown to scholars and that appears to have been annotated by Mary Sidney Herbert, the Countess of Pembroke, during her childhood. Not only do these annotations offer a new, unparalleled view into Sidney Herbert's English rendering of Petrarch's "Trionfo della Morte"; they also provide a view into the ways translation defined her literary practice more broadly, including in her closet drama *The Tragedy of Antony*. Chapter 4 examines Noël de Berlaimont's popular, widely published multilingual language manual, the *Colloquia et Dictionariolum*, scrutinizing unnoticed aspects of its typography while also focusing on copies annotated and interleaved by particular owners. Close attention to the *Colloquia*, which was compiled and published with merchants in mind, sheds new light on William Haughton's merchant comedy *Englishmen for My Money*. In chapter 5, I examine a copy of Pietro Aretino's erotic dialogues, the *Ragionamenti*, which was once owned by the playwright Ben Jonson. I reveal that this seldom-discussed volume ranks among the Continental literary materials out of which the dramatist fashioned his comedy *Epicene*. The chapters that follow discuss a host of other unique bibliographical examples—annotated multilingual dictionaries or playbooks inscribed with foreign languages mimicking the books' typographies—that show, as clearly as can be glimpsed today, early modern readers and playgoers interacting with their texts. Through this material-textual evidence, I argue, one can apprehend and analyze the workings of cosmopolitan vernaculars in early modern England.

Though it focuses on vernacular languages and translation in early modern published volumes such as these, *Theaters of Translation* also examines the productive interplay of performance and print. Indeed, though multilingual language-learning books from this era surely captured something of the spoken exchanges playing out in England's schoolrooms and streets, these publications also helped shape the staged cosmopolitanisms of the theater. My analysis therefore builds on András Kiséry and Cyndia Susan Clegg's studies of the playhouse's ability to communicate specialized knowledges to particular audiences, as well as Claire M. L. Bourne's recent analysis of the relationship between early modern book design and dramaturgy.[28] Specifically, I examine the ways works of drama delivered portions of language-learning manuals and dictionaries to playgoers, or, in the cases of closet drama or texts carefully crafted for reading (such as Jonson's *Workes*), to readers who might envision polyglot exchanges within a "theater of one's own mind." Such an approach shortens the categorical distance between language dialogues in diminutive published formats (such as John Florio's Italian-English dialogues in quarto, or Pierre Erondelle's *The French Garden* in octavo) and dramatic playbooks issued in similarly compact deliveries—sometimes by the same stationers.[29] Though they occupy ostensibly different generic categories, plays and language dialogues share a number of formal features—speech prefixes and dramatis personae catalogs, for instance—as well as thematic concerns. I therefore build on scholars' recent work on the intersections between performance and print, the mobility of texts and books in relation to the space of the theater, and performative acts of pedagogy or reading that carried multiple vernaculars out of polyglot dictionaries and language guides into playhouses and dramatic texts, and back again.[30] *Theaters of Translation* thus argues that attention to the ways cosmopolitanism on the Renaissance stage is "read" will also illuminate a broader view of printed dictionaries, grammars, and dialogues preceding it, restoring attention to the pedagogically influenced, performative nature of these books.

"Markes of Straungenesse": Defining Early Modern Europe's Cosmopolitan Vernaculars

With these approaches in hand, then, and in contrast to established narratives arguing for the triumph of English over Latin or what Benedict Anderson termed "the origins of national consciousness," this philological and bibliographical study analyzes what I am hailing as "cosmopolitan vernaculars" within a European literary-theatrical domain.[31] The critical genealogy of this term encompasses comparative work in premodern Sanskrit studies and postcolonial theory, as in the influential formulations developed by Sheldon Pollock and Homi K. Bhabha.

In his broad comparative-historical work, Pollock employs this term to describe the adoption of Sanskrit literature's cosmopolitan aesthetic among regional, vernacular courts in South Asia around the beginning of the second millennium. The result of these elite literary projects, he claims, was an array of mutually accommodating "cosmopolitan vernaculars," each characterized by assertions of regionality and supraregionality, literary value, the retrofitting of Sanskrit taxonomies, and the localization of epic space and political vision.[32] By contrast—and again, using broad strokes in his discussion—Pollock perceives in premodern *Latinitas* a project of coercion and conquest that over roughly the same centuries gave way to "vernaculars of necessity," in which the state dictated the terms of participation.[33] While concurring with Pollock's general picture, *Theaters of Translation* apprehends and analyzes the ways cosmopolitan vernaculars functioned in early modern Europe as well, in particular ways, both in aristocratic schoolrooms and in less strictly elite contexts—namely, the public theater.

Meanwhile Bhabha, taking a much more particular and human subject–oriented approach, focuses on the centuries *after* England's rise to global imperial dominance, a rise taking shape during the period with which the present study is concerned. He writes of a "double life of British minorities that makes them 'vernacular cosmopolitans,' translating between cultures, renegotiating traditions from a position where 'locality' insists on its own terms, while entering into larger national and societal conversations."[34] Pushing productively against the notion of a traditionally privileged and coercive European cosmopolitan, a notion my own analysis both inherits and acknowledges, Bhabha proposes here a subversive, subaltern cosmopolitan emerging from cultures subject to colonial oppression.

In adopting the term "cosmopolitan vernaculars," *Theaters of Translation* proffers a link between Pollock's and Bhabha's accounts. Attentive to generative, crosslinguistic vernacular communities within the specific circumstances of sixteenth- and seventeenth-century Europe, I focus carefully on the material-textual instantiations of these languages, and in a way that balances a historicized approach with an interest in both imaginative and subversive possibilities. Namely, I use "cosmopolitan vernaculars" to refer to multiple, nonclassical (i.e., "vernacular") languages in the European Renaissance that commingle and converse with each other in print and manuscript, their linguistic society modeling and fashioning border-crossing communities of belonging for authors, readers, and audiences. One can observe this phenomenon at work in the corpus of bilingual and polyglot dictionaries, grammars, and dialogue books produced in early modern Europe that are at the center of this study. Each implies a "feeling beyond one's own environment" that is linguistically structured, estranged from the modern conception of the nation-state, and which spills into drama.[35] As this chapter and others that follow show, such a pervasive, cosmopolitan practice in multiple languages takes shape in a variety of discursive domains: education, religion, economics, sex.

The terms of *Theaters of Translation* should not be understood to assume some sort of utopianist picture of languages playing freely off each other at all times. As Bosman rightly observes in the midst of his data-driven polysystem analysis of British plays, "Stressing the multilingualism and mobility of early British drama should not be taken to imply that all its languages had equal status or that movements between them were uniformly fluid."[36] The analyses of the present study take place against this background, in which the political clout, military powers, economic strength, and artistic prestige of various cultures in Europe, and beyond, were staggered. Further, even if linguistic fluidity often evinces pleasure or curiosity in or about the "other," it could also serve as cover for developing nationalistic or imperial agendas against which Bhabha's "vernacular cosmopolitan" strives. One need only think of the coercive language learning Caliban experiences in *The Tempest* ("You taught me language," he says to Miranda and Prospero, "and my profit on't / Is I know how to curse"), or Antonio de Nebrija's assertion in the first European vernacular grammar that "siempre la lengua fue compañera del imperio" (language has always been the partner of empire).[37] Within the modest glimpse into the time period it offers, *Theaters of Translation* remains aware of these more sinister aspects while uncovering the ways that dictionaries, language manuals, grammars, and drama promised worlds of words for early modern readers and playgoers. Furnishing "imagined cosmopolitanisms" in a Europe whose futures were neither inevitable nor clear, these multilingual vernacular publications and performances acquainted England's men and women—for better and for worse—with languages, literatures, people, and cultures beyond but also within their own place.

Though the present work certainly aims to engage scholars who privilege the terms *transnational* or *global*, it is *cosmopolitan* that is most essential to this study, and this word merits some particular remarks of its own. In one especially prominent genealogy of this critical keyword, an emphasis on classical and post-Enlightenment contexts typically glosses over lessons to be gathered from the early modern period; *Theaters of Translation* addresses this conspicuously neglected interval. Making the first call for the term's modern critical reconsideration, Martha C. Nussbaum recommended the "very old ideal of the cosmopolitan" (rooted in classical antiquity and later rearticulated by Immanuel Kant) as a universally applicable model for the modern world.[38] Shortly thereafter, Timothy Brennan countered such a proposal on the grounds that scholars' modern use of *cosmopolitan* merely papered over expressions of privilege and cultural imperialism.[39] In successive years, Pheng Cheah and Bruce Robbins's collection *Cosmopolitics:*

Thinking and Feeling Beyond the Nation pushed the discussion beyond this impasse and toward a useful mix of "new cosmopolitanisms," opening the door for inquiry into "minoritarian cosmopolitanisms" and "the cosmofeminine" as elaborated by Carol A. Breckenridge, Bhabha and Pollock, Dipesh Chakrabarty, and several other scholars of language, history, anthropology, and art history.[40] This rich, proliferating array of approaches confront the contradictions at the heart of the term; after all, as Jacques Derrida has discussed, modern cosmopolitan projects are troubled by a contest between the unconditional offer of hospitality (which a "city of refuge" ideally promises) and necessary conditions on that hospitality, should such a project be implemented.[41] Returning to the discussion recently, Nussbaum remarks further that the terms of cosmopolitanism—in her words, "a noble but flawed ideal"—suffer from a bifurcation between "duties of justice" on the one hand and "duties of material aid" on the other.[42]

As a critical keyword, then, *cosmopolitanism* seems to offer as many difficulties as possibilities. At different turns it is utopian, placeless, welcoming, wandering—hospitable to those far away, negligent to people nearby. In his study *Cosmopolitanism: Ethics in a World of Strangers*, philosopher Kwame Anthony Appiah remarks on the fact that *cosmopolitan* has even been an anti-Semitic or xenophobic slur deployed by ethnocentrists and nationalists, a phenomenon that has surfaced again and again, with frequency, in the years since his book's publication.[43] While taking sides again these "noisiest foes" of cosmopolitanism—I do, as well—Appiah simultaneously presents an openhanded solution to the conceptual dilemma: "Fortunately, we need take sides neither with the nationalist who abandons all foreigners," he writes, "nor with the hard-core cosmopolitan who regards her friends and fellow citizens with icy impartiality. The position worth defending might be called (in both senses) a partial cosmopolitanism."[44] This approach, to my view, provides some steady ground for further thinking. Making no all-encompassing, prescriptive claims for the term's applications, *Theaters of Translation* offers a partial cosmopolitanism delimited by its attention to several particular vernacular European languages enough within my skill to examine with care—English, French, Italian, Spanish, and, on occasion, Dutch and German—by means of their printed appearances on the page, and their staged utterances in early modern London, such as they can be assessed today.

With a few noteworthy exceptions, studies focused on cosmopolitanism largely retain an emphasis on the term's Greco-Kantian genealogy and modern applications and therefore commonly overstep the centuries between classical antiquity and the Enlightenment, including the period at the center of this study.[45] Nearly forgotten is John Dee's exhortation in 1577 to examine "the State of Earthly Kingdoms, Generally, the whole World ouer," so that one becomes "*Cosmopolites*: a Citizen, and Member, of the whole and only one Mysticall City Vniuersal."[46] In addressing phenomena associated with this early modern "cosmopolite," particularly the cosmopolitanisms that crop up among early modern vernacular languages, my analysis supplies a linguistically focused response to Amanda Anderson's call for a "rigorous genealogy of cosmopolitanism."[47] In doing so, I provide a view into early modern *linguistic* cosmopolitanisms in England between the typical classical and colonial/postcolonial accounts. Because *Theaters of Translation* focuses mainly on England's stages and Europe's languages, readers will find in these pages what Pollock identifies as "the singular, privileged location of European thought and history."[48] That is, after all, part of the legacy of the primary sources at the center of my analysis, as well as the methods structuring scholarship and discourse in the anglophone academy. However, it is the work of this study to unravel the linguistic "singular" at the core of this European history, and through the terms of cosmopolitanism to revisit the nascent and intersecting forms of vernacular languages as they appeared in print and manuscript during the sixteenth and seventeenth centuries on the way toward those more consolidated and imperialist, but by no means inevitable, forms. In this regard, *Theaters of Translation* stands not only as a series of linked claims about cosmopolitan vernaculars in English Renaissance plays but also as an invitation to further work along cultural, linguistic, and literary borders in an early modern world that had no certain or decided future.

In employing these terms along these lines, my investigation therefore examines cosmopolitanisms not only or principally in the domain of human subjects (e.g., ambassadors, travelers, go-betweens, etc.) but crucially in language itself and in the material texts and performances conveying and shaping that language for readers. In this way, I build on the object-focused investigations of scholars such as Margreta de Grazia, Maureen Quilligan, Peter Stallybrass, and Julian Yates, and crucially the philological and syntactical approaches advanced in recent years by Jeffrey Masten and Valerie Traub.[49] Indeed, early modern vernacular languages and words were often anthropomorphized in the terms of citizenship, naturalization, and denization. Not just expressive vehicles for transnational subjects, words and languages embodied the cosmopolitan conversation—meaning verbal exchanges but also intimate dwelling, commerce, and conversion—that their readers and speakers either did or could be inspired to adopt.[50] As the early modern educator William Camden wrote, linguistic mingling was the rule rather than the exception for English: "Whereas our tongue is mixed, it is no disgrace, whenas all the tongs of *Europe* do participate interchangeably the one of the other."[51] It is this interchangeable participation that these texts—language-learning publications but also plays—held out to early modern readers, theatergoers, actors, and authors. And in its mixed nature, English in this period was, to use Derrida's phrase, "a language that is not one's own."[52]

Some did not take kindly to this idea. In a 1569 treatise on orthographic reform, John Hart argued that the presence of foreign characteristics among English words "is euen as we would not haue any straunger to be conuersant, nor dwell amongst vs, though he be a free Denison . . . except . . . he shoulde weare continually some mark, to be knowe[n] whence he is."[53] Frustrated by this heterogeneous situation of "conuersant" foreigners (and hailing the example of the "Denison," a foreigner made English by royal patent), Hart ruled instead that any borrowed word should "leaue all his colours, or markes of straungenesse" (sig. E1r)—that is, to dispense with orthographic reminders of a word's foreign origins. "For so the French doe terme it," he continued, "when any forren is so receuied amongst them, they cal him naturallized" (sig. E1r). In Hart's act of personification, visible characteristics of foreign languages and the individual words borrowed from them have no place in English; rather than being accepted as denizens, they should be "naturallized" and assimilated without orthographic signs of previous attachments. (Curiously, though, Hart notes this word's French provenance, proof that the "markes of straungenesse" he sought to eliminate could cling stubbornly to their English forms, even on the watch of the most vigilant.) Ultimately, Hart seeks the assimilation of this "straungenesse," which would erase a word's multilingual and geographically migratory aspects—in other words, its cosmopolitanism.

Other writers discussed linguistic denization in more agreeable terms, offering approval for cosmopolitan vernaculars and their utility in English writing. Although she would have objected to the sinful connotations of "cosmopolite" articulated in contemporary sermons, Mary Sidney Herbert perceived her own English translations of the Psalms as immigrant texts in the foreign land of her own vernacular. As I will discuss at greater length in chapter 3, she claims in a dedicatory epistle that the "Psalmist King" David is "now English denizend, though Hebrue borne," using terms of citizenship for a religious text crossing borders, languages, and cultures.[54] Strikingly, in an England in which Jewish people had been expelled, Sidney Herbert imagines an anthropomorphic "Hebrue" text doing something a human cannot: achieve citizen's rights.

This picture applied for words and phrases as well as entire texts. In his 1606 English adaptation of a work by Giambattista Giraldi Cinzio (the same writer responsible for *Othello*'s "source"), Lodowick Bryskett begged that "you must giue me leaue to vse new words of Art, such as are proper to expresse new conceits, though they be yet strange, and not denizened in our language."[55] More than simply neologisms or "inkhorn terms," however, these "new words of Art" represent in miniature the variety of linguistic minglings shaping the vernacular landscape of Renaissance England. As a translator, a traveler, and the son of an Italian immigrant, Bryskett embodied the cosmopolitan condition of the vernaculars he dealt to readers. Decades later, Ben Jonson's friend James Howell would sustain these terms in his own English grammar, reminding readers that foreign words "do in tract of time as it were Naturalize themselfs and becom free denisons."[56] For Howell, these words join with English not on account of any human dealings but on their own; here one observes a kind of free-agent immigration, a naturalization without the state. Elsewhere, in Howell's *Lexicon Tetraglotton*, an engraving represents vernacular languages as a society of humans: "Associatio Linguarum," reads a label above the illustration, and below, "La Ligue des Langues" (figure 1.2). By advocating for the denization of "strange" words and foreign texts, authors such as Sidney Herbert, Bryskett, and Howell challenged Hart's notion of a pure, unmixed English society, exalting a cosmopolitan vernacular mingled and in play with other European and even non-European tongues.

Colloquia on Stage: Cosmopolitan Vernaculars in Shakespeare's London

Characterized by the mingling of various languages and cultures discussed by these authors, the England in which Shakespeare lived and worked was a fertile site for the cosmopolitan vernaculars that surface in his comedy *The Merry Wives of Windsor*. This work of drama will serve as an introductory site for my broader study, owing to the prominence attached to the playwright but also to the "Englishness" traditionally assigned to the comedy. An analysis of the multilingual dictionaries and language manuals circulating during Shakespeare's lifetime shows how this allegedly "English comedy" transposes the interplay of foreign vernaculars onto the stage and back into print. *The Merry Wives of Windsor*, in fact, offers up a rich portrait of translation as employed by a would-be seducer, Falstaff, as well as the ways that translation might be reversed onto the oppressor's own head by the play's prominent immigrant and female characters (with Mistress

FIGURE 1.2 James Howell, *Lexicon Tetraglotton, an English-French-Italian-Spanish Dictionary*, 1660, frontispiece engraving. Folio EC6 H8394 660I. Reproduced by kind permission of the Kislak Center for Special Collections, Rare Books and Manuscripts, University of Pennsylvania.

Quickly chiefly among them). Exhibiting thematic elements of revenge, an expressed interest in proper, pious femininity, generic elements of "city comedy," and concerns about money and sex, all on top of typographic qualities linking it to language manuals, this play lays out an assortment of topics and questions engaged, through the terms of translation, by all other chapters of this book.

Even studies that are attentive to the remarkable linguistic diversity of *The Merry Wives of Windsor*, however, often retain an emphasis on what Richard Foster Jones termed "the triumph of the English language." Recent criticism on *Merry Wives* pointing in this direction has focused on English monarchy and aristocracy, English domesticity and "middling culture," and English placeness.[57] Moreover, as Leah S. Marcus has shown, these critical tendencies have been shaped by the play's editorial tradition, which prioritizes the folio text above that of the 1602 quarto in a way that shores up a picture of Englishness.[58] What could be called an "anglocentric bias" here is contiguous with what Marjorie Rubright has termed "presumptive monolingualism": in her words, "a cultural fantasy that anyone might ever be wholly *mono*lingual."[59]

Such analyses of *Merry Wives* also propose, or at least imply, that the play's smatterings of foreign language constitute a temporary phase of linguistic chaos along the pathway to a more standardized and more modern-looking English. For example, Lynne Magnusson, attuned to the linguistic heterogeneity I discussed previously, offers a valuable exploration of the comedy's expression of changing language and shifting media, but her analysis trains its attention not on multilingualism per se but on what this "collision of micro-languages" can show about the emerging "King's English."[60] Other linguistically attuned analyses of *Merry Wives* by Deanne Williams, who discusses the play's Anglo-French dimensions, and Marianne Montgomery, who examines the comedy's use of Latin, also project an image of an ascendant English language, whether among educated or uneducated London playgoers.[61] Even as they underscore that *Merry Wives* proffers an array of "non-English" words, these interpretations shore up the singularity of English (and Englishness) against other languages circulating in the comedy.

My own discussion proposes a different avenue into *The Merry Wives of Windsor* in which the cacophonous mixture of foreign words and phrases represents precisely the play's point. Holding in focus the period's polyglot language-learning texts, I favor an approach that does not assume the inevitability of a cohesive "King's English" but rather slows down to examine the multilingual mixture circulating through the play, and through the period. What emerges is not an "English comedy" but rather a play deeply interested in the cosmopolitan mingling of foreign languages and English within the play's clearly marked English setting. My discussion builds on the work of Patricia Parker, who has uncovered an intricate network of gendered wordplay in *Merry Wives* linking tropes of translation and adultery, as well as Kathryn Vomero Santos, who proposes that *Merry Wives* exhibits an English language that is simultaneously hospitable and hostile to immigrant characters.[62] Foreign characters falter with the English language, but so do the play's English natives—and they do so in a way that may elucidate the multilingual culture in which this comedy was first acted and printed. In the remainder of this first chapter, I will argue that *Merry Wives* stages a link between translation and seduction through Falstaff's faulty attempts at romance, but also, crucially, that this discourse of translation is contested and eventually undermined by the combined powers of the play's non-English and women characters, with Mistress Quickly as a critical linguistic "go-between" among them. Exhibiting polyglossia and interpretive agility such as can be seen in Europe's multilingual dictionaries and dialogue books—particularly, Noël de Berlaimont's ultrapopular *Colloquia et Dictionariolum*—these foreign and women characters teach playgoers to see even this most unmistakably "English" of staged Englands as a cosmopolitan space for language learning, multilingualism, and fluidity between foreign and native.[63]

There is evidence that Shakespeare consulted several manuals that translated foreign languages and literatures for anglophone people; accordingly, these publications can be regarded as a context for *Merry Wives*'s linguistic commentary. It is true, as Magnusson notes, that "even the most educated could not have consulted an English grammar book before the appearance of William Bullokar's *Bref Grammar for English* in 1586 or an English dictionary before Robert Cawdrey's *A Table Alphabeticall* in 1604."[64] A variety of multilingual lexicons, grammars, and phrasebooks preceded these monoglot publications, however, setting English, French, Italian, and Spanish (and other vernaculars and classical languages, such as German and Latin) in conversation with each other for the benefit of their users. Today, these books offer a window into the period's transcultural dealings and its emergent political and discursive categories, such as nationhood or race.[65] Through studies of textual parallels, scholars have also established that Shakespeare used bilingual language manuals by John Florio, John Eliot, and Claudius Hollyband; the latter two were printed in London by Thomas Vautrollier and his successor, the Stratford-born stationer Richard Field.[66] The "discovery" of a four-language dictionary with marginal notes supposedly in Shakespeare's hand has been discredited by scholars, but multilingual dictionaries and language manuals, circulating throughout early modern London in multiple editions, were genres the playwright knew.[67]

Among the most widely circulating language-learning publications in early modern Europe was Noël de Berlaimont's *Colloquia et Dictionariolum*, a popular dictionary and language manual that, I argue, may have influenced a linguistically themed tavern scene in *Henry IV Part 1*, as well as certain elements of its "sequel," *The Merry Wives of Windsor*.[68] The *Colloquia* has an extensive publication history. In one form or another, it witnessed more than 150 editions over several centuries and across England, France, the Netherlands, Spain, Germany, Italy, and other countries.[69] Displaying as many as eight languages across its columns (vernaculars and Latin), the text often appeared in oblong, pocket-sized packaging, with its diverse tongues differentiated by typeface (figure 1.3).[70] The *Colloquia*'s most expanded form was first printed in 1598, contemporary with *Henry IV Part 1* and *Merry Wives*; it features a guide to letter writing, a pronunciation treatise, a brief dictionary, and, as Susan E. Phillips has carefully analyzed, a set of lively dialogues that engage the issues of schooling, slavery, and seduction, the last of which I will consider in more detail through this discussion.[71]

Printed with titles and speech prefixes, and preceded by short lists of speakers resembling dramatis personae catalogs, these polyglot dialogues also resemble miniature works of drama. In the first and longest of these, entitled "A Dinner of Ten Persons," rowdy supper guests engage in drinking contests, discuss language learning, and heap requests on an overtasked youth named Francis. "Francis, bring a chaire for your coosen," asks one speaker; "Francis, go you before one knocketh theare," demands another; "Francis, bring vs to eate . . . fill vs to drinke. fil for your coosen, and then round about."[72] If they were not consulting editions of the *Colloquia*—some of which, it seems, were printed in sixteenth-century London—Shakespeare and his contemporaries could also find this busybody Francis and his multilingual supper mates in *The Spanish Schoole-master*, a version of Berlaimont's text printed in 1591.[73]

This dialogue, I argue, informs Shakespeare's *Henry IV Part 1*, in which Prince Hal claims he can "drink with any tinker in his own language" and torments a busy tavern drawer named Francis.[74] Seizing on this moment's importance to the play, Richard Helgerson states that "Hal's prodigality and amendment are . . . presented as two steps in an extended language lesson," and I suggest this points to much more than merely "alehouse

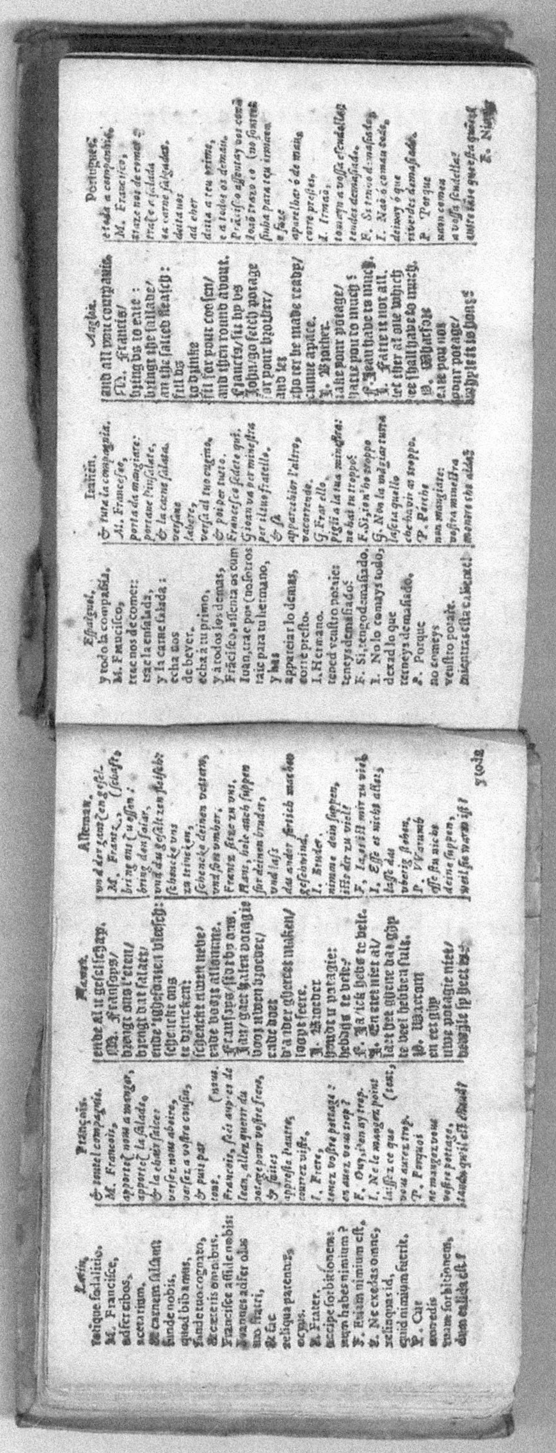

Figure 1.3 Noël de Berlaimont, *Colloquia et Dictionariolum octo Linguarum*, 1631. 418 B514c. Courtesy of the Charles Deering McCormick Library of Special Collections & University Archives, Northwestern University.

slang."[75] Indeed, with his friend Poins—who in *Merry Wives*, as I will show, frames Falstaff's wooing in the terms of translation—Hal drives the tapster back and forth across the tavern in a repeated exchange of "Francis!" and "Anon!" that amounts to "a literal as well as a figurative language lesson."[76] To top it all off, when Falstaff arrives on stage, the Prince ends the scene on a distinctly foreign-sounding note: "'Rivo!' says the drunkard" (2.4.108).[77] These common elements—deep drinking, language learning, and a character named Francis hustling "round about"—could be a coincidence, but such striking similarities open the possibility that the playwright was not only familiar with the *Colloquia* but also transposed its lively dialogues onto the stage.

If Shakespeare did use this widely circulating polyglot manual, he potentially would have known another of its dialogues that links seduction and translation in a way that shows *Merry Wives* in a new light. Indeed, as Phillips has shown—from column to column and from English to French to Italian or German—readers of this book could find the language to make a lewd advance, or to rebuff one.[78] This episode takes place in an inn, where six weary guests have gathered. A host welcomes them—"Sirs, you shall be very wel vsed," he says—and grants them stable room, good wine, and plenty to eat (sig. L1r). At the table, two guests talk about their diverse origins: "I am of Brussel," states a traveler named Sampson, "Of the linage of the Schollers" (sig. L7r–L8r). Offering multiple replies for the *Colloquia*'s readers, Sampson's interlocutor states that he is "from Fraunce, from England, and fro[m] high Dutchla[n]d," three countries corresponding to the book's languages (sig. L8r).

This conversation concluded, the dialogue takes one of these lodgers to his bed with the aid of a chambermaid or hostess named Joan. Suddenly, the lodger feels unwell: "I am very ill at ease: I sheake as a leafe: vpon thee tree," he says once they reach the chamber; "Warme my kerchif, and binde my head well" (sig. M2r). Asking Joan to put out the light, he reveals his true purpose: "My shee frinde, kisse me once: and I shall sleape the better" (sig. M4r). Realizing the ruse, the hostess confronts the lodger: "Sleape, sleape, you are not sicke seeing that you speake of kyssing, I had rather die, then to kisse a man in his bed, or in any other place" (sig. M4r). All under the multilingual rubric of a language lesson, the *Colloquia* serves up wooing strategies for inn-dwelling male travelers, as well as witty counters to hostesses or chambermaids whom men perceive as whores.[79] Rejecting this attempt at seduction—here, in up to eight languages at once—Joan ensures this dialogue's readers that if one can learn to translate an unchaste proposition, one can also learn to offer a rejection.

Other language-learning manuals circulating in Shakespeare's England presented lessons in translation through the terms of seduction, too. To be sure, seduction scenes are a staple of language instruction from the earliest *manières de langage*, but the sixteenth century witnessed the multiplication of these forms of "courtesy" in print, influencing the theater along the way. Among these are two dialogues in John Florio's Italian-English *Firste Fruites* (1578), a book that Shakespeare knew and drew upon in his playwriting. In the second chapter, a rather forward male speaker addresses a female interlocutor with "Fayre mayde, wyll you that I loue you?" and proceeds with what operates as a brief lesson in verb tenses (Italian, or English): "I haue loued you, I loue you, & wil loue you."[80] The "mayde" rejects him, however: "I haue hated you, I hate you, & I wyl hate you," she says, and when asked for her reason she responds, "I knowe not, but I cannot loue" (sig. A1v).

Although this wooing attempt ends with reconciliation and a trip "to the Theatre to see a Comedie" (sig. A2r), a suggestion of the fluid intercourse between dialogic language learning and playacting, things are not as agreeable in a later exchange. In this tenth chapter entitled "To speake with a woman"—as if the earlier chapter were not enough—a would-be suitor's greetings to a lady are taken as ridicule: "I render you a thousand thankes, I know you are courteous," he begins, to which she replies, "You are redy to mocke me," insisting finally that "I was neuer subiect vnto loue, neither seeke I to be" (sig. B4v). As with the *Colloquia*, not all of *Firste Fruites*'s dialogues dwell on wooing; as one exhausted speaker puts it, "It were labour lost to speake of Loue" (sig. S3r). However, in these chapters, as in the *Colloquia* episode at the inn, Florio's readers learn to translate (i.e., to speak or read another language) through a man's series of invitations to love—or, conversely, a woman's rejections of lechery. In these theatrical language-learning dialogues—dialogues that, like printed plays, often involve multiple speakers and speech prefixes, and are preceded by lists of dramatis personae—one witnesses a connection between translation and seduction, a connection that helps clarify *Merry Wives*'s cosmopolitan treatments of language.

Mistress Quickly stands as an especially prominent representative of *Merry Wives*'s combined interest in translation and seduction. Even before her seventeenth-century redesignation as a fast-footed German in Venice's Second Folio, this chambermaid works to derail Falstaff's seduction plots and is able to "drink with any tinker in his own language" within the play's multilingual setting. Like *Henry V*'s Princess Katherine, who "brings alive the multiplicity within English itself," and in opposition to a male-focused discourse of translation, Quickly unites foreign and women characters in *Merry Wives* through the fluid, mobile linguistic turning critics have recognized in her.[81] An emblem of the play's treatment of linguistic and national belonging, she not only stands as a "go-between" but also works in the household of a foreigner, the Frenchman Doctor Caius. In fact, comically suggesting both mental and sexual varieties of transnational mingling, Quickly states in the quarto text that the Frenchman "puts all his priuities in me."[82] Having also appeared as the polymorphous, beverage-touting "*Hostesse*" (sometimes abbreviated "*Host.*") in the speech prefixes of the Henriad's linguistically troped tavern scenes, the Quickly of *Merry Wives* can be seen as a staged variation on the savvy chambermaid-hostess "Joan" in Berlaimont's *Colloquia*, as well as a female reflection of the polyglot Host of the Garter also appearing in the comedy.[83] This servant woman's language certainly possesses comic value, but when read against the accented and foreign-language speech one finds in *Merry Wives* (and indeed, in the books and streets of Shakespeare's London), her words also assume a transnational, translinguistic quality.

Seen differently, Mistress Quickly's words are not necessarily malapropisms or errant speech but rather foldings-together of foreign and domestic terms that introduce English playgoers to phrases in polyglot dictionaries—and Continental wines—that can win, in her words, "any woman's heart" (2.2.67). This female "go-between" fits into the picture outlined by Frances E. Dolan, who emphasizes a link in the early modern period between foreign wines and the women of England's households. "Wine, largely imported, was a favored beverage in England," she writes, adding that it was consumed in taverns and palaces, often mixed or adulterated (labeled "bastard"), and accordingly a product rife with uncertainty.[84] "That uncertainty," Dolan continues, "was both associated with femininity and, occasionally, an opportunity for women who joined experiments in growing grapes and making wine in England."[85] Mistress Quickly exemplifies this connection between foreign wine, mixture and mingling, and femininity, as well as experimentation of a linguistic, if not scientific, variety. Altogether, via the words of a barkeeping Henriad hostess, Shakespeare expresses dramatically the bound-together notions of translation and seduction on display in the *Colloquia* and other foreign-language manuals and dictionaries.

In *Merry Wives*, this blend of multilingualism, wines, and women occurs most conspicuously in a speech delivered by Mistress Quickly in act 2. My remarks draw on the analysis of Barbara Sebek, who notes here "a cheeky and perhaps scandalously pointed set of Spanish wine references," though I will stretch this picture in a more cosmopolitan and translingual direction.[86] Quickly's speech is a reflection on the elegance of the court, intended as a satirical picture of Falstaff's supposed romantic effects on Mistress Ford: "The best courtier of them all, when the court lay at Windsor, could never have brought her to such a *canary*—yet there has been knights, and lords, and gentlemen, with their coaches, I warrant you—coach after coach, letter after letter, gift after gift, smelling so sweetly, all *musk*, and so *rushling*, I warrant you, in silk and gold, and in such *alligant* terms, and in such wine and sugar of the best and the fairest, that would have won any woman's heart" (2.2.59–67; my emphasis). According to Magnusson, Mistress Quickly's words in this moment "place on exhibit the linguistic products of her experience of moving between different linguistic cultures," although for Magnusson this means linguistic cultures within the domain of the emerging English language. Within such a reading, Quickly appropriates the "posh words" of aristocratic ladies whose lifestyle she wishes to imitate, her "appetite for fine expression" (which includes alcoholic beverages, an element I will emphasize) representing not malapropism or incorrect speech but rather the resourceful use of language in the zone between orality and literacy.[87] I certainly agree with Magnusson that the traditional understanding of Quickly's speech as "malapropism" is limiting, but I would also suggest that the notion of "linguistic cultures" on display here could be broadened considerably: beyond the borders of English and England, across Europe, and in a manner such as can be observed in the multiple columns of the *Colloquia et Dictionariolum*.

Indeed, with "canary," "musk," "rushling," and "alligant," Mistress Quickly does not necessarily commit malapropism; nor is she only experimenting within the English language. Rather, and as critics and editors have not fully noticed, her speech resembles that of a polyglot interpreter riffing on bilingual dictionaries, bridging national and linguistic communities with multilingual terms. It is not this character's subjectivity or personhood so much as the related domain of her language that occupies the center of my reading.[88] Specifically, Quickly's terms coincide not only with Spanish wines (as Sebek notes) but also with other foreign wines cropping up in the period's polyglot lexicons. The word "alligant" appears in both John Florio's Italian-English dictionary of 1598 and Randle Cotgrave's French-English lexicon of 1611: "Vino rosso, *red wine or alligant*," reads the one, and "Vin de rosette. *Alligant*," states the other.[89] The words "musk" and "rushling" point in the direction of foreign alcohol as well. Florio's entry for "Moscato" features "*the wine muscadine*" (sig. V3r), and the *Oxford English Dictionary* indicates that before it was adopted by English speakers in the eighteenth century, "riesling" appeared as both "Rißling" and Rußling."[90] Like the interlocutors of the *Colloquia* or the linguistically mischievous Prince Hal in the tavern, this servant woman could certainly claim to "drink with any tinker in his own language." Spoken by this mobile go-between in Shakespeare's play, a description of attempted seductions at court carries onto the stage the cosmopolitan vernaculars and multilingual beverages appearing in Europe's foreign-language lexicons.

Even in the quarto text, where Mistress Quickly does not deliver this multilingually directional speech, Falstaff connects the chambermaid with linguistic mobility, using the epithet "my good she-Mercury" (2.2.75–76). As Parker has emphasized, this moniker links Quickly—designated elsewhere as a "messenger" (2.1.143)—with a messenger-god "who is not only famously an *interpres* (go-between and translator) but a notorious conveyer, patron both of language and of thieves."[91] It also locates her among the *Colloquia* editions I have been discussing; in fact, a representation of Mercury with his winged helm makes up part of a two-faced Janus head on the frontispiece of a 1662 edition (figure 1.4). Other multilingual manuals and dictionaries in the period elaborate on this connection.

FIGURE 1.4 Noël de Berlaimont, *Dictionariolum et Colloquia Octo Linguarum*, 1662, detail from frontispiece engraving. 413 D554. Courtesy of the Charles Deering McCormick Library of Special Collections & University Archives, Northwestern University.

For instance, the definition of "Mercurial" appearing in Cotgrave's 1611 French-English dictionary includes "*prating, talkatiue, long-tongued*" as well as "*craftie, subtill, deceitfull, theeuish,*" each of which might be used to describe the speech of Shakespeare's Quickly (sig. 3F6v). As a "messenger" and "go-between" who ostensibly facilitates but in reality undermines the erotic attachments in *Merry Wives*, Quickly in her habits of language embodies the estrangement of Windsor's local environment: an interest in both translation and multilingualism.

Seductive Translations in *The Merry Wives of Windsor*

If the multilingual go-between Mistress Quickly evokes the *Colloquia*'s savvy chambermaid Joan, Sir John Falstaff offers a staged embodiment of the phrasebook's lascivious lodger. Indeed, it is also through this consumer of foreign wines, wines articulated by Quickly, that Shakespeare brings the dyad of seduction and translation upon the stage in *Merry Wives*. Windsor begins to resemble a scene in Berlaimont's polyglot dialogues: Falstaff, a lodger at an inn, a consumer of sack and canary, and known among the play's characters as a "scholar" (2.2.170), pursues women in a world populated by foreign languages, immigrant characters, and travelers. To complement his multilingual and transnational associations with feasting (e.g., a "Dutch dish" [3.5.110]), Falstaff sends duplicate love notes to his would-be lovers in a manner that evokes the *Colloquia*'s model letters to be copied out in various languages. Finally, though in his first spoken lines Falstaff protests to Shallow that he has not "kissed your keeper's daughter" (1.1.106)—precisely the *Colloquia* lodger's end-game with Joan—the quarto text reveals, upon Mistress Ford's first entrance, that "*Syr* Iohn kisses her" (sig. A4r).[92]

Within the context proffered here, while Mistress Quickly with her foreign wines stands for linguistic multiplicity, Falstaff articulates a desire for the singularity of translation.[93] Indeed, when he first devises to pursue Mistress Ford, the fat knight frames his amorous intentions as an act of linguistic turning. Referring to the "entertainment" he perceives in Mistress Ford, Falstaff asserts that his aim is to make meaning out of her obscure demeanor: "Briefly, I do mean to make love to Ford's wife. I spy entertainment in her: she discourses, she carves, she gives the leer of invitation. I can construe the action of her familiar style, and the hardest voice of her behaviour—to be Englished rightly—is: 'I am Sir John Falstaff's'" (1.3.40–45). Falstaff sees what he wants to see here, deciphering—"construing," rendering into English—Mistress Ford's signals of "entertainment." Critics perceive a variety of possibilities for the languages Falstaff is hailing in these lines.[94] I would propose that the languages do not need to be "fixed," though, for in any case, Shakespeare lays bare the more sinister side of translation as employed by men: its coercion and sexual violence. Pistol rapidly picks up on the meaning within this discourse of "Englishing," a common early modern synonym for translation; this way, he ushers the discussion into the territory of sexual activity: "He hath studied her well, and translated her will—out of honesty into English" (1.3.46–47).[95] As Kathryn Vomero Santos has demonstrated, Pistol's remark taps into the "out-of-into" language typically used in early modern discussions of translation, but it also evinces what she calls "an interpretive and transformative practice that allows Falstaff to understand the chaste and honest female will as inconstant."[96] Adopting the discourse of translation for his own sexual designs, Falstaff casts himself as an interpreter of inscrutable female behavior as he prepares to seduce Mistress Ford. In doing so, he renders "English" as distinct from (or foreign to) honesty.

Falstaff links his seduction plans not only with translingual construing but also with acts of thievery and colonial imposition associated with the word "translation." Here, Shakespeare exposes connections between male sexual coercion and the "unrequited conquests" powering Europe's exploitation of the Americas.[97] The metaphorical translations Parker has found throughout this comedy continue when Falstaff boasts about his adulterous plans for both Mistress Ford and Mistress Page: "She bears the purse too: she is a region in Guiana, all gold and bounty. I will be cheaters to them both, and they shall be exchequers to me. They shall be my East and West Indies, and I will trade to them both" (1.3.65–69). With these words, Falstaff gestures far beyond the play's English setting, casting translation as a colonial project that moves exotic goods and languages. As Parker aptly states, "To trade, here, is to be a cheater: the term carries with it the familiar sense of 'betray' as well as of the 'translation' he seeks to engage their [i.e., Mistresses Ford and Page] 'honesty' in."[98] Falstaff represents himself as both a scholar and a colonial "expansionist leader" who wields translation as a weapon against the play's women.[99] Yet in spite of these designs, what begins for Falstaff as a colonial act of translation results in a set of episodes in which he is not the agent of translation but its object.

If translation threatens to serve a seductive purpose in the hands of this play's *Colloquia* lodger-like Falstaff, *Merry Wives* ultimately offers a counter through the combined powers of foreign-born Windsor residents (in the subplot) and savvy, interpretive women (in the main plot). While the former represent the linguistic multiplicity that would challenge any seductive "translations," the latter reinterpret and employ the early modern period's capacious meanings of translation as a righteous—yet, as per the title, "merry"—measure of revenge. By drenching, beating, and humiliating Falstaff, this play's clever women take "translation" to its semantic limits and in a way that redounds upon the lasciviously intentioned knight. To refer to the title of John Florio's 1598 Italian-English lexicon, Windsor's world of seduction is also a "world of words," a world in which polyglot variety and facility with meaning, wielded by both immigrant and women characters, offer resistance against the play's native-born Englishmen.

The multilingual and immigrant population of this allegedly "English comedy" cannot receive enough emphasis. Circulating throughout the subplot with their accents and non-English words are Sir Hugh Evans, the Welsh parson who teaches Latin, and Doctor Caius, a Frenchman whom Williams calls "a walking bilingual dictionary" for his mix of French and English terms.[100] Although these speakers might be distinguishable by their accents, they trade verbal tics with each other ("Pible"), and with Mistress Quickly ("absence" for "absent"), further evincing this play's interest in linguistic mixture.[101] Above all in the subplot, though, there is the Host of the Garter, who participates in and validates the play's world of multilingualism. Using words such as "Kaiser" (1.3.9), "Cavaliero" (2.1.176, 180, 191; 2.3.67), "varletto" (4.5.62), "myn-heers" (2.1.197), "punto" and "montant" (2.3.23, 24), he samples from German, Italian, Spanish, Dutch, and French, embodying theatrically the polyglot innkeepers portrayed in Berlaimont's *Colloquia* and other such multilingual manuals. For John Michael Archer, in fact, the Host's various languages ultimately result in a Garter Inn that is "placeless" and that therefore could be, I suggest—to quote from the popular *Colloquia*—"from Fraunce, from England, and from high Dutchland."[102] The translinguistic ability seen in *Merry Wives*' characters and in the Host courses through this comedy: in act 1 alone, one finds "*Pauca verba*" (1.1.113), "A fico for the phrase" (1.3.27), and "*ma foi, il fait fort chaud*" (1.4.46). Strikingly, the play known as "Shakespeare's English comedy" abounds in non-English words.

While the Host of the Garter exhibits tendencies toward translation in a manner that would mistreat or defraud foreigners, he also commends his non-English guests and falls prey to their table-turning plots. According to Santos, the Host exists in a complex, somewhat equivocal triangular relationship with the play's two prominent immigrant characters: "The Host emphatically declares his possession of the English language at the expense of Evans and Caius and becomes a figure for English as a host language that both makes room and denies entry at the proverbial inn."[103] Indeed: he deludes the would-be combatants Evans and Caius, stating afterward that the two strangers can "keep their limbs whole and hack our English" (3.1.71). This combination of trickery and linguistic trash-talking extends into the play's fourth act, when the Host learns about the arrival of "the German," accompanied by his courtly entourage and who "desires to have three . . . horses" (4.3.1–2). The Host is quick to ask, "they speak English?" (4.3.6), wishing to converse with these visitors in his native tongue rather than in theirs.

Yet if the Host displays prejudice against the play's foreigners, he also confesses his errors and commends their positive qualities. On these grounds, critics have read him as a reconciliatory figure against the play's multicultural background.[104] Remarking on the important occupations of Evans and Caius, the Host admits, "I have deceived you both. . . . Your hearts are mighty, your skins are whole, and let burnt sack be the issue" (3.1.96–99). With this nod to "burnt sack"—a Spanish wine that could be included among the polyglot Mistress Quickly's beverages—the resolution of this episode in *Merry Wives* amounts to a toast pointing beyond England's borders.[105] Later on, moreover, the Host asserts that "Germans are honest men" (4.5.68), contesting his countryman Bardolph's allegation that the guests are "three German devils, three Doctor Faustasses" (4.5.66) who have, it seems, stolen his horses. In this case, the offstage Germans actually have turned the tables on the English, reversing the Host's original plan to trick them.[106] Immigrant interests are clearly not the Host's priority, but he remains in dialogue with Caius, Evans, and other foreigners with his steady stream of non-English words.

Seen within this "world of words," and confronted by Windsor's crafty female interpreters, Falstaff's downfall demonstrates that if translation can serve a sinister purpose, it can also be reversed and reclaimed for good. In David Landreth's words, "Windsor is Falstaff's schoolroom," a domain of instruction and punishment, though it is also a schoolroom extending from the play's fictional setting into the multilingual columns of language-learning books such as the *Colloquia*, exemplified in *Merry Wives* by Mistress Quickly, Doctor Caius, and Sir Hugh Evans, and present in the merry wives' interpretive dexterity as well.[107] Indeed: though the fat knight originally conceives his coercive project as an act of translation, the wives ultimately reverse his plot, stretching the definition of translation to its limits and effecting, through this (re)interpretation, a series of clever countertranslations.

In the first of these episodes, the servants of Mistress Ford "convey"

Falstaff out of the house in a buck basket. Parker links this episode with "verbal harping . . . throughout the play on the multiple senses of *conveyance*"—trade, bearing or carrying, linguistic transport, and theft.[108] Mistress Ford's instructions to her servants to "carry" a laundry basket prepares Shakespeare's audiences for Mistress Page's feigned advice to banish Falstaff from the house in the same terms that connect transport and translation: "If you have a friend here, convey, convey him out," she says (3.3.107–8). A suspicious Ford unwittingly picks up on the wives' language later on, using the translation code-phrases "out of" and "in" as well: "As I am a man, there was one conveyed out of my house yesterday in this basket" (4.2.137–38). In repeating the word "convey," Shakespeare's crafty women characters conspicuously reinterpret Falstaff's language of translation—his construal of the wives' gestures "out of honesty into English" and his thievery of Guiana's "gold and bounty"—to turn the link between seduction and translation, translations of all kinds, into a joke at Falstaff's expense. Rather than translinguistic clarity or colonial riches, the fat knight finds himself stewed in filthy laundry and dumped into the Thames. In this power reversal, the translator has been translated; the sexual colonizer has become the colonized—or, at least, "conveyed" away at the behest of Shakespeare's clever women and their servants.

The wives enact a second translation reversal on the foolish old knight when they disguise him as the Witch of Brentford: a sartorial translation. Admittedly, costume plots occur frequently in early modern drama, posing the risk of perceiving "translations" everywhere. Yet I suggest that this rarer instance of a male character dressing as a woman occupies another critical site of the wives' interpretive skill, enabling them to further undermine the play's link between seduction and translation.[109] With Ford arriving soon to interrupt the meeting between Falstaff and Mistress Ford, and with the buck basket and other hiding places off the table, a costume seems the only option. Mistress Ford offers the suggestion: "My maid's aunt, the fat woman of Brentford, has a gown above" (4.2.71–72). Seizing on the same "translation" that Ben Jonson hails in *Every Man Out of His Humour*, a clothing change, Shakespeare repackages his protagonist into yet another form: "I think the 'oman is a witch indeed. . . . I spy a great peard under her muffler" (4.2.182–84), observes Evans, who can see through to Falstaff's original guise.[110] Here, the foreign-born Evans seems in on the merry wives' "translation" joke. In the end, this costume change into a witch leaves Falstaff enduring a fate similar to the "translated" Bottom-turned-ass in *A Midsummer Night's Dream*; after the fact, he marvels with embarrassment at "how I have been transformed" (4.5.89).[111] With this costume change, the wives reinterpret and stretch the meaning of translation to its limits, overturning Falstaff's seductive plans in the process.

Facing a final plot involving a show of fairies and dressed—again, translated—in another ridiculous costume, Falstaff appeals to episodes of seduction in classical mythology in order to redeem his own transformed appearance. Here, the fat knight wears a horned headdress associated with a ghostly folklore figure, Herne the Hunter.[112] Uneasy with his silly getup and its cuckoldry connotations, he likens himself to Ovid's mythological Jupiter, figuring the translation of physical appearance in violent terms as a form of seduction—in this case, rape: "Now the hot-blooded gods assist me! Remember, Jove, thou wast a bull for thy Europa: love set on thy horns. O powerful love, that in some respects makes a beast a man, in some other a man a beast! You were also, Jupiter, a swan for the love of Leda: O omnipotent love, how near the god drew to the complexion of a goose!" (5.5.2–8). Here, one finds Ovid's Jupiter as a figure of sexual coercion freighted with connotations of classical transformation. Attempting to drum up confidence, the physically translated but still translation-desiring Falstaff appeals to the king of the deities and the seduction attempts that brought on two transformations, both of them, in turn, conveyed to English readers through Arthur Golding's English rendition of Ovid's *Metamorphoses*.

Rather than a bull or swan, however, the horned wooer appears here at the merry wives' request as a "Windsor stag" (5.5.12), incorporating the Actaeon myth that chases Shakespeare's characters around throughout the play.[113] Indeed, the merry wives effectively turn Falstaff into a different male character from Ovid, not Jove the protean seducer but rather a mortal figure transformed—translated—by a female goddess, Diana. This Ovidian metamorphosis dominates the scene discursively. "Who comes here? My doe?" asks Falstaff, to whom Mistress Ford replies, emphasizing the fat knight's gender, "Sir John, art thou there, my deer, my male deer?" (5.5.14–17). Even when he offers his body to Mistress Ford and Mistress Page, hoping for what Wendy Wall calls "a cross-species orgy," Falstaff seems to signal his own change into the embattled Actaeon, turned into a deer and ripped apart by his own dogs.[114] "Divide me like a bribed buck, each a haunch," he says (5.5.24). Desiring an association with one classical myth of transformation—Jupiter's sexual seizure of Europa and Leda—but forced into another by the merry wives, Falstaff becomes a failed figure of seductive translation. Here, as in the *Colloquia*'s bedchamber scene, the goddess Diana's revenge on her male voyeur plays out again in a reversal, or reinterpretation, of translation—and in a way that downs the ill-intentioned Falstaff.

Falstaff comes to this realization in a townwide humiliation scheme that involves not only the crafty interpreters, Mistresses Ford and Page, but also the polyglot inhabitants of Windsor. Women and foreigners join forces in this comedy's last hurrah, a spectacle of fairies, and they do so in a manner that qualifies the picture of masculine, triumphant Englishness critics have perceived in this play's conclusion.[115] First transformed into Actaeon at the merry wives' command, the foolish old knight is also subjected to the ridicule of the accented Evans, who is dressed as a sprite. "Heavens defend me from that Welsh fairy," cries Falstaff, adding in the folio text, "lest he transform me to a piece of cheese!" (5.5.81–82).[116] In this moment, the notorious eater Sir John faces the threat of being eaten himself, and by a foreigner, too. Meanwhile, the multilingual tinker Mistress Quickly governs the scene as the "Queen of Fairies." Putting Quickly in a role so plainly reminiscent of Queen Elizabeth possesses obvious political implications; as Pittenger recognizes, the sovereign position here is occupied by the most improper "quean" of ladies.[117] What raises the stakes here, I would add, is the fact that Mistress Quickly works in the house of a Frenchman, attends Latin language lessons, and speaks a vocabulary of foreign words and foreign wines legible in bilingual dictionaries. To return to the evocative example of the Venice Second Folio, this character, based on the Italian *mezzana*, is recast in one early reader's handwriting as "*Frau Schnellfuss*"—there, she is a fast-footed foreigner herself. In the carnivalesque conclusion of *The Merry Wives of Windsor*, interpretive women and multilingual foreigners team up against Falstaff's chauvinistic translation plot, bringing to the stage the savvy chambermaid Joan and the multilingual tinker-drinkers in Berlaimont's *Colloquia et Dictionariolum*.

Hailing transformation—or again, "translation," to keep in focus Bottom in *A Midsummer Night's Dream*—Shakespeare encourages his audience not only to laugh at Falstaff's folly but also to recognize the power of translation, wielded by non-English and women characters, to turn upon men who attempt to employ it for oppressive purposes. By the play's end, it is clear that Falstaff was never Jupiter, or even Actaeon, but rather an ass like the "translated" rude mechanical in Shakespeare's earlier comedy. "I do begin to perceive that I am made an ass," the fat knight admits (5.5.119). This series of countertranslations, moreover, has effects on the knight's facility with "scholarly" speech. In Adam Zucker's words, "With each humiliation at the hands of the Merry Wives, that ability is steadily put to the test as a mode of social performance."[118] Subjected to the interpretive maneuvers of Mistresses Ford and Page, even Falstaff's language bows to the rich multilingual texture of this play's Windsor population.

At a first glance, small-town Windsor might seem an unlikely place for cosmopolitanism. Compared to cities like London or Venice, how could such a community—with its provincial gossip and rituals—be truly welcoming to immigrants and their languages? For many critics, "Shakespeare's English comedy" has seemed the most appropriate label for a play lodged in such a domestic setting and featuring what seems like the ridicule of foreigners, especially compared with plays set in larger, multicultural cities: Thomas Dekker's *The Shoemaker's Holiday*, or Ben Jonson's *Volpone*. As Kwame Anthony Appiah notes, though, "Engagement with strangers is always going to be engagement with particular strangers."[119] To be sure, as some have recognized, Shakespeare's Windsor does have a welcoming side.[120] But, to Appiah's "particular strangers," I would also add "particular languages"—and not only English but also French, Dutch, German, Italian, and Spanish, along with the classical, scholarly Latin of Evans's lesson scene—these and other languages on display in early modern Europe's most popular language-learning book, Noël de Berlaimont's *Colloquia et Dictionariolum*.

The Drama of Translation, from Kyd to Jonson

As I have done here with *Merry Wives*, *Theaters of Translation* analyzes cosmopolitan vernaculars within a series of strategically selected works of drama staged and printed in early modern England. While remaining cognizant of medieval precedents and eighteenth-century afterlives of these phenomena, my study focuses on the turn of the seventeenth century, extending from Roger Ascham's educational treatise *The Scholemaster* in 1570 to the highly gendered language of Ben Jonson's *English Grammar*, published in 1640. Coinciding, then, roughly with the period of pre-Restoration professional theater in England (1576–1642), the interval between these linguistic-pedagogical works, I suggest, constitutes England's brief but spectacular moment of cosmopolitan vernaculars—a moment of linguistic openness and fluidity in which the "triumph of the English language" was not the inevitable, or even only possible, outcome. Taking *The Merry Wives of Windsor* as a point of departure, the rest of my study looks beyond Shakespeare to show how other playwrights made use of Renaissance England's polyglot resources, both in tragedies and in comedies, and both in stage plays and dramatic texts meant for reading.

Because early modern translation encompasses a range of discourses intersecting with language learning, grammatical practice, and lexicography, each of the four chapters that follow features a strategically chosen mode of translation: instruction, religious transcendence, exchange, and propagation. Taking my cue from the recent work of Roland Greene and Patricia Parker, which investigates "critical semantics" and "critical keywords" in early modern literary contexts, I analyze these translation modes through chains of related terms, including but not limited to *confusion*, *change*, *turn*, and *convey*, with thoroughgoing recourse to these words' appearance in early modern dictionaries and literature.[121] Coupling this philological inquiry with a variety of material-textual examples highlighting the overlapping typography, marginalia, and binding arrangements of language-learning books and dramatic publications, each chapter culminates in a fresh reading of a Renaissance play. Taken together, these chapters shed light on particular functions and uses of cosmopolitan vernaculars in Renaissance drama in England and the ways translation worked on and between the page and the stage.

Taking up a pair of highly influential early modern tragedies—one publicly acted, one written for private reading—the next two chapters illustrate how cosmopolitan vernaculars worked in pedagogical and religious domains. In chapter 2, I interpret the linguistic diversity in Thomas Kyd's *Spanish Tragedy* (a play ending with the circulation of books onstage and a deadly, multilingual play within a play) as a theatrical expression of the period's polyglot instruction as it appeared in multilingual dictionaries, grammars, and printed dialogues. Drawing on unique material-textual examples such as an annotated copy of John Baret's pedagogically motivated polyglot dictionary and Gabriel Harvey's bound-together dramatic publications and foreign-language manuals, I show how Kyd teaches foreign languages to his audiences, both through his texts and from the stage.

Mary Sidney Herbert's English translation of Robert Garnier's tragedy *Marc Antoine* is the focus of chapter 3. In discussing this closet drama, which is distinct from the plays examined in other chapters in that it was not publicly acted and that it was translated directly from a Continental source, I analyze the simultaneously worldly and religiously transcendent connotations of translation alongside the Countess of Pembroke's own role as one of the first published women dramatists in England. This chapter analyzes a bilingual Italian-English dictionary that was, it seems, owned and used by Sidney Herbert, the provenance of which has been unknown to scholars until recently. Restored attention to this material-textual object offers a new avenue into the countess's translations and literary works, including her English rendering of Petrarch's "Trionfo della Morte," her English Psalms, and *The Tragedy of Antony*. Since translation was sometimes thought of as a female genre or activity, this chapter also attends closely to the ways Sidney Herbert associates the figure of Cleopatra with translation in her *Tragedy of Antony*; in doing so, she flags her own work as a woman writer and translator and expresses a religiously transcendent connotation of translation: the sanctified soul leaving the body. Cosmopolitan vernaculars, this chapter shows, occupied functions not only in publicly performed plays but also in dramatic works primarily destined for the page.

The next two chapters address city comedy and reveal how this subgenre, widely recognized for its English "local color," actually rests on a foundation of cosmopolitan vernaculars. Specifically, I investigate how the discursive registers of money and sex interact with discussions of translation in the early modern period. In chapter 4, expanding on this first chapter's discussion of Berlaimont's *Colloquia* by way of its variety of editions, typographical conventions, and evident patterns of use, I demonstrate a commercial mode of translation present in William Haughton's *Englishmen for My Money*. Known widely as the first city comedy, this play concerns three foreign merchants whose fortunes in the marriage market depend on their linguistic skill. I show how this comedy, often taken to be xenophobic in its representation of foreign characters and languages, offers playful and ironic commentary on the mercantile tropes in language manuals such as the *Colloquia*; in fact, Haughton's play brings these dialogues onto the stage and, ultimately, into the play's printed texts.

In the fifth chapter of this book, I analyze propagation as a highly gendered mode of translation in Ben Jonson's *Epicene, or The Silent Woman*. Here, I reveal how the female "city talk" of this comedy brings to the stage, and to Jonson's carefully curated printed page, the erotic dialogues spoken among women in Pietro Aretino's *Ragionamenti*. Issued by John Wolfe with the assistance of Giacomo Castelvetro, this set of dialogues circulated both in London and across Europe. Jonson owned a copy himself, but this fact has been absent in discussions of *Epicene*, even though the comedy is based on an Aretino play entitled *Il Marescalco*. Focusing on Jonson's Collegiate ladies and their songs and riddles, I show how this comedy of cross-dressing expresses theatrically—and in spite of its Aretine "sources"—the period's gendered hostility to foreignness. In support of this analysis, I also discuss a linguistically interested university play entitled *Lingua*, which allegorically pits the five senses, all male, against a multilingual character named Lingua—the tongue—who is purposefully gendered female.

As mentioned earlier, Ben Jonson's own teacher, William Camden, wrote of the English language: "Whereas our tongue is mixed, it is no disgrace, whenas all the tongs of *Europe* do participate interchangeably the one of the other." Yet for some, it was a disgrace. And, as England grew from a parochial island into a far-reaching empire, the cosmopolitanism of dramatic works in this language would come to be reinterpreted as national and imperial ambition. A brief conclusion to *Theaters of Translation* gestures in these directions, which, although beyond the scope of my study, are relevant to it in the sense that they have shaped the nation-focused tradition of criticism with which my analyses contend. All told, these fresh readings of plays by Kyd, Sidney Herbert, Haughton, and Jonson—and, as has been seen already, Shakespeare—concerned as they are with multilingualism and "translation" in its manifold meanings, offer a view of the strangeness and estrangements of the English language in a period when its development and future were anything but certain.

| *Chapter Two* |

"For the Easier Understanding"

Language Instruction in Thomas Kyd's *Spanish Tragedy*

For euen as a hauke flieth not hie with one wing: euen so a man reacheth not to excellency with one tong.
—ROGER ASCHAM, *The Scholemaster* (1570)

The bloody climax of Thomas Kyd's sensational masterpiece *The Spanish Tragedy* (ca. 1587) both is and is not a work of translation. That is, it takes place both in English and "in sundry languages."[1] Driven into a fury on account of his son Horatio's murder, the Spanish knight marshal Hieronimo devises a plan in act 4 to obtain his revenge: a brief play entitled *Soliman and Perseda*, acted before the King of Spain and his royal company, featuring the criminals Balthazar and Lorenzo as characters, and performed in a variety of tongues. Hieronimo explains his design to his actors-to-be, including his dead son's beloved (and secretly, the knight marshal's own accomplice) Bel-imperia:

> Each one of us must act his part in unknown languages,
> That it may breed the more variety,
> [*to Balthazar*] As you, my lord, in Latin, I in Greek,
> [*to Lorenzo*] You in Italian, and for because I know
> That Bel-imperia hath practised the French,
> In courtly French shall all her phrases be. (4.1.165–70)

Balthazar responds that "this will be a mere confusion" (line 172), a claim often taken to mean that the royal audience will not comprehend what it hears—that these languages are truly, and not superficially, "unknown." For Hieronimo, however, the variety of languages is a necessary element of the revenge plot; "It must be so," he asserts (line 174). Some critics and editors question whether Hieronimo's playlet was actually staged in multiple tongues, particularly given that early quarto editions of *The Spanish Tragedy* render the playlet's multiple languages in English. Yet, in his authoritative study of the play, Lukas Erne asserts that "there are no sound reasons to doubt that the play of 'Soliman and Perseda' was ever performed in 'sundry languages.'"[2] Likely staged in multiple languages, then, but Englished in print for Kyd's literate audiences, the play's climactic moment is simultaneously foreign and native.

Despite what readers saw in the printed playbooks, however, critics tend to believe that the diverse languages performed here and used elsewhere in Kyd's tragedy would have resulted in utter incomprehension. Some propose that the play's "fall of Babylon" presented a kind of divinely ordained "Babel" or "confusion of tongues" to playgoers.[3] Others assert that *The Spanish Tragedy* evinces through its supposedly "unknown languages" a Protestant and nationalistic, if not wholly xenophobic, agenda against "Babylon-Spain."[4] With some key exceptions, these views prioritizing incomprehension constitute a general, performance-focused consensus about *The Spanish Tragedy*'s hostile approach to language, foreignness, and alien religion.[5]

Recently complicating these Protestant and nationally focused approaches to the play is Carla Mazzio, who examines Kyd's ironic reflections on English discourses of linguistic, legal, and historiographic confusion. As Mazzio argues, *The Spanish Tragedy* is as much about conditions of "linguistic incoherence and 'confusion' at home as it is about the triumph of England, and English, over classical and other vernacular languages and literary-cultural traditions."[6] If it is distinct from the anglocentric interpretations already surveyed, however, Mazzio's perspective on *The Spanish Tragedy* nevertheless sustains assumptions in earlier scholarship about the incomprehensibility and chaotic combination of the play's multiple tongues.[7] Examining Kyd's tragedy alongside contemporary debates about the unstable and corrupt nature of the developing English language, Mazzio interprets Hieronimo's playlet as "an inarticulate Renaissance in the extreme, with classical and vernacular languages coexisting but refusing to cohere," also calling it "a kind of grotesque variant of the fusion and confusion of cultural differences."[8] Though less invested in Protestantism and nationalism in favor of a new and productive focus on language itself, Mazzio's account nonetheless views Kyd's play as a disorderly and ugly hodgepodge of foreign tongues.

In this chapter, by contrast, I will argue that the polyglossia in *The Spanish Tragedy* and in Hieronimo's playlet particularly are neither as xenophobic nor as incomprehensible as these critics maintain, and that they constitute instead a dramatic expression of instructional translation well known in Renaissance England. Retaining Mazzio's central focus on language but building on Eugene Hill's emphasis on how the play "evokes, foregrounds, and enacts a *translatio studii*," my philologically and bibliographically based cosmopolitan approach further estranges (in the dual sense of "making-unfamiliar" and "making-foreign") the established, nationally focused interpretations of this play.[9] Read in parallel with a cross section of the period's pedagogical treatises, polyglot dictionaries, language-learning dialogues, and printed Continental plays, these multilingual portions of *The Spanish Tragedy* exemplify a fruitful and productive mix of cosmopolitan vernaculars and effect a linguistic variety of instruction in the theater. In making this claim, I build on the work of Marianne Montgomery, who argues Kyd's play does not simply reproduce hostile, orientalized views of Spanish hybridity but offers a knowable, theatricalized picture of the language through its auditory polyglossia.[10] Not only through these foreign "sound effects" on stage, I argue, but also by way of their circulating printed instantiations, Kyd's tragedy delivered a world of languages to London's educated playgoers and readers, advancing the discourse in England's many contemporary bilingual and polyglot manuals and dictionaries as well. Altogether, the cosmopolitan mingling of tongues in *The Spanish Tragedy* celebrates the socially elite educational roots of Renaissance translation and drama, ultimately presenting the play as both a language lesson and an epistemological space to contemplate foreign words.

Before proceeding to *The Spanish Tragedy*, this chapter will examine instructional modes of translation extant in polyglot dictionaries, grammars, and language guides of the period. Paying special attention to the ways these publications for French, Italian, and Spanish took up Roger Ascham's notion of "double translation," the discussion will then proceed to Gabriel Harvey, a university-educated sixteenth-century reader who bound his Italian grammar together with works of drama, annotating each volume copiously. Not only do Harvey's books and the broader instructional culture in which they participated offer a fresh context for examining the scattered foreign words across *The Spanish Tragedy*; they also provide a new way to understand Hieronimo's polyglot playlet and the conspicuous circulation of playtexts on stage at the tragedy's conclusion.

"Diligent Bees": Double Translation and Vernacular Instruction

In Renaissance England, instruction in vernaculars including French, Italian, and Spanish owed its methods to classical language study. In this section, I will discuss several surviving language publications—a dictionary, a dialogue book, and a grammar—that testify to this continuity. As Jason Lawrence has shown, Roger Ascham's pedagogical technique known as "double translation" offered a foundation for rapidly expanding communities of vernacular-language learning in print.[11] Discussed at some length in his treatise *The Scholemaster* (1570), translation represents "the most common, and most commendable of all other exercises for youth," and the instructor's former pupil Queen Elizabeth stands as a model student for her "perfit readines, in *Latin, Italian, French,* & *Spanish.*"[12] Desiring to improve on contemporary single-translation methods, Ascham proposes that English students of the Latin language should thoroughly construe and parse a passage, render it into English, and then translate it back into Latin again.[13]

A section in *The Scholemaster* entitled "Translatio linguarum" clarifies the method of double translation further, also implicitly justifying its use among vernaculars tongues. Despite a general emphasis on Latin and English, Ascham states that his method is "proper for euerie tong, particularly for following the steppes of the best Autors" in those languages (sig. L2v). Rooting his method in the examples of Cicero and Quintilian, he adds: "I am moved to thinke this waie of double translating, either onelie or chieflie, to be fittest, for the spedy and perfit atteyning of any tong" (sig. L2v–L3r). With the words "euerie" and "any," *The Scholemaster* extends its reach to include multiple languages, potentially including vernaculars beyond English. Moreover, despite his anxieties about contemporary Italy, Ascham states that he does not by any means "contemne, either the knowledge of strange and diuerse tonges, and namelie the Italian tonge, which next the Greeke and Latin tonge, I like and loue aboue all other" (sig. H3r). Separating Italy's linguistic and pedagogical matter from what he sees as contemporary cultural vices, Ascham opens his program to Italian and other "strange and diuerse tonges" making their way into England, including vernaculars.

While Ascham's treatise remains a conventional touchstone for discussions of early modern language and translation, John Baret's *Alvearie* (1574), a dictionary in English, French, Greek, and Latin, offers a clearer example of how socially privileged forms of sixteenth-century Latin translation pedagogy were beginning to incorporate cosmopolitan vernaculars into their fabric.[14] An instructor at Cambridge, Baret issued his dictionary as an aid to students undertaking bilingual translation exercises. Whether or not an annotated copy in the possession of modern-day booksellers George Koppelman and Daniel Wechsler belonged to William Shakespeare (and it seems it did not), this book and other surviving copies offer a window into the multilingual practice of Renaissance schoolrooms.[15] Like *The Scholemaster*, this *Alvearie* was dedicated to William Cecil, patron of learning and languages, but it was designed especially for the benefit of "yong learners."[16] If the book was made for Baret's students, it was also presented as the result of their translation efforts. Indeed, as John Gallagher notes, prefatory spaces in multilingual language-learning books often "reproduced the classroom—and its successes—in print."[17] The instructor explains in a preface: "I appoynted them [i.e., the students] certaine leaues of the same booke euery day to write the English before ye Latin, and likewise to gather a number of fine phrases out of *Cicero, Terence, Caesar, Liuie, &c.* and to set them vnder seuerall Tytles, for the more ready finding them againe at their neede. Thus within a yeare or two they had gathered togither a great volume, which (for the apt similitude betweene the good scholers and diligent Bees in gathering their wax and hony into their Hiue) I called then their *Alueari*e, both for a memoriall by whom it was made, and also by this name to incourage other to the like diligence" (sig. ⋆4). As scholars have noted, this dictionary has discernible traces of other, contemporary lexicons.[18] Yet all the same, Baret credits his Cambridge students for the book's production, offering the volume as a kind of lexicographic application—and product—of Ascham's method.

Essential to the *Alvearie*'s front matter is its discourse of bees and beehives, which joins together the categories of translation and imitation and epitomizes the mingling of various languages, both classical and vernacular.[19] In taking up this discourse, Baret likens his students to "diligent Bees," compares the book to a "Hiue," and publishes it with an elaborate beehive frontispiece (figure 2.1). Along with other contributors of commendatory verses, the Ovid translator Arthur Golding uses this same trope to emphasize the book's fitting title and Baret's great pains in bringing together these four languages in print, two classical and two vernacular (represented in the frontispiece as trees). "For vnderneath this Hyue yet small in fame," Golding writes, referring to the hive on the frontispiece, "Of fower Tungs the flowers hyued bee / In one sweet iewce to serue the turne of thee" (sig. ⋆⋆1r). That is, out of four initially separate "flowers" hived in this book's pages, Baret's students have furnished "one sweet iewce" for the use of other young learners. From this discourse of bees and the techniques associated with it, one can see how the categories of imitation, translation, "gathering and framing"—or "juicing"—and language instruction are slippery, codependent, and often hard to disentangle (indeed, the difficult syntax of Golding's verse testifies to this complexity).[20] Issued as a dictionary, however, and breaking "a number of fine

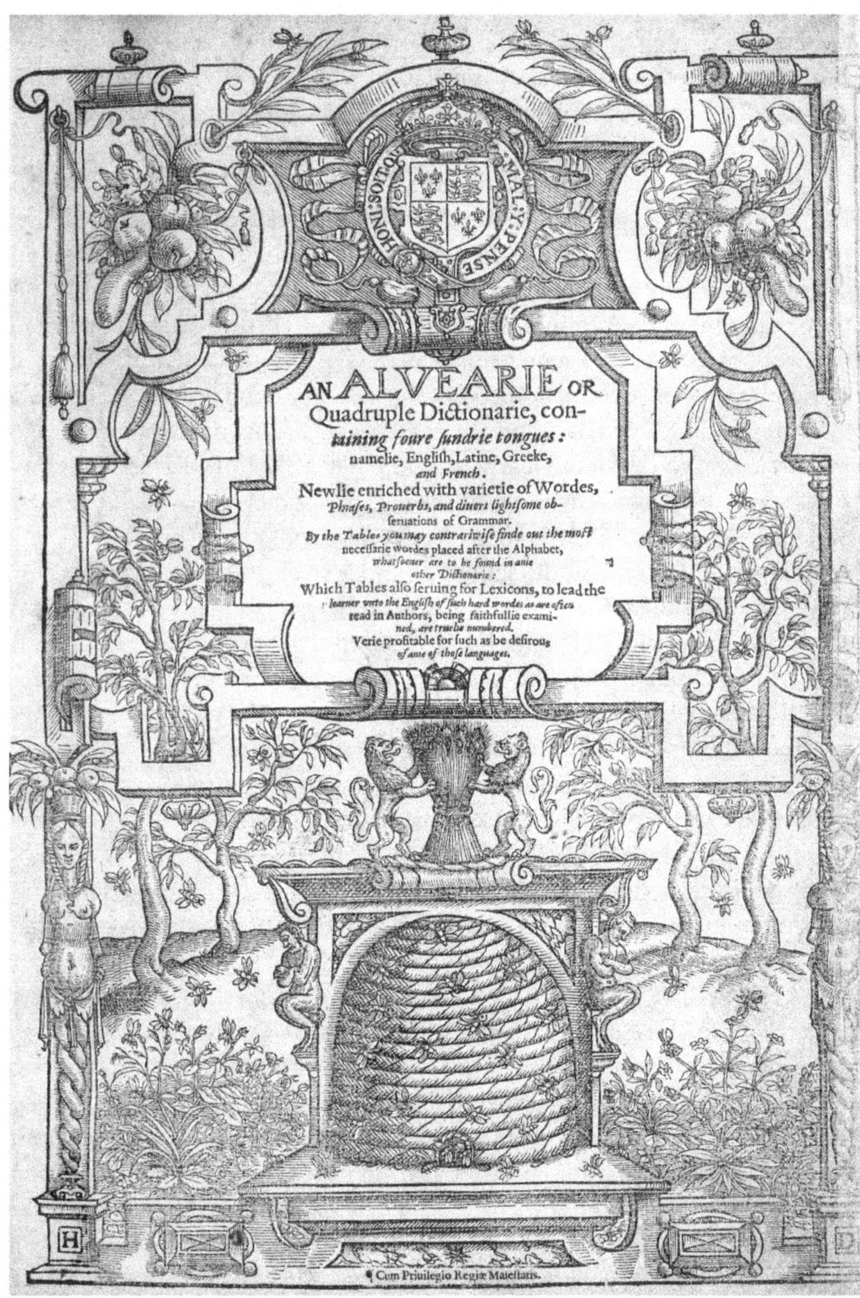

FIGURE 2.1 John Baret, *An Alvearie or Quadruple Dictionarie, containing foure sundrie tongues*, 1580, frontispiece engraving. Furness PA2364 .B35 1580. Reproduced by kind permission of the Kislak Center for Special Collections, Rare Books and Manuscripts, University of Pennsylvania.

phrases" into their constituent parts for the benefit of schoolboys, Baret's *Alvearie* nonetheless associates translation with the pedagogical technique of "gathering and framing" and a collaborative variety of multiple language education.

Surviving copies of this dictionary show how readers and "yong learners" seized on this apian discourse in the practical service of translation. In doing so, they follow the compiler's prefatory suggestions, for Baret encouraged his book's users to act like "diligent Bees" and to "place such as they reade in good authours, vnder their proper Tytles, or in the margent of this booke, for their owne priuate vse" (sig. *4v). Below this advice, an owner of the 1580 edition copied out in secretary hand a pithy sentence by Isocrates included by Baret on the same page for his readers' encouragement: "Dost thou desire to learne and know much / Loue lerning and thou shalt soone be such."[21] Writing in their copies, other users of the *Alvearie* added their own headwords to the dictionary, including "ferula, 1a, f.g. A feruler or palmer wher w^{t} the scholers hand is stroke" (i.e., a schoolmaster's rod) and "Phrontisterũ, xij n.g. is a Schoolehowse" (a place for thinking or studying; potentially an Aristophantic reference), that register lexicographically the physical discipline accompanying early modern instruction.[22] The former inscription is numbered to fit in with other entries on the page, and the latter has been added to the Latin index as well. In Koppelman and Wechsler's copy, the most concentrated handwriting appears on what the booksellers call a "trailing blank," a flyleaf containing over two hundred words in English, French, and Latin. Clearly, this book's annotators have followed Baret's suggestion to act like "diligent Bees," their inscriptions bearing out in a personalized manner the method of translation present in this polyglot lexicon more generally.[23]

The year before Baret's dictionary was first published, Huguenot refugee Claudius Hollyband issued *The French Schoolemaister* (1573), a book that shapes Ascham's methods into printed dialogues for the study of French. As critics have recognized, the title of this book clearly evokes *The Scholemaster*, and the manual's two-column layout endorses Ascham's insistence on translation for language learning, too. Furthermore, Hollyband dedicates his book to the royal tutor's own "yong learner," Robert Sackville, the eldest son of *Gorboduc* playwright Thomas Sackville and the grandson of Richard Sackville, the royal administrator whose conversations helped furnish *The Scholemaster* in the first place.[24] Robert also seems to have had some interest in the Italian language, for he owned a copy of William Thomas's *Principal Rules of the Italian Grammer*, the first primer of its kind in England.[25] If Italian and Latin were familiar to the Oxford-bound

Sackville at this time, however, Hollyband indicates that French was not: "These causes haue allured mee to dedicate this simple worke vnto you, bycause you are not entred any thinge at all into the language, but are new to learne: not that you shuld leaue of your weightier, and worthier studies in the Uniuersitie, but when your minde is amazed, and dazeled with longe readinge, you may refresh and disport you in learning this tongue" (sig. A3v). Although Hollyband's dedication shows that French, like Italian, did not yet rank among the "weightier, and worthier studies" offered officially at universities, it suggests that for young men at Oxford there was nevertheless a place for self-directed vernacular-language learning.[26] On the one hand, Hollyband's manual anticipates Sackville's political and diplomatic future, "when God, your Countrey, your Prince, and Age shall call vppon you . . . to accomplish their commaundement into the forreyne region" (sig. A3v). On the other hand, learning French could be a pastime, a pleasurable activity that "may refresh and disport you." With a mind to these literary pleasures, Thomas issued his *Principal Rules* with specific regard for "the better understandyng of Boccace, Petrarcha, and Dante." Building on the success of *The French Schoolemaister*, Hollyband published another manual, *The Frenche Littelton* (1576), dedicated again to the "yong gentilman M. Robert Sackevill."[27] These French manuals witnessed dozens of editions, ushering Ascham's instructional model into the territory of cosmopolitan vernaculars.[28]

Through imaginative exchanges among multiple characters, Hollyband's books show how techniques for classical-language learning could be adopted, or "translated," for vernacular instruction. Moreover, through their two-column presentation, they facilitate translation from one language to another. If these publications illustrate the polyglot contours of the Erasmian *copia* examined by Richard Halpern, or the emerging and outlaw notion of "vernacular eloquence" explored more recently by Jenny Mann, they also offer provocative glimpses into what Lynn Enterline calls "the theatricality of everyday life": daily techniques of imitation and performance that attended but also undermined the schoolroom's tenets of order and mastery.[29] In its second and all subsequent editions, *The Frenche Littelton* begins with a dialogue entitled "Of Scholers and Schoole / *Des Escholiers et Eschole*," which stages a variety of colloquial, pedagogically themed scenes with a cast of various speakers (in the first edition, it appears fourth). Here, a boy leaves home for school, is scolded by his instructor for tardiness, complains about his classmates, and is finally required to "*turne [his] lessons out of french into english: and then out of english into french*" (sig. C5v). Should he refuse this task of double translation, he faces the "feruler or palmer" (to use the terms of the previously discussed *Alvearie* reader). Hollyband's schoolmaster warns his students:

> *You haue not rehearsed your lessons,*
> *I perceaue it well enough: you shall be all*
> *whipped to morrow morning, if you*
> *misse in it a word onely,*
> *a syllable: a letter.* (sig. C6v)

> Vous n'avez pas répété voz leçons,
> ie l'apperçoy bien: vous serez tous
> fessez de main au matin, si vous y
> faillez vn seul mot, vne seule parolle,
> vne syllabe, vne lett[r]e (sig. C7r)

Here, the rehearsal, monitoring, and harsh physical punishment evident in the period's Latin pedagogy takes shape imaginatively in Hollyband's bilingual, two-columned vernacular lesson. Altogether, Hollyband's printed manuals illustrate how the daily study of Latin in early modern schoolrooms could be reconfigured in an imaginative and theatrical manner for French and Italian vernacular purposes.

Like Baret's *Alvearie*, the first London-published manual for the Spanish language was both a multilingual enterprise and a product of translation. Printed by John Wolfe and issued considerably later than most guides to French or Italian—most likely on account of English political tensions with Spain—John Thorius's *Spanish Grammer* (1590) delivered its language lessons to readers in English, Spanish, and French.[30] Coupling a short dictionary with grammatical instruction in areas including pronunciation, parts of speech, verbs, and correct conjugation, this manual translates Antonio del Corro's *Reglas Gramaticales para Aprender la Lengua Española y Francesa*, which had been published four years earlier at Oxford. If its current binding reflects an early modern owner's wishes, then one extant Bodleian Library copy of Thorius's translated Spanish language manual bound with John Huise's *A Perfect Survey of the English Tongue* (1624) may offer further proof for the ways communities and techniques of vernacular-language learning overlapped at Oxford.[31]

Oxford's vibrant community of vernacular-language students offers one point of origin for *The Spanish Grammer*, and John Wolfe's printing house stands as another. Like the sophisticated Italian-language books Wolfe issued a decade earlier, and which I will consider at length in chapter 5, *The Spanish Grammar* owes much to the Continentally trained printer's capable multilingual typography.[32] To differentiate between languages, Thorius states in a preface to his book, "I haue caused it to be printed in three sundry kindes of letters," referring to the italic, roman, and black-letter type that indicate separately French, Spanish, and English for readers (sig. A3v).[33] With its bilingual dictionary and polyglot typography, this

Spanish manual, London's first, extends England's culture of linguistic instruction to encompass a third vernacular, an important one at this time in English history.

Altogether, these publications exemplify clear continuities between classical and vernacular language training in Renaissance England, namely in employing Ascham's double-translation method in the service of French, Italian, and Spanish instruction in print. They also enable a kind of bilingual identification with master or student (as in Hollyband's *Frenche Littelton*) and provide visual linguistic assistance for learners through typography (as in Thorius's *Spanish Grammer*). Importantly, these books often assume a theatrical quality through the inclusion of speech prefixes, lists of dramatis personae, and scene locations, thereby anticipating conventions in early printed drama. In this way, these manuals and dictionaries constitute a linguistic bridge between Latin schoolroom practices and later works of vernacular drama composed by former students, Kyd among them.

Translated for Action: Gabriel Harvey's Grammar Drama

In the case of Kyd's contemporary Gabriel Harvey, a Cambridge scholar, student of languages, and copious annotator of printed books, the overlap of these instructional techniques and drama survives in an Italian grammar formerly bound with his vernacular playbooks. Today, portions of this *Sammelband* are held separately at the Folger Shakespeare Library, the Houghton Library, and the Huntington Library; if imaginatively reassembled and considered together as a unit, they attest to Harvey's interest in exemplary conversation, as András Kiséry has shown.[34] I would add that they also offer a view into his joint project in vernacular-language learning and dramatic reading. Unnumbered and somewhat disconnected from the scholar's other language-learning books at the Huntington is a copy of Henry Grantham's *An Italian Grammer* (1575), itself a translation of Scipione Lentulo's *Italicae Grammatices Praecepta ac Ratio* (1567). The inscription "Axiophili prima ars Linguae Italicae. Grammatica. Comoediae. Tragoediae." (Axiophilus's [i.e., Harvey's] first technique for the Italian language. Grammar. Comedies. Tragedies.) on this book's title page (figure 2.2) led Caroline B. Bourland to infer that "when Harvey owned it some Italian plays were bound with the grammar."[35] This is demonstrably true from the surviving books' evidence. According to a nineteenth-century auction catalog and matching markings on the books' fore edges, Harvey's copy of this *Italian Grammer* was once part of a *Sammelband* along with several playbooks in octavo, some in Italian, some in Latin. These

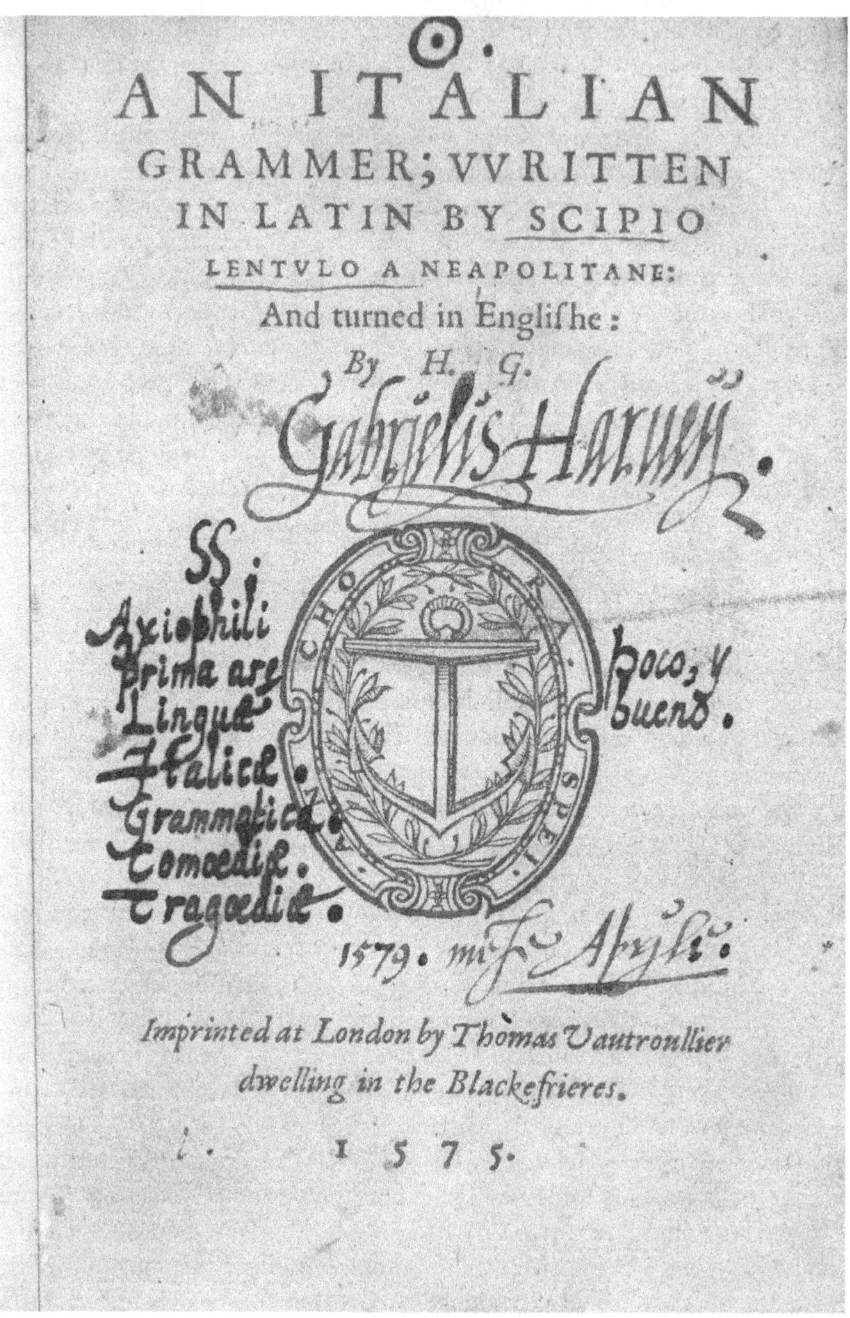

AN ITALIAN GRAMMER; VVRITTEN IN LATIN BY SCIPIO LENTVLO A NEAPOLITANE: And turned in Englishe:

By H. G.

Imprinted at London by Thomas Vautroullier dwelling in the Blackefrieres.

1575.

FIGURE 2.2 Gabriel Harvey's copy of Scipione Lentulo, *An Italian Grammer*, trans. Henry Grantham, 1575, sig. *2r. RB 62184. Reproduced by permission of the Huntington Library, San Marino, California.

are: Lodovico Dolce's *Medea* and *Thieste*, Erasmus's Latin translations of Euripides's *Hecuba* and *Iphigenia*, and an Italian edition of Terence's comedies.[36] This binding arrangement attests to the possibility of a *prima ars*, or first technique, of vernacular instruction extending through schoolbooks (in translation) into the published drama of Dolce, Euripides, and Terence (also in translation).

Harvey's choice to join an Italian grammar to Italian plays represents a personal and material manifestation of the prevalent mingling of pronunciation lessons, grammar rules, and bilingual dialogues in language manuals by instructors including Hollyband and Florio, manuals that Harvey owned and annotated.[37] The *Sammelband* also points to how these language-learning publications could be put to practical and pleasurable use along with other, similar books, at a time when nonclassical vernaculars were not part of the university curriculum.[38] At the Huntington alone, surviving language-learning publications numbered and annotated by Harvey include John Eliot's *Ortho-epia Gallica* (1593), Pierre du Ploiche's *Treatise in Englishe and Frenche* (1578), a bilingual French-English text entitled *The Images of the Old Testament* (1549), John Thorius's *Spanish Grammer* (1590), and Richard Perceval's dictionary *Bibliotheca Hispanica* (1591).[39] Bourland shows that Harvey demonstrated his familiarity with vernacular languages long before marking in these books; accordingly, such extensive use of these manuals attests to a technique of language learning that is continuous and recursive, rather than once and final.[40] Building on the work of Bourland and Virginia F. Stern, Warren Boutcher and Joyce Boro view Harvey's methods as part of a humanistic agenda geared toward social, political, and moral success.[41] Altogether, Harvey's use of these books not only extends his politically oriented "studying for action" into vernacular territory; it also evidences an interest in a less strictly utilitarian and more delightful "affective style," particularly in relation to Continental drama.[42]

Harvey's annotations in this *Sammelband* appear in English, Italian, Latin, and Spanish, and it was in this period that he was beginning to experiment with French as well. The scholar's inscriptions in the *Italian Grammer* evince clear attention to the text's lessons, repeating certain phrases in the margins, also branching out into other languages (as in the case of his use of the Spanish phrase "Poco y bueno").[43] Harvey points ahead to the volume's drama as well, writing "No finer, or pithier Exa[m] ples, then in ye Excellent Comedies, & Tragedies following: full of sweet, & wise Discourse" (sig. L2r; see figure 2.3). In the pages of Dolce's *Medea*, he praises the four included tragedies in Latin, also making mention of Ascham and the educational reformer John Cheke.[44] In English, Harvey compares George Gascoigne's rendition of *Jocasta* with those of Euripides and Dolce, showing his reflections on the history of theater crossed both classical and vernacular tongues (sig. A2v). Italian annotations in both *Medea* and *Thieste* discuss Dolce, Ludovico Ariosto, and Torquato Tasso, and also include references to the works of Luigi Contarino (sig. A3v), Pietro Aretino, and Francesco Sansovino (sig. D8v). In Harvey's Aldine copy of Euripides's plays, Italian inscriptions offer praise for Aretino's "Quattro comedie," Machiavelli's incisive and elegant *Mandragola* and *Clitia*, and Ariosto's *Suppositi*, dramatic works he could have known through his printer, John Wolfe.[45] The annotation techniques and dramatic commentary one finds across Harvey's language manuals and these Continental playbooks strongly suggest that both kinds of printed material served as sites for instruction and delight in vernacular languages ("sweet, & wise Discourse"), at least among Harvey and his learned, male associates.[46]

In this *Sammelband*'s marginalia, Harvey also indicates that dictionaries played a crucial role in his vernacular language-learning practice. Following the aforementioned comment about comedies and tragedies, he writes in his Italian grammar: "A notable Dictionarie, for the Grammer" (sig. L2r; figure 2.3). Perhaps an Italian-English dictionary such as William Thomas's *Principal Rules* was affixed to this volume; it featured a vocabulary of some eight thousand words, and Harvey considered the book in parallel with Florio's *Firste Fruites* (1578) as an inspirational guide to the language.[47] Alternatively, Harvey could be gesturing to a "homogeneal Dictionary" mentioned in his annotations in du Ploiche's *Treatise in Englishe and Frenche*; this could refer to Perceval's *Bibliotheca Hispanica*, which was bound with the same *Treatise* and which he inscribed with the words "Huc meum Dictionarium Homogenium, propriè, et merè Hispanicum" (This my homogeneal dictionary, properly and purely Spanish).[48] A final possibility could be that Harvey was referring to the dramatic octavos themselves as a kind of dictionary, a treasury of languages bound with and for the exploration of Italian grammar; if this sounds tenuous, his annotations in the index to Stefano Guazzo's *Civil Conversatione* (bound with Harvey's equally diminutive copy of Hollyband's Italian dialogues) refer to the book's contents as a "Thesoro della lingua, discorso, e Conuersatione Italiana."[49] Lexicons and indices were often known in this era as "treasuries," such multilingual wordlists providing English readers access to the drama of Dolce and other Continental playwrights. Whatever the case, both mentions of dictionaries in these language manuals suggest that when it came to language instruction among learned audiences, dictionaries and grammars not only provided assistance for the combined practice

155

Of an Interiection.

Of ioye: *Oh.*

Of laughing: *Ah, Ah.*

Of vvondring: *O, vh, vh.*

Of sorrovve: Aih, *Ah, Oyme.*

Of Desier: *Deh.*

Of dreade: *Bàco Bàco: Oh Oh Dio.*

FINIS.

Figure 2.3 Gabriel Harvey's copy of Scipione Lentulo, *An Italian Grammer*, trans. Henry Grantham, 1575, sig. L2r. RB 62184. Reproduced by permission of the Huntington Library, San Marino, California.

of vernacular language study and dramatic reading but also offered a physical space for the mingled contemplation of various vernaculars and their dramatic applications.

"When in Toledo There I Studied": *The Spanish Tragedy*'s Instructional Origins

This privileged instructional context would have been deeply familiar to Thomas Kyd. In the final sections of this chapter, I will show how the polyglossia scattered purposefully throughout *The Spanish Tragedy* not only reflected Kyd's own linguistic education and his work as a published translator but also projected into the theater the "fruitful" world of printed language instruction pointed up by Baret, Hollyband, and Thorius, among others. In this way, I offer a vernacular complement to the usual Latin-focused, schoolroom-to-playhouse models of literary influence, showing how playwrights' training in vernacular tongues also deeply informed their dramatic compositions; my approach also expands the notion of "vernacular eloquence" (as discussed in Mann's study of "outlaw rhetoric" striving against classical models) to account for French, Italian, and Spanish, which were present in England, too.[50] Finally, although I focus my attention on Kyd's learned playgoers and readers in this chapter, *The Spanish Tragedy*'s polyglot language lessons also reached broader, less-educated quarters of the playwright's audiences, for as Montgomery recognizes, the theater "makes the experience of foreign words accessible to a wider range of people, including the illiterate."[51] Even without the use of hendiadyses, verbal pairings that group an unknown word with a familiar term, Kyd offers audience members with less formal schooling a sample of foreign vernaculars circulating in London's multilingual dictionaries and grammars, as well as vernacular schoolrooms. In these ways, *The Spanish Tragedy*'s multilingual playlet and its scattered foreign words appear less as an "inarticulate Renaissance in the extreme" and more as an extension of instructional practices familiar to Kyd, offering language lessons to learned readers or playgoers and a glimpse into these techniques for more general audiences.[52]

Kyd's training at the Merchant Taylors' School, an institution directed by the educational reformer and language theorist Richard Mulcaster, easily could have furnished the playwright with a sophisticated, cosmopolitan approach to vernacular languages. Parting ways with those who desired to purify the English language from its Continental influences, Mulcaster offered approval for how English "boroweth daielie from foren tungs, either of pure necessitie in new matters, or of mere brauerie, to garnish it self with all."[53] Indeed, as Margaret Tudeau-Clayton has recently pointed out, this practice of "enfranchisement" championed by Mulcaster possessed "emancipatory force" and vast possibilities.[54] The instructor offered praise for Baret's *Alvearie* and Hollyband's *Campo di Fior* (1583); he also published his treatises at a printer frequented by Hollyband, perhaps evincing ideological affinities between the educator and communities of vernacular lexicography and instruction.[55] It was under this educator's supervision that Kyd, the son of a scrivener, possibly had his first experience with aristocratic translation and theater exercise, both in the service of Latin instruction.[56] In the years following his Merchant Taylors' education, Kyd did not proceed to university like some of his more privileged peers, but he did publish English translations of Torquato Tasso's household treatise *Padre di Famiglia* in 1588 and Robert Garnier's tragedy *Cornélie* in 1594, thereby establishing himself as a multilingual, collaborative playwright and practitioner of translation.[57] (This work also aligns him with Mary Sidney Herbert, whose poetry and closet drama I will discuss in the next chapter.) The foreign languages in *The Spanish Tragedy*—in particular, the "sundry languages" of the culminating playlet—therefore function as a dramatic deployment and expansion of Kyd's sustained interest in foreign vernaculars and their translation for instructional and literary purposes.

The Spanish Tragedy's early printed editions feature a small but significant number of words in non-English languages: three words in Spanish, thirty-three in Italian, and 193 in Latin.[58] This is something more, I am arguing, than a "fallen model of hybridity."[59] For Janette Dillon, this mix of languages throughout the play suggests the rise of the vernacular over Latin, a narrative one often finds in established studies of language, print, and nationhood.[60] Reading Kyd's play in relation to sixteenth-century England's hostility toward foreigners, Dillon perceives specific connotations for each of these languages. Latin represents authority and singularity, while "alien vernaculars" represent "slipperiness and unreliability. . . . English [is] in the position of strength, firmly allied with plainness and transparency. Spanish and Italian . . . take the action into a world of swift decisions, calculated treachery and Machiavellian intrigue."[61] Without dismissing these connotations, which were surely present to some degree in early modern London, I suggest greater consideration for the ways these foreign languages offered something less nationalistic and more cosmopolitan both to readers and to playgoers. In the early quartos, for instance, these words and phrases are singled out with italic type, an indication of foreignness common to the period's language manuals and multilingual dictionaries.[62] In this way, the comprehensible, auditory "mixture of languages" that Montgomery finds in *The Spanish Tragedy*'s staged performances had a textual complement in the early quartos' typography, but as I will show in detail later on, these books can be understood as much more than mere "recording device[s]" for performance, for they also shaped the playgoing expectations of readers.[63]

In addition to sharing typographic conventions with drama, the period's bilingual dictionaries and language manuals provided relatively stable guides for these words, opening their meaning in print to English readers with some schooling. According to Dillon, when Hieronimo utters the phrase "*Pocas palabras*" (few words) (3.14.119), two out of the play's three Spanish words, "he too has by now become a double-dealer."[64] Though this Spanish phrase might indeed seem charged with treachery to some playgoers or readers, particularly given England's tense political relationship with Spain at this time, Hieronimo expresses a desire for revenge long before this moment in the play, rendering these words' "turning-point" status open to question. Furthermore, the use of these Spanish words locates the tragedy among the Spanish dictionaries and manuals in Kyd's England, thereby offering a theatrical site for linguistic contemplation. For example, someone with access to Harvey's language manuals and dictionaries could find "Poco, a little" (sig. S1v) and "Palabra, a word" (sig. S1r) in Thorius's *Spanish Grammer*, while "Poco, little, *Parum, paulùm*" and "Palabra, a word, *Verbum*" appear in Perceval's *Bibliotheca Hispanica* (sig. S4r, R4r). In John Minsheu's Spanish-English dialogues, an exchange between friends at a banquet features Hieronimo's words exactly. When one interlocutor makes a witty request for wine, another speaker replies, "A buen entendedór pocas palabras, de lo sant Martin quiére v.m." ("*To a good vnderstander a worde is enough, you woulde haue that of Saint Martin*").[65] Even if the playwright lacked Spanish fluency, Kyd's tragedy joins these instructional publications in presenting "*Pocas palabras*" to an English audience. A host of other plays in England followed suit, engraining Kyd's foreign utterance into London's dramatic fabric as "the commonest Spanish catch-phrase" in the theater.[66]

Literate audience members also could have associated the sententious Italian phrases in Kyd's play with proverbs listed in foreign-language phrasebooks or works of translation. Both Lorenzo's "*E quel che voglio io, nessun lo sa. / Intendo io; quel mi bastera*" (And what I want, no one knows. I do know; that is enough for me) (3.4.83–84) and Hieronimo's "*Chi mi fa più carezze che non sole / Tradito m'ha, o tradir vole*" (He who gives me more caresses than usual has betrayed me or wants to betray [me]) (3.14.170–71) employ the two-part structure of numerous proverbs set among the

Italian-English dialogues in Florio's *Firste Fruites*. In fact, in this book's nineteenth chapter, "*Prouerbii* / Prouerbes," one interlocutor nearly utters the words spoken by Hieronimo: "*Chi mi fa meglio che non sole, tradito m'ha, ò tradir mi vole*," rendered into English as "Who doth vnto me better then he is woont, he hath betrayed me, or els wyl betray me" (G4r).[67] Readers of *The Spanish Tragedy* noticed these proverbs. One of Q4's two surviving copies features early annotations not translating but copying out this Italian phrase in the margin (figure 2.4). Inscribed in an italic hand mimicking the printed text's italic letterforms, the writing most likely evinces an educated or educationally aspirational reader.[68] This, I suggest, evinces a "Harveian approach"—or a kind of "study for action"—to vernacular language in the physical space of Kyd's playbook; it is, one could say, a handwritten enactment of the *imitatio* or repetition of *sententiae* one finds in Renaissance schoolrooms.[69] The proverb here can also be traced back both to an English translation of Lodovico Guicciardini's *L'Hore di Ricreatione* (1573) and to a phrase attributed to a "subtill Italian" in George Puttenham's *Arte of English Poesie* (1589), showing that in one way or another, English readers could associate Hieronimo's Italian words with language manuals or

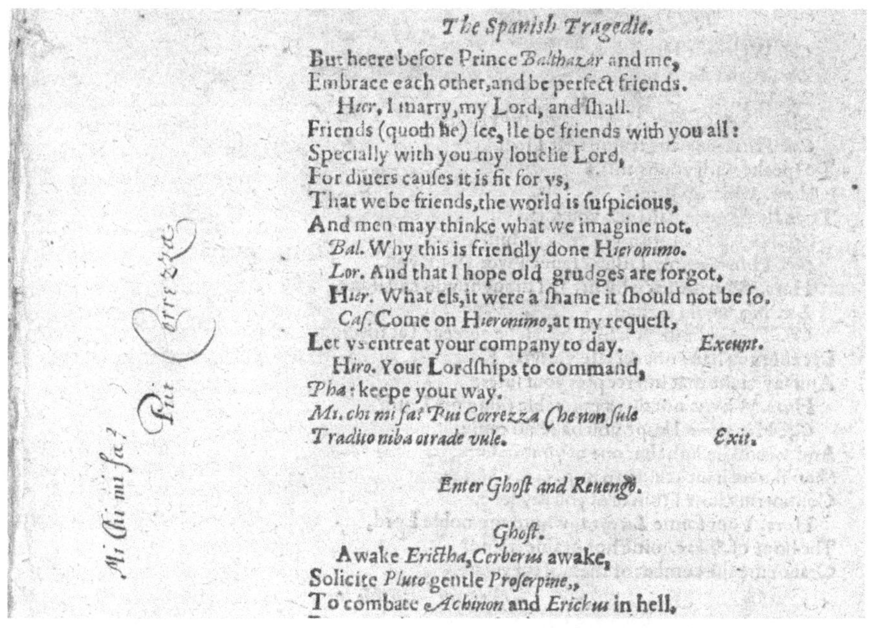
The Spanish Tragedie.

But heere before Prince *Balthazar* and me,
Embrace each other, and be perfect friends.
Hier, I marry, my Lord, and ſhall.
Friends (quoth he) ſee, Ile be friends with you all:
Specially with you my louelie Lord,
For diuers cauſes it is fit for vs,
That we be friends, the world is ſuſpicious,
And men may thinke what we imagine not.
Bal. Why this is friendly done *Hieronimo*.
Lor. And that I hope old grudges are forgot.
Hier. What els, it were a ſhame it ſhould not be ſo.
Caſ. Come on *Hieronimo*, at my requeſt,
Let vs entreat your company to day. *Exeunt.*
Hiro. Your Lordſhips to command,
Pha: keepe your way.
Mi. chi mi fa? Pui Correzza Che non ſule
Tradito mi ha otrade vule. *Exit.*

Enter Ghoſt and Reuenge.

Ghoſt.

Awake *Erictha*, *Cerberus* awake,
Solicite *Pluto* gentle *Proſerpine*,
To combate *Achinon* and *Erickus* in hell.

FIGURE 2.4 Thomas Kyd, *The Spanish Tragedie: Containing the lamentable end of Don Horatio, and Bel-Imperia: with the pittifull death of olde Hieronimo*, 1602, sig. K1v. C.57.d.5. Reproduced by permission of the British Library.

works of translation.[70] Bilingual dictionaries and language manuals published in England offered a ready path into the italicized foreign languages in *The Spanish Tragedy* quartos, a path that some readers took up directly, pen in hand.

The fragments of foreign vernaculars in Kyd's play prepared readers and playgoers for Hieronimo's spectacular polyglot conclusion, which accomplishes the protagonist's desired revenge for his son Horatio's death. It must be emphasized that the knight marshal's plans emerge from a clearly indicated pedagogical and dramatic context. As Mazzio states, "The learned context of the playlet is important because it raises questions about how the multilingual dimensions of humanism and the law may have impacted popular dramatic innovation."[71] As knight marshal, Hieronimo is a step below other aristocratic characters, but citizens praise him "for learning and for law" (3.13.51), and the masque in act 1 establishes his dramaturgical aptitude (1.4.138–73). In fact, it is supposedly for this latter reason that the King requests another performance to celebrate Balthazar and Bel-imperia's impending marriage. Formally introducing the play to Bel-imperia and his son's murderers Lorenzo and Balthazar, Hieronimo explains the tragedy's origins in his own youth and education:

> When I was young I gave my mind
> And plied myself to fruitless poetry,
> Which, though it profit the professor naught,
> Yet is it passing pleasing to the world. (4.1.69–72)

Here, Hieronimo looks back to his youthful days as a scholar—that is to say, a student, a "yong learner" not so different from the pupils of Baret, Minsheu, or Mulcaster. Though a practitioner of law during the play, Hieronimo admits his past devotion to "fruitless poetry" (a subject to which I will return). He continues, presenting a copy of his work to his three auditors:

> When in Toledo there I studied,
> It was my chance to write a tragedy–
> See here, my lords–
> *(He shows them a book.)*
> Which, long forgot, I found this other day. (4.1.75–78)

Like Polonius in *Hamlet* ("I did enact Julius Caesar"), Hieronimo draws a link between the instruction of young men and the acting of drama, a connection essential to training in classical tongues but equally salient for supposedly "fruitless" vernacular tales.[72] In doing so, the protagonist traces a literary history especially familiar to Kyd, whose career in vernacular literature rested on a foundation of bilingual instruction and performance at the Merchant Taylors' School. Hieronimo further flags the link between schoolroom and playhouse when he specifies that his tragedy "was determined to have been acted, / By gentlemen, and scholars too, / Such as could tell what to speak" (lines 98–100). Being able to "tell what to speak" stands here as a key characteristic of men with a certain learned status—whether gentlemen and students, or Balthazar's "princes and courtiers" (line 101)—and indeed, the ability of "tongues" to "tell" receives thoroughgoing attention throughout the play at large (Hieronimo bites out his own tongue at the tragedy's end, rendering further confession impossible).[73] The retrospective nature of the knight marshal's account and his emphasis on his youthful studies establishes the play within a play already as a kind of instruction.

Furthermore, for some "gentlemen, and scholars" attending or reading Kyd's play, Hieronimo's reference to Toledo would have been rich with historical connotations of polyglossia and translation. Although no universities were located in Toledo, the scholarly group known as the Escuela de Traductores Toledanos thrived during the twelfth and thirteenth centuries and was widely known during the Renaissance.[74] It was precisely the multilingual character of this group—a group which included Englishmen—that contributed to Toledo's reputation as a major center for scholarship and translation, along with its substantial collection of manuscripts by writers including Aristotle, Ptolemy, and Galen. Evidence also suggests that, centuries before Ascham, a kind of double-translation method accompanied the Escuela's practice.[75] In directly referencing Toledo in *The Spanish Tragedy*, both Hieronimo, whose name already calls to mind the Biblical translator Jerome, and Kyd, a published translator himself, locate themselves within a longer trajectory of instruction, polyglossia, and the translation that made literature available to other cultures.[76]

If this medieval context seems obscure, such an allusion to Toledo would still resonate with instructional and linguistic significance for some "yong learners" or educated playgoers familiar with Spanish language manuals and literature published in Kyd's England. In a conversation included in Minsheu's Spanish-English dialogues, for example, two Englishmen named Giles and William discuss the benefits of speaking with Spaniards, making a clear reference to Toledo:

E. Vámos a la lónja, adonde me estan esperando dos amígos Españ-	*G. Let vs goe to the Exchange where two Spanyards very discreete men my*

óles, muy discretos, gustaréis de su buena conversación.	*friends are tarrying for me, you shall haue a taste of their good conuersation.*
G. Háblan ynglés?	*W. Speake they English?*
E. Vn poquito, peró pues vos entendéis bien el Español, y yo tanbien no ympórta.	*G. A very little, but seeing you vnderstand well the Spanish and I also, it makes no matter.*
G. Huelgo me de yr, aunque no séa, mas de por aprendér algunas buenas frásis Españólas.	*W. I am glad to goe, though it be but to learne some good Spanish phrases.*
E. Essas sé yo que las tiénen buenas,	*G. Those I knowe they haue and good ones,*
porque son de *Tolédo* donde es la príma de la lengua Española. (sig. n6v–o1r)	*bicause they are of* Toledo *where it is the prime of the Spanish toong.*

This moment leading up to "buena conversación" ("*good conuersation*") might seem lost within the greater bulk of Minsheu's dialogues, to say nothing of the same volume's appended dictionary and grammar, but it makes a plain statement about Toledo's linguistic preeminence. As "la príma de la lengua Españóla" ("*the prime of the Spanish toong*") this city stands as an important source for the "buenas frásis Españólas" ("*good Spanish phrases*") that Minsheu's two English interlocutors hope to hear—and "*learne.*" Moreover, this exchange corroborates the commentary available in Juan Huarte's *Examen de Ingenios* and the widely published and translated prose romance *Lazarillo de Tormes*, both of which Harvey mentions in his language-manual annotations.[77] Translated into English as *The Examination of Men's Wits* by language critic Richard Carew, a passage in Huarte's treatise addresses language acquisition directly: "if a Biscane of 30. or 40. yeeres age, come to dwell in *Castilia*, he will neuer learn this language: but if he be but a boy, within two or three yeares you would thinke him born in *Toledo*."[78] English readers of *Lazarillo*'s second part, meanwhile, would encounter the protagonist's disputation with learned doctors and his ensuing desire to "set vp a schoole in *Toledo*" and to become "the inuenter of a new language neuer knowne before among men."[79] Though that plan never comes to pass, Lazarillo's dream sustains the associations between learning, language, and Toledo that one finds in Minsheu's dialogues. And, whether they knew it or not, English readers of the period's most widely published polyglot language manual were consulting the work of a Toledan scholar, Francisco de Villalobos (I will discuss this manual at greater length in chapter 4).[80] In calling attention to both "gentlemen, and scholars" and "Toledo," Kyd prepares his playgoers and readers for the cosmopolitan vernaculars soon to issue from Hieronimo's tragedy.

In spite of the emphasis on "gentlemen," these cosmopolitan vernaculars also offer a place for socially elite and literate women. Addressing his accomplice Bel-imperia, the knight marshal states that "for because I know / That Bel-imperia hath practised the French, / In courtly French shall all her phrases be" (4.1.168–70). Many scholars have rightly recognized a sexual pun in "practised the French," but a pedagogical context lies here as well. As Juliet Fleming has shown, language manuals published in England often associated the French vernacular with women and femininity, even if their ostensible target audience was male.[81] This, at least, is the case for Pierre Erondelle's *The French Garden*, which claims on its title page to have been designed "for English Ladyes and Gentlewomen to walke in." While Fleming finds potent evidence that this manual "reaffirms a woman's duty to be chaste, while offering the male reader a titillating scrutiny of what the text represents as female sensuality," the study of French was not inaccessible to women in Renaissance England, and one may take this title page as an indication of some verifiable historical practices (including proof that women read this book).[82] Along with Queen Elizabeth, whose language skills were well known by the 1590s, Mary Sidney Herbert, who will be discussed at length in the next chapter, was a reader and translator of both Italian and French; like Kyd, she rendered into English a play by Robert Garnier (though for the printed page, rather than the public stage), and she evidently consulted language-learning manuals in the course of her translation work. Furthermore, Mulcaster recommended the instruction of "young *maidens*" as well as boys, and the annotations of women such as Anne Chamberleine, whose signatures appear on extant copies of Hollyband's *Frenche Schoole-maister* (1582) and Robert Sherwood's *French Tutour* (1625), testify to women's engagement with French language instruction.[83] In giving Bel-imperia the French-language role, Kyd draws on a salient gendered dimension of this pedagogical context, broadening the instructional technique of translation to include women.

Additionally, in avowing that Hieronimo's play will be "passing pleasing to the world" and gesturing to Italian and French dramatic traditions, Kyd also sets the knight marshal's drama in dialogue with the broader, cosmopolitan contours of early modern European theater, which stretch far beyond England's socially privileged schoolrooms. For Anston Bosman, these transnational contours constitute "Renaissance intertheater," a worldview in which *Hamlet*'s play within a play (set in Vienna, written in Italian, and performed in Denmark by traveling players) would not be the exception but the rule.[84] With stately hopes for their production, Hieronimo and Lorenzo praise the skillful performance of "Italian Tragedians . . . so sharp of wit" (4.1.157) and "French Tragedians" (line 161), and in doing so, they seize on the border-crossing tendencies of early modern theater and printed drama. Importantly, these foreign players (and practitioners of commedia dell'arte, as many editors suppose) remind Hieronimo of the playlet's peculiar but crucial polyglossia:

HIERONIMO. In Paris? Mass, and well remembered!
There's one thing more that rests for us to do.
BALTHAZAR. What's that, Hieronimo? Forget not anything.
HIERONIMO. Each one of us must act his part in unknown languages,
That it may breed the more variety. (4.1.162–66)

Some critics have judged Hieronimo's words here as a "lame and queer explanation," or as "seemingly gratuitous" in an alleged intention to obfuscate meaning.[85] Mazzio emphasizes these lines' importance but argues that they mark Hieronimo "as complicit in the process of vernacular corruption," viewing him—and Kyd—through the anxious eyes of sixteenth-century orthographic theorists.[86] From another perspective in keeping with Mulcaster's more permissive theory of language, however, the knight marshal can be seen instead to celebrate not corruption but rather the cosmopolitan "breeding" of these languages—a production akin to the "hyuing" of four languages into "one sweet iewce" in Baret's dictionary. Here, the *copia* in Renaissance schoolrooms does not equal, as Halpern alleges, "the neutralization of foreign ideology" but rather its purposeful expansion and use.[87] With specific references to language learning and in relation to his multilingual, Toledo-born tragedy, Hieronimo aims here to wield instruction as a variously bred and fully matured tool for revenge, in spite of its formerly "fruitless" nature.

"Fruitless Poetry": Kyd's Profitable Translation

It is by this very phrase, "fruitless poetry," that Hieronimo and Kyd tap into a widespread pedagogical discourse of cultivation, gardening, and profitability in a way that furthers the revenge plot. As Christopher Crosbie has recognized, the playwright's engagement with these tropes evinces sustained interest in *oeconomia*, or household management.[88] I suggest this language simultaneously strengthens the polyglot playlet's connection to multilingual language manuals, linguistic debates, and poetic *copia* in Renaissance England as well. On a parallel with Baret, whose *Alvearie* deploys the related "apian metaphor" to express the profitable gathering and framing of separate languages into a single hive, the language instructor John Florio adopts the discourse of "fruits" in the titles and prefaces of his bilingual manuals, *Firste Fruites* (1578) and *Second Frutes* (1591). Prefaces and commendatory verses in these volumes play on this metaphor repeatedly, resembling the way verses accompanying the *Alvearie* refer again and again to bees, flowers, and "sweet iewce." If the "fruits" in Florio's first manual seem "too too vnripe, sower, and vnsauerie" (sig. *4r), for example, the instructor promises—and in considerably more violent terms—a more mature product in his 1591 volume: "I haue for these fruites ransackt and rifled all the gardens of fame throughout Italie . . . if tra[n]slated they do prosper [(]as they flourished vpon their natiue stock) or eate them & they will be sweete, or set them & they will adorne your orchyards."[89] When Kyd's instructor Mulcaster approved English orthography in his *Elementarie* on the basis of use and custom (rather than encouraging a reformed alphabet), he asked along similar lines, "Is natur therefor baren in vs, which was frutefull in them, bycause we maie not inuent, and put somwhat to theirs? No forsoth" (sig. M1v). This language of cultivation, maturation, and coming-to-fruition provides a discernible background for Hieronimo's claim that his own poetry was "fruitless," without profit for himself, but "passing pleasing to the world." It also illustrates such a remark's relation to broader discussions about language enrichment, instruction, and poetics in Renaissance England.

Additionally, the association of "fruits" with progeny and reproduction elsewhere in the play establishes the multilingual playlet as a poetic surrogate for the deceased Horatio, a vengeful monument that will outlast the players on stage. Through this language, the formerly "fruitless" poetry of Hieronimo comes to maturity, "breed[ing] the more variety" as a productive execution of multilingual, vigilante justice.[90] Early in the play, Lorenzo stabs Horatio in the garden, declaring, "these are the fruits of love" (2.4.54). In a grotesque visual pun, he then leaves the body hanging in the arbor (represented on the title page of the Q8 text of 1615, and later editions; see figure 2.5). Hieronimo takes up this discourse again shortly thereafter, not only to express his inexplicable grief ("mine unfruitful words" [3.7.67]), but also to cherish his deceased son explicitly as his own offspring. The 1602 additions to *The Spanish Tragedy* include a scene in which the knight marshal commiserates with the painter Bazardo, who has also experienced the death of a son. Commenting on the gallows-like arbor upon which he found Horatio's body, Hieronimo recounts how "it bore thy fruit and mine. O wicked, wicked plant!" (3.12A. 71).[91] In these scenes, Kyd associates the discourse of "fruits" with Hieronimo's progeny in a way that will prepare audiences for the knight marshal's allegedly "fruitless" poetry (which, in the end, is quite mature and productive after all).

The fury toward this fatal arbor reaches its apex in a brief but crucial scene that converts—or translates—the discourse of fruitlessness into the violent "breeding" of Hieronimo's polyglot playlet. Importantly, Kyd situates this scene right between the moment when Hieronimo introduces his play and when it is staged. Here, the knight marshal's wife Isabella cuts down the arbor upon which Lorenzo and Balthazar hung the dead Horatio; critics read this as an enactment of vengeance.[92] "I will not leave a root, a stalk, a tree, / A bough, a branch, a blossom, nor a leaf, / No, not an herb within this garden plot" (4.2.10–12), she vows, listing off arboreal and

FIGURE 2.5 Thomas Kyd, *The Spanish Tragedy: Or, Hieronimo is mad againe. Containing the lamentable end of Don Horatio, and Belimperia; With the pittifull Death of Hieronimo*, 1623, title page, detail. Case Y 135 .K984. Reproduced by permission of the Newberry Library, Chicago, Illinois.

floral terms in a poetic expression of *copia* one expects to find in dictionaries by Hollyband or Florio. "Fruitless forever may this garden be" (4.2.14), she proclaims, "And as I curse this tree from further fruit, / So shall my womb be cursed for his sake" (4.2.35–36). With this, she stabs herself in a manner that recalls Horatio's murder but that also anticipates the carnage of Hieronimo's playlet, in which Horatio's body will reappear as a "fruitful" gloss on the polyglot performance. Keeping in mind Lorenzo's initial act, Isabella's scene reunites the play's discourse of fruit with bodily violence, also rendering the "garden plot" (4.2.12) into Hieronimo's plot ("already in mine head" [4.1.51]) and its material instantiation as a book ("Look upon the plot," says the King [4.4.32]).[93] By associating "fruit" with progeny, and Horatio in particular, Kyd brings Hieronimo's originally "fruitless" poetry to maturity, and in a way that will "breed the more variety" for the sake of copious revenge.

In effecting this pedagogically inspired, polyglot vengeance before the King and other royal officials, Hieronimo—and Kyd—endorse the virtue not only of "breeding variety" but also "confusion" as a joining-together of multiple languages. These elements go hand in hand, gesturing also to the play's cosmopolitan linguistic texture and multinational range of characters from both Spain and Portugal.[94] When Balthazar expresses concerns about the polyglot nature of the play, Hieronimo has an answer ready for him:

BALTHAZAR. But this will be a mere confusion,
And hardly shall we all be understood.
HIERONIMO. It must be so, for the conclusion
Shall prove the invention and all was good.
(4.1.172–75)

Here, critics often seize on a modern, pejorative sense of "confusion" that includes "the action of confounding, confusing, or throwing into disorder: *spec.* in reference to the 'confusion of tongues' at the tower of Babel."[95] In this way, the word would anticipate Hieronimo's soliloquy reference to "the fall of Babylon, / Wrought by the heavens in this confusion" (lines 186–87), thereby suggesting something destructive and apocalyptic in connection with the book of Revelation, the book of Daniel, or the Tower of Babel.[96] According to this reading, Balthazar objects to "mere," or pure and unalloyed, confusion on the basis that it would be "hardly," that is, barely, understood (*OED*, "mere," 1a; "hardly," 8a).

However, approached differently, Hieronimo's defense of "a mere confusion" emphasizes his play's origins in Toledan polyglossia and communities of learning in sixteenth-century England, also celebrating the mixture and mingling of multiple languages generally. He views "a confusion"—and the article "a" is key—not solely as something that confounds or throws into disorder, but in a more approving sense as "con-fusion": "Mixture in which the distinction of the elements is lost by fusion, blending, or intimate intermingling" (*OED*, 7a). Rather than referring to any misunderstandings, then, Hieronimo's pronouncement "It must be so" points up this augmentation and joining of languages, the same variety breeding that Mulcaster observed as both "frutefull" and a "necessitie" for the English language. In this way, the ending of the play, in Hieronimo's words, "shall prove the invention and all was good," an endorsement of language's tendency to invent—to "find out" words from other tongues and "garnish it self with all" (again, using Mulcaster's words). Balthazar's objection can be read in less hostile terms, too. "Mere" stands not only as an intensive (pure, unalloyed) but also as "only what it is said to be" (*OED*, 5a). Furthermore, "hardly," rather than meaning "scarcely; barely; not quite," could suggest something closer to "not easily or readily; with difficulty," holding out a possibility for comprehension, even to those audience members for whom these tongues seem at first "unknown" (*OED*, 5b). In both Hieronimo and Balthazar's own words, "confusion" is synonymous not only with perplexity but also with the pouring-together of multiple languages, and for useful ends.

In aligning "confusion" with "conclusion" and "understood" with "good," Hieronimo also shapes his exchange with Balthazar into the first two lines of a quatrain, hailing already the versified language of the upcoming multilingual play that will please his supernatural audience. Indeed, in spite of the tragic ending for the King, the Duke, and other audience members, the Ghost of Don Andrea later commends Hieronimo's polyglot vengeance as "spectacles to please my soul" (4.5.12). On that count, if the world of this play is one of "predetermined fate," as Thomas McAlindon has suggested, then this "fall of Babel" may indeed be "wrought by the heavens in this confusion," "heavens" indicating both the supernatural realm and the space in the theater perhaps occupied by Don Andrea's Ghost and Revenge.[97] This tragedy, in spite of the "Babel" that many critics have associated with it, is therefore both "passing strange" ("strange" simultaneously summoning connotations of exceptionality, unfamiliarity, and foreignness [*OED*, 8, 7, 1a, 1b]) and "wondrous plausible"—that is, both pleasing and worthy of the supernatural and theatrical audience's applause (*OED*, 1a, 3) (4.1.82–83).

"This Is the Argument of That They Show": Sundry Languages in Print and Playhouse

Alongside the many bilingual and multilingual language manuals and dictionaries in Kyd's London, early printed editions of *The Spanish Tragedy* opened up an epistemological space for the contemplation and comprehension of the play's "sundry languages," a polyglot variation on Robert N. Watson's view of the theater as a "one-large-room schoolhouse."[98] Indeed, much like Harvey or the unknown polyglot annotator of the British Library's Q4, a mingled reading and playgoing audience could have used their printed editions of *The Spanish Tragedy* to ponder these foreign words in the playhouse. Understanding the interplay between print and performance in the theater is crucial here and clarifies what would otherwise seem to be groundless speculation. According to Tiffany Stern's suggestive account, "Written texts—in performance—filled the playhouse, and 'literature' was regularly intruded into the theatrical space before the play began."[99] If this was so, book owners, booksellers, title and scene cards, and commonplace books would have been prevalent sights in theater precincts, adding a textual dimension to the theater's performative space. While Stern's work provokes a range of further questions—for instance, "was there a direct relationship between performances and playhouse-books or a casual and random one?"—there is evidence to suggest that playgoers provided not only a plausible market for published plays, but, in her words, "the most obvious market."[100] After all, published plays' paratextual or prefatory materials often anticipate readers familiar with staged productions. The title page of the Q4 text, for example, indicates "the Painters part" and also mentions (as many dramatic quartos do) that the play has "of late been diuers times acted."[101] Taken alongside Stern's productive speculations, *The Spanish Tragedy*'s printed editions may offer a context for its performances, their circulation within the playhouse or near it opening interpretive possibilities for audiences at Kyd's tragedy.

The substantial number of printed editions and performances of Kyd's tragedy in Renaissance England and on the Continent increase the likelihood that playgoers could have considered published copies as context for productions. To intensify this suggestion, though somewhat speculatively, playgoers could even have brought *Spanish Tragedy* playbooks to performances of the ultrapopular play. First composed by Kyd sometime around 1587, the play witnessed eleven editions before the Restoration (and it appears that there were other editions that have not survived).[102] Altogether, these numbers mark *The Spanish Tragedy* as one of the most in-demand printed plays of the period, equaling *Henry IV Part 1* and falling short only of the comedy *Mucedorus*, with sixteen known surviving editions.[103] Kyd's play witnessed success in performance too, which suggests that there were plenty of stagings and revivals to which one could bring along the playbook, or at least recall it. Altogether, *The Spanish Tragedy* would come to be performed by as many as four companies in at least six venues by 1604, and Philip Henslowe's diary records twenty-nine performances between 1592 and 1597 alone.[104] Kyd's tragedy also attained popularity in Continental Europe. Six versions—or "translations"—of the play in German and Dutch survive, some of which saw as many as nine reprintings through the early eighteenth century.[105] This was a play that circulated widely in print, in various languages, that was set in various places (Spain, Portugal, and a supernatural other world), and that was performed in a range of geographical locations, too. It stands to reason, based on the evident demand for *The Spanish Tragedy* by way of its numerous editions and performances throughout Europe, that the book could certainly have accompanied playgoers to early stagings. Presumably, this is what Thomas Middleton expected when he hoped his 1611 *Roaring Girl* playbook "may bee allowed . . . Gallery roome at the play-house."[106]

Ben Jonson's comedy *Every Man in His Humour* offers a suggestive view of what this could have looked like. In a scene from act 3, playgoers quite possibly could have seen a quarto copy of *The Spanish Tragedy* in the theater as a stage property, along the lines of what Sarah Wall-Randell has discussed in her recent analysis of "staged books."[107] If not, this moment at least encouraged audiences to imagine the playbook on stage, in the hands of actors speaking lines from the frequently performed and much-quoted tragedy.[108] In this scene of *Every Man in His Humour*, a washed-up fencing master named Bobadilla notices that his visitor, the foolish versifier Matheo, has brought a book along with him. In their ensuing exchange, one learns that it is a copy of *The Spanish Tragedy*:

BOBADILLA. What new book have you there? What, 'Go by, Hieronimo!'
MATHEO. Ay, did you ever see it acted? Is't not well penned?
BOBADILLA. Well penned? I would fain see all the poets of our time pen such another play as that was.[109]

As the scene continues, Matheo proceeds to read some "fine speeches" from the playbook to the delight of both characters (lines 107–19). According to Stern, Jonson resourcefully incorporates textual material at the theater in a variety of his works, playing a "double-game on stage for the literate and illiterate."[110] This is what one sees here in *Every Man in His Humour*, for both Bobadilla and Matheo insist repeatedly on the "penned" (rather than "played") nature of Kyd's tragedy, riffing on one of the most famous lines in early modern drama as well, lines Jonson himself had spoken on stage.[111] This is not only an act of recitation, but an act of reading in the theater, quite possibly with a "new" quarto edition of Kyd's play "playing itself" on stage and forging a link between dramatic works.[112] In addition to hailing those playgoers who brought their playbooks into the theater and recited "fine speeches" from them, Jonson's nod to *The Spanish Tragedy* collapses the distinction between player and playgoer (a technique Kyd himself deploys, as I will show), seizing all the while on one of London's most familiar—and multilingual—works of drama.

Following this logic, if the polyglossia issuing from the stage was ever truly "unknown" or "hardly . . . understood," early published quartos of *The Spanish Tragedy* offered a compensatory English version—a "translation"—of Hieronimo's play.[113] Considering the exclusively French-language exchange in Shakespeare's *Henry V*, or the long passages in Spanish and Dutch in Jonson's *The Alchemist* and Thomas Dekker's *The Shoemaker's Holiday*, it is striking that this scene was printed entirely in English. Frank Ardolino perceives in this choice "the passage from Babylonian confusion to the clarity of English, a process effected by God."[114] Yet, such a decision could be understood alternatively as offering a language lesson to playgoers and readers, for the polyglot performance and the English playtext could merge in the minds of Kyd's audiences as a mixed-media theater of translation.

Indeed, this is the epistemological space in which polyglot dictionaries, language manuals, and conversation guides exist in relation to drama, a place where playgoers could either look at or remember copies of Kyd's playbook during *The Spanish Tragedy*'s multilingual scenes. When the playlet known as *Soliman and Perseda* begins, Kyd's text includes a note to the reader: "*Gentlemen, this play of* Hieronimo *in sundrie Languages, was thought good to be set downe in English more largely, for the easier vnderstanding to euery publique Reader.*"[115] Without directly attributing this paratextual device to any individual author, printer, or publisher, one can associate these "gentlemen" with the "gentlemen, and scholars" mentioned earlier by Hieronimo. Using terms strikingly similar to Thomas's Italian dictionary "for the better *understandyng* of Boccace, Petrarcha, and Dante," Hollyband's "*easie*" way to learn French, or Minsheu's Spanish guides assuring that readers "not onely *vnderstand* them [i.e., speeches, phrases, and proverbs], but by them *vnderstand* others," this translation notice makes legible the play's connection to what Jeff Dolven diagnoses as the early modern "preoccupation with *understanding*."[116] In this way, the several quarto editions of *The Spanish Tragedy*—in the hands of theatergoers, or in their memories—opened the stage's polyglossia to a literate audience, presenting translation as a mode of language instruction. In helping audiences to set performance and print in mental parallel columns, the book itself served as a kind of theatrical "schoolmaster," guiding playgoers through Hieronimo's polyglot playlet by way of "known" English.

All surviving quarto editions of *The Spanish Tragedy* recommend this instructive approach to Kyd's play through a series of stage directions and by positioning "princes and courtiers" (to use Balthazar's words) as models for readers and playgoers. In analyzing these often overlooked paratextual features, I take my example from Margreta de Grazia, whose suggestive interpretation of *Hamlet*'s Q1 text raises important questions about material texts on stage. What if, de Grazia proposes, the King's line "see where hee comes poring vppon a booke" means scholars should understand the ensuing "To be, or not to be" as read out of a book?[117] Like Q1's Hamlet, Hieronimo appears onstage several scenes before his fatal tragedy "with a book in his hand" (sig. H1r), and based on the knight marshal's subsequent lines, it seems this is a book of Senecan drama.[118] According to Mazzio, this is a moment of translation signaling the indebtedness of the English present to the Latin past (a past, I will add, often mediated by contemporary vernacular traditions).[119] Though it might signal a decline in Hieronimo's rhetorical skill, as Mazzio contends, this moment also foreshadows Hieronimo's own polyglot play and its representation in the form of a material book. When Hieronimo first mentions his play to Bel-imperia, Balthazar, and Lorenzo, one finds in the early quarto texts the stage direction "He shewes them a book" (sig. I4r), which can be associated with Hieronimo's Senecan playbook and now his own polyglot playlet ("See here, my lords," he says). Later, after recounting the "argument," or summary of the play, he also hands to his auditors "several abstracts drawn" (4.1.135), which suggest what the characters' roles are like.[120] Similar to Jonson, who emphasizes the "penned" nature of the *Spanish Tragedy* playbook handled onstage by Matheo and Bobadilla, Kyd presents Hieronimo's tragedy not only as a momentary performance but also as a material text that aids in the comprehension of multiple languages, both for the onstage audience and for Kyd's own playgoers with quartos in hand or in mind.

In the ensuing polyglot tragedy, an event characterized by the pervasive circulation of texts, Hieronimo's playbook empowers literate playgoers by opening to them the play's "sundry languages." Following the death of his wife, Isabella, the knight marshal arrives before the Duke of Castile with his playbook (possibly the same one from the previous scene) and the "argument" or summary. "Let me entreat your grace / To give the King the copy of the play," Hieronimo says to Castile, adding, "This is the argument of what we show" (4.3.5–7). Almost repeating his words verbatim later on, the King hands the book to the Duke before the performance, saying "Here, brother, you shall be the book-keeper. / This is the argument of that they show" (4.4.8–9). The quarto's stage direction following the King's words, "He giueth him a booke" (sig. K3r), leads the reader on to the publisher's notice, effectively placing them in the position of the royal audience. As Montgomery states in her examination of the play's theatricalized representation of Spanishness, this paratextual device "is a note for two books: the text in front of the reader *and* the prop that Hieronimo passes to his royal audience onstage."[121] Indeed, for the duration of the playlet, the Duke, the Viceroy, and the King comment on the performance and its actors, "look[ing] upon the plot" (4.4.32) and making comments on the action in ways that Kyd and his contemporary playwrights would recognize, not always fondly, among their own audiences. Not merely "author and actor in this tragedy" (4.4.146), Hieronimo is also the publisher of its material instantiations, and he offers this object to his audience in preparation for the fatal performance.[122] "See here my show, look on this spectacle," he says to the royal officials after the playlet's conclusion (4.4.88), encouraging audiences not only to "see" but also to "look on," as one would look on the text of a book. In locating Hieronimo's play in a material object, as Q1 *Hamlet* does for "To be, or not to be," early quartos of *The Spanish Tragedy* enabled readers and playgoers to reflect on the role of the text in relation to the theater, and, I suggest further, opened an epistemological space for the parallel contemplation of polyglot performance and printed English translation.

Altogether, as this chapter has demonstrated, the polyglossia in Thomas Kyd's *Spanish Tragedy* expresses theatrically the multiple vernaculars present in Renaissance dictionaries, dialogues, and grammars. In this way, it brings an instructional mode of translation to bear upon the experience of readers and playgoers alike. Compiled by educated men including John Baret, Claudius Hollyband, and John Thorius, the period's many language publications extended vernacular lessons to both "yong learners" and university scholars like Gabriel Harvey, who bound and used his copies together with works of published Continental drama. As a beneficiary of Richard Mulcaster's progressive teachings on vernacular languages, Kyd was deeply influenced by this context. Taken together with these manuals and dictionaries, *The Spanish Tragedy*'s scattered words in Spanish and Italian—whether phrases like "*Pocas palabras*," or Italian proverbs—do not point solely to grotesque perplexity but also to profitable education in multiple languages. Through the inclusion of these utterances, the multilingual playlet at *The Spanish Tragedy*'s conclusion gathers up and reissues, both from the stage and in early quarto editions of the play, a "fruitful" array (or perhaps, in Florio's terms, "ransackt . . . gardens") of foreign vernaculars extant in bilingual and multilingual language publications. A violent yet cathartically productive performance staged in multiple tongues and printed in English "*for the easier vnderstanding to every publique Reader*," this scene and the play more generally participates in a broad economy of translation and instruction that opened Renaissance England to cosmopolitan vernaculars.

| *Chapter Three* |

Mary Sidney Herbert's "Fatall Change"

The Tragedy of Antony and the Countess of Pembroke's Religious Translation

We thy Sydnean Psalmes shall celebrate,
And, till we come th'Extemporall song to sing,
(Learn'd the first hower, that we see the King,
Who hath translated these translators) may
These their sweet learned labours, all the way
Be as our tuning. . . .

—JOHN DONNE (1635)

In a moment, in the twinkling of an eye at the last trumpet: for the trumpet shall blowe, and the dead shal be raised vp incorruptible, and we shal be changed.

—1 CORINTHIANS 15:52, THE GENEVA BIBLE (1560)

In the fifteenth sonnet of *Astrophil and Stella*, Philip Sidney's poetic persona discusses the relationship between foreign literary sources and poetic composition in English, suggesting that ideally, the two should remain separate. In a mocking tone, he criticizes writers who "search for euerie purling spring" and harps on "you that do Dictionaries methode bring / Into your rimes, running in rattling rowes."[1] Here, it seems, the poet simply takes issue with incapable and derivative versifiers. But from another perspective, with "bring / Into" pointing figuratively at the process of translation (i.e., the "bringing" of a text from one language into another) and a jibe at the "rattling rowes" of double-alphabetic entries, Sidney's speaker gestures toward the numerous bilingual and multilingual lexicons published "for the better understandyng of Boccace, Petrarcha, and Dante," as dictionary maker William Thomas promised.[2] In fact, singling out the second of these Italian poets in particular, *Astrophil and Stella* 15 offers special caution to English writers "that poore *Petrarchs* long deceased woes /With new-borne sighes and denisend wit do sing."[3] Opposing not only the *Canzoniere*'s commitment to the "love malady" tradition but also its foreign origins—as I discussed in the first chapter, "denizen" refers in this period to a foreign-born resident guaranteed English rights by royal patent—Sidney's speaker suggests that proper, muse-inspired verse in England has little room for foreign literatures or the multilingual publications offering access to them.[4] These, as Astrophil clarifies, are not domestic aids, but "far-fet [i.e., far-fetched] helpes" imported for artificial poetic efforts and destined to end in "wrong waies," a "want of inward tuch," and the eventual exposure of "stolne goods."[5] Even if some called Philip Sidney the "*English* Petrarke," authentic poetic inspiration in this sonnet comes not from Petrarch at all but rather from one's own muse—within one's own mind, as well as within one's own linguistic and national borders.[6]

This chapter argues not only that Philip Sidney's sonnet offers a limited picture of the interplay among foreign languages, multilingual lexicons, and literature in Renaissance England but also that "Dictionaries methode" and "denisend wit" rest at the foundation of his sister Mary Sidney Herbert's religiously inflected project in literary translation. A poet and dramatist well-versed in several classical and vernacular tongues, the Countess of Pembroke admits and engages with the complex denization that her brother, or at least his poetic voice, holds at bay (both in *Astrophil and Stella* and in his *Apologie*). In fact, she asserts in a dedicatory verse to her English Psalm translations that the "Psalmist King" David is "now English denizend, though Hebrue borne," illustrating in a brief but telling manner how a foreign work can cross boundaries and have a new habitation in a new language.[7] Along with these Psalms, Sidney Herbert translated Petrarch's "Trionfo della Morte," Philippe de Mornay's philosophical treatise *Un Discours de la Vie et de la Mort*, and, my main focus here, Robert Garnier's tragedy *Marc Antoine*.

In *The Tragedy of Antony*, I argue, the Countess of Pembroke combines devotional discourse with linguistic practice to convey to her readers a sense of literary translation as religious transcendence. Distinguishing her work from the sinful connotations of "worldliness" and adopting an approach that transports drama across the world's languages and borders—and from a Catholic, stage-play context into a Protestant, closet-drama one—she finds a divinely sanctioned application for cosmopolitan vernaculars in Renaissance England. Even without being publicly acted, then, as were the dramatic works analyzed in other chapters of this study, *The Tragedy of Antony* nonetheless recruits a border-crossing approach to languages for its particular ends, developing a "theater of translation" in the reader's mind, if not on a stage. Within these circumstances, without costumes, music, or other trappings afforded a stage play, the particularities of language arguably carry a greater weight, a weight which Sidney Herbert took on not just in monolingual terms but as a translator, and one with devotional aims.

In recent decades, critics have understood *The Tragedy of Antony* as a self-effacing enterprise in women's writing, a Stoic expression of grief belonging to the *ars moriendi* tradition, and a pointed expression of concern about English royal succession, to name three influential views.[8] Continuing this inquiry beyond England's borders, Margaret P. Hannay and Victor Skretkowicz have helped to clarify how *The Tragedy of Antony* brought Continental historical tragedy to England and contributed to a transnational Protestant movement.[9] Rerouting these border-crossing approaches through the multilingual lexicography underpinning Sidney Herbert's practice as translator, poet, and dramatist, this chapter will demonstrate how the countess showcases a cosmopolitan discourse of translation as religious transcendence, a changeless change operating simultaneously and inseparably on linguistic and religious levels. This, I am suggesting, is what John Donne points to (in this chapter's first epigraph) when he celebrates the deceased Mary Sidney Herbert and her brother Philip as "translated translators."[10]

Gender plays a critical role in the way Sidney Herbert both participates in the work of translation and figures it religiously for herself and her readers. Indeed, if the previous chapter's picture of translation as instruction centers on schoolboys and educated men, this chapter highlights the ways a woman writer employed Europe's cosmopolitan vernaculars for her own literary and religious advancement, and for that of a reading, if not playgoing, dramatic audience. Many critics have remarked on the "faithful" or "literal" qualities of Sidney Herbert's translation from Garnier, and indeed, a close examination of both texts reveals her careful attention to the French tragedian's language.[11] These terms of fidelity or literalness come with limitations, though, for they place the original text in a paternal position, leaving the translator in a "femall" and "secondhand" place, to use the terms employed by none other than language master and translator John Florio.[12] As Jonathan Goldberg has provocatively suggested in a challenge to previous treatments of Sidney Herbert's "Triumph of Death," "If the countess's poem is a faithful translation, it faithfully translates . . . complex routes of identification, across literary texts, across sites of imitation, across sites of identification that include cross gender identification as well."[13] Though she adopts translation as a conservative and gender-appropriate entry into literary practice, Sidney Herbert also offers throughout her writing a network of religious figures of translation, inviting her readers to interrogate the very techniques she employs as a woman author. The question that matters, I am proposing, is not how "faithful" or "literal" her translation is but rather *how* Mary Sidney Herbert employs translation and encourages its meta-analysis in a religious key.

Indeed, existing among Goldberg's "complex routes of identification," a mode of translation as religious transcendence occupies a central place in Sidney Herbert's efforts to "bring" foreign languages into "denizend" English. The word "translation" in Sidney Herbert's England was not limited to a linguistic or educational register, for it also signified "ascending or being received into heaven or the afterlife."[14] Specifically, I will demonstrate that the Countess of Pembroke's closet-drama translation of *Marc Antoine* showcases the inseparability of religious and literary translation to readers of her play. As she transforms French words into English, she hails religious connotations of *translation* and *change* and renders Garnier's tragedy into a reflection on death that is both devotional and cosmopolitan; this reflection transcends Catholic and Protestant confessions, too. Altogether, stretching Goldberg's already-capacious interpretation of Sidney Herbert's "faithful translation" to include the work of *faith*-ful, or religiously attuned, translation, I argue that *The Tragedy of Antony* mobilizes the overlapping and sometimes contradictory religious and linguistic connotations of translation in a manner that both advances Sidney Herbert's literary vocation and establishes a religious site and practice for cosmopolitan vernaculars in England.

"Enok is Translatid": Devotional Change in Renaissance England

Though in early modern England the word *translation* also possessed today's familiar linguistic connotation, the term occupied a specialized position in devotional contexts. Much of this discourse originates from a discussion of faith in the New Testament's Letter to the Hebrews, specifically the miraculous example of Enoch passing in a blessed state from the earthly realm to heaven. Rendering the Latin Vulgate's mobile sense of "translatus est" in English for the first recorded time, the Wycliffite Bible states that "Bi feith Enok is translatid, that he schulde not se deeth; and he was not founden, for the Lord translatide him."[15] This use of the word was sustained in later bibles during Sidney Herbert's lifetime, and throughout the seventeenth century religious literary translators including John Milton would employ it in precisely this sense.[16] Furthermore, a vast number of sermons, treatises, and commentaries—like the Bible, many of these being linguistic translations themselves—either address this passage or adopt its particular definition. For example, a translated sermon by Andreas Hyperius discusses the aspiration of believers to "perfectly know god" so that "when they die and depart this life, they might be translated to life eternal."[17] Likewise, in a Protestant treatise translated from Latin into English, Hermann Rennecher states that God's elect proceed in their everyday existence "vntill that their glorification being fully ended and finished, they be made happy both in body and soule together, and translated into the heavenly rest."[18] Often the product of linguistic translation in its own way, this religious discourse of translation reached English readers through an array of bibles, commentaries, treatises, and sermons.

For Sidney Herbert's readers, the word *change* took part in this religious discourse of translation, accommodating a sense of holy alteration as well and thus signifying at times both translocation and transformation.[19] Like *translation*, *change* could gesture to the transition or moving-across from the earthly world toward death or the life beyond: as the *Oxford English Dictionary* has it, "Death, considered as a substitution of one state of existence for another" (*OED*, "change," *n.*, I.3b). In the 1560 Geneva Bible, the book of Job offers this specific, sanctified meaning in the context of great suffering: "If a man dye, shal he liue againe? All the dayes of mine appointed time wil I waite, til my changing shal come" (sig. 2L2v; Job 14:14).[20] Here, for the patient believer Job, and especially as interpreted through a Christian typology, "change" points to a long-awaited reward at the end of earthly affliction, a virtuous and divinely sanctioned exit from the trials of human life. This use of "change" appears in the New Testament as well, and in more exuberant circumstances. Linking both the transformation of the flesh and blood and the death of the righteous believer to the resurrection of Christ, Paul's First Letter to the Corinthians in the Geneva Bible asserts that "we shal not all slepe, but we shal all be changed. . . . the dead shall be raised vp incorruptible, and we shal be changed" (sig. 2X2v; 1 Corinthians 15:51–52). Different from the Lucretian "sea-change" in *The Tempest* that turns King Alonso's bones into coral and his eyes into pearls, a secular transformation making no mention of a soul at all, this scripturally situated "changing" stands for both a divinely ordained sanctification of the human spirit and its raising-up from the earthly corruption of the world.[21] Like the passage of Enoch's soul to heaven in Hebrews, this translation is a holy transport to the realm beyond, part transformation in substance and part translocation in place. It is a blessed resurrection that ends in a heavenly union with God.

In their mingled gestures to physical transport to heaven and to the alteration of one's own substance in death, *translation* and *change* cohered and converged beyond these explicitly religious contexts and with a variety of interconnected terms. In fact, early modern bilingual dictionaries defining *alteration*, *mutability*, and *variety*—words often associated with the practice and concept of linguistic translation—routinely included *change* among their definitions and headwords. For example, John Baret's *An Alvearie or Triple Dictionarie* features the entries "to Change: to translate" and "A mutation: a changing: an alteration," while at the end of the sixteenth century, John Florio's Italian-English dictionary lists "Mutare" as "*to change, to translate, to turne, to disguise, to shift, to alter, to remoue, to transforme.*"[22] Shakespeare signals this rich interplay of terms to his playgoers and readers during Bottom's transformation in *A Midsummer Night's Dream*: "O Bottom, thou art changed," cries Snout, with Peter Quince glossing further, "Bless thee, Bottom, bless thee! Thou art translated."[23] Indeed, *Midsummer* audiences had many opportunities to contemplate this word, for the play's supernatural subplot concerns the theft of not just any boy, but a "changeling" boy transported—or, translated—from India into Athens. In these lexicographic and dramatic contexts, "change" pointed not only to substitution or reciprocal giving but also to the processes of alteration, mutation, and variation associated ubiquitously with linguistic applications and related connotations of divine transport.

For Sidney Herbert's readers, however, the kind of alteration or variety in substance associated with "change" could often point to inconstancy, faithlessness, and doctrinal heresy. This is clear from other entries in the period's multilingual dictionaries. In his maze of glosses for the headword "to Change," Baret includes the entry "Changeablenesse, wauering, mutablenesse, vnconstancie," signaling connotations of instability and inconsistency (sig. M3v). Likewise, Florio's definition for "Variabile" includes "*variable, changeable, mutable, diuers, fickle, vnconstant, subiect to change*" (sig. 2O4r), and John Minsheu's Spanish-English dictionary explains "Alterár" as "*to alter, to change, to remooue,*" but also "*to growe angrie, prooue inconstant.*"[24]

These connotations often appeared in highly gendered contexts as well, as in discussions of an allegorized "Lady Fortune," the feminine associations of the moon, or the personified, female figure of Mutability or Inconstancy. "What man that sees the euer-whirling wheele / Of Change, the which all mortal things doth sway," Edmund Spenser writes in his *Mutability Cantos*, "But that therby doth find and plainly feele / How Mvtability in them doth play / Her cruell sports, to many men's decay?"[25] Meanwhile, in a Catholic context hailing examples from the book of Job, Nicholas Caussin figures a female and personified Inconstancy, who is "sometymes great, sometymes little, sometimes grosse, sometymes slender, sometymes strayght, sometymes crooked."[26] Here, Spenser's Mutability and Caussin's Inconstancy stand for the female-gendered fickleness and perverse variety associated more broadly with *change* in the early modern period. As Caussin's treatise suggests, this range of negative meanings surfaced in religious sermons and commentaries as well, usually directed at believers—Catholic or Protestant—whose faith was seen to be inconstant. While striving for a divinely sanctioned change or translation to heaven, then, devout Christians hoped to shun the sinful meanings associated with that other change, earthly mutability and variety. "Our faith shoulde not be changeable, and wee become wauering, for the altering of our mynde and opinion," wrote one translator of John Calvin's sermons, but "that wee shoulde goe on continually in the right way, vntil such time as we haue finished our course."[27]

Even more odious than this weak-mindedness in Protestant England, however, was the Catholic doctrine that theologians viewed with utter skepticism: transubstantiation. Thomas Wilson, for instance, defines transubstantiation in his *Christian Dictionary* as "A change of one substance into another: as of Bread into the Body of Christ; of Wine, into the bloud of Christ, according to that monstrous doctrine of Popery."[28] Likewise, in a commonplace book possessed by the Danby family of Yorkshire, a discussion about how "Bread is turned into the very naturall body of Christ" casts scorn upon the "variety of garm[en]ts, alteracons of gestures, & change of voice" that accompany the practice, inscribing the Catholic ritual at the center of an assortment of mutable appearances and actions.[29] Although "change" could point to the translation of the righteous into God's kingdom, these waverings of the mind or conversions of the bread and wine into the body and blood of Christ could constitute "monstrous" religious applications of the word, especially in a Protestant context.

These conflicting connotations of "change" as either divine transport or as mutability and fickleness help to shed light on the notion of the worldly *cosmopolite*, an embattled epithet genealogically linked to the modern term *cosmopolitan*. As I noted in chapter 1, John Dee recommended in 1577 that his readers examine "the State of Earthly Kingdoms, Generally, the whole World ouer," so that each becomes "*Cosmopolites*: A Citizen, and Member, of the whole and only one Mysticall City Vniuersall."[30] Here, Dee advocates the border-crossing openness associated with cosmopolitanism today and which implies a kind of physical transport ("the whole World ouer"). In spite of this progressive view, others including Protestant divines understood *cosmopolite* with contempt, for the same term also gestured to people encumbered by a great variety of sins and worldly pleasures. The theologian Thomas Adams asserted to his listeners and readers that the "vanities of carnall ioyes, the varietie of vanities, are as bitter to vs, as pleasant to the Cosmopolite or worldling."[31] Connecting the cosmopolite's worldly sinfulness with the "varietie" appearing throughout the discourse of translation and change, Adams embraces here the stability and constancy of the devout Protestant believer and his God. Adding to this rhetoric four years later in *A Prospective Glasse to Looke Into Heaven*, John Vicars criticized his opponents as "carnall *Worldlings*, proud *Cosmopolites*."[32] Both divines would have objected to controversial Catholic publications and editions of Pietro Aretino's scandalous dialogues—which I will discuss in chapter 5—issued with the imprint "Cosmopoli."[33] For the cosmopolite and the consumer of these publications, according to these arguments, the only possible life is a life of worldly indulgence and eventual suffering; the changeable world and its variety exist in opposition to the divinity and constancy of heaven, proving a "carnall" obstacle to the transcendent aspirations of God's true believers. It is within this context—the Protestant deprecation of worldly variety and its association of inconstancy with women (as one sees in Spenser and Caussin), *and* the simultaneously laudatory valuation of change and translation into heaven—that Sidney Herbert wrote between languages.

The Countess of Pembroke's Religious Translation

In her literary translations and in her "Dictionaries methode," Mary Sidney Herbert adopts this copious and often contradictory discourse of translation and change, briefly entertaining its worldly connotations but ultimately emphasizing its inseparably religious and linguistic substance to readers. This strategy is evident in her English translation of Petrarch's "Trionfo della Morte," which survives today in a single, nonauthorial manuscript copy.[34] In this two-part poem, Petrarch first observes Laura visited by Death and a multitude of departed souls, and then engages in a dialogue with the deceased Laura, who instructs him on the joyful blessings of death. As Gary F. Waller observes, "Laura's attitude to Death has the serenity of transcendence."[35] Alive in the first part of the poem but deceased in the second, she appears in these verses in the midst of a translation between worldly and heavenly domains. This is clear in the first part already from Sidney Herbert's invocation of "earth" and "world," domains that both define and cannot define the still-living Laura. According to the speaker, Petrarch's beloved takes "no earthlie march, but heavenly" (1.22), though when Death confronts her, the speaker reminds the reader that Laura "in the world was one," still susceptible to Death's grasp (1.51). Enlisting the discourse of translation and change deployed in contemporary sermons and treatises on the death of the righteous, Sidney Herbert renders Petrarch's Laura into English in a way that bridges linguistic concerns with religious vocabulary.

In the poem's second part, Laura assuages Petrarch's concerns about the pain of death and the transition from earthly life to the heavenly existence beyond.[36] At first, Petrarch has doubts and fears about death: "When this or light to end doeth growe, / which we calle life (for thow by proofe hast tryde) / Is it such payne to dye? That, make me knowe" (2.28–30). Acting as a kind of sanctified schoolmaster, Laura responds to these questions, urging Petrarch to resist the temptations that characterize his life on earth. The "vulgar" offer a misleading path, she warns, and she offers a recommendation: "Of lothsom prison to eache gentle mynde / Death is the end: And onelie who employe / Their cares on mudd, therin displeasure finde" (2.34–36). This terzina encourages Petrarch to take comfort in a divinely approved, religious mode of translation. Although the corrupt—those "who employe / Their cares on mudd"—will be damned, the righteous "gentle mynde[s]" will experience delight in their transport to the afterlife. Here, the world in Sidney Herbert's verse stands for something corrupt, not the rich and interesting "State of Earthly Kingdoms" appreciated by John Dee but rather its base and earthy substance, "mudd." Indeed, this is the world of suffering and vanities in which Job must wait "til my changing shal come." Here, Sidney Herbert's translation dovetails with Vicars's and Adams's theological arguments against the "vanities of carnall ioyes," and Laura urges Petrarch—and the reader—to pursue the sanctified path. However, the countess's poem cannot divest itself from "change" in the broadest sense, for even as it attempts to divorce itself from the earthly mutability of "carnall *Worldlings*," it nonetheless adopts, even celebrates, a change or translation toward the heavenly life beyond. Such a paradox is clear from Petrarch's assessment of Laura's transformed state: "Changeless to me, though chang'd thy dwelling were" (2.174). While remaining free from the variety of "carnall ioyes," Laura has undergone a divinely sanctioned translation (or change)—that is, a moving-across that is free from the cosmopolite's "varietie of vanities," a holy change without change.

A bilingual Italian-English dictionary possessed and inscribed by women in the Sidney family demonstrates that both this particular Petrarchan terzina and a kind of "Dictionaries methode" lie at the foundation of Sidney Herbert's religiously motivated career in literary translation. In fact, the evidence suggests it was used by the countess herself during her youth. Unknown to modern scholars until recently, this second-edition copy of William Thomas's *Principal Rules of the Italian Grammer* (1562) features a blank leaf inscribed with three Italian lines from Petrarch's "Trionfo della Morte" and is undersigned with the name "Maria sidney" (figure 3.1).[37] Any attempt to attribute the handwriting with certainty is complicated by the fact that there are three generations of women known at one point or another as "Mary Sidney": Mary Sidney (née Dudley), Mary Herbert (née Sidney, later Countess of Pembroke), and Mary Wroth (née Sidney); in a way, here stands a reproduction—or translation—of a name in its own way across the family's history. Yet, the connection to Mary Sidney Herbert's known translation of Petrarch, I believe, tilts the balance in her favor. Although this signature does not offer a perfect match for any of the Countess of Pembroke's extant signatures I have seen, the date of the book and its physical features suggest it belonged to her mother during the sixteenth century, rendering all the more likely the idea that the Countess of Pembroke consulted this book during her youth and that the "Maria sidney" signature is hers.[38] Written elegantly in an italic hand, the terzina delivers Laura's advice to Petrarch—namely, as already discussed, to turn from the pleasures and temptations of the world:

> La morte e fine d'una prigion oscura
> a gl'animi gentili a gl'altri e noia
> Ch'anno posto nel fango ogni lor cura
> MARIA SIDNEY

The Petrarch of the *Trionfi* is not the sighing poet mocked in *Astrophil and Stella*, but this careful inscription registers nonetheless the interest of a Mary Sidney in the Italian poet's works, bilingual dictionaries, and a "denisend wit" beyond England's borders.[39]

Confirming the Sidney family provenance, a sixteenth-century hand elsewhere in the volume reads "This boke ꝑtainit [i.e., pertaineth] too the righte honorable and my good Lady the lady Sidnay," trailing off into unfinished, iterative letterforms (sig. L3v).[40] Though the identity of this other annotator seems more elusive, the messy, inconsistent handwriting and locution suggest a person of lesser status or education in the household—a servant or a child. One cannot rule out, for instance, that the inscription signals a young Mary Sidney, future Countess of Pembroke, acknowledging the dictionary's possession by another Mary Sidney, her mother.[41] Whatever the case, this book's Italian handwriting not only reproduces and rehearses Laura's religious lesson to the worldly Petrarch but also offers a powerful indication that the "Trionfo della Morte" circulated among women in the Sidney household decades before the late 1590s, the moment traditionally associated with the Countess of Pembroke's translation on account of the date inscribed upon the Petyt manuscript: December 19, 1600. Contrary to the picture proposed by Jason Lawrence, it appears there was a strong connection between language-learning practice and the countess's Petrarch translation.[42]

Especially because of their multilingual character and interest in the art of dying well, the Petrarch marginalia in this bilingual dictionary can be reasonably associated with other books possessed and inscribed by Sidney women. An extant copy of *Concetti di Girolamo Garimberto* features Mary Dudley Sidney's autograph, household records mention at least one

FIGURE 3.1 Lines from Petrarch's "Trionfo della Morte" inscribed in William Thomas, *Principal Rules of the Italian Grammer*, 1562, back flyleaf, detail. STC 24021. Reproduced by permission of the Houghton Library, Harvard University.

"French book," and other printed volumes demonstrate Lady Sidney's continued practice in Continental vernaculars.[43] For instance, adopting an approach shared by other women annotators of foreign-language manuals, she wrote "Escript par la maine d'un ffemme heureuse" (Written by the hand of a happy woman) in her copy of Edward Hall's *union of the two noble and illustrate famelies of Lancastre & Yorke* (figure 3.2). Judging by other, surrounding inscriptions in the book, Mary Dudley Sidney wrote this French phrase in 1551, the year of her marriage to Henry Sidney. Furthermore, Henry Sidney added to his wife's annotations here, copying down educational and Stoic-minded verses asserting the superiority of death over life, a theme that would be important to their daughter's literary career. Copious marginalia throughout the volume in secretary and italic hands in English and in Latin ultimately couple Henry and Mary Dudley Sidney together in the book, and in material-textual terms. "We should not underestimate the impact this fact might have made on a young Philip, Mary, or Robert as they leafed through the pages of their parents' *Chronicle*," advises Andrew Strycharski.[44] Indeed, the Sidneys stocked their residences with books printed in and inscribed with foreign languages in a manner that served not only their virtuoso poet son, the "*English* Petrarke," but also their translator and dramatist daughter, the eventual Countess of Pembroke.

Other annotations in the Sidneys' Italian-English dictionary show that this family's multigenerational engagement with foreign languages crossed paths not only with the Stoical *ars moriendi* but also with devotional lyric. Written laterally along the book's fore edge, a narrow, carefully manicured italic inscription consists of two lines copied from Thomas Sternhold's versified translation of Solomon's proverbs: "By Souch as I haue heald full dear, haue sett my frendshype light" and above it, "My duraunce doth perswade, of fredome suche dispaire," the latter trimmed, but which can be inferred from Sternhold's verse as it appears in an extant printed volume (sig. T3r [missigned M3r]).[45] Significantly, the devotional subject matter of these verses anticipates Sidney Herbert and her brother Philip's collaboratively produced English translations of the Psalms (an effort Sternhold had undertaken decades earlier). I will discuss the Sidney Psalms in more detail subsequently, since they constitute an especially important element of the countess's combined commitment to linguistic translation and the translation of the sanctified soul. What is significant here is that the Sidney family's contemplation of Sternhold's religious poetry surfaces in the pages of a bilingual dictionary and in dialogue with what seems to be Mary Sidney Herbert's youthful consideration of Petrarch's "Trionfo della Morte."

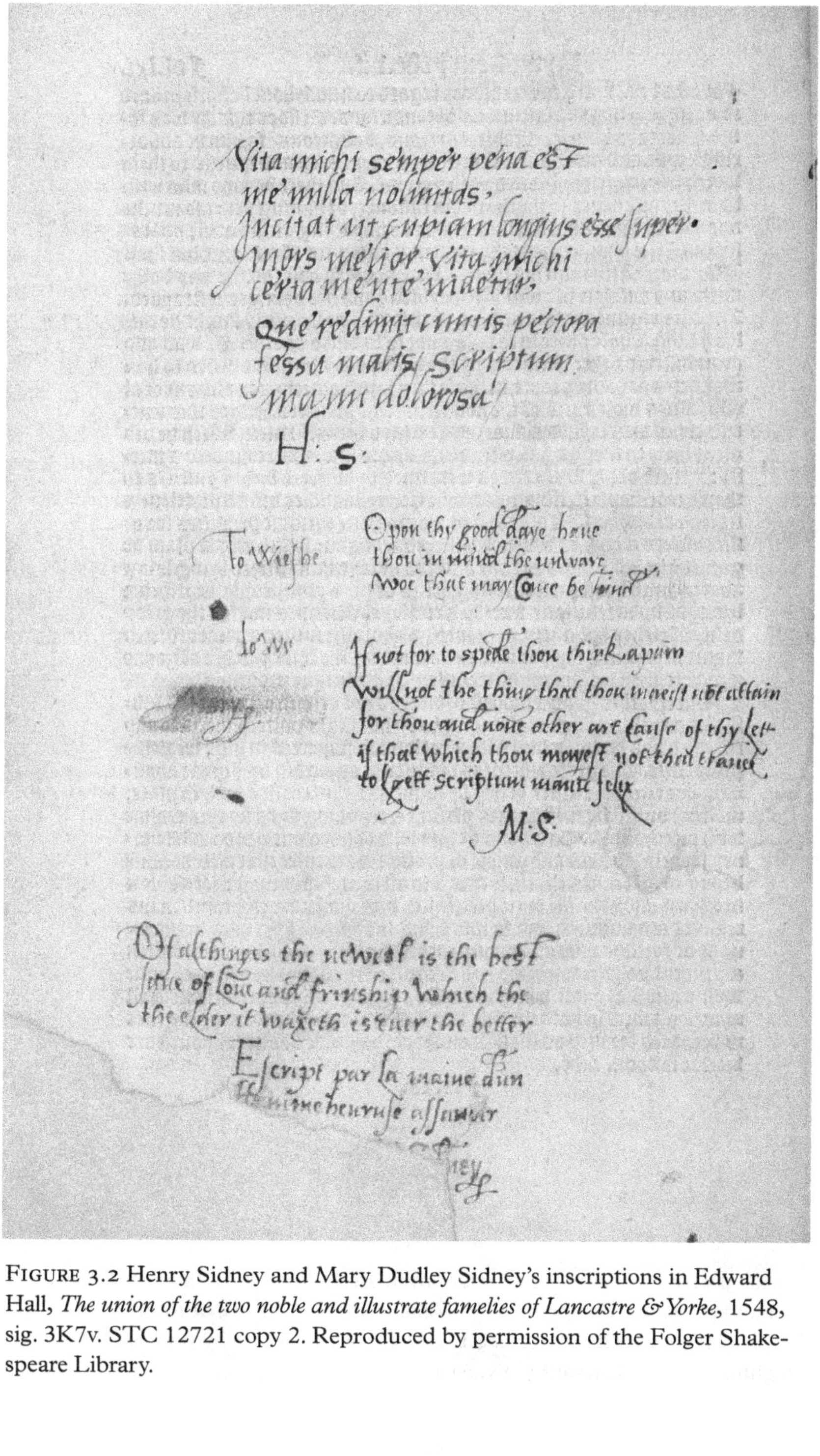

FIGURE 3.2 Henry Sidney and Mary Dudley Sidney's inscriptions in Edward Hall, *The union of the two noble and illustrate famelies of Lancastre & Yorke*, 1548, sig. 3K7v. STC 12721 copy 2. Reproduced by permission of the Folger Shakespeare Library.

Other inscriptions in the Sidney copy of *Principal Rules of the Italian Grammer* include both new headwords and further glosses on the religious connotations of translation permeating "The Triumph of Death." On the other side of the leaf with the "Maria sidney" inscription and the lines from Petrarch's "Trionfo della Morte," for example, there appears a list of thirty-one Italian headwords and their English translations in a hasty, informal italic hand and in a different ink. It seems this same hand crops up throughout the dictionary's text as well.[46] Although there is no clear evidence connecting these inscriptions to the Sidney family, one annotation is striking nonetheless, for it offers in quite literal terms a further gloss on the religious meanings of translation characterizing the Countess of Pembroke's works. This inscription appears beside Thomas's entries "*Trappassare*, to die or departe" and "*Trappassato*, deade or departed." "Trappassare to exced or passe," the reader glosses further in an italic hand, with a secretary hand adding three more words in a manner that mimics the book's typography: "or to transgresse" (figure 3.3). Just above this inscription, Thomas's printed text features "*Transitorie*, transitorie or passyng" and "*Transmutare*, to chaunge," enriching this page and this particular user's ability to reflect on it with further connotations of change and translation

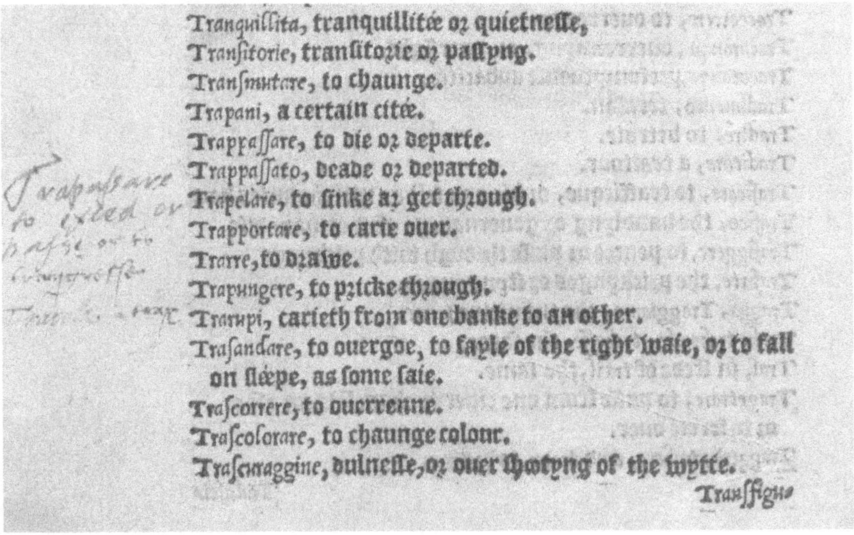

Tranquillita, tranquillitée or quietnesse,
Transitorie, transitorie or passyng.
Transmutare, to chaunge.
Trapani, a certain citée.
Trappassare, to die or departe.
Trappassato, deade or departed.
Trapelare, to sinke or get through.
Trapportare, to carie ouer.
Trarre, to drawe.
Trapungere, to pricke through.
Trarupi, carieth from one banke to an other.
Trasandare, to ouergoe, to fayle of the right waie, or to fall on slépe, as some saie.
Trascorrere, to ouerrenne.
Trascolorare, to chaunge colour.
Trascuraggine, dulnesse, or ouer shotyng of the wytte.
Trasfigu

FIGURE 3.3 An early reader's annotations in an informal italic hand and a secretary hand glossing "Trappassare" in William Thomas, *Principal Rules of the Italian Grammer*, 1562, sig. 2L4v, detail. STC 24021. Reproduced by permission of the Houghton Library, Harvard University.

animating both the Petrarch lines copied into the book and Sidney Herbert's works more generally. Other marginalia in the book—"prison" (sig. G1r), echoing the passage from Petrarch, or "marigoldo" (sig. T4v), a known epithet for the Countess of Pembroke—leave open the possibility of a Sidney connection with this annotation.[47] Speculation aside, though, these marks suggest at least that someone used this Sidney family dictionary to contemplate the notion of *trappassare*—not merely the mutability and change attending human life but also the ability of the soul to change, to "exced or passe" or transcend worldly baseness in death.

Altogether, this annotated copy of Thomas's bilingual lexicon offers proof for the Sidney family's religiously inflected interest in the "Trionfo della Morte," and, it seems, decades before the date traditionally associated with the Countess of Pembroke's translation. This would not be surprising, for the countess's parents provided her an outstanding family education in classics, the church fathers, and Latin, French, Italian, and possibly Greek and Hebrew, too, along with a possible language tutor known as "Mistress Maria, the Italian."[48] One may have to speculate, but perhaps the dynamics legible from these annotations also inform the literary bonds scholars have noted between Sidney Herbert and her niece Mary Wroth.[49] If the bilingual dictionary's annotations indeed feature the hand of Sidney Herbert, as I have been suggesting, then this book demonstrates that the Countess of Pembroke's contemplation of the "Trionfo della Morte" anticipated and influenced her later translations, rather than merely reflecting or accompanying them. In the most modest terms, the handwriting here illustrates that at least two generations of women in the Sidney household studied these Italian verses.

The notion of a sanctified, changeless change evident both in "The Triumph of Death" and in the pages of this bilingual dictionary also surfaces in Sidney Herbert's triumphant devotional work: her English Psalm translations. Again, it was for these "Sydnean Psalmes" that John Donne celebrated the deceased Countess of Pembroke and her brother Philip Sidney as "translated . . . translators," hailing the very discursive link that the woman poet and playwright explored again and again in her literary practice. For this collaborative endeavor, Sidney Herbert edited the first forty-three Psalms originally translated by Philip and then completed Psalms 44 through 150 on her own; seventeen surviving manuscripts testify to a protracted period of writerly and revisionary labors.[50] For Elaine V. Beilin, these formally innovative English Psalms represent the culmination of Sidney Herbert's independent career as a divine poet: "By translating the Psalms into a wide range of verse forms, experimenting with meter and rhyme to find the most apt expression and faith for each song, Mary Sidney [Herbert] sought to play her part in the encouragement of godliness among her peers."[51] Such an effect is clear from the testimony of Edward Denny, who placed Sidney Herbert "in the quier of Heaven," as well as from the abundant praises of John Harington, Samuel Daniel, and John Davies, among others.[52] Indeed, in a Simon van de Passe engraving, Sidney Herbert appears holding a book of "Davids Psalmes," her triumphant, religious work as a translator represented visually, with pride (figure 3.4). All told, the countess's Psalms offer translation to her readers as both devotional product and technique.

Significantly, these achievements in religious versification took place contemporaneously with Sidney Herbert's translations from vernacular works and were considered as belonging to a broader literary project by those close to the countess. Indeed, John Harington presented three of Sidney Herbert's Psalm translations to Lucy, Countess of Bedford, along with the sole surviving manuscript copy of "The Triumph of Death."[53] Additionally, the countess's physician Thomas Moffett advised her in print to "let Petrarke sleep, give rest to Sacred Writte," urging her to set aside her practice in literary translation during a period of ill health.[54] Here, it seems Moffett understood both the Petrarch and the Psalm translations not as separate projects but together (though as a composite strain on Sidney Herbert's wellness). Considered together in this way, these translated works evince not only the Countess of Pembroke's linguistic aptitude, but also her broader, thematic concern with the ability to transcend worldliness.

The themes of worldly mutability and change, as well as the mode of translation as religious transcendence, surface conspicuously in the text of these "Sydnean Psalmes" as well. Examples are numerous, freighted with both the religiously motivated "language of ruination" and, as in Psalm 57, an evocation of "the distance between the mutable world and the unchanging heavens."[55] This is the case in Psalm 77's penitent admiration of God, which seems an echo or rehearsal of Petrarch's praise for Laura: "That chang lies in his hand, / who changlesse sittes aloft."[56] Furthermore, each of the three Psalms included in the Petyt "Triumph of Death" manuscript offers some commentary on the trope of mutability powering Sidney Herbert's literary productions: the desire to be divinely purged of sins, changed from spotted leprosy to white snow (Psalm 51); praise for God's steadfast nature and his dominion over earth's vicissitudes and variability (Psalm 104); and a wish for God to quash worldly oppressors in the foreign land of Babylon (Psalm 137). As mentioned, Sidney Herbert also asserts in an original dedicatory poem to Queen Elizabeth that the "Psalmist King" is

FIGURE 3.4 The Countess of Pembroke holding a book of "Davids Psalmes," engraved by Simon van de Passe. © National Portrait Gallery, London.

"now English denizend, though Hebrue borne," articulating a transition in King David's nationality or residency status and indicating that she considered her own devotional translations as possessing a kind of spatial moving-across while retaining their core essence, a paradoxically changeless change (lines 29–30).[57] Altogether, then, and in a way that bridges her Psalms to "The Triumph of Death" and, as will be seen, *The Tragedy of Antony*, what Donne referred to as Sidney Herbert's "sweet learned labours" highlights the boundaries and transitions between the mortal world and the holy life beyond. It is here that one finds the coinciding and inseparable notions of translation as both worldly practice and heavenly passage to the life beyond, a simultaneously linguistic and devotional concept that surfaces again and again in the countess's works and underwrites her literary productions.

"Changing and Rechanging": *The Tragedy of Antony* in English

The Countess of Pembroke's closet drama *The Tragedy of Antony* foregrounds a preoccupation with the changeable world and humanity's susceptibility to waver in allegiances and affections, but also the translation of the soul away from the realm of suffering. Indeed, Waller finds in this translated tragedy a world characterized by "continual uncertainty and mutability," thematic elements that Sidney Herbert adopted as an author and translator and sponsored as a patron figure.[58] Shortly before *Antony* saw print, the countess was the dedicatee of Edmund Spenser's *Ruines of Time*, published in 1591 by her preferred stationer William Ponsonby and dealing in the same discourse of ruination. "I haue conceiued this small Poeme, intituled by a generall name of the worlds Ruines," states Spenser, also gesturing to Sidney Herbert's recently deceased brother Philip ("that most noble Spirit, which was the hope of all learned men"), and offering a thematic picture of the volume's lyrics.[59] The poet expanded on this discourse in his *Mutability Cantos*, in which the allegorical figure of Mutability brandishes her changeable nature in a rhetorical battle against the Gods. "Nothing doth firme and permanent appeare," she claims, "But all things tost and turned by transuerse."[60] Read against this context of inevitable change and things "turned by transuerse," *The Tragedy of Antony* is both an example of and a thematic commentary on early modern translation in its overlapping linguistic and religious dimensions. That is, it exhibits a figurative, religious mode of translation even as it delivers a product of literary translation—as a work of closet drama—to readers.

Antonius, as it was originally titled, first appeared in a 1592 quarto volume along with the countess's translation of Philippe de Mornay's *Discours de la Vie et de la Mort*, which offers further context for the tragedy. Considered together, these texts display a women-centered variation on the *ars moriendi* tradition.[61] In a passage that offers a striking parallel to Petrarch's questions about mortality in "The Triumph of Death," Mornay's treatise asks rhetorically, "Yea but you will say, it is a payne to die. . . . You will say, there is difficultie in the passage" (lines 692–95). Responding to these queries about the "passage" from one life to the next and elaborating his navigational and mercantile comparisons, Mornay offers a picture designed to comfort the reader. The Countess of Pembroke renders the response as follows: "So is there no Haven, no Porte, whereinto the entraunce is not straite and combersome. No good thing is to be bought in this worlde with other then the coyne of labour and payne. The entraunce indeede is hard, if our selves make it harde, comming thither with a tormented spirite, a troubled minde, a wavering and irresolute thought. But bring wee quietnesse of mind, constancie, and full resolution, wee shall not finde anie daunger or difficultie at all" (lines 695–702). Here, in the same key as Protestant divines in English translation or her translated Petrarch or Psalmist, Sidney Herbert follows Mornay in opposing "a wavering and irresolute thought" with "quietnesse of mind, constancie, and full resolution." In translating the Stoic philosophy of Mornay, a radical Protestant colleague and friend of her brother Philip, she addresses again what is a central theme of her literary works: the mutability and suffering of the world and the peace guaranteed to the steadfast soul in death.[62] When read alongside this philosophical treatise, Sidney Herbert's English version of Garnier's tragedy becomes, in part, "a play illustrating the worldly life against which de Mornay inveighs," as well as a testament to the countess's translationally inclined Protestant and diplomatic initiative.[63] "Both done in English by the Countesse of Pembroke," states the title page in terms that signal the foreign-language provenance of both texts and the labor of translation that occasioned their appearance "in English."[64] For this volume, if one is to take the closet drama as enacting a theatrical spectacle in one's own mind, Mornay's musings can be seen to occupy the role of a prefatory "performance." Altogether, the coupling of *The Tragedy of Antony* and this philosophical treatise on death engaged readers with the multidirectional discourse of translation and change permeating Sidney Herbert's literary projects more broadly, including *Antony*, as I will show.

From its very first scene, *The Tragedy of Antony* presents a world overtaken by change and inconstancy, and not for the better. Indeed, as Beilin notes, the play opens with a vision of Antony "acting out his passionate, worldly life with its inevitable end."[65] Speaking in the aftermath of the Battle of Actium, he specifies that his engagements with the Egyptian monarch Cleopatra have caused him to waver in precisely the manner discussed at length by Mornay. "For her have I forgone / My Country," he says, confessing a foregoing or passing-by of his marital and political obligations, surrendering his status as "late maister of so many nations" (lines 8–9, 131). Antony's capriciousness begets further changes, for his wife Octavia has since "mov'de my Queene (ay me!) to jealousie" (line 11), yet another departure or "move" from harmonious order toward chaos. In a catalog comparing how things were then with how things are now, Antony illustrates how his love for Cleopatra, borne of his own wavering, effected a transformation from military valor to pastoral pleasures:

> Since then the *Baies* so well thy forehead knewe
> To Venus mirtles yeelded have their place:
> Trumpets to pipes: field tents to courtly bowers:
> Launces and Pikes to daunces and to feastes. (lines 68–71)

In this soliloquy spoken by her titular character, Sidney Herbert displays this tragedy's particular commitment to the discourse of change, mutability, and alteration. With this syntactic structure ("to . . . to . . . to"), Antony relates the Circean changes that Cleopatra has wrought upon him, a conversion that has substituted power with pleasure, fanfare with luxury, weapons with courtly delights. Significantly, Cleopatra comes from beyond Antony's borders. Much like Christopher Marlowe's King Edward II, for whom the Frenchman Gaveston orders up "wanton poets" and "Italian masques by night" to celebrate his reunion with the English ruler, Antony stands at the center of a conflict between foreign and sexual desires on the one hand and political commitments at home on the other.[66] Having tarnished his honor, disrespected his friends, and declared war against the Empire, he now longs for death. "It's meete I dye," he says a mere eight lines into the play, adopting Job's desperation but with only himself to blame (line 8). In Antony's words, and after so many changes and transitions, death constitutes a refuge that will, once effected, "have / Bounded . . . the course of my unstedfast life" (lines 44–45)—both in the senses of "binding" and "creating boundaries" that will put an end to such inconstancy, foreign romances, and ceaseless motion.

The vocabulary of change and mutability—and of foregoing, movement, and unsteadfastness—serves paradoxically as the rhetorical foundation of

Antony's speech and, consequently, the countess's English translation of the play more broadly. Indeed, it is precisely through this language that "the play dismantles Antony's identity as a great warrior/hero."[67] As a coping mechanism, Antony projects his own inconstant behavior onto Cleopatra in words that are italicized in the early editions for their sententious or aphoristic value: "*But ah! by nature women wav'ring are, / Each moment changing and rechanging mindes*" (lines 146–47). Without endorsing such a misogynistic generalization about the influence of women on otherwise steadfast male minds, the play's chorus echoes the complaint that the world is a corrupting, inconstant, and transitory place (and I will address the chorus's remarks on such matters in greater depth momentarily). Delivered to English readers by the Countess of Pembroke, Garnier's titular character grapples with the mutability that led him away from his own country to Cleopatra and that resulted from his pleasurable encounters with her. His lament primes Sidney Herbert's readers for further commentary on change and mutability, "translations" upsetting the usual order of *Antony*'s political and moral universe.

Meanwhile, commenting on the miserable changes that have befallen Egypt in the play is Philostratus, Garnier's rhetor figure who amplifies the closet drama's generally negative connotations of change. Strictly an observer and commentator, he has "no interaction whatever with other characters" but offers commentary on the action.[68] In a soliloquy following the change-focused chorus of act 1, Philostratus reports that the land is overrun with foreign soldiers and war, atrocities that would have been all too common to the French playwright's contemporary readers. After all, as Garnier suggests in the play's prefatory materials, sixteenth-century France was overwhelmed by "nos dissentio[n]s domestiques, & les malheureux troubles de ce Royaume, auiord'huy despouillé de son ancienne splendeur, & de la reuerable maiesté de nos Rois, prophanee par tumultueses rebellions" (our domestic conflicts and the unfortunate troubles of this kingdom, which today is robbed of its ancient splendor, and of the reverend majesty of our kings, which is profaned by tumultuous rebellions).[69] If there is any escape from the violence represented in the tragedy, says Philostratus, it is also by way of change, namely a change in Caesar's heart. He encourages the Egyptians to offer sacrifices "not our selves to save, / But soften *Caesar* and him piteous make / To us, his pray: so that his lenitie / May change our death into captivitie" (lines 277–80). Even Caesar, it seems, is susceptible to a change of heart; overcome with foreign might, the Egyptians must force one change in order to attain another for themselves. Again in this passage, change represents the governing principle of *The Tragedy of*

Antony, whether for good or, more often, for ill. From Philostratus's speech, it is also clear that the notion of change in the play is commonly bound up with the miseries of foreign subjection.

Indeed, an important dimension of this tragedy's concern with change as either mutability or as divinely sanctioned transport from suffering revolves around the worldly threat of domination by foreign or "strange" powers. It is this threat that the possibility of the soul's passage to the afterlife addresses and seeks to counter. The inevitability of worldly bondage is especially evident in the chorus's lines in *Antony*, offering further proof of the inconstant and unpredictable nature of the mortal world. Here one learns that the Nile, which began all life and supplies it with nourishment, has lately been subjected to the imperial Tiber. Describing this miserable state of affairs, the chorus offers praise for freedom, which "inflame[s] couragious mindes" (line 810). However, there is much more to say about bondage:

"But if force must us enforce
"Nedes a yoke to undergoe,
"Under foraine yoke to goe
"Still it proves a bondage worse.
"And doubled subjection
"See we shall, and feele, and knowe
"Subject to a stranger growne. (lines 811–17)

Both early editions of Sidney Herbert's translation feature this passage with printed commonplace marks, emphasizing the sententious wisdom of these statements on "forc[ing]" and "enforc[ing]," as well as "bondage" to a "stranger." Readers of the Geneva Bible might have recalled the book of Job, in which "His armies came together, and made their way vpon me, & camped about my tabernacle," and "mine acquaintance were stra[n]gers vnto me" (sig. 2L4r; Job 19:12-13). Critics often note how many of Sidney Herbert's most striking alterations to Garnier's text occur in the chorus, but the translator retains here the playwright's focus on foreign subjection ("vn ioug estranger" [sig. H5r] [a foreign yoke] and an "estrange nation" [sig. H5r] [foreign nation]) and its miserable consequences.[70] Life has inevitable vicissitudes, the play suggests, and these changes include the passage of foreign armies across borders—another kind of translation or movement rooted in the mutability of mortal life on earth.

Although to Elizabethan readers this lament may have seemed "darkly resonant amid fears of renewed Spanish onslaught," it constitutes more generally a sermon on mutability, the brevity of human life, and the "fatall change" awaiting all mortals.[71] Flowers will wither and die, the chorus says, buildings will burn and fall. This inevitability of death, itself a kind of metamorphosis or change, applies to all things:

> All things fixed ends do staie,
> Ends to first beginnings fall.
> And that nought, how strong or strange,
> Chaungles doth endure alwaie,
> But endureth fatall change. (lines 868–72)

In words that resemble the arguments in Spenser's *Mutability Cantos*, this chorus discloses not merely "the steady trudge of historical time," as Karen Raber contends, but also *The Tragedy of Antony*'s central preoccupation with "fatall change"—specifically, change at the moment of death and which "nought" (i.e., naught, nothing) can escape.[72] This is the divinely sanctioned notion of translation or change surfacing in Hebrews, Job, and 1 Corinthians. Significantly, "fatall" has no analog in the French text, evincing Sidney Herbert's concentrated thematic commitment to death—that is, the religious mode of translation—underpinning this tragedy and her other translated works. By adding this word, she foreshadows the deaths of Antony and Cleopatra, reflects on Petrarch's "Trionfo della Morte," and connects her dramatic work with her English versions of the Psalms and Mornay's *Discours*. Especially striking here, too, is the complicated syntax Sidney Herbert deploys to render Garnier's verse into English: "All things fixed ends do staie," she writes, words that might evoke either the certainty of death ("fixed ends") to comfort or support all living creatures, or, possibly, for all things on earth to rest upon or trust in such "fixed ends" (see especially *OED*, "stay," *v.*2, 1b, 3b). In any case, this "fatall change" applies to all things, "how strong or strange" ("strange" being another key addition by Sidney Herbert), pointing even to the powerful foreign forces responsible for Egypt's subjection. There is faith, then, in this "fatall change," a comfort that one sees as well in Sidney Herbert's presentation of Petrarch's Laura and Donne's eulogized treatment of the "translated" Mary Sidney Herbert and Philip Sidney. This is a translation of the soul that frees humanity from the world's mutability and suffering, also laying low foreign oppressors.

The chorus of act 3 advances this focus on mutability and the *ars moriendi* tradition, countering the vicissitudes of earthly life with religious translation into the holy life beyond. Here, the play points toward a solution to the negative connotations of inconstancy and fickleness attending the word "change," countering them with a divinely approved release from worldly suffering, also a "change" (or translation). In just the first few lines, the chorus addresses the "blinde desire / To staie our life from flieng" (lines 1263–64), associating ignorance and folly with the impulse to "staie" death, to hold it at bay. Far preferable, the chorus asserts, is death, which "rather healthfull succor gives" and "rather all mishapps relieves / That life upon us throweth" (lines 1268–70). With a chain of rhetorical questions, this portion of the play elevates the comfort of death above the various and shifting burdens of worldly existence, foreshadowing the solution that will occur to Cleopatra at the end of the tragedy. "O *Antonie* with thy deare mate / Both in misfortunes fortunate!" the chorus exclaims, suggesting the paradoxical relief of death as an exit from tumultuous earthly affairs (lines 1340–41).

"Not Yet Transformed": Cleopatra Translated-in-Translation

Before I address this conclusion, however, the character of Cleopatra requires some consideration as the linchpin for the play's mixed discourse of linguistic and religious translation. Plutarch's *Lives* emphasizes Cleopatra's facility with languages already, and as Skretkowicz points out, this is also the case for Garnier's text, which offers a foundation for Sidney Herbert's English version.[73] Furthermore, at the end of the second act, Diomed—designated specially as secretary to Cleopatra in the playtext's list of "Actors"—recites in soliloquy a blazon of the Egyptian queen, offering comparisons between her physical characteristics and precious stones or metals: an alabaster face, coral lips, golden hair. Surmounting these physical features—rather European for an African queen, it ought to be noted—are Cleopatra's exquisite social graces and eloquence:

> Yet this is nothing th'e'nchaunting skilles
> Of her caelestiall Sp'rite, hir training speache,
> Her grace, hir Majestie, and forcing voice,
> Whither she it with fingers speach consorte,
> Or hearing sceptred kings embassadors
> Answer to eache in his owne language make. (lines 727–32)

In terms that are present already in Garnier's text (sig. H3v–H4r), Diomed emphasizes here the qualities that make Cleopatra an elegant and capable ruler, ending on the multilingual facility so valuable for exchanges with foreign dignitaries. Though other early modern portrayals denigrate the Egyptian queen as adulterous, Sidney Herbert delivers a Cleopatra who merits praise not only for her appearance (figured as such already by Garnier) but also for her "enchaunting skilles," multilingual interpretation among them, and her "training speache," employment of her voice in a manner that persuades but also extends, draws, and leads (*OED*, "train," *v.*1, I.1b, 2a, 3b, 4).[74] Able to "move"—or transport—her audiences in this manner with her multilingual facilities, Sidney Herbert's translated Cleopatra is a translator, too. "Certainly this queen," state Sidney Herbert's Clarendon editors, "would be an appropriate model for a woman translator."[75] Furthermore, this mention of multilingualism could be interpreted during the 1590s as a reminder of Queen Elizabeth's capable polyglossia, which had been praised by Roger Ascham and Richard Mulcaster and which set her apart from the monoglot King Philip II of Spain.[76] Without directly associating the monarch with Cleopatra, then, Sidney Herbert illustrates the political advantages of foreign-language study for a ruler such as Elizabeth. Altogether, in a manner that is at once both metadramatic and metatextual, Sidney Herbert commends the very ability that furnishes the translated text in the hands of her readers.

However, as a translated translator, Cleopatra is stubbornly resistant to change at first, rejecting the wavering characteristics of this tragedy's universe and staking out a stable and unyielding place for herself and her love for Antony. In her resolution, she earns Mary Ellen Lamb's designation as a "constant heroine."[77] Early in the play, during a conversation with her handmaidens Charmion and Eras—labeled Cleopatra's "women" in the playtext's paratext—the Egyptian queen assumes blame for the current crisis and imagines her beauty to be partly responsible.[78] Rejecting Charmion's advice to forsake Antony and to make amends with Caesar, however, she professes her unyielding affection for the play's titular character. This love, she proposes, withstands the changeable tendencies of the protean world characterizing the tragedy more generally. "In that faire fortune had I him exchaung'd / For *Caesar*, then," she says, "men would have counted me / Faithles, unconstant, light" (lines 580–82). Here, closely following Garnier's "changer" and "leger, / Infidelle, inconstant" (sig. H1v) (exchange . . . light, / Unfaithful, inconstant), Sidney Herbert equates the exchange of political affiliations with the notion of romantic infidelity often associated with women in early modern Europe. For Cleopatra, however, turning from Antony to Caesar would signal not only inconstancy but bitter betrayal:

> If I, whome alwaies more then life he lov'de,
> If I, who am his heart, who was his hope,

Leave him, forsake him (and perhaps in vaine)
Weakly to please who him hath overthrowne?
Not light, unconstant, faithlesse should I be,
But vile, forsworne, of treachrous crueltie. (lines 586–91)

Here, the Egyptian queen offers further contributions to the play's general discourse about fluctuating circumstances and allegiances, making a bid to resist both. While her servants argue for her to change political sides and thereby to take part in the "faithles, unconstant, light" behavior that onlookers might observe with scorn, Cleopatra insists on steadfastness, claiming furthermore that such mutable behavior is "vile, forsworne, of treachrous crueltie." At this moment in the tragedy, virtue lies in loyalty and constancy to love; in change, vice. In her fidelity to Antony, Cleopatra takes arms against shifting political and affective ties, also defying misogynistic expectations about what actions she might take.[79]

Yet, for all its anxiety about mutability and the fleeting nature of political and affective bonds, *The Tragedy of Antony* ultimately seeks resolution in the sanctified mode of change or translation treated consistently in Sidney Herbert's works. This conclusion surfaces with Cleopatra, who after Antony's death departs from her usual discourse of constancy and steadfastness to plead for divinely ordained physical transformation and eventual transport to the afterlife. In this way, as Liz Oakley-Brown recognizes, "the lamenting Cleopatra is aligned with several Ovidian figures of despair who lose their identities as women."[80] Facing Antony's death and straddling the earthly and heavenly domain in her despair, Cleopatra compares her state to that of sorrowful women in Ovid's *Metamorphoses*, beginning with Niobe in book 6. Here, she addresses Niobe in an apostrophe:

a sencelesse rocke
With griefe become, on *Sipylus* thou stand'st
In endles teares: yet didst thou never feele
The weights of griefe that on my heart do lie.
Thy Children thou, mine I poore soule have lost,
And lost their Father, more then them I waile,
Lost this faire realme; yet me the heavens wrathe
Into a Stone not yet transformed hath. (lines 1911–18)

Boasting of her own misfortunes and claiming that they surpass Niobe's, Cleopatra envies the mythological heroine, craving or at least expecting (signaled by the small, but significant and thrice-repeated word "yet") a transformation of her own: the softening of Caesar's heart. Though she retains Garnier's "transforme" (sig. I1 1v) (transform) in her English rendering, the Countess of Pembroke makes a striking departure when referring to Niobe's metamorphosis. The French text's apostrophe to "Larmoyante Niobe" (Weeping Niobe) testifies that "tu sois faitte vne roche immobile" (sig. I1 1v) (you were made an immobile rock), but Sidney Herbert's "become" (line 1912) presents the transformation in more voluntary terms, offering to readers a threefold, multilayered translation at the levels of word, text, and character. Indeed, Cleopatra envies the change that Niobe has endured in her deep sorrow for her children, whether by divine order ("faitte" [made]), or voluntarily wished ("become"). Having witnessed the loss of her lover, she desires an equivalent Ovidian translation by "heavens wrathe" but at this moment remains "not yet transformed." Rendered from Garnier's French into English and modified at the level of the sentence, the notion of translation here—not Bottom's comic change into an ass or Falstaff's desired comparison with the shape-shifting Jove, but Niobe's somber metamorphosis into a durable stone—offers an ideal passage from suffering, and at multiple levels, too. As an escape hatch from the torments of the world into material stability, it is highly desirable: a glimpse of a resolution (both resolving and becoming-resolute) for the play.

After comparing herself to Niobe, Cleopatra makes yet another appeal to a classical exemplar of sorrowful translation. Here, she adopts—or translates further—a segment in book 2 of the *Metamorphoses*, in which the sisters of Phaeton are changed into poplar trees:

> *Phaetons* sisters, daughters of the Sunne,
> Which waile your brother falne into the streames
> Of stately *Po*: the Gods upon the bankes
> Your bodies to banke-loving Alders turn'd (lines 1919–22)

Arthur Golding's translation of the *Metamorphoses* makes clear that this transformation is a painful and violent one, but in Cleopatra's retelling, Phaeton's sisters find some relief in the all-seeing gods' initiative.[81] As in Niobe's case, this kind of translation affords escape from worldly suffering and lamentation. Modifying the neutral "Aulnes riuagers" (sig. I1 1v) (shore-dwelling Alders) into "banke-loving Alders," Sidney Herbert confers a sense of comfort and even peace upon the transformed sisters, who become part of their natural surroundings and cling to them for stasis. Here, one could ponder the biographical significance of this passage for the countess, a sister in mourning herself.[82] For my purposes though, with the word "turn'd," Sidney Herbert renders Garnier's "transmuerent" (sig. I11v)—a word which Claudius Hollyband's bilingual lexicon glosses as "*to change*"—into yet another term at the center of early modern discourses about translation (and which I will discuss at greater length in the next chapter).[83]

This translated state is what Cleopatra envies, for in contrast to Ovid's women, the Egyptian queen feels scorned and mocked by the Gods. "For me, I sigh, I ceasles wepe, and waile," she says, "And heaven pittiles laughes at my woe, / Revives, renewes it still" (lines 1923–25). Without such an Ovidian change available, the translation awaiting her is not an earthly metamorphosis into a rock or "banke-loving" tree, but rather death: "In the ende," she states, the Gods "doth death for comfort lende" (lines 1925–26). Here, she begins to sound a bit like Job, who in the Geneva Bible prays for the "change" of death before his friends: "Oh that I might haue my desire, & that God wolde graunt me the thing that I long for!" he says (sig. 2K4r; Job 6:8). But instead, Cleopatra begs for a place in the *Metamorphoses* among Niobe and Phaeton's sisters, who were—to her eyes, Sidney Herbert's translation suggests—mercifully translated from their mortal state of mourning. Equally miserable but scorned by the Gods, Cleopatra finds in death the only feasible translation available to her. In converting these lines from French into English, and in transporting and resettling Cleopatra's longing for death among Ovidian episodes of women "transformed" and "turn'd," Sidney Herbert exposes the multiple layers and meanings of early modern translation to the view of her readers. Showcasing both the inseparable linguistic and religious qualities of translation, she extends a legible and cosmopolitan act of devotional contemplation that transcends confessions and borders, urging English Protestants to consider the *ars moriendi* through a newly "denizend" French tragedy originally penned by a Catholic playwright.

Striving against the very constancy and stability she once claimed for herself, Cleopatra wishes for her soul's passage to the realm beyond the worldly domain and in a manner that transcends languages and opens new worlds for Sidney Herbert's readers. Although Beilin suggests Cleopatra's last act is "to confirm her earthly passion" and Danielle Clarke understands it as "resistance to Caesar, to tyranny, and to normative constructions of the political woman," this scene also echoes with the religiously resonant connotations of translation as transport to the divine afterlife.[84] In articulating her desire not to stay in the earthly realm of human suffering but rather to become one with Antony in the life beyond, Cleopatra adopts a mode of religious translation, a divine passage of the soul made possible in turn by the Countess of Pembroke's border-crossing accomplishments in literary translation. As with Laura and Petrarch in "The Triumph of Death," here lies the promise of mingled souls in the sanctified afterlife:

> Die *Cleopatra* then, no longer stay
> From *Antonie*, who thee at *Styx* attends:
> Goe joine thy Ghost with his, and sobbe no more
> Without his love within these tombes enclos'd. (lines 1927–30)

For the Egyptian queen, translation offers not only comfort from life's suffering but also the promise of a peaceful reunion with one's own beloved—in this case, not God or Petrarch, but the Roman Antony.[85] This joining of "Ghost[s]" or souls can be read as cosmopolitan, both in the way it transcends the shifting political boundaries of the world and in the way the countess ushers the tragedy's text from one vernacular to another (transcending Catholic-Protestant divisions, too). The final line of Sidney Herbert's Englished tragedy further encapsulates this religious mode of translation, granting Cleopatra an escape from her worldly sorrows: "Fainting on you, and fourth my soule may flow" (line 2022). Reworking Garnier's "mon ame vomissant" (sig. I12v) (my soul spewing) into "my soule may flow," Sidney Herbert confers a more heroic significance upon the passage of the queen's soul from one world into the next.[86] Additionally, in supplanting the French participle with "may flow," a verb conferring a sense of permission or possibility, the translator-playwright provides a sense of fluid *and* voluntary transport to the realm beyond. Concluding with a vivid example of melded linguistic and religious translation, Sidney Herbert invites her readers into a new world and a new movement between worlds, urging them to flee worldliness in its usual, sinful sense and to ascend into the cosmopolitan "world of words" championed by other literary translators (Florio chiefly among them). Challenging the indulgent "cosmopolite" but employing an approach to translation that is simultaneously devotional and linguistic, *The Tragedy of Antony* expands the conceptual sense of what a "world" can be within the realm of Europe's cosmopolitan vernaculars—here, enacted not on the public stage but within the minds of Sidney Herbert's readers.

Though it has traditionally been discussed in modern scholarship as either a feeble example of "closet drama" or as an instance of early modern "women's writing," *The Tragedy of Antony* witnessed in its own time a second edition and also inspired a genre of its own, evidence for its importance at a crucial turning point in the history of English drama. Indeed, although her translation of Mornay seems to have seen higher contemporary demand, Sidney Herbert's version of *Marc Antoine* was influential and invited further contributions to—or, translations of—the "Antony and Cleopatra" genre from Samuel Daniel, William Shakespeare, and others.[87] This tragedy-in-translation deserves attention not only for its position in literary history, however, but also for the way in which it attains that position: its poetic recruitment of the inseparable religious and linguistic discourses of early modern translation. This project constitutes a devotional application of cosmopolitan vernaculars and for an audience of dramatic readers.

What underlies the countess's work, as I have argued in this chapter, is a mode of translation operating jointly in linguistic and religious registers in *The Tragedy of Antony*—a "faithful translation" that is also a "*faith*-ful translation." On the most literal level, Sidney Herbert "Doo[es] into English" a French tragedy by Robert Garnier, changing a text from one language into another. At the same time, however, she furnishes this work with a rich discursive texture resonating with changes, translations, and religious significance. This discourse can refer at times to the inconstancy and fickleness of the world and the "varietie of vanities" enjoyed by the pleasure-seeking cosmopolite, but at the same time it points to a transcendent and divinely approved passage to the holy life beyond. My own rediscovery of the 1562 Italian-English dictionary in which it appears a young Mary Sidney Herbert inscribed lines from Petrarch's "Trionfo della Morte" offers a striking connection between this linguistic context—a kind of "Dictionaries methode" mocked in *Astrophil and Stella*—and the "fatall change" characterizing the countess's literary practice more broadly. In drawing together these religious vocabularies of alteration, mutability, change, and the transport of the soul in righteous death, and in employing them in a work of dramatic translation, Mary Sidney Herbert illustrates with *The Tragedy of Antony* the inseparability of linguistic and religious translation as the act and site of devotion. In company with her "Triumph of Death" and her Psalms, the translator-playwright's rendition of Garnier's tragedy both figures and enacts a mode of translation as change and transcendence, merging the faith-filled discourse of "fatall change" with faithful linguistic practice to inspire and religiously transform its readers.

| *Chapter Four* |

"O, the Generation of Languages"

Exchanges and Interchangeabilities in William Haughton's *Englishmen for My Money*

Tourner. *To turne; conuert, alter, change; exchange, giue in exchange . . . also, to translate.*
—RANDLE COTGRAVE, *A Dictionarie of the French and English Tongues* (1611)

French—Italian—Dutch. Listing off the languages of merchant characters in rapid succession, William Haughton's comedy *Englishmen for My Money* (1598) renders theatrically the array of foreign tongues displayed and translated in early modern Europe's marketplace-themed language manuals. In act 2, following the introduction of three "outlandish" traders at the Royal Exchange—the economic center of Haughton's London—a clever servant and clown named Frisco conducts an interview with the schoolmaster Anthony, a native Englishman.[1] Newly disguised as a French tutor, Anthony hopes to win his way back into the home of the Portuguese, but fluent anglophone, usurer named Pisaro:

ANTHONY. I am nominated Monsieur Le Mouche, and rest at your *bon* service.

FRISCO. I understand him partly yea and partly nay. Can you speak French? *Content pore vous Monsieur Madamo.*

ANTHONY. If I could not, sir, I should ill understand you. You speak the best French that ever trod upon shoe of leather.

FRISCO. Nay, I can speak more languages than that. This is Italian, is it not: *Nella slurde Curtezana*?
ANTHONY. Yes, sir, and you speak it like a very natural.
FRISCO. I believe you well. Now for Dutch: *Ducky de doe watt heb yee gebrought.*
ANTHONY. I pray, stop your mouth, for I never heard such Dutch before brocht. (2.2.25–37)

This dialogue anticipates other episodes in the play involving French, Italian, and Dutch patois, a strategy enabling monolingual playgoers to apprehend non-English languages in the theater.[2] This convention does, as Emma Smith observes, "heighten the comic effect" in what is often hailed as the first "city comedy," arranging the conflict humorously over matters of linguistic compatibility.[3] Simultaneously, the technique also stages dramatically—or "translates"—the polyglot and multicolumned mise-en-page observable in language manuals issued partly for the use of traders. Indeed, in spite of his earlier suggestion to a ragtag trio of English suitors not to "suffer a litter of languages to spring up amongst us" (1.2.105), the surprisingly capable Frisco does the opposite here, unfolding a variety of foreign words in a comic pattern in order to mock Anthony and delight Haughton's readers and playgoers. With the epithet "*Monsieur Madamo*"—which after 1609 could remind audiences of Shakespeare's "Master Mistress"—the clown also edges in a remark about the codependent indeterminacies of gender and language, which come to play a crucial role in Haughton's comedy, too. Ultimately, it is the "frisky" Frisco who stands as an emblem of the broader patterns of interchangeability in *Englishmen for My Money*, patterns that encompass languages, typefaces, habits, and people. Though both speakers here are presumably English and possess limited fluency, this scene's catalog-like presentation of stage French, Italian, and Dutch, its concentration on understanding ("I understand him partly yea and partly nay"), and its discourse about languages ("Can you speak French?") bring to the stage the period's widely known polyglot manuals and their marketplace tropes.

Moving from the educational and religious translations in the tragedies of Kyd and Sidney Herbert, it is the work of this chapter to show how the comedy *Englishmen for My Money* extended the cosmopolitan vernaculars in Europe's mercantile-themed language manuals to English playgoers and readers. This dynamic, I maintain, happens both on the stage and in print, and takes place specifically through the discourse of exchange and interchangeability, a discourse evident in Noël de Berlaimont's *Colloquia et Dictionariolum*, the popular multilingual language manual I treated in chapter 1 and will examine in more depth here.[4] My analysis therefore builds on the work of Nina Levine, who has analyzed connections between Haughton's play and the immigrant-suffused culture of language education in early modern London.[5] First acted in 1598, *Englishmen for My Money* concerns Pisaro's attempts to set up his three half-English daughters with a trio of rich foreign traders: a Frenchman, an Italian, and a Dutchman. With aid from the clever clown Frisco and the sly schoolmaster Anthony, however, three less wealthy Englishmen marry the ladies instead. While addressing the play's London-specific setting, much recent criticism has gravitated toward either financial concerns or the techniques by which Haughton represents national identity.[6] The latter approaches, which have focused on topics ranging from Pisaro's status as "crypto-Jew" or "denizen" (i.e., a foreigner made English by royal patent) to the "mother tongue" and the degree to which Haughton sympathizes with foreigners, persist in interpreting the play's foreign languages and accents as indicative of a predominantly anti-alien or at least nationalistic spirit.[7]

Other recent analyses, however, have turned from the nascent nationalism within Haughton's comedy to the ways the play comments ironically on language and nationhood, opening possibilities to view the play's linguistic exchanges in a more cosmopolitan light. Scott Oldenburg, for example, urges critics to reconsider how *Englishmen for My Money*'s London is "a multilingual home to English, Dutch, Portuguese, and Italians," while Marjorie Rubright recognizes how the typography in the play's printed versions "proved a sliding signifier of . . . linguistic difference," opening potential for slippage in language and nationhood in the very structures designed to distinguish and order them.[8] Most recently, Kelly J. Stage suggests that even as this comedy affirms anglocentric outcomes, it also "produces a fluid, alien, uncontrolled space of urban experience."[9] While I also perceive a fluid, alien quality in the play, I believe more remains to be said specifically about its peculiar linguistic dimensions. In interpreting the multiple languages in Haughton's comedy as theatrical expressions of the printed foreign vernaculars in the period's market-themed polyglot manuals, and in shifting the emphasis from the human subject (e.g., "identity") to the related domain of language, this chapter directs the critical discussion about *Englishmen for My Money* beyond both England's borders and the established subgeneric terms of "city comedy." It also examines the ways the play's translingual elements function within a discursive channel of homosocial amity that gives way, though not entirely so, to a picture of heterosexual couplings. Analyzed freshly in this way, Haughton's play can be seen as a *cosmopolitan* comedy, its tropes of mercantile exchange rooted in the connotations of interchangeability underwriting early modern translation throughout Europe and gesturing forward to emergent systems of global capital.

"Proposes of Marchandise": Visual and Textual Exchanges in the *Colloquia*

Characterized by the dramatis personae catalogs, speech prefixes, and scenes amounting to brief narratives I discussed in chapter 1, the widely published language dialogues of Noël de Berlaimont both anticipated and overlapped formally with the dramatic works of Haughton and his contemporaries.[10] As I noted in the first chapter's discussion of Berlaimont's *Colloquia et Dictionariolum*, critics sometimes refer to these polyglot language-learning manuals as "dramatic" or "theatrical," but this chapter, along with this book's other chapters, considers this paradigm in reversible terms, also recognizing segments of plays as *staged language-learning dialogues*. By placing this polyglot emphasis on the plays, one can perceive more clearly the workings of cosmopolitan vernaculars within and against Europe's emergent ideologies, among them the notions of international trade legible in Haughton's fictional setting. These, to repeat this book's title, were "theaters of translation."

As a language manual, the *Colloquia et Dictionariolum* can be viewed as representative for the period on account of its extensive and long-running circulation. According to Susan E. Phillips, the *Colloquia* "was easily one of early modern Europe's best sellers and certainly its best-selling dictionary, appearing in at least 149 editions from Lisbon to Warsaw during its 278 years in the early modern marketplace."[11] Over time, the book grew from a brief Dutch-French vocabulary with three dialogues and religious passages to a variety-filled manual including seven dialogues, a letter-writing guide, a pronunciation treatise, and a brief dictionary arranged alphabetically by Dutch entries. In its most expansive instantiations, Berlaimont's book sported eight languages: Latin, French, Dutch, German, Spanish, Italian, English, and Portuguese. What often remained constant across these versions was the *Colloquia*'s diminutive, portable size, its oblong format (commonly in 8° and 16°, but sometimes in the unusual 10°) and its horizontally arranged, parallel-column mise-en-page, which ultimately became an industry standard for the genre.[12] While this typographic arrangement displays the pattern of "compressed translation" discussed recently by A. E. B. Coldiron, in which "multiple language versions of a work are . . .

brought into one textual space," the book's extensive textual genealogy and its transnational publication record also join it to the translation patterns she terms "catenary" (texts translated in chains of succession over a long period of time) and "radiant" (translated texts fanning out to diverse linguistic communities from a single origin point, within a relatively short period).[13] Both anticipating and accompanying the development of early modern theater in England, the *Colloquia* delivered market-themed language lessons on an international scale, and with conventions that would come to characterize dramatic publications, too.

Berlaimont's manual was partly directed toward merchants, the historical counterparts of Haughton's foreign characters, though it also implies the mingling of merchants with other kinds of figures. As John Gallagher has recently discussed, polyglot manuals such as this one commonly relayed "commercial competence" to readers, as well as linguistic abilities: buying, selling, bartering, and exchanging coin.[14] To that purpose, the *Colloquia*'s title page—itself printed in multiple languages—often specifies that its dialogues are "tres profitables & vtils, tant au faict de marchandise, qu'aux voiages & aultres traffiques / *seer nut ende profitelijck tot der coopmanschap, reyse, ende andere handelinghen*" (very profitable and useful, as much for the doing of trade, for voyages, and other exchanges).[15] A version of this book published in London in 1639 mentions "MERCHANTS and SEAMEN" in its extended title as well. Furthermore, two other editions feature engraved frontispieces portraying eight figures—one for each language—some delineated by their dress and physiognomy, others negotiating alongside their goods (figures 4.1 and 4.2). It seems clear that merchants constituted an important audience for editions of this utility-focused polyglot manual, which perhaps served "as cribs for travelers and merchants" more than providing detailed linguistic instruction.[16] But if merchants do appear on this book's engraved frontispieces, they are often indistinguishable from figures representing other languages and audiences—schoolboys, courtiers, and soldiers, for instance.

These engravings deserve attention because together they exemplify the tension between circumscribed order and indiscriminate mingling that characterize both Berlaimont's manual and, as I will show, *Englishmen for My Money*. While the 1631 Amsterdam edition distinguishes each figure from the others, the 1662 Antwerp edition's frontispiece emphasizes similarity, offering up a scene of cosmopolitan amity for the book's users. Since the two manuals were issued in cities less than one hundred miles apart, perhaps the later edition with its new engraving was intended to supplant or at least complement the 1631 illustrated edition of the *Colloquia*; in any

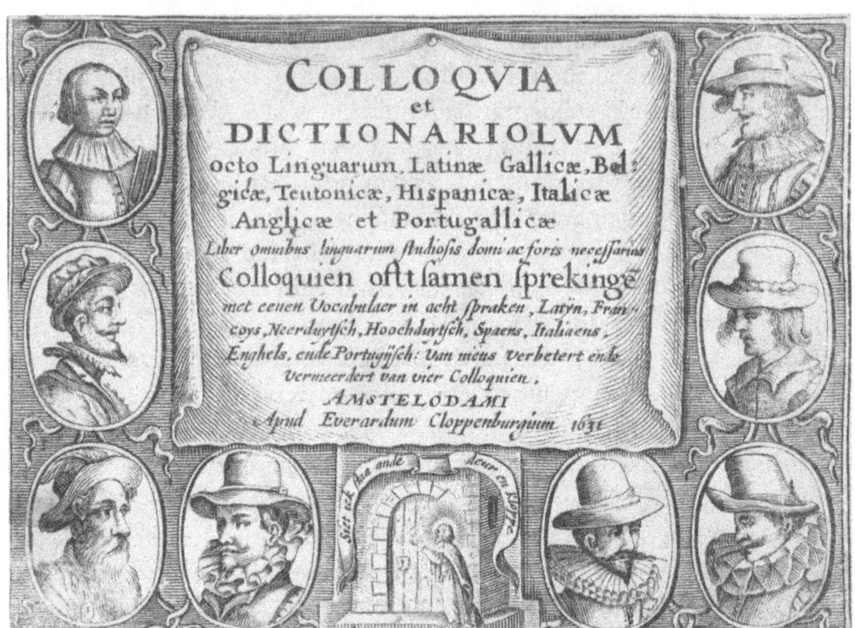

FIGURE 4.1 Noël de Berlaimont, *Colloquia et Dictionariolum octo Linguarum*, 1631, frontispiece engraving. 418 B514c. Courtesy of the Charles Deering McCormick Library of Special Collections & University Archives, Northwestern University.

FIGURE 4.2 Noël de Berlaimont, *Dictionariolum et Colloquia Octo Linguarum*, 1662, frontispiece engraving. 413 D554. Courtesy of the Charles Deering McCormick Library of Special Collections & University Archives, Northwestern University.

case, they offer together a provocative glimpse into the varied possible uses of this book. As Phillips notes, the earlier frontispiece "takes the particularity and peculiarity of nations to an extreme," associating the men's fashions with national identity ("a German hat, a Spanish moustache, an Italian ruff") and leveling languages, but keeping each distinct from the others.[17]

Confined to separate spaces by a grid of oval borders, these figures make no eye contact or exchanges with each other. In contrast, the 1662 engraving features a scene of polyglot dialogue between virtually indistinguishable traders; compared to the figures in the earlier engraving, it is difficult to tell them apart by their facial features.[18] Grouped in conversation, these figures touch one another, overlap, and intermingle, and though perhaps unintentionally, the engraver's craftsmanship sometimes makes it difficult to associate body parts with corresponding figures. Summing up this engraving's interests in interchangeability, border crossing, and language practice is the central bust of a Janus-Mercury-Mars figure, featuring two faces, armor, and a winged helmet. To build further on chapter 1's discussion of Mistress Quickly, these representations mobilized connotations of passages, transitions, and travel, as well as eloquence, merchandise, thievery, and the "friendly war" of trade, all qualities which surface in Berlaimont's text.[19] In its symbolism, this book's title page delivers a picture of the book's possible audiences and the ways in which those audiences—including merchants—may mix and mingle with each other.

With their heads and bodies inclined toward each other, rather than set apart in the style of the 1631 miniatures, the shuffled figures on this title page also come off as friends, representing male homosociality as a site for cosmopolitan exchange. One pair on the right resembles two figures in Robert Vaughan's engraving of "ACQVAINTANCE," which decorates the title page of Richard Brathwait's *The English Gentleman* (1630) (figure 4.3). In a fold-out leaf meant to accompany Vaughan's frontispiece, a text there glosses this image in language that could describe the 1662 *Colloquia*'s engraved figures: "ACQVAINTANCE is in two bodies individually incorporated . . . no lesse selfely than sociably united."[20] Taking up this trope of amity, several *Colloquia* editions' prefaces address a "Beloved reader" (in other language columns, "*Amy Lecteur*," or "Amigo Lector") and ask, "Wo hath euer ben able to fet with one speach, the frindship of sundry nations?"[21] The book's content witnesses the frequent coming and going of friends as well. "It is a friend, open the dore" (sig. C7r), commands an interlocutor at a banquet, while a vendor asks, "Frinde, what will you buye?" (sig. G5r). Picking up visually on these and other "friendly" cues, the 1662 *Colloquia*'s engraved frontispiece highlights the polyglot, same-sex interchangeability or "sociable union" intended by the book's dialogues (if not its other textual elements), thereby making clear a departure from the 1631 edition. Here, friendship is the groundwork for exchanges, interchangeabilities, or *intercourse*—in the early modern sense of reciprocal, nonhierarchical, two-way transit, associated with male-male contexts.[22]

Although merchants only constitute a portion of Berlaimont's audience, this polyglot manual's dialogues repeatedly marshal tropes of merchandise to serve a general schema of linguistic interchangeability. In this way, one can understand the indistinguishable figures in the engravings as visual glosses. In the second chapter, "For to learne to buye and sell," a trader named Margaret declares that "God will send vs some marchantes" (sig. G5r), and the remainder of the dialogue consists of tense negotiations over cloth. Two speakers in the fourth dialogue, "For to aske the way," remark on "marchants" who appear on the road before them (sig. K2r). And

FIGURE 4.3 Richard Brathwait, *The English Gentleman*, 1630, detail from frontispiece engraving. 17th-41 RHT. Courtesy of Princeton University Library Special Collections.

in the sixth dialogue, one learns "It is not late, the machauntes haue not yet opened their shoppes, nether their ware vnfolde" (sig. M8r). Further episodes of buying, selling, and price negotiation appear in the seventh dialogue, "Proposes of marchandise," along with units on foreign currency and model letters for financial requests and debt dealings. Merchants populate the polyglot landscape of Berlaimont's *Colloquia*, and more generally these dialogues recognize mercantile exchange as a prominent discursive site for both language and translation among all sorts of speakers.

One especially striking element of these dialogues is the range of negotiations that accompany these scenes of mercantile exchange. Often, during conversations about buying and selling, both parties fear the prospect that they will "lose" in the final agreement. In the second dialogue, the merchant Daniel pays a visit to shopkeepers Katherine and Margaret, and after asking the prices of several products ("How much shall I pay for an ell of this cloth?" "What is the quart of this wine worth?" [sig. G7r–G8r]) remains stingy to the dismay of both sellers. "It is te much," he says (sig. H1r). Katherine directs him to cheaper items, explaining that she shall not be able to live by his pay—"I should loose therby" (sig. H3r)—and that the would-be buyer is "to harde" (sig. H5r). "That I am indeede," Daniel replies (sig. H5r). The two reach an agreement, but their conflict over the price of goods reflects the greater mercantile purposes of the book. Rather than representing straightforward dealings at the market, the scenes in Berlaimont's dialogues seem to play out almost every possible outcome, however rude or confrontational, and to enable those exchanges across multiple languages.

Language Shufflers: The *Colloquia*'s Typography, Mise-En-Page, and Polyglot Uses

The ways these multiple languages were represented for readers and users of the *Colloquia* deserve attention, particularly in terms of typography and mise-en-page. As I mentioned in chapter 2, scholars have discussed how typeface often served a linguistic purpose in publications featuring multiple languages, and one can observe this practice in Berlaimont's dialogues, too.[23] In fact, in this and other examples of compressed translation, "printers' chosen formats and typography may have sometimes articulated implicit relationships among the cultures represented by each language."[24] To that end, *Colloquia* editions illustrate patterns that appear to have become established with passing decades and in certain contexts. According to my survey of extant editions featuring English, printers of the *Colloquia* employing typographic variety used black-letter type exclusively for German, English, and Dutch, and particularly for the latter two, especially after 1630. Italic was used for Spanish, French, and Italian, but much more frequently for the latter two, thereby associating roman more closely with Spanish. Mise-en-page mattered as well. All the editions I have seen position Dutch and German on the verso, while Spanish, Italian, and Portuguese appear on the recto; this ordering may speak to the *Colloquia*'s ideal readers and language groupings.[25] Indeed, at a broad scale, the numerous editions of Berlaimont's dialogues associate particular typefaces and positions on the page with certain languages, arguing for neat and structured relationships between and among the multiple languages. Typographic borders, which divide languages into distinct columns in all the *Colloquia* books I have surveyed that were printed after 1620, help to enforce this orderly picture, delineating French, Italian, and Dutch from each other and from other languages with heavy black rules or dashes.

Yet despite this seemingly structured typographic representation of languages in print for generations of European readers and language learners, there remain exceptions pointing toward the cosmopolitan coinvolvement of multiple tongues. Referring to this phenomenon as "typographic relativism," Marjorie Rubright proposes that the nature of typographic organization in these and other wordbooks offered readers a visual picture of the languages at hand, but one that was subject to change and dependent on context. For this reason, black-letter type could gesture not solely to Englishness but also to the "jumbled" nature of the Dutch and English languages.[26] This effect, I would argue further, both anticipates and doubles the mingled but amicable representation of merchants on the 1662 edition's frontispiece, mixing up representations of languages into a homosociably polyglot hodgepodge. English and French drift from recto to verso in certain editions; Dutch appears sometimes in italic and other times in roman, even though English appears in black letter; Venice and Bologna editions of the *Colloquia* feature all languages in roman type. One finds this fluctuation in typography not only among various editions but also in the dialogues' text, too. For instance, as it often happens in printed drama, phrases uttered in foreign languages stand out to the reader in deliberately different typefaces, disrupting each column's normalized stream of italic, roman, or black-letter text to signal a linguistic change. This is the case when revelers in the first dialogue recite the Latin prayer "De tali convivio," which remains untranslated across all columns, briefly rupturing the established typographic patterns (sig. F8v–G1r). (For the Latin column, a change from roman to italic indicates a tonal shift, if not a linguistic difference.) In such cases, when Berlaimont's speakers change languages, the book's typography changes also.

Furthermore, the very printing techniques responsible for this book's production resulted in the folding-together of various tongues. According to Coldiron, catchwords, ubiquitous guides provided by printers to aid in the binder's organization of the sheets, unsettle the straightforward reading of particular language columns in John Wolfe's "compressed translation" edition of *The Book of the Courtier*. Although she also proposes that "not all multilingual column-format books have such a directive effect," including "polyglot phrasebooks and dictionaries, where the eye may comfortably stay in one column," on a closer look, the *Colloquia*'s mise-en-page indicates that its readers could not pursue purely monoglot paths without difficulty.[27] On almost every page, catchwords shuffle syllables, words, and phrases of Berlaimont's languages across the gutter or over the leaf from recto to verso or vice versa, resulting in mixed types and tongues in what are otherwise typographically and linguistically homogenous columns. In the 1598 Delft edition, Spanish words in roman (e.g., "Amigo") spill across into the German, which otherwise appears in italic; in the 1616 Antwerp edition, French phrases in italic (e.g., "*ie n'ay*") find themselves lumped at the bottom of a black-letter English column; the italic Portuguese column harbors Latin words in roman (e.g., "volente") at the foot of the page in the 1631 Amsterdam edition (see the first of these examples in figure 4.4). There are countless other examples. Like the figures on the 1662 engraving, the catchwords in dozens of extant *Colloquia* editions tilt, nearly touch, and stray beyond their appointed typographic borders, following the standard procedures of printing but destabilizing the order proposed by the book's columned arrangement. And though some editions figure these columns typographically with borders (especially after 1620), many others do not, enabling French words or Latin words or Spanish words to butt up against each other on the page. Even if they remained invisible to readers as an expected printing convention, the *Colloquia*'s catchwords nonetheless challenge the orderly structure of the grid, bridging language to language and scrambling positional, if not typographic, associations. It seems the very production of this book demands the interchangeability and shuffling-together of diverse languages, resulting in "sociably united" tongues, a typographic variation on the figures pictured in the 1662 *Colloquia* engraving.

If the *Colloquia*'s typography and mise-en-page offer both orderly and intermingling notions of linguistic variety for readers, surviving copies of the *Colloquia* provide evidence of the specific ways early users could

Latin,	François,	*Flamen.*	Alleman,
R. Amicus,	*R. C'eſt amy,*	R. Het is vrient/	*R. Ein freundt,*
aperi oſtium.	*ouurez l'huys.*	doet de deure open.	*thue auff.*
F. Tune es Rogere?	*F. Eſtes vous la Rogier?*	F. Sijdy daer Rogier?	*F. Seydt ihr da Rogier?*
R. Etiã, hic ego adſum	*R. Ouy, ie ſuis icy:*	R. Ja ick ben hier:	*R. Ia, ich bin hie:*
eſt pater tuus domi?	*voſtre pere eſt-il à la*	is u vader thuys?	*iſt dein vatter daheim?*
F. Eſt, & item	*F. Ouy, & (maiſon?*	F. Ja hy/ ende	*F. Ia, vnd*
mater mea:	*ma mere auſsi:*	mijn moeder oock:	*mein mutter auch:*
ingredere,	*entrez dedans,*	coemt binnen:	*kompt her ein,*
dicam patri	*ie diray a mon pere*	ic salt mijn vader seg-	*ich wils meinẽ vatter ſa*
te veniſſe.	*que vous eſtes venu.*	gẽ dat ghy comẽ zijt.	*das ihr kommẽ ſeydt. (gẽ*
P. Franciſce,	*P. Francoys,*	P. Fransoys/	*P. Frantz,*
fac parentur omnia	*appreſtez tout*	maect al gereet	*mache alle ding fartig*
vt accumbamus.	*pour aller manger.*	om te gaen eten.	*das wir eſſen.*
F. Pater,	*F. Mon pere,*	F. Vader/	*F. Vatter,*
omnia parata ſunt,	*tout eſt preſt,*	tis al gereet/	*es iſt alles fertich,*
vbi voles, accumbere	*vous pouez aller mãger*	ghy meucht gaen eten/	*ir moegt zum eſſen gehẽ,*
licebit.	*quand il vous plait.*	alst u belieft.	*wan es euch geliebet.*
P. Bene habet,	*P. Bien, ie vien*	P. Wel/ ick come	*P. VVol, ich will*
continuò iſthic adero,	*encontinent,*	terstont:	*van ſtund an kommen,*
voca pueros.	*appellez les enfans.*	roept de kinderen.	*ruffe den kinderen.*
F. Faciam libẽs pater,	*F. Bien mon pere,*	F. Wel mijn vader:	*F. Ich wils thun lieber*
heus Ioannes,	*Iean, où eſtes vous?*	Jan/ waer zijdy?	*Horſtu Hans, (vatter:*
veni diſcubitum:	*venez manger:*	ghy sout comen eten?	*komme zum tiſch:*
			R. Amigo,

FIGURE 4.4 Noël de Berlaimont, *Colloquia et Dictionariolum Octo Linguarum*, 1598, sig. C6v. MINI00415. Reproduced by permission of the Rare Book & Manuscript Library, University of Illinois at Urbana-Champaign.

engage with foreign vernaculars as well. Indeed, as Gallagher has shown, such signs of use offer a window into how printed texts and handwriting techniques could work in parallel with the oral and auditory dimensions of early modern language training.[28] A striking example of this can be found in a 1616 Antwerp edition of Berlaimont's manual held today at the Folger Shakespeare Library, which contains in several blank leaves over three hundred inscribed English words along with their French equivalents (figure 4.5). According to ownership markings, this copy belonged to the Englishman Henry Delves, Second Baronet of Cheshire (1597–1663), and the evidence suggests he had the book bound with extra leaves for personalized lexicographic practice.[29] Other surviving polyglot manuals and dictionaries I have seen indicate this was not an unusual approach, and the manual's portable size made its blank leaves a convenient place to write. Almost 90 percent of the English words inscribed in this book's extra leaves, nearly all of which are infinitive verbs and nouns, already appear in the *Colloquia*'s printed wordlist in some way (several of them more than once). In rewriting these entries, Delves reshuffles them alphabetically by English, rather than by Dutch as in the book, thereby rendering the volume more useful for an anglophone in need of French terms. Beginning on the printed book's final verso, continuing on the added leaves, and winding around to the front after he runs out of space, the annotator also marks certain corresponding entries in Berlaimont's wordlist and includes a non-alphabetic "catch-all" leaf at the front of the volume for assorted verbs, nouns, and adjectives. On account of not only the rearranged entries but also the carefully ruled columns and guide letters mimicking the printed book's mise-en-page, this copy of the *Colloquia* illustrates Delves's attention to the content of Berlaimont's manual, as well as the ways in which the book's format "formats" his approach to the material. Here, one observes a mercantile-themed polyglot conversation guide prompting an Englishman to further practice in translation.

Other surviving copies illustrate how readers could use the *Colloquia* to translate information about money and exchange rates. At the University of Illinois, a copy of a 1623 Amsterdam edition features a sequence of what appear to be monetary conversions, all in the same early hand (figure 4.6).

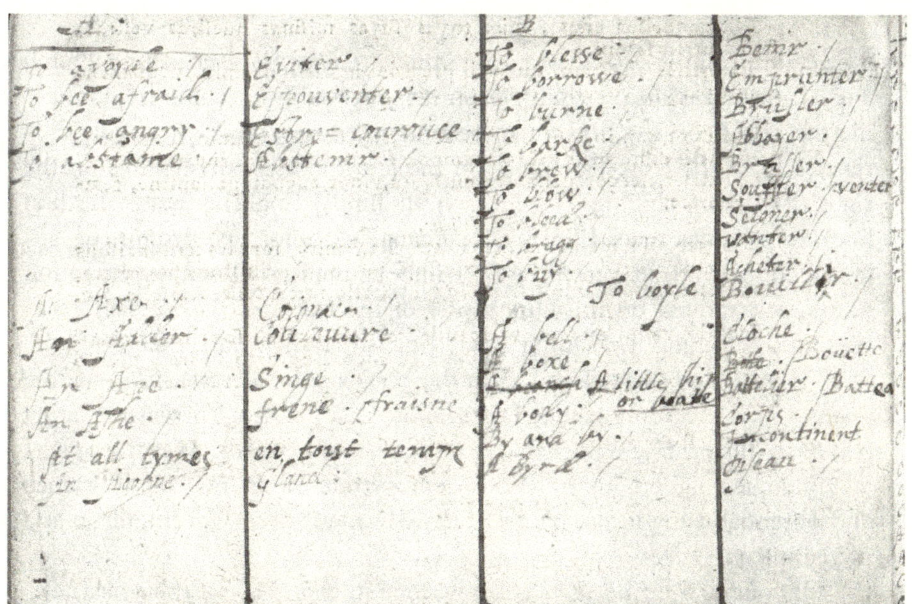

FIGURE 4.5 Noël de Berlaimont, *Colloquia et Dictionariolum Septem Linguarum*, 1616, back flyleaf. STC 1431.86. Reproduced by permission of the Folger Shakespeare Library.

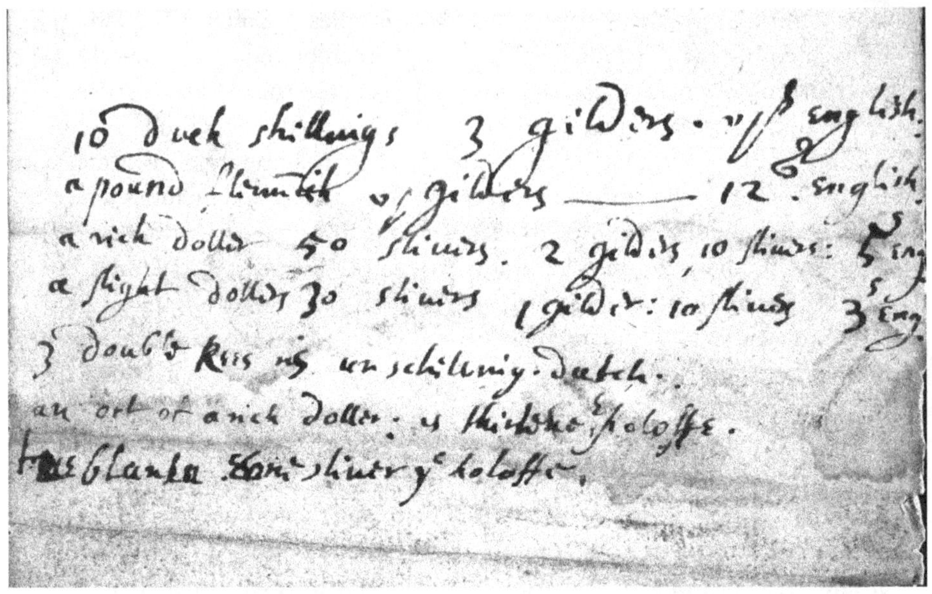

FIGURE 4.6 Noël de Berlaimont, *Colloquia et Dictionariolum Octo Linguarum*, 1623, flyleaf. Baldwin 0706. Reproduced by permission of the Rare Book & Manuscript Library, University of Illinois at Urbana-Champaign.

These inscriptions enable one to picture a *Colloquia* user setting Dutch and English currencies against each other, roughly in columns mimicking the book's design, and for mercantile purposes, too.[30] Arranging currencies from the Low Countries on the left and English shillings on the right ("10 duch shillings 3 gilders vj s[hillings] English," reads the first line), these notes record financial exchange rates for two prominent language communities targeted by Berlaimont's manual. Based on the round numbers arranged on the Dutch side of the leaf and the English spellings used throughout ("Dutch" and "English" rather than "Neerduytsch" or "Vlaems" and "Engelsch" as in the book's printed text), it seems the owner was an anglophone like Delves or at least that English was the target language. Illustrating evidence of practice on appended leaves, these surviving copies of Berlaimont's book demonstrate the manual's importance and potential value in the hands of early modern users, for linguistic and mercantile purposes.

Of course, the *Colloquia* was not alone in charting out rhetorical relationships between mercantile practice, translation, and polyglot exercise, nor was it unique in encouraging readers to take up these activities.[31] Other Renaissance-era language publications adopt a mercantile discourse of translation as well, including John Minsheu's massive eleven-language dictionary, *Ductor in Linguas* (1617). To Minsheu, the book's purpose was obvious. "What vse Merchants may make of this Booke," he states in an epistle to the reader, "especially those that are in person to traficke in forreine Countreys and Tongues, I need not here set downe, when it approues it selfe so plaine to euery mans vnderstanding."[32] An Oxford project initiated around the time of *Englishmen for My Money*'s first production, Minsheu's dictionary was laboriously compiled at the hands of a polyglot committee of scholars. Later in the epistle, Minsheu compares his lexicographic endeavor to a merchant's delivery of foreign goods: "And seeing I haue made so dangerous a voyage, and aduenture, in so many tempests in an Ocean of trauailes, troubles, and hard sufferings, and wants, the greater part of this twenty yeeres, to bring this tossed Barke vnwreckt, which here vnlades, and layes in order to your viewes the Commodities that are in the same" (sig. A4r). As Edmund Valentine Campos aptly states, "Minsheu portrays himself as a commercial adventurer recently returned from foreign lands to offer his wares for the good of the commonwealth."[33] Indeed, the lexicographer adopts here the same tropes that the poet Samuel Daniel employed for explicitly colonial purposes: "T'enrich vnknowing Nations with our stores" of language, and across "strange shores."[34] Likening his own work to the "aduenture" of merchants, Minsheu offers his dictionary to readers as a "tossed Barke" full of foreign "Commodities"—that is, words—all to advance their fortunes. In making this parallel between polyglot lexicography and foreign trade, and especially for a folio towering over Berlaimont's diminutive manual at almost a half-meter tall, Minsheu serves up a mercantile variation on the rhetoric of heroism coursing through many of the period's Continental dictionaries.[35]

Not only is *Ductor in Linguas* a book for merchants, however, for Minsheu clarifies that these traders also inspired his life's work in languages. In another preface, he offers an anecdote reflecting on his past, his journeys, and his exchanges with international traders: "In my yonger time, aboue thirty yeeres since, by meanes of some worthy Merchants . . . I was first furnished according to my then great desires, to trauell into forreine Countreys, and get the knowledge of some of the Tongues (which I haue professed) and at their seruices here present, and truely affirme, that not onely my furnishing forth, my supplie when I wanted abroad, and my transporting from one Countrey to another, as also my comming home (when I had beene taken prisoner) was still by Merchants" (sig. A4r). Not only has Minsheu designed his dictionary for merchants and compared it to their "tossed Barke" full of "Commodities." Here, he also acknowledges the influence that merchants have had on his own travels and learning. It is thanks to merchants, he writes, that he was first able to travel, to learn languages, and to return home to set about his life's work. *Ductor in Linguas* cost a fortune to produce and left Minsheu in financial ruin, but it stands nonetheless as a multilingual effort inspired by and designed for merchants, also offering a precedent for subscription publication.[36]

Decades later, this merged discourse of merchandise and multilingual lexicography surfaced in Giovanni Torriano's bilingual *Vocabolario Italiano & Inglese* (1659). Inheriting the scholarship of John Florio, who had been preparing a third edition of his own dictionary, Torriano "Revised, Corrected, and Compared" his predecessor's work alongside that of the Accademia della Crusca, also dedicating it specifically to merchants.[37] A preface to Andrea Riccard and William Williams, governor and vice governor of the Company of Turkey Merchants in London, precedes this large dictionary's text and is followed by another dedication by the book's stationers to London merchant James Stanier. In the latter, the publishers ask Stanier's permission to issue the volume "to all the World, and to be so just as to endeavour, that not only in ENGLAND, but in the PARTS BEYOND SEA, where your Correspondents have daily experience," hoping also that "our Gratitude may travell as farr as the use of this Book will carry it."[38] In a final preliminary address, Torriano echoes Minsheu's comment about the obviousness for such a dictionary, particularly "when . . . excellent Books do travell into all Nations" and "when all Merchants that traffique into the *Levant*, must Trade by that Language [i.e., Italian]" (sig. b2r). Issued for Turkey merchants in particular, Torriano's dictionary adopts Minsheu's discourse of trade (via Florio) and projects forward into mercantile territory in and beyond Europe. Other English-Italian works by Torriano followed a similar trajectory.[39] Along with Berlaimont's pocket-sized *Colloquia* editions, these massive dictionaries employ the discourse of merchandise in the service of polyglossia and translation. Both works encouraged merchants—among students, courtiers, and others—to take part in a multilingual world of words.

"I'll Learn to Speak this Gibberish": Language Lessons and Markets on Stage

By beginning *Englishmen for My Money* with a scene of instruction and placing high stakes on the search for a language tutor, Haughton positions his comedy within this world of words, particularly among mercantile-themed polyglot language manuals such as the *Colloquia*. Many critics have addressed Pisaro's opening monologue, but few have remarked on how the ensuing episode represents a lesson between Pisaro's daughters and their schoolmaster, Anthony.[40] This scene concerns moral philosophy and not language, but Anthony's recollection that "my mother Oxford (England's pride) / Fostered me pupil-like, with her rich store" (1.1.40–41) calls attention to one of England's most vibrant communities of polyglot scholars and lexicographers. In addition to John Minsheu, the names of Antonio del Corro, John Florio, and John Thorius were familiar at Oxford during Haughton's time (see my discussion in chapter 2), and the phrase "rich store" seizes on the discourse of rhetorical *copia* that encompassed not merely English but other languages as well.[41]

In spite of this pedagogically themed opening, Pisaro's half-English daughters reject philosophical schooling and turn—that is, translate—the play's world of pedagogy into a mingled world of commodities and romance. In this way, they help to inaugurate the notion of women's "city talk" first analyzed by Karen Newman, though in a manner engaged with the discourse of contaminating foreignness explored more recently by Diane Cady.[42] Like Shakespeare's Bianca, who wishes in *The Taming of the Shrew* to "learn my lessons as I please myself," Pisaro's daughters reconfigure the pedagogical scene into a stage for their own erotic fantasies.[43] Not the dedicated pedant Pisaro desired, the schoolmaster Anthony encourages this redirection, partly because of his own vested interests. Accommodating his pupils, Anthony modifies his teaching into "a lecture of more pleasing worth" (line 67), placing emphasis on both pleasure and value, and doles out gifts from his friends, the English suitors Harvey, Heigham, and Walgrave. These gifts include a letter scorning education ("every line repugns philosophy" [line 69)]), a purse full of "golden circle[s]" (i.e., coins) (line 72), and a pair of gloves. Along with the play's proverbial subtitle, *A Woman Will Have Her Will*, the phrase "I need not to instruct; you can conceive" (2.3.322, 4.1.177) becomes an anthem throughout this comedy, spoken both to Pisaro's daughters and the English suitors and flagging a transition from education to romance, sex, and reproduction. Altogether, in this early scene, commodities and the ensuing discussion of romance and dowries overtake instruction, foreshadowing the emphasis on interchangeability throughout the play.

Following Anthony's articulation of the mercantile matters bound up with romance, Pisaro's daughter Marina expresses the translation of schoolroom into marketplace much more plainly, melding the discourses of affection and money in the process. In couplets, she discusses Harvey's romantic letter to her in economic terms:

> There's not a word of this, not a word's part,
> But shall be stamped, sealed, printed on my heart.
> On this I'll read, on this my senses ply,
> All arts being vain, but this philosophy. (1.1.105–8)

For Marina, the moral philosophy her father would have her and her sisters learn makes an alchemical transformation into the economic and affective philosophy of Harvey's letter. "Not a word," not even part of a word—and in whatever language—is separable from financial concerns in this play. Employing overlapping tropes of coinage and letter writing ("stamped, sealed, printed"), Pisaro's daughter figures her romance as a kind of economic exchange that one can "read," a new philosophy at odds with the schoolroom she and her sisters so despise. Laurentia and Mathea support their younger sister's claim with more couplets, the former naming her beloved Ferdinand Heigham "an angel of more price" (line 112) and advancing the combined discourse of affection and money with an allusion to contemporary currency. In accepting Anthony's tokens from the English suitors Harvey, Heigham, and Walgrave, Pisaro's daughters effect a translation of learning into the combination of romance and money that will come to dominate the plot (and which are legible already in the play's extended title).[44]

Pisaro has other ideas, however, and attempts to steer his daughters' affections toward three foreign merchants by way of a language tutor. "I have o'er-heard your vile conversions" (line 127), he cries, stepping forward and condemning the lesson's transition toward monoglossia and English romance.[45] In this way, the search for a polyglot instructor becomes, however briefly, the driving motivation of both the protagonist and the play at large. Breaking up the lesson and scorning Anthony's encouragement of the prodigal Englishmen, Pisaro enlists the clown Frisco to find an instructor who may help his daughters to communicate better with his desired sons-in-law:

> Give diligence, enquire about
> For one that is expert in languages,
> A good musician, and a Frenchman born,
> And bring him hither to instruct my daughters—
> I'll ne'er trust more a smooth-faced Englishman. (1.1.162–66)

By insisting on both an "expert" and a "Frenchman born" (rather than a young and inexperienced Englishman like Anthony), Pisaro refers to a specialized industry of language instructors that emerged in London during the late sixteenth century. Indeed, by the time of *Englishmen for My Money*'s first performance, this community of foreign vernacular educators was well established and had begun to witness conflicts with native Englishmen taking up the same trade.[46] Pisaro delegates the search to his mobile and protean servant, Frisco, who with a range of parroted foreign-language sounds ("awee awee" [line 174] and "*Haunce butterkin slowpin frokin*" [lines 182–83]) comically convinces the usurer that he has adequate skills for the task. If Frisco's imperfect linguistic expertise or his ironic commentary on the play's action seem to align him with the English characters rather than Pisaro, his name and his playfulness gesture in a far more foreign direction, as I will show later on. For this reason, Pisaro's maintenance of Frisco makes sense. At the scene's end, the usurer aligns himself with the "several languages" (line 217) of the merchants, pitting polyglot education and his own marriage-market designs against the monoglot romance prized by his daughters, who desire the English suitors instead.[47]

Pisaro's half-English daughters and their English suitors display xenophobic attitudes to foreign languages and the stranger-merchants who speak them, but these hostile views need not be accepted without a sense of irony, particularly on account of early modern London's polyglot environment. In act 2, Mathea asks her Continental suitor, "Think you I'll learn to speak this gibberish, / Or the pig's language?" (2.1.97–98); later, Laurentia offers the Dutchman, Vandal, a parting shot: "If needs you marry with an English lass, / Woo her in English, or she'll call you ass" (2.3.159–60). As Smith observes, the daughters' resistance to the foreigners is "repeatedly figured in terms of linguistic incompatibility," and the English rival suitors add to this ridicule with threats of physical violence.[48] Critics have perceived in these cruelly comic episodes "a blindness to one's own national weaknesses," "a fantasy of English *cultural* superiority," and "a singularly English point-of-view."[49] However, Levine and Rubright have suggested that in spite of all this hostility and jingoism, the play's relentless interest in diverse accents also comments on the mingled nature of foreign languages in London, English among them; among other critics, Oldenburg offers a reminder that Pisaro's daughters are half-foreign themselves.[50]

These alternative views of *Englishmen for My Money*'s xenophobic humor would have appealed to segments of London's mixed theatergoing audience, which included foreign traders, travelers, and dignitaries. In fact, non-English strangers are responsible for many firsthand accounts of theater spectacles in early modern London: the Frenchman Jacques Petit, who attended a production of *Titus Andronicus*; the Italian priest Horatio

Busino, who witnessed John Webster's *Duchess of Malfi*; and the Dutchman Johannes de Witt, to whom is owed the only contemporary drawing of an Elizabethan theater's interior, to name only three.[51] Writing for audiences in London which included or would be familiar with such foreigners in some way, Haughton offers a variety of opportunities to reflect on the shifting boundaries between foreign and native, ultimately effecting a kind of defamiliarization akin to what Stage observes within the play's sense of space: "The stage comes to embody the strangeness of the larger city."[52] More specifically, though, I suggest these reflections on foreign and native take place through the notion of interchangeability illustrated in Berlaimont's widely published dialogues. Altogether, rather than simply forcing anti-immigrant laughter upon its audiences, *Englishmen for My Money* not only highlights the bitterness and violence attending that laughter but also manifests more broadly the cosmopolitan linguistic engagements characterizing and pointing beyond early modern London, across Europe.

If some of Haughton's audiences—both native and non-English—could resist a straightforwardly xenophobic interpretation of the comedy's foreign accents, then the play's Englishmen attempting foreign languages can be read against the grain, too. As Levine notes, the comedy again and again "turn[s] attention to the fumbling linguistic performances of the English themselves," thereby highlighting merchants' and travelers' desperate need for foreign languages.[53] One instance of the play's ironic treatment of anglophones occurs in act 2 when Anthony, disguised as "Monsieur Le Mouche," has a rather difficult encounter with the Frenchman Delion. With foreign text flagged in italic for readers, the merchant-suitor asks, "Monsieur, *Vous estes tresbien venu, de quell pais estes vous*."[54] The English schoolmaster answers not immediately, but after some reflections, spoken aside: "*Vous*, thats you: sure he saies, how do men call you," followed by his tentative, and incorrect, response: "Monsieur *le Mouche?*" In the quarto's typography, readers can follow Anthony's translation of "*Vous*" into the English "you" through the passage from italic to roman. If the schoolmaster's foolish attempt to render French into English resembles the work of a fastidious dictionary user—something like Philip Sidney's pejoratively named "Dictionaries methode"—his French alias can be found in the same domain, for in his 1593 bilingual dictionary, the French language master and lexicographer Claudius Hollyband defines "Maistre-mouche" (set in roman) as "*a nicke name describing a craftie and subtil fellow, also a merie and ingenious or wittie one*" (set in italic).[55] Anthony aspires to be just such a "craftie and subtil fellow" in his French guise, but even his new name—the only foreign word he can muster, it seems—leans on a bilingual dictionary compiled by a foreign-born French teacher. Meanwhile, Frisco's running epithet, "Master Mouse" (e.g., 2.2.39), translates this Englishman back into a cowardly fool, driving home Haughton's ironic commentary on the linguistic ineptitude of his countrymen.

Although Delion intends his question as an act of courtesy to a countryman, it comes off as a language exam administered by a foreign merchant, an exam that extends beyond the stage to readers and playgoers. More is at stake here, I am arguing, than merely "a bilingual struggle between French and English," though this is certainly a part of the picture.[56] This is also the case when Alvaro acts as his own interpreter to the advantage of both Marina and less-learned audience members: "Bella madona, dare is no language so *dulce*—'*dulce*': dat is 'sweet'—as de language dat you shall speak" (2.1.34–35). Indeed, in paying for a book or for admission to the playhouse, Haughton's audiences gained entry to a staged performance of Berlaimont's *Colloquia.* There is much stock for laughter in these exchanges, but the scene offers much more than a simple comedy routine. By allowing the audience to overhear Anthony's attempt to translate "*Vous*" and to follow Delion's explanation of "*dulce*"—a process rendered typographically for readers familiar with conventions in Berlaimont's and other language manuals—Haughton dramatizes the linguistic challenges and failures experienced not only by foreigners in London but also by Englishmen themselves, and in the same London streets. Fortunately for Anthony, the three English suitors distract Pisaro with a mention of their debts, saving the schoolmaster from having to perform the French language. Even if the comedy tends toward the perspective of the Englishmen, as many critics have shown, it figures linguistic practice and translation as techniques that unite foreigners and natives, drawing them together to mingle and speak, such as one sees on the 1662 *Colloquia* frontispiece. These, also, are mercantile language lessons that do not end on stage but extend to Haughton's playgoers in the theater space, and to readers via print.

"Whither Frisk You at This Time of Night?" Haughton's Cosmopolitan Servant-Clown

As one can see already in the Delion-Anthony language lesson, the quarto editions of *Englishmen for My Money* pose challenges to the xenophobia perceived by so many critics, illustrating typographically the variety of languages deployed in the comedy. Rubright observes: "The typographic arrangement of the speech of the play's Englishmen makes plain that italic indicates foreign languages, not foreign characters."[57] In this way, the early quartos' typography presents foreign languages visually, regardless of the speaker's origins, and in a way that resembles the material-textual displays in bilingual and polyglot language manuals like the *Colloquia.* Even in this scene, though, there are exceptions exposing the seams between and among languages, resulting in their commixture and interchangeability. With the word "brocht," for instance, spoken by Anthony and which straddles linguistically and typographically the boundary between English and Dutch (it appears in the quartos in roman, a typeface that registers normatively as English against the foreign and mock-foreign words' italic), Haughton either delivers a foreign word in the guise of a naturalized one or dresses an English word in Dutch's foreign spelling. The boundary between these languages, that is, often becomes unclear.[58] Here, the playwright also accommodates the period's capacious definitions of *translation*, which in multilingual dictionaries often included the notion of "bringing."[59] Haughton's deployment of this lexicographically resonant translation keyword signals not only the blurriness between languages but also their tendency to change from one into the other. Like Minsheu's polyglot dictionary, this play "vnlades, and layes" the "Commodities" of foreign languages to the view of readers and audiences who may take them up and use them, regardless of the words' origins.

Furthermore, the disguises and mistaken identities in *Englishmen for My Money* attest to the interchangeable nature of foreign and native and the ease with which one could be "translated" into the other. Even if the foreign languages in Haughton's comedy are sometimes delineated on the page (in italic) or on the stage (through "stage language" or patois), one finds a precursor to the indeterminacy represented decades later on the 1662 *Colloquia* frontispiece. As the play goes on, Lloyd Kermode observes, "there seems to be less and less difference between a 'real' foreign character and one national character disguised as another," and critics' careful treatment of Pisaro has illustrated how tenuous the boundaries between Jew, Spaniard, Portingale, and Englishman could be.[60] Accordingly, the schoolmaster Anthony is able to change himself into Monsieur Le Mouche, donning a disguise and ensuring that Frisco will recognize a foreigner by it: "For in this borrowed shape / Must I beguile and overreach the fool," he says, taking up the translation keyword "borrowed" to flag further foreign connotations (1.2.66–67). The ambiguously named Frisco adopts this approach as well, stealing Vandal's cloak and posing as the Dutchman under the daughters' window. "Now look I as like the Dutchman as if I were spit out of his mouth," the clown says with synesthetic flair, adding "I'll straight home and speak groote and broode, and toot and gib'rish" (3.1.10–12), practicing his foreign speech before performing the role. Though Frisco's disguise might be "comic in that it creates yet another opportunity to gull the foreigner," as A. J. Hoenselaars contends, I agree with Levine that it also more seriously invites the audience to question the supposed distinction or tension between Englishman and foreigner.[61] Through their "borrowed shape" and parroted speech, Anthony and Frisco enable Haughton's audiences and readers to interrogate supposedly fixed linguistic boundaries—such as one sees in the cordoned-off portraits of the 1631 *Colloquia*—as well as their stereotypical assumptions.

As a "frisky" go-between who "frisks" among foreign traders and English suitors and unsettles identity distinctions, Frisco deserves special attention. Indeed, Jean E. Howard recognizes that the clown stands as a "vehicle for much of [the play's] linguistic commentary," and I would add that it is commentary that resists the comprehensive endorsement of a particular language or country.[62] Admittedly, the servant's laughter often comes at the foreign merchants' expense, but his thoroughgoing interest in the exchange and multiplication of languages situates him somewhere in between the poles of foreign and native; as Stage aptly notes, his character can be defined by its "slipperiness."[63] Asked where he is going early on in the play, Frisco responds, "How shall I tell you when I do not know my self, nor understand my self?" (1.2.73–74). Does the clown mean he is uncertain of his destination or his identity? Or both? It is this ambiguity that underwrites Frisco's experimentation with foreign languages and accents, particularly when he disguises himself with Vandal's cloak and attempts to speak "groote and broode, and toot and gib'rish." Here, Haughton invites his audience to ask if the clown has been changed at all by donning the Dutchman's cloak, or if he was ever truly English to begin with; he certainly seems "in the know" during his exchanges with Anthony, another slippery character. Frisco, to use Phillips's apt designation for the *Colloquia*, is an "equal-opportunity offender."[64] He makes jibes at the foreigners and leads them literally astray in London's streets but undermines the English suitors' language and designs as well (he reveals their plans to Pisaro in act 2 for the sake of amusement).

Even Frisco's name challenges audiences and readers to think about the fluidity and continuous exchanges of language and culture. Recalling "fresh" or "new" (Italian and Spanish, "fresco"), "Frisco" gestures beyond "Harvey" and the topographically derived "Heigham" and "Walgrave" toward the Continent and the languages spoken by the English suitors' rivals.[65] The word *frisk* resonates in this name as well, and according to the *Oxford English Dictionary*, *frisco* might be understood as a pseudo-Italian variation on this term (as both noun and verb).[66] Across early modern drama, *frisk* signals turning, dancing and playfulness, from Simon Eyre's command to "frisk about, and about, and about" in *The Shoemaker's Holiday* to Polixenes's "twinned lambs that did frisk i' th' sun" in *The Winter's Tale*.[67] In *Englishmen for My Money*, the verb "frisk" points most obviously to the perpetual turning of Pisaro's servant during a scene of travel through London's darkened streets: "Ho, Frisco! Whither frisk you at this time of night?" (3.3.68) asks the local Bellman. One hears in these words the collapse of "Frisco" and "frisk you"—perhaps resulting in "frisky"—thereby opening erotic channels within the discourse of male friendship discussed earlier. By this point, the servant has not only taken Vandal's clothing and mimicked his language but is also jumbled together with Alvaro and Delion, frisking about in the intimate dark where a person's language distinguishes him before his appearance. Discussing this scene, Stage remarks that "Frisco, in his intermediary role, guides the audience as well as Delion and Alvaro into heightened states of confusion."[68] Yet I would suggest that this scene of nightly travels through London also communicates a point about the interchangeability of foreign and native, and the pleasures that might accompany that interchangeability. In other words, attending to the play's emphasis on the fluid boundaries of language, nation, and culture gestures toward a "friendlier," even erotic, and certainly less xenophobically hostile reading.

Here, the polyglot merchants and Frisco could be character types extracted from Berlaimont's dialogue "For to aske the way," wandering aimlessly and asking others for directions. "I turned down on the left hand, and so lost him," says the clown, recounting to Pisaro his sinister separation ("sinister" in both leftward and morally suspect senses) from Vandal in the dark streets and hailing the "turning" that characterizes his name and his interest in the protean qualities of language (4.1.247–48).[69] In the exchange with Pisaro that follows, the word "turn" echoes repeatedly: "Why, then you turned together, ass!" "Why, turned you not both on the left hand?" "On which hand turned ye?" (4.1.249, 251, 255). As a go-between who accompanies foreign merchants through the streets of London, trades languages with them, and takes on their appearances through disguise, Frisco is the embodiment of bringings, turnings, and conversions—or "friskings"—that occur between and among languages in Haughton's cosmopolitan comedy and in early modern language manuals like the *Colloquia*. Drifting queerly across the linguistic borders proposed by this play's native Englishmen, he is a borrowed word himself.

Like Anthony and Frisco, the foreign and English suitors in Haughton's comedy also take on disguises, emphasizing metatheatrically the tendency of cultures and languages to "turn" into each other. As critics including Daniel Vitkus and Jonathan Burton have shown, early modern English drama witnessed a considerable amount of discourse on ethnic "turning," which expressed both emerging imperial fantasies and cultural anxieties about religious conversion.[70] My discussion shifts these studies' emphases from the religiously shaped human subject toward related linguistic connotations, however, "turning" in its own way from Othello's question "Are we turned Turks?" to Benedick's remark about the love-struck Claudio in *Much Ado About Nothing*: "Now is he turned ortography; his words are a very fantastical banquet."[71] In this way, I wish to unpack the continuum between social identities and languages and to assess how linguistic concerns emerge at the center of the question. In Haughton's comedy, Pisaro recommends English costumes to Alvaro, Delion, and Vandal, who attempt to advance their suits with his daughters through both a bed trick and a more naturalized appearance (even if their accents betray their identities). Haughton also attaches metatheatrical meaning to these disguises. In act 2, Pisaro refers to his plot as "a jest / Worth the telling—nay, worth the acting" (2.3.218–19) and, like a Portuguese Hieronimo working in reverse, casts the foreign merchants in native, English roles: "Each one shall change his name. / Master Vandal, you shall take 'Heigham,' and you / 'Young Harvey,' and Monsieur Delion, 'Ned'" (2.3.237–39). Finding out about these plans, the Englishman Harvey reflects on his rival with the same terms: "Well, neat Italian, you must don my shape. / Play your part well, or I may 'haps pay you" (3.2.5–6), punning on both the dowry he hopes to win and the beating with which he threatens the foreigners.

As the comedy develops, this playacting multiplies, and across genders, too. When Anthony advises Laurentia to "play Anthony in my disguise" (4.2.45) and Walgrave dresses as the neighbor Susan, these cases of cross-dressing remind audiences of both the theater's gendered costuming practices and the gender politics accompanying translation. "All translations are reputed femalls, delivered at second hand," wrote John Florio, and in a context of gender politics that I will examine more fully in the next chapter.[72] Through these metatheatrical means, Haughton exposes the channels by which the interchangeable languages and speakers in manuals like Berlaimont's "turn" their way in and through the theater to paying audiences and readers.

Although he initiates this metatheatrical "device" (2.3.241), even Pisaro fails to distinguish the Englishmen from the foreigners, referring to both groups at various times as "strangers" and employing the word "turn" in the midst of a mix-up at the Royal Exchange. Here, in a scene with elements resembling the *Colloquia*'s dialogue "Proposes of marchandise" or its model letters for greedy lenders or stalling debtors, one finds the Portuguese usurer meeting with merchant colleagues, discussing investments and prices, and fetching correspondence from the post carrier. Although Stage suggests this scene exhibits the diminishment of class anxiety in favor of "heightened anti-alien sentiment," I suggest one can nonetheless perceive in it further commentary on the ability of foreign and native to be exchanged or mistaken for each other.[73] Distraught by the news of his ships' seizure by pirates, the usurer takes Harvey, Heigham, and Walgrave to be his foreign merchant "friends" and invites them to dine with him:

PISARO. Master Vandal, I confess I wrong you,
But I'll talk a word or two with him, and straight
turn to you.
. . . .
HEIGHAM. Turn to us? Turn to the gallows if you will.
HARVEY. 'Tis midsummer-moon with him; let him alone.
He calls Ned Walgrave Master Vandal. (1.3.208–13)

At surface level, Pisaro merely talks here of "turn[ing]" to *face* Heigham, Harvey, and Walgrave after speaking a word with his merchant colleague, but in doing so, he unwittingly "turns"—that is, translates—the Englishman Walgrave into the Dutchman Vandal. For Pisaro, it is "midsummer-moon," the same time during which Shakespeare's Puck turned the carpenter Bottom into an ass.

In a play so concerned with foreign languages and interchangeable identities, I argue that this act of turning cannot be taken lightly, particularly during a scene at the Royal *Exchange*. Indeed, Heigham's repetition of "turn" ("Turn to us? Turn to the gallows if you will") renders legible or audible the "bringing, turning, and converting" known as translation (as spelled out in Florio's dictionary) and which blurs the boundaries between languages and identities in this play. Furthermore, though today it signals willful destruction, the name "Vandal" resonated in the early modern era with connotations not only of Germanic heritage but also of wandering or placelessness: "The *Vandales* . . . haue gotten that name by their much wandring from place to place," asserts Richard Verstegan in *A Restitution of Decayed Intelligence in Antiquities* (sig. B4v). To be called "Master Vandal" was to have one's rooted Englishness—an Englishness flagged in the play's original title—invested with foreign and meandering qualities,

qualities embodied by both Frisco and the night-wandering "strangers." Here, Haughton's irony is clear. Like Anthony and Frisco, the two trios of foreign and native suitors take on disguises and are mistaken for each other, emphasizing the play's metatheatrical interest in "turning" and the manifold exchanges between native and foreign.

Partly through all this turning and playacting, Haughton's comedy entertains the potential for "sociable union" between foreign and native through the discourse of male friendship. Rendering theatrically the "friendship of sundry nations" discussed in Berlaimont's manual or represented in the intermingled figures on the 1662 *Colloquia* engraving, Pisaro often refers to Delion, Alvaro, and Vandal as friends. In fact, throughout the comedy, he uses the word more times than all the other characters combined. The usurer's first mention of the foreign traders hails them as "All strangers, and my very special friends" (1.1.212), and at the Exchange, he addresses them as "loving friends" (1.3.3). Later, in his home, Pisaro explains to his half-English daughters, "They are my friends, your friends, and our well-willers" (2.1.7). Haughton counterbalances these Portuguese, French, Italian, and Dutch merchant-friends with the English foursome of Anthony and the suitors, who often refer to each other in similar terms. Yet, in spite of Pisaro's bilingual warning to Alvaro about Walgrave—"that 'grande amico' is your grand inimico" (2.1.85)—these two groups of friends ultimately prove to be porous and subject to exchange. As I have already discussed, Pisaro mistakes the English suitors for the foreigner Vandal "and your friends" (1.3.218); later on, the disguised Vandal impersonates Heigham, proposing himself to Pisaro's daughters—not without an accent—as "your grote vriend" (3.4.10); and the crafty Anthony, knowing Pisaro can overhear them, suggests to the Englishmen that the usurer "H'ath been a friend to you" (4.1.185). By error, by disguise, or by an act, the notion of male friendship drifts from foreign to native and back again throughout *Englishmen for My Money*.

The mobile and linguistically flexible Frisco shuttles between these "friends" as the play proceeds, strongly suggesting an erotic dimension to these transcultural relationships. Already, his malleable name ("Frisk-you"/"Frisky") points in the direction of the frisking, friskiness, and playfulness that characterizes the play's "sociably united" homosocial bonds. Frisco's friendships are undiscriminating, if not promiscuous—what I perceive, ultimately, as a far cry from anti-alien "manipulations."[74] Disguised as Vandal, he refers to his Portuguese employer as "my groute friend" (3.2.125), expressing the amity between the Dutchman and his own master but inhabiting the relationship and challenging class boundaries as well as linguistic ones. Exiting the scene, he turns the discourse of friendship on the Englishman Heigham, who is blocking his path: "Fare de well good frend" (3.2.151–52). Later, while "frisking" in the dark, the clown spreads terms of amity to Alvaro and Delion as well: "Come, honest friends, will ye go to our house?" (3.3.88), offering with "our" a species of cross-cultural communal belonging. Shortly thereafter, the clown reports to Pisaro that "It was so dark I could not see on which hand we turned—but I am sure we turned one way" (4.1.256–57), melding the already-examined discourse of "turning" with "friendly," and erotic, terms (one need only recall Desdemona's alleged "turning" in *Othello*). Through his impersonations of languages and identities, Frisco extends the discourse of friendship in an indiscriminately cosmopolitan fashion to Portuguese denizens, native Englishmen, and foreign merchants, rivaling the 1662 *Colloquia* frontispiece in its display of intermingled figures. In Haughton's comedy, homosocial intimacy operates as a channel for the cosmopolitan mode of interchangeability, and Frisco is the "friend" who best exemplifies its potential for queer attachments.

"Vile Conversions": Haughton and Cosmopolitan Comedy

The conclusion of *Englishmen for My Money* is contingent on "translation" broadly understood: a woman disguised as a polyglot schoolmaster, a man cross-dressed as a woman, and a feigned "translation" of a soul into heaven. In this way, I argue, even if the comedy's resolution favors the English suitors, it depends on bringings, turnings, and conversions, all subsets of the broad network of meanings accompanying the word *translation* in early modern England. As I have discussed elsewhere in this book, corporeal or sartorial translations occur in early modern drama with regularity, activating this expansive set of connotations for Haughton's theater audiences and readers. "Bless thee, Bottom, bless thee! Thou art translated," says a confounded Peter Quince in Shakespeare's *A Midsummer Night's Dream*, while Cordatus hails Fungoso as "the translated gallant" in Ben Jonson's *Every Man Out of His Humour*.[75] In other contexts, the word could signal a kind of religious transport between the earthly realm and a spiritual world beyond—"To take or convey . . . to heaven or the afterlife" (*OED*, II.10). As I discussed in the previous chapter, Mary Sidney Herbert played on this flexible meaning of the word in her English translation of Robert Garnier's tragedy *Marc Antoine*, interrogating the terms of translation through which she presented herself as an author, poet, and dramatist. Along similar lines, Anthony, the three English suitors, and Pisaro's crafty daughters test the semantic limits of translation through their plans to outwit the Portuguese usurer and his outlandish "friends."

Even if Haughton never names them explicitly as such, variations on translation writ large can be found among all three couples in *Englishmen for My Money*, namely in dress and in religious transport to the afterlife. Two of the pairs take up the sartorial definition, joining the foreigners and Anthony in the practice of disguise. First, Laurentia clothes herself in the schoolmaster's garb in order to elope with Heigham. "You must play Anthony in my disguise" (4.2.45), says the schoolmaster to Laurentia, offering his identity to her. In a second couple, sartorial translation surfaces in Walgrave's decision to cross-dress as the neighboring girl Susan in order to sneak into Pisaro's house. During an encounter with the overly flirtatious Pisaro, who takes a liking to this "Susan" (or, possibly, the Englishman underneath the costume), Walgrave muses in an aside that "I must turn womankind altogether / And scratch out his eyes" (4.3.61–62). This, audiences would realize, is the second time Pisaro mistakes Walgrave for someone else. As before, Haughton deploys the word "turn," this time yoking together the feminine connotations of translation with the act of cross-dressing, both for Walgrave specifically and for an audience that could discern boys underneath the costumes of Pisaro's daughters. Finally, the English suitor Harvey pretends to be suddenly ill, his soul on the verge of being "translated" into the life beyond. "My soul is labouring for a higher place / Than this vain, transitory world can yield," he says (5.1.123–24). Since Harvey's death would cancel his debt with Pisaro, the usurer now needs him to remain alive as long as possible in order to wed him to his daughter Marina, all to protect his financial interests. In this way, Pisaro, who once championed translation and the polyglot instruction of his daughters, now opposes translation of a different variety—the "soul . . . labouring for a higher place." Of course, the usurer's efforts eventually come to nothing, only facing more "vile conversions" from the three daughters and Anthony. Although critics rightly call attention to the ways this play's outcome favors the English suitors over the foreign merchant-friends, the ending requires the native victors to engage with and embrace "translation" in its broadest sense, even as they double down on their Englishness. In this sense, *Englishmen for My Money* offers a conditional endorsement for the translational mode of interchangeability, granting it considerable space but enabling its straightforward success only for certain parties—Pisaro's daughters and the English suitors, and also Frisco.

Observing Walgrave's particular case of cross-dressing as "turning," Frisco offers further comment on polyglossia in *Englishmen for My Money*, this time hailing foreign interchangeability as a "dialogue" and figuring the play's sequence of foreigners in gendered and material-textual terms. It is here, I argue, that one can witness most suggestively this comedy's dramatic rendering of Berlaimont's *Colloquia* and other manuals like it as a playful speculation on linguistic and cultural mingling.[76] After watching Pisaro's attempts to woo "Mistress Susan," Frisco mocks their exchange, unable to see through the disguise but playing on the age discrepancy: "Lord, what a dialogue hath there been between Age and Youth!" (4.3.84–85). From this categorization of the exchange as a polyglot "dialogue" between Portuguese and English, the clown proceeds to list the foreign merchants one by one, speculating on how they might engage Pisaro's half-English daughters in the bedroom. I quote it at length: "You do good on her? Even as much as my Dutchman will do on my young mistress! . . . I'll lay my cap to twopence that he will be asleep tomorrow at night when he should go to bed to her. Marry, for the Italian, he is of another humour, for there'll be no dealings with him till midnight; for he must slaver all the wenches in the house at parting, or he is nobody. . . . Yet for my money, well fare the Frenchman. O, he is a forward lad, for he'll no sooner come from the church, but he'll fly to the chamber. . . . O, the generation of languages that our house will bring forth! Why, every bed will have a proper speech to himself and have the founder's name written upon it in fair capital letters, 'HERE LAY—,' and so forth" (4.3.85–102). Yet again, Frisco offers a catalog of foreigners and their expected stereotypes (a sleepy, drunk Dutchman, a lascivious Italian, a duplicitous Frenchman, etc.). This go-around, however, he also weaves in financial concerns. With "I'll lay my cap to twopence" and "Yet for my money," the servant makes these sexual liaisons a site for commercial gain, which they are, and at the expense of the play's women, too—Walgrave boasts grotesquely that he, Heigham, and Harvey will "cancel all our bonds in their great bellies" (4.1.115).[77]

Ultimately, the implication is that, along with the amorous ventures of these foreign merchants into Pisaro's household, the Continental market creeps into the English bedroom, and according to distinct—and gendered—metaphors of material textuality, translation, and reproduction. To this point, Frisco figures these advances and their corresponding reproduction as a textual product. The phrase "bring forth," joined with "the founder's name," conjures the mixed reproductive and printing discourses of the period, articulating each foreign merchant in masculine terms as a kind of printer or typesetter leaving his imprint on the blank sheets of Pisaro's daughters.[78] Like the "Commodities" discussed by Minsheu in *Ductor in Linguas*, these part-foreign, part-English children will be "laye[d] in order to your viewes." Furthermore, "bring" once again summons up connotations of translation present in the earlier exchange between Frisco and Anthony, for to "bring forth" generations of languages is to reproduce them, to render them in other tongues. Kermode associates Frisco's image of polyglot "bed[s]" marked by "fair capital letters" with the grave.[79] Yet, it could alternatively evoke—more playfully—the columned arrangement of widely published polyglot language manuals in the minds of readers and playgoers, each one topped with a running title indicating a particular language: "François." "Flamen." "*Italien*." Each of these beds, says the clown, has a "proper speech to himself," resulting in a polyglot nursery of words begotten by the multilingual exchanges that Haughton's play simultaneously summons up and strikes down. Through these means, Frisco's speech takes up the epistemological frameworks present in Berlaimont's *Colloquia* and other mercantile language manuals, remarks on Pisaro's conversation as a "dialogue," and figures the foreign merchants in sequence yet again, this time in textual and gendered terms.

Ultimately, though Pisaro's designs fall through, the "frisking" or "turning" servant Frisco creates an imaginative space for audiences and readers to contemplate the foreign traders' "success" with Pisaro's daughters (however unrequited or unwanted), or at least the ways they would attempt to woo the ladies. This possibility is only more apparent in the play's denouement, when the clown proposes to "now let Mouche put on her [i.e., Laurentia's] apparel and be married to the Dutchman" (5.1.232–33). This is a comic suggestion, to be sure, but one that bridges together foreign and native, crosses borders and languages, and mixes genders altogether. Expressing surprise that "Mistress Susan" ended up being Walgrave, Pisaro asks Frisco for further comment, and the clown responds with an image of same-sex female intimacy to match the earlier remark: "Yet now I remember me, she did not lie here; and the reason is because she doth lie here, and is now abed with Mistress Mathea" (5.1.268–70). Although *Englishmen for My Money* ultimately translates its "friendly" male homosociality into pairings between men and women, Frisco's commentary at the end of the play reanimates the same-sex friendship that accompanies the comedy's cosmopolitan contours, this time opening a channel for women, too.[80] As in the case of a cross-dressed Nerissa at the end of Shakespeare's more famous merchant-centered comedy (and Gratiano's wish to be "couching with the doctor's clerk"), Haughton's audience is left with alternative fantasies.[81] Even after the failed attempts to woo Pisaro's daughters, there remains an expectation for the same-sex coupling, or at least the cosmopolitan jumbling-together, of English and Dutch "friends."

Finally, in emphasizing the cosmopolitan linguistic contours of *Englishmen for My Money*, this chapter proposes a solution to the variety of subgeneric labels the play has accumulated over the last several decades. Often laying a focus on the play's local concerns, urban setting, and financial discourse, scholars have associated the play with "city comedy," "London comedy," and "usury plays."[82] While these terms differ, most accounts agree on one thing: Haughton's play signaled the initiation of a new dramatic form, a subgenre often centered on an urban setting and intrigues among gallants, citizens, wives, widows, whores, and servants. This thread of scholarship cannot receive enough emphasis, for it has conditioned decades of criticism on the comedy. The variety of subgeneric labels attached to *Englishmen for My Money* raises several questions, though. How spatially specific must a city comedy be for it to become a *London* comedy? How many city comedies are also usury plays, and is Haughton's drama unique or more representative in this respect? And importantly, how shall one account for the variety of languages and accents that crop up in city comedies? Because *Englishmen for My Money* is widely regarded as the first of its kind, the stakes of these questions seem high, with implications for dozens of comedies set in London and featuring witty exchanges scattered with foreign words—plays penned by Thomas Dekker, Ben Jonson, Thomas Middleton, and others. Ultimately, I ask, what is a "city comedy," particularly when it uses so promiscuously languages located within, but originating beyond, these playwrights' city?

In response to this situation, on account of Haughton's extensive commentary on vernacular interchangeability, translation, and the relationship between foreign merchant and native, *and* because of the striking parallels one can observe between his play and the widely published polyglot dialogues of Noël de Berlaimont, I propose *Englishmen for My Money* ought to be recognized as a cosmopolitan comedy of European languages. I offer this proposal not merely to add another subgeneric label to the mix but to gather up the terms that have inhabited the critical discussion all along. After all, though each of the surveyed generic labels offers a useful path into the comedy's urban and financial dimensions, they obscure the broader implications of what Albert Croll Baugh, early on, termed the "national element" in the play.[83] I would revise this phrase to read as the *cosmopolitan* linguistic elements (plural) in the play, elements with a politics that would help lay the groundwork for systems of international capital even as they respond to cross-cultural curiosities and attachments.

Haughton's comedy registers a transition from the schoolroom to the market; it features foreign vernaculars on stage and in print spoken by both foreign Europeans and native Englishmen; and it deals repeatedly with key thematic elements in the period's most important polyglot language manuals—negotiations in the marketplace, for instance, or conversations "on the way." Moreover, this play comments ironically on the interchangeability of strangers from Continental Europe and native English people at home, particularly as this interchangeability can be observed and experienced through language. It is true that *Englishmen for My Money* includes a significant quantity of details about known London places and includes a usurer as its protagonist. However, if one expands the focus from England or London to the Europe beyond and within, not merely through the subjectivity of the merchants but also by way of the foreign languages and words they speak, the generic labels "city comedy," "London comedy," or "usury play" become increasingly inadequate on their own. Altogether, I suggest Haughton's *Englishmen for My Money* demands reconception as a cosmopolitan comedy on account of its theatrical projection of the polyglot exchanges for merchants circulated in Noël de Berlaimont's *Colloquia* and other multilingual manuals and lexicons dealing in mercantile tropes. From its so-called origins, both reveling in exchanges of early modern languages and anticipating the long shadow of financial markets in Europe and beyond, "city comedy" as it is traditionally known is always already cosmopolitan, and one might attend profitably to the ways other and later plays of this sort exhibit non-English or translinguistic elements.

| *Chapter Five* |

"All Translations Are Reputed Femalls"

The Propagation of Women's Speech in Ben Jonson's *Epicene*

These be the inchantementes of *Circes*, brought out of *Italie* . . . fonde bookes, of late translated out of *Italian* into English, sold in euery shop in London . . .
—Roger Ascham, *The Scholemaster* (1570)

The final act of Ben Jonson's comedy *Epicene, or The Silent Woman* (1609) opens with a series of translations. After watching as Sir Dauphine Eugenie humiliates both Sir John Daw and Sir Amorous La Foole with several blows and witty remarks, Mavis is the first among the independent and intellectually inclined Collegiate ladies to express her desire for him. Addressing Daw, La Foole, and Clerimont, she asks, "Gentlemen, have any of you a pen and ink? I would fain write out a riddle in Italian for Sir Dauphine to translate."[1] Daw responds that he can supply the writing materials and accompanies Mavis offstage, where she composes her "Italian riddle" (5.2.34). When the Collegiate returns, she hides the paper from the other women ("You shall not see it, i'faith, Centaur"), and then presents it to Dauphine: "Good Sir Dauphine, solve it for me. I'll call for it anon" (5.2.34–36). As she exits, Clerimont snatches the paper and decodes the message for what it truly is: a secret invitation to sex. Conveyed—here, one could also say transported and translated—both from character to character on stage, *and* in italic type for readers of Jonson's 1616 Folio, the letter reads:

> *"Sir Dauphine,*
> *I chose this way of intimation for privacy. The ladies here, I know, have both hope and purpose to make a collegiate and*

> *servant of you. If I might be so honoured as to appear at any end of so noble a work, I would enter into a fame of taking physic tomorrow and continue it four or five days or longer, for your visitation.*
> *Mavis." (5.2.47–53)*[2]

Clerimont, whose very name evokes a desire for clarity (evoking the French "clairement," i.e., clearly), is amazed by the forwardness of this erotic proposal: "Call you this a riddle? What's their plain dealing, trow?" (5.2.54–55). The Folio's accompanying marginal note "*He reades the paper*" (sig. 3D1r) might signal that Mavis composed this letter in English; in this sense, "Italian" would merely be a ruse signaling the message's sexual implications. Alternatively, however, the act of reading on stage, signaled textually by a typographic marginal note instancing what Claire M. L. Bourne hails as Jonson's "continued investment in typography as a means of mediating the theatricality of his plays," suggests that Clerimont is actually "Englishing"—that is, translating—the Italian-language contents of the written erotic proposal.[3] For readers of *Epicene*, moreover, the Collegiate lady's epistle appears not in the play's usual roman type but in italic, a type associated with Continental vernaculars in the period and which turns Mavis's letter visually, if not linguistically, into a foreign tongue.[4] What stands here, altogether, is a variety of "translations" folded together for the playgoing and reading audiences of Ben Jonson, an author deeply attentive to the staged and textual possibilities of his plays.

Indeed, Clerimont's attempt to "clearly" decipher Mavis's Italian message—and in a play entitled *The Silent Woman*—gestures toward the copious early modern connotations of the word "translation," connotations that often intersected with the idea of women's speech and writing. As was seen already with Mary Sidney Herbert in chapter 3, translation was an acceptable avenue for certain educated and privileged early modern women authors, particularly when it came to religiously themed texts and, if playwriting was involved, in circumstances apart from the public theater. In Tina Krontiris's words, "Religion actually creates one of the paradoxes of the sixteenth century: on the one hand women were enjoined to silence while on the other they were permitted to break that silence to demonstrate their faith and devotion to God."[5] In *Epicene*, Mavis is an educated authorial figure and a translator; it is she who asks for "a pen and ink," stating plainly that she "would fain write out a riddle," not in English, presumably her native language in *Epicene*'s London setting, but "in Italian." Yet the context here is far from godly. This Italian riddle, situated as it is in a male-authored public play, points away from the sanctified and socially approved domains of women's translation—away from Mary Sidney Herbert's psalms and closet drama—and toward the sexualized voices of women in Continental texts from beyond England's shores.

Discussions of translation among male writers in the period—including Ben Jonson, as I will show—deal in heavily gendered tropes. As I have noted in prior chapters, John Florio—whom Jonson named a "worthy Freind"—famously commented that "all translations are reputed femalls, delivered at second hand."[6] Deploying pointed gendered language here, Florio names these translations "femalls," their gendered status not given, but "reputed," reflecting the reputation, gossip, or slander accompanying discourses about women in the period. Furthermore, Florio dresses the translated text in the language of birth and reproduction ("delivered") and figures the translator—in this case, male—as a kind of multilingual obstetrician responsible for the resulting "second hand" product. Florio continues this gendered and maternal treatment of translation in his reader's epistle, remarking that "from translation all Science [i.e., knowledge] had it's of-spring" but also articulating the fear that "his Mistresse should be so prostitute"—that is, that this knowledge might become too common and extend beyond its proper linguistic and sexual bounds (sig. A5r). According to Patricia Parker, Florio's deployment of gendered, reproductive, and educational language in these pages exemplifies a paradox in which "women, excluded from the study of rhetoric, figure curiously and prominently in Renaissance English discussions of rhetoric, and particularly in relation to questions of decorum and control."[7] Although women sometimes *were* involved in the study of rhetoric, and although Jonathan Goldberg has questioned critical tendencies to take Florio's dedicatory remarks at face value, the translator's use of—and participation in—this gendered trope offers an indication that the work of translation can involve a complex and dynamic gendered relationship between a male translator, the original text he strives to adapt for another language, and the resulting "femall" translation.[8] Here, in the era before Lawrence Venuti's modern notion of "the translator's invisibility," discussions of translation are bound up with questions of gender hierarchy and proper order.[9]

Using Florio as a starting point, this final chapter will analyze the gendered discourse of translation as propagation as it finds expression in early modern drama in England, specifically in Ben Jonson's *Epicene*. At stake, as I will demonstrate, is this comedy's designation as a London-based "city comedy," as well as Jonson's own position between a classicized anglophone tradition and more modern cosmopolitan vernaculars, and across performance and print. Defined in Florio's 1598 Italian-English dictionary as "*an increase, a multiplying, an extending, a continuing*," the term "propagation" facilitates a critical analysis of multiplicities—reproduction, expansion, copiousness/*copia*, and vernacular polyglossia—attending the deeply gendered discourses of translation in this play.[10] Indeed, Jonson's comedy exhibits what one could call a Florian perspective on gender, seizing on and strengthening a link between translation and the propagation of women's speech, both within and across languages. Focusing on the ways this notion of propagation accompanies the Italianate cosmopolitan vernaculars (rather than classical and English texts) influencing Jonson as a playwright, I argue that *Epicene*, itself a product of translation and multiplicities, also advances and multiplies this reproductive mode of translation for readers and playgoers in England, both from the page and from the stage. Seen this way, the "local color" of this comedy begins to look foreign, and not solely in the classical, Latinate sense usually noticed by scholars. On top of this, and in spite of Jonson's efforts to obscure his own translinguistic writing, *Epicene* demonstrates how vernacular linguistic cosmopolitanism in Europe's Renaissance, however celebratory in its transnational mixings and minglings, harbored deeply gendered hostilities and misogynistic motives. Beginning this analysis with early modern discussions of language and the allegorical treatment of women's speech and translation in Thomas Tomkis's university comedy *Lingua*, I will then move to the women's voices in Pietro Aretino's *Ragionamenti*, a previously unrecognized Italian "source" for Jonson's play. Unveiling *Epicene*'s foreign, Italianate contours, I show in this chapter how "city comedy" becomes increasingly fragile as a subgeneric term when the investigation presses on the intersecting notions of translation, multilingualism, and women's speech.

"Exceeding Plentifull": Translation and Linguistic Multiplicity in Thomas Tomkis's *Lingua*

Florio's gendered treatment of translation as propagation surfaces not only in his English Montaigne but also in his bilingual dictionaries. Here, the very word strains against a singular definition, exhibiting, as Marjorie Rubright has shown, a gendered epistemology of scattered meanings.[11] In a lengthy dictionary entry deeply relevant to my thoroughgoing analysis, the translator-cum-lexicographer defines the Italian *tradurre* first according to the word's physical connotations of change and movement ("*to bring, to turne, to conuert, to conuay from one place to another*") and second, almost as an afterthought, in the sense most familiar today ("*Also to translate out of one tongue into another*") (sig. 2N3v).[12] This notion of "turning" overlaps with the terms of Florio's definition of "Volubilità," explained unfavorably as "*mutabilitie, ficklenes, vnco[n]stancie . . . the turning of a thing. . . . Also a round or quicke speaking without impediment*" (sig. 2P6v). Here, Florio taps into early modern discourses associated with women's speech and which surface in the theater, too. For instance, a translation lesson between the chambermaid Alice and Princess Katherine in Shakespeare's *Henry V* exemplifies both the notion of voluble speech between women and the "turning" of one language's vocabulary into sexual terms, while *The Taming of the Shrew*'s daughterly duo of Katherine and Bianca embodies both unrestrained female speech and women's desire in the context of a language lesson (to "learn my lessons as I please myself").[13] As one can see in Florio's dictionary and on stage, the word *translation* and its associated terms participate in an expansive, highly gendered discursive field encompassing the notions of volubility, inconstancy, and promiscuity, each of which were often associated with women and their access to or use of language.

This joint notion of propagation and translation also found expression in treatises addressing the English language and the multilingual variety within it. "Englishes" plural, as Margaret Tudeau-Clayton describes it, may be a more apt term for what one observes within this copious linguistic terrain.[14] Though they rarely deployed the intensively gendered rhetoric one finds in Florio, these writers saw the English language itself as a product of translation, speaking many tongues and embodying their distinctive characteristics. As seen already in the first chapter, the educational reformer Richard Mulcaster suggested that this condition was a result of word borrowing, which he termed "enfranchisement." "I know no other diuision of *enfranchised* words," he stated, "then after the tungs from whence we borow them, as *Latin*, *Greke*, *Hebrew*, *Italian*, *French*, *Spanish*, *Dutch*, *Scottish*, &c. Which ar freid [i.e., freed] amongst vs, as the present nede of either them with vs, or vs with them, doth sew [i.e., shew] to be incorporate."[15] Still recognizable as belonging to their original languages, these enfranchised words are borrowed and "made free"—that is, granted citizens' rights within the English language. The outcome here can be viewed as a reciprocal and "incorporate" (i.e., joined to the body of English) cosmopolitan relation between Europe's early modern languages. Writing decades later, Richard Carew proposed that the English tongue's sweet and copious substance was a result of such a hybrid nature: "Seeing then we borrow (and that not shamefully) from the *Dutch*, the *Britaine*, the *Romane*, the *Dane*, the *French*, the *Italian*, and the *Spanyard*," he says, "how can our stocke bee other then exceeding plentifull?"[16]

While adopting Mulcaster's more progressive approach, however, Carew acknowledged the objection—voiced by Balthazar in Kyd's *Spanish Tragedy*, as was seen in chapter 2—that an English enriched by translation might be seen as a so-called Babel-like "confusion," or incoherent. Other writers perceived folly in this propagation of tongues, and made opposition. George Puttenham, for example, objected to "that which . . . we may call the *mingle mangle* as whe[n] we make our speach or writinges of sundry languages vsing some Italian word, or French, or Spanish, or Dutch, or Scottish, not for the nonce or for any purpose (which were in part excusable) but ignorantly and affectedly."[17] Although some linguistic borrowing is permissible for Puttenham—"in part," he clarifies, and "for the nonce," for a particular purpose—experimentation with foreign words in the English language amounts to verbal foolishness or showiness ("ignorantly and affectedly"), resulting in what he calls "intollerable vices" (2E4r). Decades later, Richard Verstegan objected to this linguistic growth and mixture as "the scum of many languages," arguing for a plainer and purified version of the English language rooted in its Germanic origins.[18] But whether they did so with praise or condemnation, England's linguistic commentators could agree that the propagation of foreign tongues—that is, their dissemination across borders and into the orbit of English—had come to shape their native language.

First acted during this period of linguistic change and expansion, Thomas Tomkis's university play *Lingua: or, the Combat of the Tongue and the Five Senses for Superiority* (ca. 1602) links the notion of copious speech with a transgressive and deviant variety of translation.[19] The play—first acted in the male environs of Cambridge—accomplishes this dynamic in distinctly gendered terms, consisting of an allegory in which the tongue (the protagonist Lingua, purposefully female) pleads for a place among the five senses of the body (Visus, Auditus, Olfactus, Tactus, and Gustus, all figured as male characters). Initially undermining the five senses' authority, Lingua faces imprisonment when her plots are discovered. In her analysis of *Lingua*, Carla Mazzio focuses on "the phenomenology of the 'inarticulate'" expressed in the comedy, particularly in relation to the character Tactus (Touch), who exposes failures of eloquence in the play.[20] Meanwhile, in an argument attentive to tropes of translation in the comedy, Ellen Ellerbeck analyzes how Lingua's eventual censure constitutes a dramatized variation on hostilities between educated men at Cambridge and the less-learned men and women in the surrounding town. "A contribution to the academy's politicization of the vernacular," she states, "this play warns the laity that scholarship is inaccessible, held firmly in place by linguistic and gender barriers."[21] Though it ostensibly rejects the propagation or transmission of masculine knowledge to an effeminate or vulgar public—for to publish such knowledge would be profane—Tomkis's play (paradoxically in vernacular English, rather than Latin) enacts this increase or reproduction through a focus on Lingua's speech and translation, skills that unsettle the play's masculine hierarchy.

Indeed, Tomkis presents Lingua as a learned, multilingual speaker who threatens the masculine authority of the five senses. As Ellerbeck observes, Lingua appears as "a powerful and learned orator" when she makes her initial petition.[22] Though scorned by Auditus as an "idle prating Dame," Lingua reminds the audience that she furnishes a variety of pleasing languages, not only classical and ancient ones but also the "*Tuscane* graue, / The Brauing *Spanish* and the smooth-tongd *French*, / These pretious Iewells that adorn thine eares."[23] In issuing a descriptive catalog of tongues, Lingua deploys a technique common to numerous early modern linguistic treatises (Mulcaster's and Carew's among them), resembling also what one observes with Haughton's clown, Frisco. What is especially remarkable about Lingua's speech, however, is that she is not merely fluent in these languages but claims them as her own offspring. Indeed, in nearly Florian terms, Tomkis's protagonist asserts herself as the progenitor of languages. First, she indicates that Auditus "by my meanes conceiust as many tongues," positioning the tongue as the reproductive agent and the sense of hearing (also her auditor during this speech) as the conceiving function; then, she claims that Auditus is "rauisht with my words," casting their sexual relationship in violent terms (sig. A4r). Lingua figures herself as an authoritative speaker and multilingual seducer, if not assailant, of audiences. With a striking reversal of the Aristotelian model of sex and gender (with the male as agent and the female as passive recipient), Tomkis regenders the processes of both speech and reproduction with a female agent.

Later on, Lingua makes a bolder claim for the propagation of multiple languages, openly demonstrating her linguistic talents before her auditors. Coming before Common Sense to plead her case for inclusion among the five senses, she delivers a macaronic declamation in various languages, a performance of the linguistic aptitude she alluded to in the play's first scene. Not only English appears here, but also Latin, Greek, Italian, and French: "My Lord, though the *Imbecillitas* of my feeble sexe, might drawe mee backe, from this Tribunall, with the *habenis* to wit *Timoris* and the *Catenis Pudoris*, notwithstanding beeing so fairely led on with the gratious *ἐπιέικεια* of your *iustissimæ* δικαιοσύνης[.] *Especially so aspremente spurd' con gli sproni di necessita mia pungente*, I will without the helpe of Orators, commit the *totam salutem* of my action to the *Volutabilitati* τόν γυναικέιον λόγον, *which (auec vostre bonne plaiseur)* I will finish with more then *Laconicâ breuitate*" (sig. F2r). While this moment can be read as what Mazzio calls a "hilarious display of inarticulacy," it also serves as something more—an expression, however comically exaggerated, of the cosmopolitan vernaculars Lingua described as her generated offspring.[24] Much like the vengeful Hieronimo in *The Spanish Tragedy* or the crafty Anthony in *Englishmen for My Money*, Lingua deploys here a "confusion"—that is, a mixture or combination—of foreign tongues as an expression of her unique capabilities, and boldly, "without the helpe of Orators."[25] Seen this way, the terms "*Volutabilitati*" (a Latinism evoking, at once, both "voluntary" and "volubility") and "γυναικέιον λόγον" (Greek, signaling women's speech) point toward a learned capacity to *translate* the terms of the debate on women's speech so crucial to this play and to the period's discussions of translation. Although she caters to her male auditors with an admission of her "feeble sexe," Lingua makes an assertive, multilingual appeal to belong among the senses in this scene. For her, "tongue" points not in one direction, to speech and the body, but rather in multiple directions to various languages.[26]

Unappeased, however, the five senses scorn this multilingual discourse as effeminate babble and accuse Lingua as an unauthorized purveyor of translations. In this way, Tomkis's comedy voices a cultural discourse linking transgressive facility with languages and translation to women. As Douglas Bruster asserts, these complaints in the play ultimately amount to "a literal thesaurus of misogynistic commonplaces concerning women's speech."[27] "Here's a Gallemaufry of speech indeed," states Common Sense after hearing Lingua's multilingual remarks, hailing the linguistic mingling that Carew addressed in more favorable terms as "exceeding plentifull."[28] Foremost among the accusations levied against Lingua is "high treason . . . for vnder pretense of profiting the people with translations, shee hath most vilye prostituted the hard misteries of vnknowne Languages to the prophane eares of the vulgar" (sig. F3r–F3v). With her capabilities with various languages, assets both to herself and to "the people" to whom she transmits "hard misteries," Lingua poses a threat to the exclusive authority of male senses. Strikingly, these allegations cast linguistic transgression in scholarly *and* sexualized terms, tapping into broader associations between sex and women's speech; the secrets of these languages, it is pronounced, "shee hath most vilye prostituted."[29] Much like Puttenham, Verstegan, and other conservative language critics of Tomkis's London, Common Sense and his colleagues urge Lingua to abandon her "Gallimaufry" and also to censure the transgressive translations her multilingualism helps to reproduce.

Even as they banish the play's protagonist, though, the five senses of *Lingua* strengthen a discursive link between language, femininity, and sex, locating each of these under the rubric of translation for Tomkis's readers and playgoers. In this allegorized representation of women's speech, that is, one also finds the discussions of *copia* powering early modern commentary on language and the gendered tropes preceding and following Florio's Montaigne—"all translations are reputed femalls."

From "Source" to "Theatergram" in Jonsonian Drama

Ben Jonson's *Epicene, or The Silent Woman* is a comedy that articulates, in subtler terms than *Lingua*, a similarly gendered politics of translation and language. This play engages with Europe's world of cosmopolitan vernaculars in order to explore the mingled discourse of promiscuity and women's speech. In doing so, I contend, it broadcasts to playgoers, as well as to readers of Jonson's carefully planned text, a mode of translation as linguistic propagation. In fact, by returning to *Epicene* and reflecting freshly on the fluctuating state of the English language and Florio's capacious definition of "translation," Clerimont's ability to "translate" a woman's Italian riddle into Jonson's London setting reproduces in miniature the playwright's efforts to bring an originally Italian comedy onto the English stage. As early as 1881, John Addington Symonds suggested that *Epicene*'s plot owed something to Italian theater, specifically Pietro Aretino's comedy *Il Marescalco*, which was performed at court in Mantua shortly before its 1533 publication in Venice.[30] Like Jonson's comedy, this play features a protagonist tormented by his colleagues after the duke orders him to marry, and who finally claims impotence as an excuse before learning that his wife is actually a boy in disguise. Adopting this text, Jonson redeploys Italian drama in English for his theatergoing audience, as well as for readers envisioning the action in their minds. In weaving together different languages and literary traditions dealing with women's speech, this "city comedy," as it is often known, engages with what I have been referring to as cosmopolitan vernaculars—specifically, by way of early modern Italian riddles, songs, dialogues, and plays.

As a "source" for Jonson's play, *Il Marescalco* has been studied in detail by Oscar Campbell, who traced shared elements between the two comedies in 1931. It seemed to Campbell that Aretino's comedy, rather than any classical work of literature, was the principal source for Jonson's play, and his analysis compares the two plots accordingly.[31] However, Campbell used a rather narrow definition of what a "source" can be or do, and his argument did not account for the provocative presence of the Collegiate ladies, an element with no analog in Aretino's homosocially masculine comedy.[32] Louise George Clubb offers a useful and more flexible way to account for these shared elements through her concept of "theatergrams": as I mentioned in this book's first chapter, these are various units, figures, or patterns that can be reconfigured for specific effects in plays.[33] Extending this concept beyond the theater to include "theatergrammatical" elements engaged with the playhouse—riddles, songs, and dialogues—I will demonstrate that the eroticized discourse of women's speech stands in *Epicene* as an important and previously unremarked Jonsonian engagement with Aretino. Here, one sees an effort on the part of the playwright to translate, but also to silence, the sexualized language circulating among female interlocutors in a different Aretino text: the *Ragionamenti*, a series of erotic dialogues, riddles, and verses exchanged among women speakers. Building on scholarship that moves beyond the strictures of "source studies" into more flexible analyses of imitation, adaptation, and originality, I propose that *Epicene* takes up the theatergrammatical discourse of women's speech to comment on the ways that Continental riddles, songs, and erotic dialogues propagated in early modern England through the gendered terms of translation: as Florio's bilingual dictionary had it, fickleness, mutability, and volubility ("*to bring, to turne, to conuert.*")[34]

Though they sometimes document Ben Jonson's substantial engagement with Aretino's *Il Marescalco*, most critical interpretations of *Epicene* forestall any consideration of the Collegiates' Aretine origins. Debates about the play have been dominated instead by an interest in "city comedy," a critical category that, as I discussed in the previous chapter, comes with interpretive limitations. Karen Newman's influential essay on "city talk" cogently demonstrates important relationships in *Epicene* among "monstrous" women, sexual desire, and consumerism, but it generally confines any discussion about the Collegiates to an English context.[35] This approach to the play has been strengthened in recent studies examining *Epicene* against a distinctive London topography characterized by English ballrooms, academies, wit or language, and anxieties about androgyny.[36] Strikingly, even accounts of the play's Italian connections tend to assimilate Newman's London-centered interpretation of the Collegiates and their "hermaphroditical authority."[37] Modern editions of the play shore up these biases, too. For example, Richard Dutton's Revels edition of *Epicene* acknowledges Aretino briefly, but it includes appendixes that represent Jonson primarily as an English classicist.[38] More recently, David Bevington's edition within the 2012 *Cambridge Edition of the Works of Ben Jonson* views *Il Marescalco* as

Jonson's "chief dramatic model," but it omits Aretino from its appendixes and regrettably incorporates Dutton's incorrect information on the editions of the play available in Jonson's London.[39] If they receive any mention in the criticism, the Collegiates are usually discussed in anglocentric, if not London-centric, terms. A deeper analysis of Mavis's "Italian riddle," however, complicates the (classically informed) Englishness of the Collegiates and their presence and purpose in *Epicene.* Translation, I will show, is the key to the variety of female voices that *The Silent Woman* simultaneously proffers and silences.

"*Ditemi Ciò Che Ella È*": Aretino's School of Sex

The letter composed by Mavis points directly to an academic and erotic tradition of Italian riddling in which Aretino's *Ragionamenti* participates, and which I will consider as a vital theatergrammatical context for Jonson's *Epicene.* Conveyed from one character to another in the comedy's fifth act, the translated letter signals both the erotic riddle's transmission from Italy to England and the connotations of movement and exchange accompanying the term "translation" more broadly. The early modern Italian riddle occupied an aristocratic function among humanist societies, and its content was often erotic in nature; for Michele De Filippis, writing in 1948, "one of the most pronounced characteristics of Italian riddles is their obscenity."[40] The Catholic Church often found it appropriate to censure these erotic texts, such as those of Tommaso Stigliani, who composed dozens of enigmas in octaves and sonnets. Also falling under this category of erotic Italian riddles are the verses of Pietro Aretino.[41] Altogether, Italian riddles constituted an important part of learned communities in Renaissance Europe, and in a manner that included the work of the infamous satirist and sometime playwright, Aretino.

Some of these Italian riddles were available in Renaissance London, often keeping company with songs and epistolary forms and occasionally mixing with commentary on morality and gender. Two books in particular allow one to trace the movement of Continental riddles into English print: Humfrey Gifford's *A Posie of Gilloflowers* (1580) and the unattributed *Riddles of Heraclitus and Democritus* (1598). The former delivers the compiler's mix of "french and Italian toyes as I haue translated," relaying works by Claudius Ptholomaeus and Clément Marot, and concluding with four leaves of riddles and their solutions.[42] Many of these enigmas traffic in tropes of gender and sex; some allude to changes from male to female, others to parthogenetic birth. Worrying that his readers might pick out a "badde sense" in these translated riddles, Gifford assures them in a prefatory verse that "all of them carry a good and cleane meaning" (sig. T3r). About two decades later, similar concerns occupy the compiler of *Heraclitus and Democritus*. Explaining an obscure riddle in the appendix to his book, the compiler states that "I had the substance of this riddle from Italie," suggesting it should be understood to reprehend political rulers for sowing division, lawyers for injustice, and "women for their impudence."[43] Then, lest his English readers jump to conclusions, the compiler clarifies that such women live "onely in Italie," adding further that "we hold it in England, that a shamelesse woman, wanteth the properest ornament of her sex" (sig. *4r). Distinguishing English morals from Continental shamelessness, *Heraclitus and Democritus* nonetheless draws the "substance" of this riddle from Italy and presents it before the "we" of English readers. Mingled with songs, letters, and other verse forms, Italian riddles were circulated, translated, and printed in early modern England.

First published during the same decades as the original Italian riddles translated by Gifford and the compiler of *Heraclitus and Democritus*, Pietro Aretino's *Ragionamenti* included a number of erotic enigmas and songs within a rhetorical context of lessons between women about sex.[44] In the notorious first book of the *Ragionamenti*, Nanna recounts to Antonia her experiences as nun, wife, and whore, declaring the last to be best. However, it is in the dialogues of the second book that Aretino's female speakers exchange a variety of erotic rhymes and riddles while repeatedly characterizing their sexual gossip as academic instruction.[45] Nanna's conversation with Pippa at the beginning of the second book details a whore's proper training. Exhorting the young woman to listen, Nanna fashions herself as a schoolmaster: "*Dico che tu mi attenda senza trasognare, e fa conto, che io sia il maestro, e tu il fanciullo, che impara a compitare. . . . Ma se vuoi essere il fanciullo, ascoltami, come fa egli quando ha paura di non andare a cauallo*" (I tell you to listen to me and quit daydreaming. I want you to realize that I'm the teacher and you're the pupil who is learning her alphabet. . . . And if you really want to be a good girl, listen to me as a pupil who doesn't want to get flogged).[46] While figuring herself and Pippa as masculine-gendered teacher and student (*maestro*, *fanciullo*), Nanna is also relentlessly didactic and prescriptive. She recites from experience a litany of dos and don'ts that Pippa must master if she is to become a successful whore: shows of modesty and etiquette among clients; the importance of gold, recipes, and cosmetics; and rules pertaining to the desires of old men, aristocrats, Jews, and foreigners. "*Mi marauiglio Mamma*," says an overwhelmed Pippa, "*che voi non teniate scola, a dotterando la gente in cosi fatte galenterie*" (I'm amazed,

Mama, that you don't start a school and teach women all these lovely tricks) (sig. D2r; Rosenthal, 192). The second dialogue extends Nanna's lesson to include warnings about the treachery of men, and the fixation on educational language carries on through the third and final dialogue shared by a wet nurse and a midwife (in Aretino's text, Balia and Comare), figures of reproductive significance who relay these narratives, to use Florio's words, "at second hand." Here, Nanna and Pippa are a silent audience as this pair discusses the art of being a procuress, which the midwife compares to the profession of a learned physician (sig. P8r–Q1r; Rosenthal, 310–12).

Over the course of this academically inflected "*disputa*" (dispute) (sig. P7v; Rosenthal 310), the wet nurse and the midwife recite over fifteen letters, riddles, and verses that fit into the broad tradition of early modern erotic writing.[47] Comare the midwife establishes her credibility as an expert procuress early on and recites the contents of a "*letterina in su le gratie*" (graceful little missive) (sig. S2v; Rosenthal, 332) she once composed in order to fool a gentleman into expecting a sexual encounter with a certain lady:

> *Signor mio, quando scontero io mai l'obligo, che io ho con la fortuna, con le stelle, co Cieli, e co pianeti, i quali mi han fatta degna, di esser seruitrice de la dolcezza vostra? . . . Le Signore de la Cittadi mi douerebbero inuidiare cotanto amore, del qual godendo non cambiaria sorte con la sorte imperiale. E caso che istanotte non veniate doue, & a le quante hore vi dira la fedele apportatrice di questa, ecco che io mi amazzero. (Sig. S3r)*

> (My dear Sir: When shall I ever be able to pay my debt to fortune, the stars, the heavens, and the planets, which have made me worthy of being the servitor of your sweetness? . . . Ladies in all the towns must envy this love which, if I may enjoy it, I would not change my lot with that of an empress. And if perchance you do not come to the place and at the hour of which the trusted bearer of this letter will inform you, I shall surely kill myself.) (Rosenthal, 332–33)

The midwife then explains that she delivered the forged note to the gentleman who, frustrated that his lady never appeared, indulged the procuress in compensatory sex (sig. S5v; Rosenthal, 335). Anecdotes like this one about the erotic tricks that women ostensibly used to defraud men constitute a large portion of the dialogues between women in the *Ragionamenti*.

This erotic letter in particular anticipates the scenario of Mavis's "Italian riddle" in *Epicene*, discussed earlier.

As the midwife imparts her sexual wisdom to the wet nurse, Nanna, and Pippa, she relates an increasingly provocative array of verses and riddles exchanged between whores, gentlemen, and procuresses. While telling a story about a merchant, Balia the wet nurse suggests that money would be a preferable alternative to the "*carte, e versi*" (paper and verses) (sig. X2v; Rosenthal, 362) men offer to women in courtship. The midwife admits this may be true, but that the custom of giving courtesies and songs was nonetheless once "*molto vsate*" (quite the fashion) (sig. X2v; Rosenthal, 362). In fact, Comare says, "*Quella che non ne hauesse saputo vna frotta de le piu belle, e de le piu nuoue, se ne faria vergognata, e cotal piacere tanto era ne le Puttane, come ne le Ruffiane*" (A woman who did not know a batch of the newest, most beautiful songs would have been ashamed, and whores as well as bawds enjoyed them) (sig. X2v; Rosenthal, 362). The midwife continues, telling her audience that Nanna benefited greatly from riddles and songs, including this one:

Io ho donne vna cosa.
Che quando Amore vn solo fa di doi
L'hauete anchora voi.
L'è bianca, e il capo ha d'ostro,
I capei, come inchiostro,
Drizzasi s'un la tocca,
E sempre ha il latte in bocca.
Cresce, e scema souente,
Non ha orecchie, e sente,
Dunque per vostra fè
Ditemi ciò che ella è. (Sig. X2v)

(I have, oh ladies, a thing that's mine.
But when love makes one of two
This thing belongs also to you.
Its head is red, its body fair,
And black as ink its hair.
Its mouth forever brims with milk
It rears when teased by hands of silk.
Often it grows or diminishes,
And, though dumb, knows when it finishes.
Now by my faith in thee,
Tell me what it might be.) (Rosenthal, 362)

It takes no time for the wet nurse Balia to guess the answer: "*So ben, tu vuoi dire quella da la coda*" (I know you're talking about that certain tail) (sig. X2v; Rosenthal, 362). Aretino's colleague and rival Niccolò Franco would also engage in this tradition of "cock-riddles," a tradition limning the boundary between educated and popular erotic writing in early modern Italy.[48] Stigliani's erotic riddles soon followed.

Although Aretino attributes these verses and riddles to the female interlocutors of the second book's final dialogue, he associates them with his own name as well. This technique, which Richard Andrews names "gratuitous . . . self-publicity," constitutes part of the multivalent, cross-gendered identification between Aretino and his female speakers.[49] I would suggest it also blurs the boundary between dialogue and drama. Shortly after the penis riddle, the midwife recounts another episode in which a disguised friar reads a series of erotic rhymes out of "*vn libretto*" (a little book) (sig. X8v; Rosenthal, 369). All five verses are included in the dialogue's text, enabling readers to join in the laughter about inexpensive prostitutes. Whether this "*libretto*" is meant to be a printed volume or a manuscript, Aretino establishes himself as the author of these erotic songs through a clever act of ventriloquism. The wet nurse comments after the final verse, "*Egli è in canto, e parla de l'amor diuino, cosi dice il maestro, che quando era discepolo, lo fece con quelli, che hai detti, e dirai*" (This madrigal has been set to music and speaks of divine love; so says Maestro Aretino who, when he was still a student, composed it together with those you've chanted and will still chant) (sig. Y2r; Rosenthal, 372). As Comare clarifies in her response—and as Rosenthal reveals already in his modern translation—this "*maestro*" once composing erotic madrigals as a schoolboy is none other than "*Il flagello de Principi*" (sig. Y2r), an epithet associated with Aretino on the title page to the *Ragionamenti* and elsewhere. This moment stands as a kind of authorial metariddle, emphasizing for readers Aretino's authorship of materials that are ostensibly created by and shared among women.

"How Then Ayme We at *Peter Aretine*": The *Ragionamenti* in Jonson's England

Although there were no early modern attempts to render Aretino's dialogues into English print, these erotic riddles and songs between women were legible in England to anyone who could access the book and read Italian. These proliferating dialogues exemplify another site of translation, as they spread beyond geographical boundaries through print, proffering cosmopolitan vernaculars to England's readers. After returning from Italy, where he had learned the art of printing, John Wolfe prepared in London an Italian-language edition of the *Ragionamenti* (1584), which he issued for sale on the Continent as well as in England.[50] Crucial to this project was Italian émigré Giacomo Castelvetro, who acted as a humanistic editor, buyer, and agent for Wolfe up until the year 1591.[51] With the imprint "Bengodi" rather than "London," Wolfe signaled to readers both a sense of pleasure ("godere bene," to enjoy well) and the copious variety of Aretino's language (Bengodi also being a fictional land of plenty in Boccaccio's *Decameron*). A preface in this volume also promised to publish the satirist's "ingeniose Comedie" (sig. A2v), and within four years Wolfe and Castelvetro introduced English readers to Aretino the dramatist—and his *Marescalco*—by way of a publication, in 1588, entitled *Quattro Comedie.*

Although in 1570 Ascham had already bemoaned the "fonde bookes, of late translated out of *Italian* into English, sold in euery shop in London," a number of English writers revived his complaints and leveled them at Aretino's books.[52] Gabriel Harvey's brother Richard unloaded a dense attack on Aretino in *A Theologicall Discourse of the Lamb of God and His Enemies*, calling the Italian "the arrogantest rakehell, and rankest villen."[53] In John Eliot's *Ortho-epia Gallica*, London has become infiltrated by Italians, some of them "*wicked heads . . . who have empoysoned by the venime of their skill, our English nation, with the bookes of* Nicholas Machiauell *and* Peter Aretine, *replenished with all filthiness and vilanie; who deserue for their pains a few swings of the strapado, or some bastinadoes, and to be banished out of the kingdome of England*"[54] With this flourish of foreign torture terms ("*strapado*," "*bastinado*"), Eliot seems to mean Wolfe's editions specifically, although many others, including John Davies and Gervase Markham, conflated the *Ragionamenti* with the sonnets Aretino had composed for a set of engravings depicting sexual positions.[55] Ultimately, Aretino's name came to stand for sexual license in England, signaling both erotic riddles and lurid visual representations of sex.

Readers registered these associations in early editions of Aretino's *Ragionamenti.* The user of one 1584 Wolfe edition singled out particularly erotic passages in ink, underlining and adding glosses both in Italian and in English. At one point early in the first book, this reader marks a passage where newly arrived nuns are shown paintings of Saint Nafissa ("the patron saint of whores," glosses Rosenthal, 14), whose facial expression Nanna interprets as singing a song entitled "*Che fa lo mio amore che non viene*" (What Is My Love Doing That He Does Not Come) (sig. B5v; Rosenthal, 15). At the bottom of the page, the reader has written "The preacher of ye monastery going into ye cha[m]ber w[i]th them, shew them ye deuise of euery picture" (figure 5.1). Here, in a passage of the dialogues registering both auditory and visual elements of the *Ragionamenti*'s erotic content, this reader flags the "picture[s]" that might recall the engravings associated with Aretino's very name. This particular reader might be English, but Wolfe's edition of Aretino's dialogues proliferated from Italy to England and elsewhere, reproducing the satirist's most notorious work across Europe. Decades later, this transnational quality would be especially clear in a 1660 Italian-language edition of the *Ragionamenti* based on Wolfe's and issued with the striking imprint "Cosmopoli" (figure 5.2), an imprint the stationer Richard Field had employed in English Catholic publications.[56] Such a placeless imprint announces to readers that these dialogues, riddles, and songs exchanged by Aretino's women belonged not to one nation or culture but rather occupied a *cosmopolitan* position among the vernaculars of Renaissance Europe. It was not any place in particular but Europe's cosmopolitan interest in the transnational circulation of Italianate eroticism that brought Aretino's dialogues to seventeenth-century readers.

Despite so much polemic in London, or possibly because of it, Wolfe's editions facilitated numerous imitations of Aretino's work in English prose, satire, and drama, cross-generic adoptions which can be understood under the capacious rubric of translation.[57] Flying in the face of moralistic critics, Thomas Nashe praised Aretino in *The Unfortunate Traveller* as "one of the wittiest knaues that euer God made."[58] Later, in *Lenten Stuffe*, he promoted the Italian author's name more plainly, claiming that "of all stiles I most affect & striue to imitate *Aretines*."[59] Nashe also deployed Aretino's name during a heated pamphlet exchange with Gabriel Harvey, and it seems that there was an especially high degree of interest in Aretino at Cambridge, where Nashe and Harvey, as well as Edmund Spenser, were educated.[60] (The anti-Aretino critic Richard Harvey had been a student there, as well.)

John Florio played an important role in England's increasing interest in Aretino, an interest which was channeled into the theater. Along with his occasional editorial assistance in Wolfe's printing house, Florio offered readers of his bilingual Italian-English lexicon a key into the language in the *Ragionamenti*'s erotic dialogues. The early owner of one highly annotated 1598 edition of *A Worlde of Wordes* took notice, underlining twelve Aretino titles in the lexicographer's list of sources.[61] Without such a dictionary, Florio asked in his lexicon's dedicatory epistle, "How then ayme we at *Peter Aretine*, that is so wittie, hath such varietie, and frames so manie new words?" (sig. A4r).[62] Recruiting what could be read as an Aretine register for his own, earlier language-learning dialogues in *First Fruites*, Florio also used the chapter title "*Ragionamenti*," and more than once.[63]

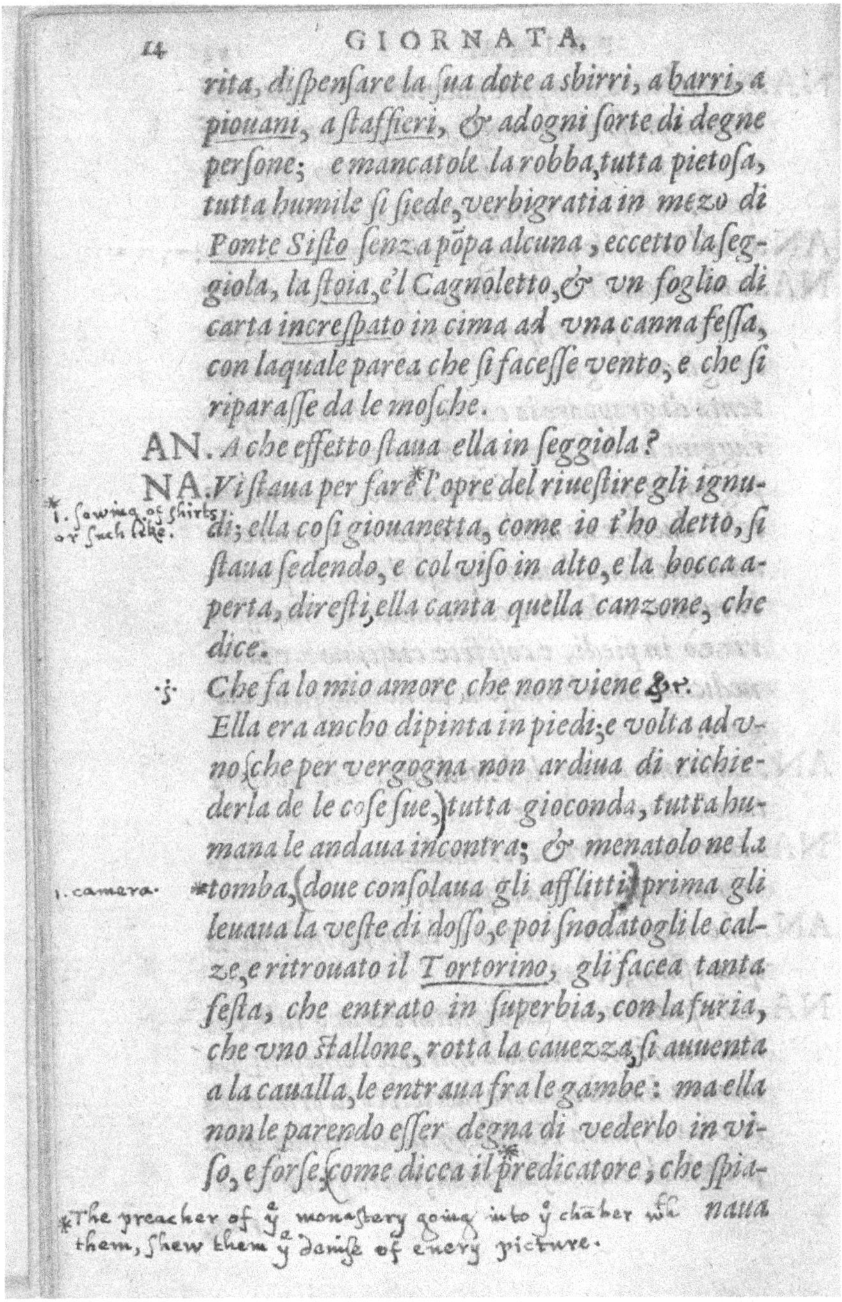

14 GIORNATA.

rita, diſpenſare la ſua dote a sbirri, a barri, a piouani, a ſtaffieri, & adogni ſorte di degne perſone; e mancatole la robba, tutta pietoſa, tutta humile ſi ſiede, verbigratia in mezo di Ponte Siſto ſenza pōpa alcuna, eccetto la ſeggiola, la ſtoia, e'l Cagnoletto, & vn foglio di carta increſpato in cima ad vna canna feſſa, con laquale parea che ſi faceſſe vento, e che ſi riparaſſe da le moſche.

AN. A che effetto ſtaua ella in ſeggiola?

NA. Vi ſtaua per fare* l'opre del riueſtire gli ignudi; ella coſi giouanetta, come io t'ho detto, ſi ſtaua ſedendo, e col viſo in alto, e la bocca aperta, direſti, ella canta quella canzone, che dice.

*i. sowing of shirts or such like.

Che fa lo mio amore che non viene &c.

Ella era ancho dipinta in piedi; e volta ad vno, che per vergogna non ardiua di richiederla de le coſe ſue, tutta gioconda, tutta humana le andaua incontra; & menatolo ne la *tomba, (doue conſolaua gli afflitti) prima gli leuaua la veſte di doſſo, e poi ſnodatogli le calze, e ritrouato il Tortorino, gli facea tanta feſta, che entrato in ſuperbia, con la furia, che vno ſtallone, rotta la cauezza, ſi auuenta a la caualla, le entraua fra le gambe: ma ella non le parendo eſſer degna di vederlo in viſo, e forſe, come dicea il *predicatore, che ſpianaua

i. camera.

*The preacher of ye monastery going into ye chāber with them, shew them ye deuise of every picture.

FIGURE 5.1 Pietro Aretino, *La Prima . . . Seconda Parte de Ragionamenti di M. Pietro Aretino*, 1584, sig. B5v. B85 Ar3. Reproduced by permission of the Rare Book & Manuscript Library, Columbia University in the City of New York.

CAPRICCIOSI & PIACEVOLI

RAGIONAMENTI

DI

M. PIETRO ARETINO,

Il Veritiere e'l diuino, cognominato il flagello de' Principi.

NUOUA EDITIONE.

Con certe postille, che spianano e dichiarano euidentemente i luoghi & le parole più oscure, & più difficili dell' opera.

STAMPATI IN COSMOPOLI.

L'Anno 1660.

FIGURE 5.2 Pietro Aretino, *Capricciosi & Piacevoli Ragionamenti di M. Pietro Aretino*, 1660, title page. Elz O 111. Reproduced by kind permission of the Kislak Center for Special Collections, Rare Books and Manuscripts, University of Pennsylvania.

To add to this picture, John Marston, Edward Guilpin, and several other authors adopted elements of Aretino's writing in their satires, which were then censored and burned by the English bishops in 1599. As Lynda Boose has argued, this so-called Bishops' Ban was largely a reaction to a "newly available form of moral transgression" associated with Aretino's writing in general and Wolfe's editions of the *Ragionamenti* in particular (although these editions were not actually included in the burning). She suggests that, following this act of censorship, the erotic and misogynistic style of Aretino found a new home on the Jacobean stage.[64] Not merely adaptations or imitations, these theatergrammatical deployments of Aretino's female speech constitute a variety of textual translation—a carrying-over from Italian to English, from page to stage—both a commentary on and rehearsal of the propagation of cosmopolitan vernaculars in Jonson's England.

Just as *Epicene* translates *Il Marescalco*'s Italian plot into an English setting, the comedy, as I've begun to suggest, also translates the promiscuous female speech of the *Ragionamenti* into the theatrical loquaciousness of the Collegiate ladies. Here, translation functions as propagation through the reproduction of Italian women's erotic dialogues, songs, and riddles. This connection is no coincidence, for a London edition of the *Ragionamenti* inscribed with Jonson's signature and motto (both now overwritten) testifies to the playwright's familiarity with Aretino's dialogues (figure 5.3).[65] Like the 1588 edition of *Quattro Comedie*, this book was issued under the auspices of John Wolfe. No direct evidence survives to trace Jonson's engagement with the text of *Il Marescalco*, but given his known ownership of the *Ragionamenti* and the circulation of the *Quattro Comedie* in these circles, it seems more than possible that Jonson also had access to Wolfe's edition of the play. Frances A. Yates suspects that the playwright also benefited from the help of Florio, one of Aretino's greatest philological champions in England.[66]

While one might be inclined to focus on the generic and typographic differences between these two London versions of the Aretino texts, similarities between dialogue and drama facilitated Jonson's translation of these texts' theatergrammatical elements into *Epicene*'s dramatic landscape. As *Theaters of Translation* has repeatedly underscored, Europe's cosmopolitan vernaculars circulated between plays and language-learning publications in Renaissance England, and Aretino's dialogues can certainly be considered as a site for language learning among English readers desiring to peruse the erotic exchanges (especially via Florio's lexicon). Wolfe's editions offered readers *Il Marescalco* as a play in roman type and the *Ragionamenti* as a

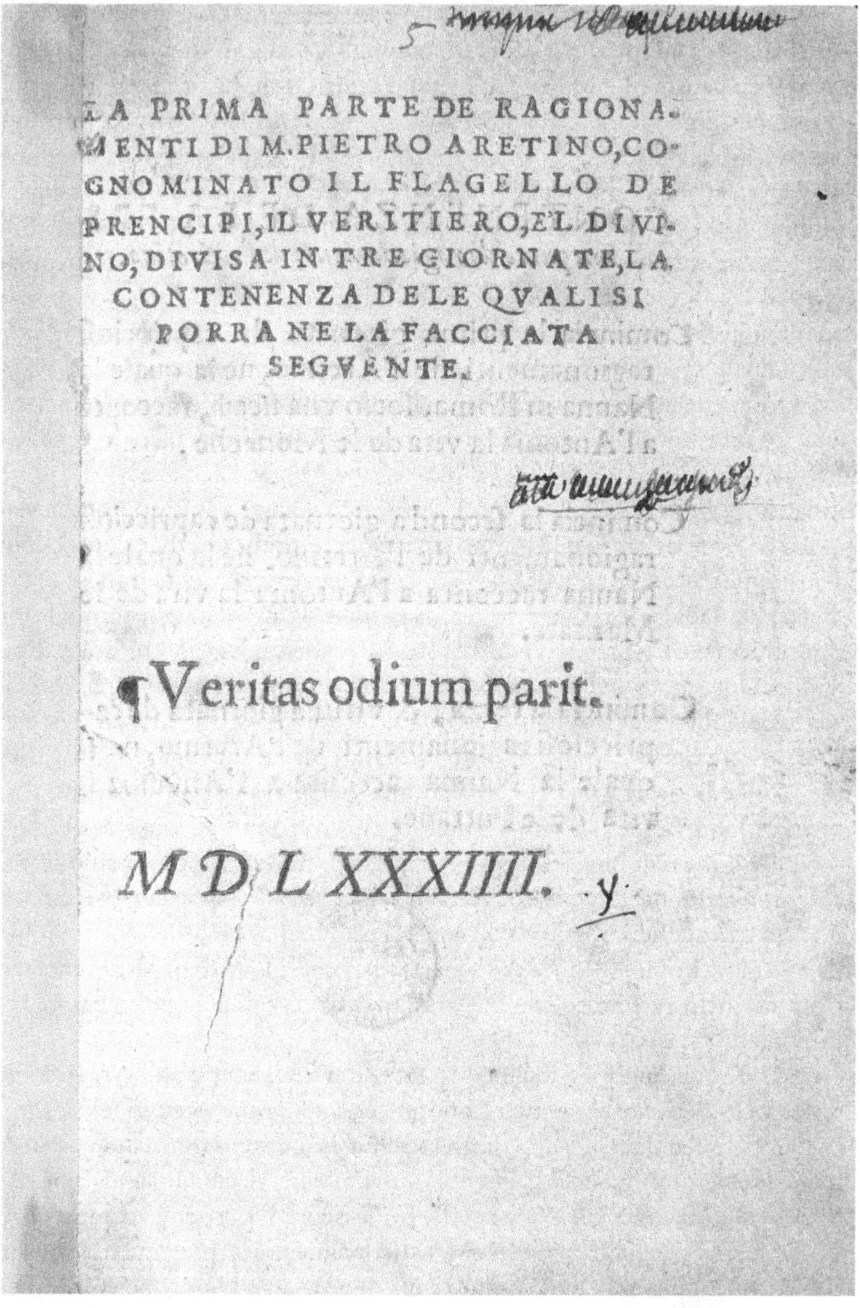

LA PRIMA PARTE DE RAGIONAMENTI DI M. PIETRO ARETINO, COGNOMINATO IL FLAGELLO DE PRENCIPI, IL VERITIERO, E'L DIVINO, DIVISA IN TRE GIORNATE, LA CONTENENZA DE LE QVALI SI PORRA NE LA FACCIATA SEGVENTE.

¶Veritas odium parit.

M D L XXXIIII.

FIGURE 5.3 Pietro Aretino, *La Prima . . . Seconda Parte de Ragionamenti di M. Pietro Aretino*, 1597?, sig. 1A1r. Douce A. 642. Reproduced with permission of the Bodleian Libraries, University of Oxford.

set of six dialogues in italic, but both are written in prose, and these books' shared status as censored literature on the Continent—and suspicious literature in London—calls into question the fixity of generic boundaries. Moreover, the erotic dialogues in the *Ragionamenti* have an unruly, theatrical format; Aretino places his women speakers on a rhetorical stage and allows them to speak freely, without decorum. "Doubtless," asserts David Frantz, "his experience as a dramatist served him well here."[67] In a historical context that forbade the performance or printing of Aretino's work on the European continent, the English stage—here understood as belonging to Bosman's "Renaissance intertheater," in which consideration of multiple languages was the rule rather than the exception—granted not only space but also a linguistically cosmopolitan dimension to Aretino's playful, bountiful language.[68] Playwrights such as Jonson brought this cosmopolitan dimension of language into being through the work of translation, in the several senses of translation I have explored, across languages but also across genres. If the *Ragionamenti* had been denied to European readers, John Wolfe and Giacomo Castelvetro facilitated the book's return to print, and Jonson transformed the dialogues into English theater to be heard publicly by way of the Collegiates and scrutinized textually in printed editions of *Epicene*.

"Hermaphroditical Authority": How Jonson Translated Aretino's Female Academy

Jonson's translation of the *Ragionamenti*'s female interlocutors into the sexualized, academic community of Collegiate ladies occurs as early as *Epicene*'s first act. As Howard has recognized, the early modern notion of an academy for women had deep associations with frivolity and promiscuity, but here it also evinces the work of translation responsible for these characters and their erotic inclinations.[69] Speaking with Clerimont, Truewit comments on the "hermaphroditical . . . authority" of these women: "A new foundation, sir, here i'the town, of ladies, that call themselves the collegiates: an order between courtiers and country madams that live from their husbands and give entertainment to all the wits and braveries o' the time" (1.1.63, 58–61). Soon, Morose's preference for silent women emerges, and Truewit torments him with the thought of garrulous ladies who "censure poets and authors and styles . . . or be thought cunning in controversies or the very knots of divinity . . . and answer in religion to one [question], in state to another, in bawdry to a third" (2.2.86–91). "Oh, oh!" cries Morose (line 92) in response to this already-sexualized portrait of the Collegiates (notice "cunning" and "knots"). Here, Jonson "Englishes" the outburst of Aretino's protagonist in *Il Marescalco,* who cries "O, o, o" upon hearing Ambrogio's misogynistic rants.[70] Not only do these women talk endlessly about literature and sex, Truewit says; some "may have made a conveyance of her virginity aforehand, as your wise widows do of their states before they marry. . . . Or if she have not done it yet, she may do, upon the wedding day, or the night before, and antedate you cuckold. The like has been heard of in nature" (lines 105–9). At this moment, some bilingual theatergoers, or readers, would have been reminded not solely of "nature" but also of the erotic conversations in Aretino's *Ragionamenti,* especially in the second dialogue of the first book, about wives. Furthermore, with the word "conveyance," Truewit—and, one can say, Jonson too—hails the link between the sexual behavior of loquacious ladies and the period's broad definition of *translation.* As Florio's entry for *tradurre* states, "*to bring, to turne, to conuert, to conuay from one place to another*"; "convey" in *Epicene* thus points to the translation and circulation of the Collegiate ladies, their riddles, and their alleged sexual activity, as well as the theft that Dauphine hopes to accomplish by the play's end.[71]

Jonson's conspicuous inclusion of a book of verses and madrigals in *Epicene* evinces his translation of the *Ragionamenti* as well, complementing the "Italian riddle" conveyed from Mavis to Dauphine in act 5 and offering a further indication of his comedy's fabrication out of Europe's circulating cosmopolitan vernaculars. Indeed, Jonson adopts in this moment the "*libretto*" (little book) of madrigals Aretino associates with his own name. In one early conversation between Epicene and three of the gallants, Clerimont asks, "Pray, Mistress Epicene, let's see your verses," rhymes and madrigals composed by the lady's "servant," Daw (2.3.11–13). Though written by a male character, these Continental-style verses now remain concealed by Epicene; the gallants ask her to make them public, effectively to "publish" them.[72] "Show 'em, show 'em, mistress; I dare own 'em," implores Daw (line 16), taking possession of the verses and pledging to read them aloud, too. The first of these is a "madrigal of modesty" (line 19), which adopts an established Italian lyric form while remarking on the sexuality of its subjects or listeners.[73] In the ensuing exchange littered with the names of classical poets, Clerimont and Dauphine mock Daw's ignorance of literary tradition, indexing, as Zucker puts it, the gallant's "inappropriate relationship to the . . . print marketplace."[74] However, this moment simultaneously hints at a grotesque vernacular style that opposes and threatens the classical literary establishment, and which can be traced back to Aretino's "madrigali." Indeed, this scene helps establish Daw's effeminacy and reveals the other male characters' general rejection of the conjoined ideas of the vernacular (as opposed to things classical), femininity, and alleged pseudointellectualism.

Daw's final recitation deals explicitly with questions of gender, sexuality, and reproduction. Here, the *Ragionamenti* shows through even clearer. Partly a response to Dauphine's question about women's silence ("Your reason, sir" [2.3.104]), the lines traffic in the discourse of gender reversal secretly powering the play all along:

> "Nor is't a tale
> That female vice should be a virtue male,
> Or masculine vice a female virtue be;
> You shall it see
> Proved with increase.
> I know to speak, and she to hold her peace." (2.3.105–10)

"Do you conceive me, gentlemen?" (line 111) concludes Daw, extending the poem's sexual vocabulary ("tale," "increase") into the erotically charged conversation that follows. Taking the bait, the gallants label this verse "a madrigal of procreation" (line 116). In doing so, they seize again on the gendered discourses inseparable from this play's consideration of speech and silence, driving home the link between propagation and translation in this comedy more generally. At the end of the scene, Epicene takes this madrigal back into her possession with other verses by Daw. Composed by men and possessed by women (i.e., Epicene), these Italianate verses resonate not only with an English courtship custom but also with the songs and riddles circulating and propagating among the female interlocutors of the *Ragionamenti*, including those marked as Aretino's own in the "*libretto*." As theatergrammatical texts, they illustrate Jonson's uses of cosmopolitan vernaculars and their eroticized passage from page to stage. Here, one witnesses the translation of Continental riddles and Italian prose dialogues about sex, gender, and reproduction into the English theater.

When an all-female academy—as opposed to the literary forms associated with one in Aretino—finally appears on stage, the Collegiates dominate their husbands and banter among themselves about marriage and sex. Here are the *Ragionamenti*'s erotically motivated interlocutors: emerging from the transnational tradition of late medieval women's gossip, translated from Italy to England, and made to speak a different language.[75] Haughty and the other Collegiates live apart from their spouses and cultivate power through independence, while Mistress Otter holds her husband to a strict set of domestic instructions: "I would be princess and reign in mine own house, and you would be my subject and obey me" (3.1.24–26).[76] After Morose finds Epicene to be surprisingly garrulous, the Collegiates induct her into their community, and she joins Mavis aside in a private, woman-to-woman dialogue to which the audience is not privy. The very secrecy of this dialogue—its staging literally *ob-scene*, oblique to the center of the action—may mark it as erotic, certainly in relation to earlier traditions of comedy, including Aretino's, that employ the technique of "partial enclosure" for female characters.[77] Thus, Jonson effectively stages a passage from Aretino to which English people familiar with Wolfe's editions do not yet have access, or cannot yet decipher.

Desiring access to this gossip among women, Jonson's audience listens in on this contentious female discourse during the fourth act, ultimately overhearing in English lessons that could be apprehended imaginatively as translated extracts from Aretino's dialogues. Haughty, Mavis, Centaure, and Mistress Otter advise the new Collegiate Epicene on how to rule her husband properly, to "learn to chastise," in Daw's words (4.3.7).[78] The Collegiates address Epicene as "Morose" according to masculine custom and invite her to live apart from her husband and to visit "Bedlam . . . the china houses, and . . . the Exchange" (line 19). One already perceives in these local places extensions beyond conventional or normative boundaries: a prison-hospital, vendors of East Asian goods, and the center of foreign trade and merchants discussed in the previous chapter, the Exchange. Moreover, the encouragement to wander, to stray beyond one's home, offers a thematic link to the notion of a "puttana errante" (wandering whore) that came to be associated with Aretino.[79]

The Collegiates speak among themselves in this scene in a way that an audience familiar with Aretino would interpret as full of sexualized puns. Mistress Otter describes Morose with "a huge long naked weapon in both his hands," echoed by the desire that men "draw their weapons for our honours"; a sexually inclined Centaure assures Epicene that her journeys across the city "will open the gate to your fame" (lines 2–3, 38–39, 20).[80] When Epicene questions the lawfulness of having multiple lovers ("plurality of servants") and the need to "do 'em all graces," Mavis replies that "She that now excludes her lovers may live to lie a forsaken beldame in a frozen bed" (lines 24–25, 34–35). In that case, Epicene inquires about the "excellent receipts . . . to keep yourselves from bearing of children" (lines 45–46) and to conceal the reproductive evidence of extramarital affairs.[81] Read in these terms, Jonson's presentation of the Collegiates in the play, characterized by a series of erotic conversations and anecdotes between women about sex and gender, translates its dialogue and activity out of Aretino's female academy. These women characters, their speech, their madrigals and their letters—each of these "Englished" theatergrammatical elements—are manifestations of the expansive, border-crossing properties of Europe's cosmopolitan vernaculars.

"To Turne, to Conuert" a Renaissance Play

Although, as I have been arguing, Jonson translates the sexual discourse of the *Ragionamenti* onto the English stage through the Collegiates, he simultaneously attempts to mute its Italian provenance and silence the propagating discourse of the Collegiates themselves, including by way of the printed text's appearance. This dissimulative technique of imitation—or again, one could say, translation—reinforces the efforts Jonson made to style himself, in Richard Helgerson's words, as a "laureate dramatist" in England.[82] Even though he demonstrably shared Nashe's interest in the *Ragionamenti*, Jonson also had lofty aspirations that did not fit comfortably with the intertheatrical essence of his plays. His treatment of Italianate elements in *Epicene* thus demonstrates a conflicted effort to balance the high and the low, the civilized and the grotesque dimensions of his work as he cultivated an authorial persona that would see its fullest performance in the publication of his *Workes*. The stakes here were great, for critics have recognized this folio's production in 1616 as an important event in the history of drama in England, the rise of authorship as an idea, and the development of the "bibliographic ego."[83] As Peter Stallybrass has maintained, early modern efforts to civilize required the regulation of female openness, and it is for similar reasons that Jonson takes pains to regulate and to some degree obscure *Epicene*'s "femall" translation—as foreign practice and product—of Aretino's dialogues.[84] The traditional tendency to read Jonson as a classically focused English author—a tendency that Jonson himself desired—has hidden from view what playgoers and readers familiar with the *Ragionamenti* would have found in plain sight.

Jonson's enclosure of women's speech in *Epicene* finds a persistent voice in the play's deep-running misogyny and Latinate legal discourse, a classicized, masculine register designed to quiet the comedy's delight in cosmopolitan vernaculars. "Why, all their actions are governed by crude opinion, without reason or cause," Truewit says of the Collegiates; "they have a natural inclination sways 'em generally to the worst when they are left to themselves" (4.6.54–55, 58–59). Male spectators could share Truewit's bitter sentiments about the Collegiates, though Howard has suggested that *Epicene* could have enabled educated female playgoers to join in the ridicule as well.[85] Even if they feign their expertise, this play's men traffic in Seneca, Plutarch, and Livy, while the women characters draw physic from vernacular texts such as *Greene's Groatsworth of Wit*. Indeed, in a scene of legal consultation conducted in botched but purposefully selected Latin (set in italic type for the 1616 Folio to distinguish it from vernacular English), Jonson opposes a masculine and classical discourse to the sexualized vernacular gossip of the Collegiates. The slight attention that Jonson would give to Italian in his classically oriented *English Grammar* deploys this fictional stance toward language and civility in a more straightforward manner: "Wee free our Language from the opinion of Rudenesse, and Barbarisme," he writes in a preface to the linguistic treatise, "wherewith it is mistaken to be diseas'd."[86] By locating Italian and other non-English vernaculars under the rubric of "Rudenesse, and Barbarisme," Jonson puts his native tongue on par with Latin and Greek. Likewise, in *Epicene*, he censures the unruly, female, vernacular, and Italianate voices of the Collegiates propagating among male and female spectators—and, importantly, readers, too. The epigraph from Horace on the play's title page in Jonson's *Workes* could only have strengthened these associations, and indeed, the play's title itself speaks to a classically inclined audience.[87] Some extant copies of the *Workes* register such an approach in marginalia left by early readers that effectively retrace the playwright's steps through authors from

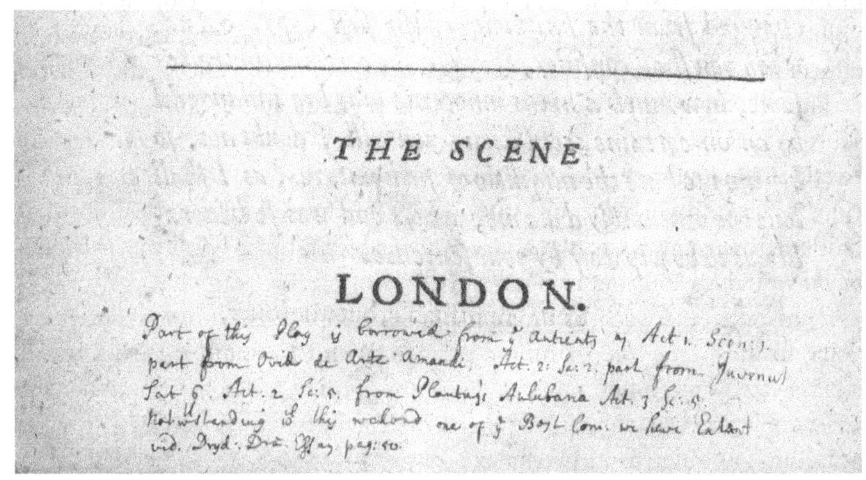
THE SCENE

LONDON.

FIGURE 5.4 An early reader's references to Ovid, Juvenal, and Plautus in Ben Jonson, *The Workes of Benjamin Jonson*, 1616, sig. 2X6v. RB 606577. Reproduced by permission of the Huntington Library, San Marino, California.

classical antiquity such as Virgil, Horace, Juvenal, and Ovid (figure 5.4). For these scholarly readers, the classical frame for *Epicene* is one the playwright desired to accomplish, and did.[88]

In order to civilize the grotesque, feminine, and Italian elements of *Epicene*—in other words, to transform the fluid interplay of European cosmopolitan vernaculars into a singular, native, classicized English discourse—the final act of the play silences the Collegiates with a surprising twist: another act of translation. Florio's capacious definition of the word *tradurre* includes "*to turne, to conuert*," and this is precisely what happens when Truewit removes Epicene's wig. Before an audience, onstage and off, that has taken Epicene for a woman throughout the play, Truewit translates her into a boy. Under her costume, Epicene has been a boy all along, but this is a change that ranks alongside Bottom's translation into an ass in *A Midsummer Night's Dream* or other magical or sartorial transformations on the Renaissance stage, including Falstaff's in *The Merry Wives of Windsor*. Although Jonson mostly obscures his own efforts in translating Aretino's play and dialogues, he slyly alludes to this project when he translates Epicene from female to male, thus disparaging the idea of a foreign, female-voiced text, congratulating himself for masculinizing and "Englishing" it, and covering his tracks in the process. Connecting the gender translation of Epicene to the fact that all the Collegiates on stage are boy actors, Jonson suggests the very impossibility of a female-voiced text.

As can already be perceived, this deployment of translation has clear political implications. While Bottom's translation is part of an "interlude of disorder," Epicene's stages before audiences (in Patricia Parker's words) "the disposition [i.e., settling, stabilizing] of a potentially wayward or unruly female *materia*," a process related to both gender and hierarchical order.[89] No longer obvious as a "femall" technique, Epicene's translation shores up the play's classical and masculine elements instead. Here, Epicene changes from a feminine display of propagation into an economical—and anatomically masculine—singular point. This metamorphosis reverses Florio's conception of translation, moving from "femall" and "second hand" to male and originary.[90] At any rate, Epicene's surprising change leaves the women speechless. A triumphant Truewit exclaims, "Madams, you are mute upon this new metamorphosis!" (5.4.197), almost a command rather than a reaction. What was once Aretino's erotic Italian discourse among women interlocutors is now an English-language comedy entitled *The Silent Woman*.

Despite such a masculine ending, *Epicene* as a whole performs a broader translation in preserving—however subtly—the erotic energy of Aretino's

Ragionamenti. In this sense, a complete division between "classical/English" and "vernacular" ultimately cannot hold. Jonson does not merely moralize, sterilize, or allegorize Italian materials here; he translates them onto the English stage in the full view of his audiences and figures this action textually for readers in his carefully planned out text. Although no betrothals accompany the play's conclusion, it exemplifies the coupling of Italian dialogue and English drama in a manner consistent with Bosman's notion of Renaissance intertheater: a theater of the in-between, both "international and multilingual."[91] Mavis's "Italian riddle" for Dauphine thus figures as an erotic proposition while commenting simultaneously on the acts of translation underlying the entire play. In company with Haughton's *Englishmen for My Money*, *Epicene* cannot be understood solely as a city comedy or a London comedy, for not only does the play already feature a reassembly of theatergrams from Aretino's *Il Marescalco*; it also reworks the theatergrammatical female voices of the *Ragionamenti* into the "city talk" of the Collegiates. The latter element, as I have sought to show here, constitutes a complex and thoroughgoing, if previously unacknowledged, Jonsonian translation of Aretino. What indeed is city talk in this translingual, transnational setting in which Continental books are printed by English stationers, sold on London bookstalls in foreign tongues, and translated into English plays? Such a place might be called "Cosmopoli."

Coda

Toward a "New World of Words," from John Florio to Samuel Johnson

"*William Thomas* hath done prettilie," remarks John Florio in the preliminaries of *A Worlde of Wordes*, his Italian-English lexicon.[1] Here, one finds Florio—dictionary maker, language instructor, and the translator of Montaigne's French *Essais*—evaluating Thomas's *Principal Rules of the Italian Grammer*, the first bilingual grammar and lexicon for Italian printed in England. Issued "for the better understandynge of Boccace, Petrarcha, and Dante," this manual opened new pathways for early modern English learners of Italian vocabulary and grammar.[2] Given these comments in *A Worlde of Wordes*, it is striking that what appears to be Florio's own copy of *Principal Rules* survives today at Cambridge University, bearing witness to the language instructor's lexicographic reflections and his work as a translator and instructor.[3] Like Roger Ascham's student Robert Sackville and the translator-dramatist Mary Sidney Herbert, whom I discussed in prior chapters, it seems Florio inscribed his name in this book: "libro di Iohanni florio," reads an italic inscription across the title page, with "questo libro e da me Iohanni florio" scribbled on the verso (figure C.1).

A variety of other inscriptions throughout this book offer what could be a view into Florio's pedagogical scene. Indeed, "Iohanni florio" is not the only name to appear in this volume's pages; one also finds the signatures of Samuel Whitly, John Whitly, Robert Woodrington, John Kennett, and John Spark, individuals who may have been Florio's students. Written in both secretary and italic styles, the book's annotations appear in English, French, Italian, Greek, and Latin, mingling languages through grammatical notes ("on fait toujours une apostrophe"), new vocabulary words and definitions ("mela an appel"), and translations of the printed text (at "*Io amo*, I loue," there appears the French annotation "j'aime").

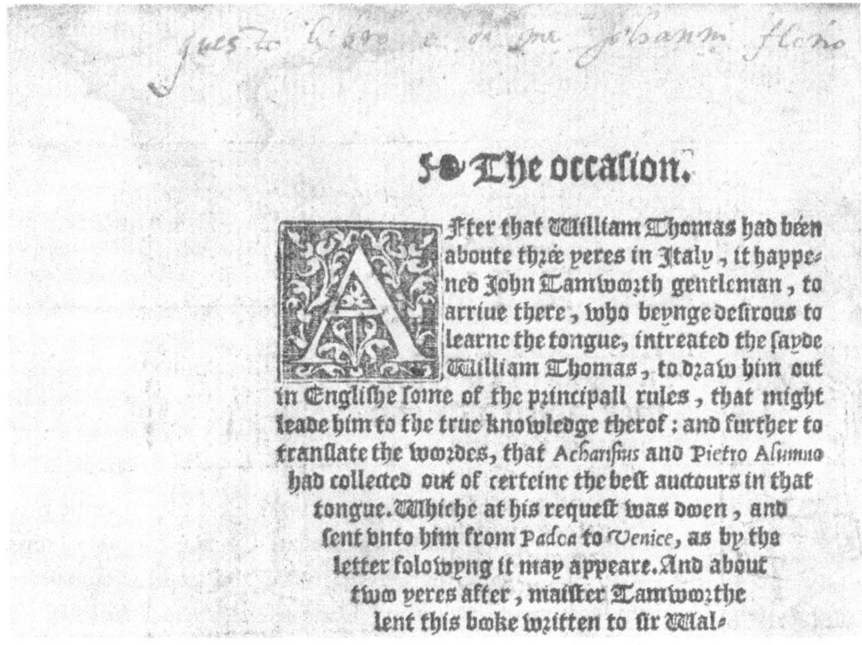

The occasion.

After that William Thomas had béen aboute thrée yeres in Italy, it happened John Tamworth gentleman, to arriue there, who beynge desirous to learne the tongue, intreated the sayde William Thomas, to drawe him out in Englishe some of the principall rules, that might leade him to the true knowledge therof: and further to translate the wordes, that Acharisius and Pietro Alunno had collected out of certeine the best auctours in that tongue. Whiche at his request was doen, and sent vnto him from Padoa to Venice, as by the letter folowyng it may appeare. And about two yeres after, maister Tamworthe lent this boke written to sir Wal-

FIGURE C.1 Inscription reading "questo libro e da me Iohanni florio" in Thomas, *Principal Rules*, 1562, title page verso, detail. Peterborough G.6.40. Reproduced by kind permission of the Syndics of Cambridge University Library.

These inscriptions, it seems, indicate a pedagogical purpose well-suited to Thomas's manual and embodying the Latin-based vernacular practice of schoolrooms in early modern England—those of Florio himself, Claudius Hollyband, and John Eliot, to name just a few.

For John Gallagher, the array of markings in this copy of *Principal Rules* is "a reminder that to learn the grammar of a foreign language was a social and conversational undertaking—not merely a scholarly and silent activity, but one in which texts and their readers engaged with the multilingual oral and aural cultures of early modern England and Italy."[4] For both language-learning publications and works of drama, *Theaters of Translation* has adopted a both/and approach to the question here, considering the ways surviving texts printed and inscribed with multiple foreign languages do not just *index* a lively, multilingual social exchange or theatrical spectacle but also add in their own way, textually, to what I have been referring to as a culture of cosmopolitan vernaculars in early modern Europe.[5] Indeed, preserved in the pages of language-learning books and printed plays are handwritten Italian proverbs, French owners' markings,

Spanish words, and other overlapping and mingling linguistic traces that, along with the multilingually attuned typographies and book-making conventions of the period (e.g., italic fonts, or bindings drawing together linguistically diverse texts), attest to the multilingual culture of Europe's early modern moment—on the stage, and in the streets—while also contributing to that same moment.[6] This was the world of John Baret's *Alvearie*, Noël de Berlaimont's *Colloquia*, and the bilingual instruction of Florio, Hollyband, and others. And it is against the backdrop of this culture that Shakespeare, as well as Thomas Kyd, Mary Sidney Herbert, William Haughton, and Ben Jonson lived, spoke, wrote, and *translated*, in the manifold sense of that word.

Indeed, considering pedagogy, print, and performance together in a single narrative, *Theaters of Translation* has shown how cosmopolitan vernaculars in this period functioned *between* the polyglot page and multilingual stage, in multiple ways. The playhouse itself, as I have argued, provided a site for pedagogical discourses, among others, that accompanied the work of translation, as well as a place where book design and dramaturgy mingled in the minds of playgoers and readers. Such imaginative considerations could also be done in regard to a work of closet drama or any printed play taken on its own terms, within what might be called a "theater of one's own mind." The overarching picture here differs from the views conditioned by influential studies such as Richard Helgerson's *Forms of Nationhood*, which read the nation backward onto the early modern era, resulting in a literary history that appears as always already English. Instead, building on more recent studies attuned to the transnational and translingual qualities of the period, I have demonstrated how the multiplicities of vernacular languages in early modern European language manuals, dialogue books, and dictionaries overlapped extensively with England's dramatic works—tragedy and comedy, designed to be staged or read, or with both in consideration—and in ways that engage with the period's discourses of education, religion, commerce, and gender, among other subjects.

These cosmopolitan vernaculars emerged from Latin schoolroom practices, extending instructional traditions through print and manuscript into the contemporary territory of French, Italian, and Spanish, among other languages of Europe—and their literatures, too. At this time, simultaneously, the English language itself was multilingual; to use Jacques Derrida's formulation, it was "a language that is not one's own," pieced together with "denizened" words and "naturalized" phrases.[7] Rather than viewing this polyglot condition of English and its influence on drama as either incoherent or as a striving toward an inevitable cohesiveness, I perceive in more reparative terms a linguistically cosmopolitan moment in which various vernaculars mixed and mingled together, fashioning for readers, authors, and playgoers forms of translinguistic belonging. Working against a view of incipient English exceptionalism and across manuscript, print, and the stage, these languages, I claim, were cosmopolitan vernaculars.

This critical reorientation causes one to perceive differently not only Shakespeare's "English comedy" as something more foreign—as this book has demonstrated, it has implications for a range of other dramatic works as well. Kyd's *Spanish Tragedy* looks less like a commentary on English-Spanish politics, or a display of inarticulacy, and more like a double-translation language lesson; Sidney Herbert's closet drama *The Tragedy of Antony* appears not only as a translated playtext but additionally as a commentary on translation's religious connotations, in a domain apart from the public theater's environs. Meanwhile, city comedies in this context emerge as much more multilingual and foreign-oriented than previously or usually understood. In Haughton's *Englishmen for My Money*—typically viewed as an unapologetically xenophobic play—disguises, accents, and a frisky servant named Frisco showcase the mingling of English with other European languages; and, despite Jonson's attempts to "silence" the Continental vernacular substance of his own comedy *Epicene*, his female "Collegiates" speak in a style indebted to Italy's most notorious erotic author. In each of these works, playgoers and readers are treated to distinctly linguistic forms of cosmopolitanism that move between and among English, French, Italian, Spanish, and other European languages.

The dynamics of cosmopolitan vernaculars analyzed in this book emerged from their medieval precedents—scholastic activity and religious discourse in Latin, for instance—but they also anticipate, not in any sort of predestined way, the development of England into a powerful imperial force throughout the world. From Falstaff's suggestion that the titular women of *The Merry Wives of Windsor* are "my East and West Indies" to *Epicene*'s mention of "china houses" and "the Exchange," the particularized translingual dealings observed in *Theaters of Translation* gesture already toward that wider world of colonialism and global domination, truly a "new world of words," in which the English language would play an increasingly conspicuous role on the way to its status as today's international lingua franca.The plays of Shakespeare's moment, accordingly, came to occupy a new position relative to the English language within the imperial era, and at the hands of that titan of English lexicography, Samuel Johnson.

As decades passed, not only Thomas's "prettilie" done *Principal Rules* but also Florio's own *Worlde of Wordes* dictionary began to look increasingly unruly. Taking issue with shaggy or repetitive definitions, dubious etymologies, and headwords in not-quite-alphabetic order, England's lexicographers adopted new standards more closely mirroring those of today. Triumphing above all attempts was the English dictionary of Samuel Johnson, a lexicographer who also edited Shakespeare's dramatic works. Rather than opting for a polyglot approach, Johnson sought to provide England's response to the French and Italian academies' grand monolingual lexicons.[8] And, while rooted in literary examples and the early modern practices of indexing and commonplacing, his work essentially arranged the English language into a catalog of knowledge.[9] Published in 1755, the *English Dictionary* must also be contextualized against the backdrop of the British Empire and the prosperity and oppression precipitated by the African slave trade. While working on the dictionary, in fact, Johnson took into his home an enslaved Jamaican boy of about ten years named Francis Barber (born Quashey); Barber took up residence among the scholar's amanuenses and other household servants.[10] One can picture the young Afro-Caribbean carrying slips of paper across the floor of the household's lexicographic laboratory known as "the garret." Johnson ultimately made Barber his heir, but the Jamaican perceived his bondage to be in effect until after a year after the dictionary's release.[11]

Once characterized by bilingual lexicography rooted in Latin schoolroom exercises and immigrant language instructors, England's dictionary landscape had become a monoglot product of the European Enlightenment, driven forward by a white London scholar aided by an enslaved Black boy from Jamaica. And in the *English Dictionary*'s pages, Shakespeare appeared repeatedly as one of the most-cited literary examples. Shortly after completing the dictionary, Johnson turned his attention to editing Shakespeare's plays, prominently shoring up the author's reputation as the transcendent "poet of nature." In his preface, he trumpeted, "The Poet, of whose works I have undertaken the revision, may now begin to assume the dignity of an ancient, and claim the privilege of established fame and prescriptive veneration."[12] And that, arguably, is precisely what happened. All told, Johnson's lexicon pointed forward, though not inevitably so, toward a world in which English would serve as an international lingua franca, and for which Shakespeare would be viewed as a singularly important linguistic wellspring. More than 250 years after Johnson's labors, other playwrights—Sidney Herbert, for instance, or Haughton—and contemporary language-learning instructors and dictionary makers, such as Florio, have drifted out of focus, along with the culture of multilingualism and translation inspiring their works.

Theaters of Translation: Cosmopolitan Vernaculars in Shakespeare's England has restored attention to that culture through its analysis of an array of multilingual dictionaries, grammars, and dialogue books from the period, along with early editions of its printed drama. Taken together, these materials offer an alternative, translinguistic view of early modern English literary history, one which is able to glimpse behind the towering legacy of Samuel Johnson's *English Dictionary* and the British Empire that carried Shakespeare to the heights of fame, at the expense of his playwright contemporaries. Importantly, this book also shows how a combined method consisting of multilingualism and translation studies, the history of books, and the history of theater and performance may productively complicate a long-lived scholarly preoccupation with national categories, a preoccupation that has shaped the siloed-off nature of academic language departments and that continues to shape the field of early modern studies, broadly conceived. The story of the nation, even if it is more story than fact, does not easily loosen its grip. But by attending to what I have called cosmopolitan vernaculars in Shakespeare's moment, *Theaters of Translation* tells a different story, revealing that linguistic and cultural mixing, rather than national cohesiveness, lies at the early modern foundations of the English language's development, and its drama.

Attention to early modern Europe's dictionaries, grammars, and language-learning books of all kinds demonstrates that the world in which William Shakespeare, Thomas Kyd, Mary Sidney Herbert, William Haughton, and Ben Jonson lived and wrote had different linguistic assumptions than those widely assumed today. Here, the stage and the page worked together to broadcast mingled and overlapping cosmopolitan vernaculars to readers, playgoers, actors, and authors, modeling and fashioning border-crossing and translinguistic forms of belonging. In the terms of Florio's bilingual lexicon of 1598, this England was a "world of words."

Notes

Chapter 1

1. On this label for the comedy, see Jeanne Addison Roberts, *Shakespeare's English Comedy: "The Merry Wives of Windsor" in Context* (Lincoln: University of Nebraska Press, 1979), esp. 51–60. On divergences between folio and quarto texts of this play, see Leah S. Marcus, *Unediting the Renaissance: Shakespeare, Marlowe, Milton* (London: Routledge, 1996), 68–100.

2. Patricia Parker, *Shakespeare from the Margins: Language, Culture, Context* (Chicago: University of Chicago Press, 1996), 116–18; Elizabeth Pittenger, "Dispatch Quickly: The Mechanical Reproduction of Pages," *Shakespeare Quarterly* 42, no. 4 (1991): 396–406. For a reading of this scene supposing that Mistress Page decorously ignores this sexualized discourse, see David Landreth, "Once More into the Preech: The Merry Wives' English Pedagogy," *Shakespeare Quarterly* 55, no. 4 (2004): 435–41.

3. William Shakespeare, *The Merry Wives of Windsor*, ed. Giorgio Melchiori (London: Arden Shakespeare, 2000), 4.1.50–55; as I mentioned, the passage quoted here appears only in the 1623 folio text, and I will remain alert to the relationship between the folio text and the 1602 quarto text throughout my analysis. All subsequent quotations from *Merry Wives* will be taken from this edition and will be cited parenthetically. Meanwhile, following the first reference within each chapter of my broader study, all early printed books will be cited parenthetically by signature.

4. For a sample of critical pronouncements along these lines, see: Parker, *Shakespeare from the Margins*, 122; Pittenger, "Dispatch Quickly"; Landreth, "Once More," 426; Richard Helgerson, "Language Lessons, Linguistic Colonialism, Linguistic Postcolonialism, and the Early Modern English Nation," *Yale Journal of Criticism* 11, no. 1 (1998): 296–97; and Wendy Wall, *Staging Domesticity: Household Work and English Identity in Early Modern Drama* (Cambridge, UK: Cambridge University Press, 2002), 93.

5. Margaret Tudeau-Clayton, *Shakespeare's Englishes: Against English* (Cambridge, UK: Cambridge University Press, 2020), e.g., 186–87.

6. William Shakespeare, *Mr. William Shakespeares Comedies, Histories, and Tragedies* (London: Isaac Jaggard and Ed. Blount, 1632), sig. D4v. This book is Biblioteca Nazionale Marciana Rari 0139, and it belonged for some time to the Venetian poet and librettist Apostolo Zeno (1669–1750). For their help with this inscription, I am grateful to James Siemon, Mara Wade, and Heather Wolfe.

7. Although Melchiori "corrects" Caius's word to read as "*Dépêche*" (1.4.49), fixing it as italicized "French," the appearance of both "*de-peech*" and "*quickly*" in italic type together offers an inverse of what one sees in the quarto playbooks of *Henry V*, where, according to Marjorie Rubright, "the polyvocal din of tongues within and across England's borders is pressed into conjunction, printed alike in a shared roman face"; see "Incorporating Kate: The Myth of Monolingualism in Shakespeare's *Henry the Fifth*," in *The Oxford Handbook of Shakespeare and Embodiment: Gender, Sexuality, and Race*, ed. Valerie Traub (Oxford, UK: Oxford University Press, 2016), 487. On the ways *Merry Wives*' "cozen Germans" blend with the comedy's broader discourse of translation, see Parker, *Shakespeare from the Margins*, 127–31.

8. Christopher Marlowe, *The Troublesome Raigne and Lamentable Death of Edward the Second, King of England* (London: for Henry Bell, 1622). Österreichische Nationalbibliothek, 19.V.22. I am grateful to Jeffrey Masten for this reference.

9. Anston Bosman, "Renaissance Intertheater and the Staging of Nobody," *English Literary History* 71, no. 3 (2004): 564.

10. Louise George Clubb recognizes Mistress Quickly as a "freelance mezzana" from the Italian theater; see *Italian Drama in Shakespeare's Time* (New Haven, CT: Yale University Press, 1989), 24.

11. John Considine has produced a series of dictionary-focused studies, including *Dictionaries in Early Modern Europe: Lexicography and the Making of Heritage* (Cambridge, UK: Cambridge University Press, 2008); *Small Dictionaries and Curiosity: Lexicography and Fieldwork in Post-Medieval Europe* (Oxford, UK: Oxford University Press, 2017); and *Sixteenth-Century English Dictionaries* (Oxford, UK: Oxford University Press, 2022). See also John Gallagher, *Learning Languages in Early Modern England* (Oxford, UK: Oxford University Press, 2019), esp. 55–100; putting less emphasis on the aural and oral aspects of language learning in favor of a focus on literary imitation is Jason Lawrence, *Who the Devil Taught Thee So Much Italian? Italian Language Learning and Imitation in Early Modern England* (Manchester, UK: Manchester University Press, 2005).

12. See the established account in Richard Foster Jones, *The Triumph of the English Language: A Survey of Opinions Concerning the Vernacular from the Introduction of Printing to the Restoration* (Stanford, CA: Stanford University Press, 1953); on this tidal moment of change for the English vernacular, see Jenny C. Mann, *Outlaw Rhetoric: Figuring Vernacular Eloquence in Shakespeare's England* (Ithaca, NY: Cornell University Press, 2012); and Paula Blank, *Broken English: Dialects and the Politics of Language in Renaissance Writings* (London: Routledge, 1996). On the long history of multilingualism in performance, see Marvin Carlson, *Speaking in Tongues: Language Play in the Theatre* (Ann Arbor: University of Michigan Press, 2006); for Renaissance examples, see especially pp. 34–43.

13. Lynn Enterline, *Shakespeare's Schoolroom: Rhetoric, Discipline, Emotion* (Philadelphia: University of Pennsylvania Press, 2012); see also Jeff Dolven, *Scenes of Instruction in Renaissance Romance* (Chicago: University of Chicago Press, 2007).

14. Gallagher, *Learning Languages*, 15.

15. Jacques Rancière, *The Ignorant Schoolmaster: Five Lessons in Intellectual Emancipation*, trans. Kristin Ross (Stanford, CA: Stanford University Press, 1991), 13; Jacques Rancière, *The Emancipated Spectator*, trans. Gregory Elliott (London: Verso, 2009), esp. 1–23. Also focusing on the pedagogical significance of the book-as-

thing, and in an early modern context, though with a coinciding emphasis on failures and breakdowns, is Julian Yates, *Error, Misuse, Failure: Object Lessons from the English Renaissance* (Minneapolis: University of Minnesota Press, 2003), xi–xx.

16. Carla Mazzio, *The Inarticulate Renaissance: Language Trouble in an Age of Eloquence* (Philadelphia: University of Pennsylvania Press, 2009), 11–12. The emphasis is Mazzio's in regard to Thomas Kyd's *Spanish Tragedy*, which I will discuss in chapter 2.

17. Tudeau-Clayton, *Shakespeare's Englishes*, 2–3; the phrase "discursive struggle" appears on p. 9.

18. See Richard Helgerson, *Forms of Nationhood: The Elizabethan Writing of England* (Chicago: University of Chicago Press, 1992); Andrew Hadfield, *Literature, Politics, and National Identity: Reformation to Renaissance* (Cambridge, UK: Cambridge University Press, 1994); Claire McEachern, *The Poetics of English Nationhood, 1590–1612* (Cambridge, UK: Cambridge University Press, 1996); and Cathy Shrank, *Writing the Nation in Reformation England, 1530–1580* (Oxford, UK: Oxford University Press, 2006).

19. See, for instance, Noémie Ndiaye, *Scripts of Blackness: Early Modern Performance and Culture and the Making of Race* (Philadelphia: University of Pennsylvania Press, 2022); Patricia Akhimie and Bernadette Andrea, eds., *Travel and Travail: Early Modern Women, English Drama, and the Wider World* (Lincoln: University of Nebraska Press, 2019); Kasey Evans, *Colonial Virtue: The Mobility of Temperance in Renaissance England* (Toronto: University of Toronto Press, 2012); Roland Greene, *Unrequited Conquests: Love and Empire in the Colonial Americas* (Chicago: University of Chicago Press, 1999).

20. See A. E. B. Coldiron, *Printers Without Borders: Translation and Textuality in the Renaissance* (Cambridge, UK: Cambridge University Press, 2015); Marjorie Rubright, *Doppelgänger Dilemmas: Anglo-Dutch Relations in Early Modern English Literature and Culture* (Philadelphia: University of Pennsylvania Press, 2014); Michael Wyatt, *The Italian Encounter with Tudor England: A Cultural Politics of Translation* (Cambridge, UK: Cambridge University Press, 2005); and Kathryn Vomero Santos, "Staging Translation in Early Modern England" (PhD diss., New York University, 2013). For a sample of recent work addressing the "transnational," "cosmopolitan," and "global," see Ayesha Ramachandran, *The Worldmakers: Global Imagining in Early Modern Europe* (Chicago: University of Chicago Press, 2015); Andreas Höfele and Werner von Koppenfels, eds., *Renaissance Go-Betweens: Cultural Exchange in Early Modern Europe* (Berlin: Walter de Gruyter, 2005); Alison Games, *The Web of Empire: English Cosmopolitans in an Age of Empire* (Oxford, UK: Oxford University Press, 2008); and Jyotsna G. Singh, ed., *A Companion to the Global Renaissance: English Literature and Culture in the Era of Expansion* (London: Wiley-Blackwell, 2013).

21. Bosman, "Renaissance Intertheater," 566. The emphasis is Bosman's.

22. See, for instance, Kelly J. Stage, *Producing Early Modern London: A Comedy of Urban Space, 1598–1616* (Lincoln: University of Nebraska Press, 2018); Nina Levine, *Practicing the City: Early Modern London on Stage* (New York: Fordham University Press, 2016); Adam Zucker, *The Places of Wit in Early Modern English Comedy* (Cambridge, UK: Cambridge University Press, 2011); Jean E. Howard, *Theater of a City: The Places of London Comedy, 1598–1642* (Philadelphia: University of Pennsylvania Press, 2007); and Karen Newman, *Cultural Capitals: Early Modern London*

and Paris (Princeton, NJ: Princeton University Press, 2007). Although most of the plays and much of the printed material I consider in this book emerged in London, my emphasis lies less on London as a space for cosmopolitanism and more on the mobilities, border crossings, and translations that nourished this cosmopolitanism, especially in European linguistic contexts.

23. Clubb, *Italian Drama*, 1–26; I employ this approach most specifically in chapter 5. See also *Transnational Exchange in Early Modern Theatre*, ed. Robert Henke and Eric Nicholson (Aldershot, UK: Ashgate, 2008), as well as M. A. Katritzky and Pavel Drábek, eds., *Transnational Connections in Early Modern Theatre* (Manchester, UK: Manchester University Press, 2020).

24. The Frankfurt catalog entry is quoted in W. W. Greg, *The Shakespeare First Folio: Its Bibliographic and Textual History* (Oxford, UK: Oxford University Press, 1955), 3–4.

25. See William H. Sherman, *Used Books: Marking Readers in Renaissance England* (Philadelphia: University of Pennsylvania Press, 2008); Jeffrey Todd Knight, *Bound to Read: Compilations, Collections, and the Making of Renaissance Literature* (Philadelphia: University of Pennsylvania Press, 2013), 16. See also Heidi Brayman Hackel, *Reading Material in Early Modern England: Print, Gender, and Literacy* (Cambridge, UK: Cambridge University Press, 2005).

26. Stephen Best and Sharon Marcus, "Surface Reading: An Introduction," *Representations* 108, no. 1 (2009): 1–21. Regarding these "depths," I owe some of my thinking to the series of papers given by Claire M. L. Bourne, Joshua Calhoun, Megan Heffernan, Adam G. Hooks, Aaron T. Pratt, and Sarah Werner at the 2019 MLA roundtable "Depth of Field: New Dimensions in the Study of Early Modern Books."

27. The term *rediscovery* is more apt than *discovery* throughout this work, since a vast array of library-science research has gone into the conservation and making available of these volumes for scholars today.

28. See András Kiséry, *"Hamlet"'s Moment: Drama and Political Knowledge in Early Modern England* (Oxford, UK: Oxford University Press, 2016), 1–33; Cyndia Susan Clegg, *Shakespeare's Reading Audiences: Early Modern Books and Audience Interpretation* (Cambridge, UK: Cambridge University Press, 2017); and Claire M. L. Bourne, *Typographies of Performance in Early Modern England* (Oxford, UK: Oxford University Press, 2020).

29. For instance, Edward Allde printed the 1592 quarto of Thomas Kyd's *Spanish Tragedy* and George Delamothe's *French Alphabeth* (1595) in octavo. For larger books, Edward Blount published John Florio's Italian-English dictionary (1598, 1611), John Minsheu's Spanish-English dictionary (1623), and Shakespeare's First Folio (1623).

30. For a sample of recent work here, see Lukas Erne, *Shakespeare and the Book Trade* (Cambridge, UK: Cambridge University Press, 2013); Tiffany Stern, ed., *Rethinking Theatrical Documents in Shakespeare's England* (London: Arden Shakespeare, 2020); Tiffany Stern, "Watching as Reading: The Audience and the Written Text in Shakespeare's Playhouse," in *How to Do Things with Shakespeare: New Approaches, New Essays*, ed. Laurie Maguire (Malden, MA: Blackwell, 2008), 136–59; Robert N. Watson, "Shakespeare's New Words," *Shakespeare Survey* 65 (2012): 358–77.

31. Benedict Anderson, *Imagined Communities: Reflections on the Origin and Spread of Nationalism* (London: Verso, 1991), 37–46.

32. Sheldon Pollock, "The Cosmopolitan Vernacular," *Journal of Asian Studies* 57, no. 1 (1998): 6–37, esp. 28. As Pollock makes clear, a process of "philologization" involving grammars and dictionaries was central to these developments (25–26). On vernacularization, see also Sheldon Pollock, "India in the Vernacular Millennium: Literary Culture and Polity, 1000–1500," *Daedalus* 127, no. 3 (1998): 41–74, as well as Pollock's broader study, *The Language of the Gods in the World of Men: Sanskrit, Culture, and Power in Premodern India* (Berkeley: University of California Press, 2006).

33. Sheldon Pollock, "Cosmopolitanism and Vernacular in History," *Public Culture* 12, no. 3 (2000): 591–625, esp. 596.

34. Homi K. Bhabha, "The Vernacular Cosmopolitan," in *Voices of the Crossing: The Impact of Britain on Writers from Asia, the Caribbean and Africa*, ed. Ferdinand Dennis and Naseem Khan (London: Serpent's Tail, 2000), 139.

35. Pollock, "Cosmopolitanism and Vernacular," 604.

36. Anston Bosman, "British Drama as a Polysystem: Visualizing Multilingualism and Mobility," *Shakespeare Studies* 48 (2020): 48.

37. William Shakespeare, *The Tempest*, ed. Virginia Mason Vaughan and Alden T. Vaughan (London: Arden Shakespeare, 1999), 1.2.364–65. On Nebrija and *The Tempest* together, see Stephen Greenblatt, *Learning to Curse: Essays in Early Modern Culture* (London: Routledge, 1990), 22–51; the English translation used here appears on p. 17.

38. Martha C. Nussbaum, "Patriotism and Cosmopolitanism," in *For Love of Country?* (Boston: Beacon, 1996), 4.

39. Timothy Brennan, *At Home in the World: Cosmopolitanism, Now* (Cambridge, MA: Harvard University Press, 1997).

40. Pheng Cheah and Bruce Robbins, eds., *Cosmopolitics: Thinking and Feeling Beyond the Nation* (Minneapolis: University of Minnesota Press, 1998); Carol A. Breckenridge et al., eds. *Cosmopolitanism* (Durham, NC: Duke University Press, 2002); see also Bruce Robbins and Paulo Lemos Horta, eds., *Cosmopolitanisms* (New York: New York University Press, 2017).

41. Jacques Derrida, "On Cosmopolitanism," in *On Cosmopolitanism and Forgiveness*, trans. Mark Dooley and Michael Hughes (London: Routledge, 2001), 22–23.

42. Martha C. Nussbaum, *The Cosmopolitan Tradition: A Noble but Flawed Ideal* (Cambridge, MA: Belknap, 2019), 5–7.

43. Kwame Anthony Appiah, *Cosmopolitanism: Ethics in a World of Strangers* (New York: W. W. Norton, 2006), xvi.

44. Appiah, *Cosmopolitanism*, xvi–xvii. The rise of right-wing nationalist movements, leaders, and governments across the world since the publication of Appiah's book causes these words to read somewhat differently than they did in 2006. For my own purposes, the take-home point is centrally about cosmopolitanism attending to particular contexts rather than making sweeping claims for "the global" or rejecting the concept altogether, on whatever grounds.

45. An exception is the discussion of the work of Hugo Grotius in Nussbaum, *Cosmopolitan Tradition*, 97–140.

46. John Dee, *General and Rare Memorials pertayning to the Perfect Arte of Navigation* (London: John Daye, 1577), sig. G3v. Quoted in Alan B. Farmer, "Cosmopolitanism and Foreign Books in Early Modern England," *Shakespeare Studies* 35 (2007): 61–62.

47. Amanda Anderson, *The Way We Argue Now: A Study in the Cultures of Theory* (Princeton, NJ: Princeton University Press, 2006), 71. Writing from the viewpoint of nineteenth-century British literary studies, Winter Jade Werner observes that Anderson's call remains mostly unanswered today, strangely in spite of the term's rich multiplicities; see *Missionary Cosmopolitanism in Nineteenth-Century British Literature* (Columbus: Ohio State University Press, 2020), 21.

48. Pollock et al., "Cosmopolitanisms," in Breckenridge et al., *Cosmopolitanism*, 9–10.

49. See Margreta de Grazia, Maureen Quilligan, and Peter Stallybrass, eds., *Subject and Object in Renaissance Culture* (Cambridge, UK: Cambridge University Press, 1996); Yates, *Error, Misuse, Failure*; Jeffrey Masten, *Queer Philologies: Sex, Language, and Affect in Shakespeare's Time* (Philadelphia: University of Pennsylvania Press, 2016); and Valerie Traub, *Thinking Sex with the Early Moderns* (Philadelphia: University of Pennsylvania Press, 2016).

50. On the varied meanings of "conversation," see Masten, *Queer Philologies*, 83–86.

51. William Camden, "The Languages," in *Remaines, concerning Britaine: But especially England, and the Inhabitants thereof*, ed. William Camden (London: John Legatt for Simon Waterson, 1614), sig. E3r.

52. Jacques Derrida, *Monolingualism of the Other: or, The Prosthesis of Origin*, trans. Patrick Mensah (Stanford, CA: Stanford University Press, 1998), 5.

53. John Hart, *An Orthographie, conteyning the due order and reason, howe to write or paint thimage of mannes voice, most like to the life or nature* (London: [Henry Denham?] for William Seres, 1569), sig. D4v.

54. Mary Sidney Herbert, "Even Now That Care," in *The Collected Works of Mary Sidney Herbert, Countess of Pembroke*, ed. Michael Brennan, Margaret P. Hannay, and Noel J. Kinnamon, 2 vols. (Oxford, UK: Clarendon, 1998), 1:92–104, lines 29–30.

55. Lodowick Bryskett, *A Discourse of Civill Life: Containing the Ethike part of Morall Philosophie* (London: [R. Field] for William Aspley, 1606), sig. G2v.

56. James Howell, *A New English Grammar, Prescribing as certain Rules as the Language will bear, for Forreners to learn English* (London: for T. Williams, H. Brome, and H. Marsh, 1662), sig. A6r. On Howell's dictionary work, see Werner Hüllen, *English Dictionaries 800–1700: The Topical Tradition* (Oxford, UK: Clarendon, 1999), 202–43.

57. On the ways the play reflects English gender and class tensions, see Peter Erickson, "The Order of the Garter, the Cult of Elizabeth, and Class-Gender Tension in *The Merry Wives of Windsor*," in *Shakespeare Reproduced: The Text in History and Ideology*, ed. Jean E. Howard and Marion F. O'Connor (New York: Methuen, 1987), 116–40; on its sense of English history, see Richard Helgerson, *Adulterous Alliances: Home, State, and History in Early Modern European Drama and Painting* (Chicago: University of Chicago Press, 2000), 57–76; for its articulations of English domesticity, see Wall, *Staging Domesticity*, 90–93, 112–26, as well as Natasha Korda, *Shakespeare's Domestic Economies: Gender and Property in Early Modern England* (Philadelphia: University of Pennsylvania Press, 2002), 76–110; for its sense of English place, see Zucker, *Places of Wit*, 23–53. The play's English middle-class setting, its expressions of sexuality and desire, and the merry wives' agency receive emphasis in

Evelyn Gajowski and Phyllis Rackin, eds., *"The Merry Wives of Windsor": New Critical Essays* (London: Routledge, 2015).

58. Marcus, *Unediting the Renaissance*, 84–88. John Michael Archer discusses how the folio text amplifies city language—including references to non-English people—even as it squeezes out the quarto's distinctive urban scenery; see *Citizen Shakespeare: Freemen and Aliens in the Language of the Plays* (New York: Palgrave Macmillan, 2005), 46–59; see also Zucker, *Places of Wit*, 47–48. Reversing the usual understanding, Elizabeth Zeman Kolkovich examines both texts in relation to England's tradition of regional royal pageants, suggesting the quarto may evince more plainly an appeal to Queen Elizabeth; see "Pageantry, Queens, and Housewives in the Two Texts of *The Merry Wives of Windsor*," *Shakespeare Quarterly* 63, no. 3 (2012): 328–54. For a focused look at the quarto text, see Helen Ostovich, "Bucking Tradition in *The Merry Wives of Windsor*, 1602: Not a Bad Quarto, Really," in Gajowski and Rackin, *New Critical Essays*, 96–106.

59. Rubright, "Incorporating Kate," 473. As Gallagher notes, "Ideas about the past (and the present) which assume the existence of a monoglot nation are at best incomplete and at worst dangerous"; see *Learning Languages*, 211.

60. Lynne Magnusson, "Language," in *The Oxford Handbook of Shakespeare*, ed. Arthur F. Kinney (Oxford, UK: Oxford University Press, 2012), 244–45.

61. Deanne Williams, *The French Fetish from Chaucer to Shakespeare* (Cambridge, UK: Cambridge University Press, 2004), 216; Marianne Montgomery, *Europe's Languages on England's Stages, 1590–1620* (Farnham, UK: Ashgate, 2012), 109–17. See also the English-focused reading in Landreth, "Once More."

62. Parker, *Shakespeare from the Margins*, 116–48, and Kathryn Vomero Santos, "Hosting Language: Immigration and Translation in *The Merry Wives of Windsor*," in *Shakespeare and Immigration*, ed. Ruben Espinosa and David Ruiter (Farnham, UK: Ashgate, 2014), 59–72; with Santos, I employ the term "immigrant" anachronistically to hail non-English outsiders, as well as the terms "stranger" and "foreigner" (the latter could refer to someone from either beyond England or from elsewhere within England). My discussion is also informed by the work of Scott Oldenburg, who argues that in addition to presenting a picture of Englishness, *Merry Wives* "participates in a counter discourse of worldly domesticity whereby multicultural elements find their way into the English home"; see *Alien Albion: Literature and Immigration in Early Modern England* (Toronto: University of Toronto Press, 2014), 149.

63. A longer version of this argument attending more closely to the play's various subplots appears in Andrew S. Keener, "Windsor's World of Words: Multilingualism in *The Merry Wives of Windsor*," *English Literary Renaissance* 51, no. 3 (2021): 409–41.

64. Magnusson, "Language," 248.

65. Margo Hendricks, "Race: A Renaissance Category?," in *A New Companion to English Renaissance Literature and Culture*, ed. Michael Hattaway, 2 vols. (Malden: Blackwell, 2010), 1:536–38.

66. J. W. Lever, "Shakespeare's French Fruits," *Shakespeare Survey* 6 (1953): 79–90; Joseph A. Porter, "More Echoes from Eliot's *Ortho-epia Gallica*, in *King Lear* and *Henry V*," *Shakespeare Quarterly* 37, no. 4 (1986): 486–88; Naseeb Shaheen, "Shakespeare's Knowledge of Italian," *Shakespeare Survey* 47 (1994): 161–69; and Timothy Billings, "Two New Sources for Shakespeare's Bawdy French in *Henry V*," *Notes &*

Queries 52, no. 2 (2005): 202–4. It is intriguing that Field hailed from Shakespeare's hometown and printed both *Venus and Adonis* and *Lucrece*, but Adam G. Hooks offers cautions to critics attempting to link the stationer directly to Shakespeare; see *Selling Shakespeare: Biography, Bibliography, and the Book Trade* (Cambridge, UK: Cambridge University Press, 2016), 35–65.

67. Michael Witmore and Heather Wolfe, "Buzz or Honey? Shakespeare's Beehive Raises Questions," *Collation* (blog), April 21, 2014.

68. Many critics have considered *Merry Wives* and the second tetralogy together; see the prominent example of Williams, *French Fetish*, 211–16. On *Merry Wives*'s date, see Melchiori, ed., 18–30. For my purposes, these plays can be treated as contemporary; see also the language-focused analysis treating the plays together in Tudeau-Clayton, *Shakespeare's Englishes*, 46–92.

69. The most extensive study of the *Colloquia* is R. W. R. Verdeyen's in Noël de Berlaimont, *Colloquia et Dictionariolum Septem Linguarum*, ed. R. W. R. Verdeyen, 3 vols., Vereeninging Derantwerpsche Bibliophilen, Uitgave Nr. 39, 40, 42 (Antwerp: Nederlandsche Boekhandel, 1925–1935), 1:xciii–cxv. On other imprints and for a summary of Verdeyen's account in English, see Caroline B. Bourland, "*The Spanish Schoole-master* and the Polyglot Derivatives of Noël de Berlaimont's *Vocabulare*," *Revue Hispanique* 81, no. 1 (1933): 283–318; see also Hüllen, *English Dictionaries*, 106–18. On Southeast Asian variations of Berlaimont's text, see Su Fang Ng, "Speaking Transnationally: Early Modern European Linguistic Exchanges with Islamic Southeast Asia," *Genre* 48, no. 2 (2015): 289–313.

70. This book and its typography reflect the pattern of "compressed translation" discussed by Coldiron, in which "multiple language versions of a work are not sent out to various readerships, but instead are brought into one textual space"; see *Printers Without Borders*, 26. On the ways this book's columned arrangements facilitated oral practice, see Gallagher, *Learning Languages*, 97; on the relationship between English and Dutch signaled by the typographical strategies of the *Colloquia* and other polyglot wordbooks, see Rubright, *Doppelgänger Dilemmas*, 140–61.

71. Susan E. Phillips, "Schoolmasters, Seduction, and Slavery: Polyglot Dictionaries in Pre-Modern England," *Medievalia et Humanistica*, n.s., 34 (2008): 129–58.

72. Noël de Berlaimont, *Colloquia et Dictionariolum Octo Linguarum* (Delphis [Delft]: ex officina Brunonis Schinkelii, 1598), sig. C6r, D1r. I cite from this orthographically imprecise edition because it is contemporary with both *Henry IV Part 1* and *Merry Wives* and because it was the first complete eight-language version; on this "final form" of the text, see Phillips, "Schoolmasters, Seduction, and Slavery," 130. I cite the English for convenience, but the text appeared in up to eight languages.

73. William Stepney, *The Spanish Schoole-master. Containing Seven Dialogues, according to every day in the weeke, and what is necessarie everie day to be done, wherein is also most plainly shewed the true and perfect pronunciation of the Spanish tongue, toward the furtherance of all those which are desirous to learne the said tongue within this our Realme of England* (London: R. Field for John Harison, 1591), sig. F5v, F6v. There is evidence of several London *Colloquia* editions; see the headnote in STC, s.n. Barlement, Noël van, as well as Phillips, "Schoolmasters, Seduction, and Slavery," 132, and Kathleen Lambley, *The Teaching and Cultivation of the French Language in England during Tudor and Stuart Times* (Manchester, UK: Manchester University Press, 1920), 241–42.

74. William Shakespeare, *King Henry IV: Part 1*, ed. David Scott Kastan (London: Arden Shakespeare, 2002), 2.4.18. All subsequent references to this text will be made parenthetically by act, scene, and line.

75. Helgerson, "Language Lessons," 294.

76. Steven Mullaney, *The Place of the Stage: License, Play, and Power in Renaissance England* (Ann Arbor: University of Michigan Press, 1995), 79.

77. Editors have associated "Rivo" ("Riuo" in quarto and folio) with Spanish and Italian; at any rate, Hal is claiming that this foreign word is something that a drinker would say. As Gallagher notes, language-learning manuals often hailed drinking rituals for the benefit of a reader's cultural competence; see *Learning Languages*, 131–35.

78. Phillips, "Schoolmasters, Seduction, and Slavery," 142–45. While I follow Phillips in emphasizing these dialogues' disorderly and subversive elements, Joyce Boro attends to the link between wooing and language learning in this and other vernacular manuals as evincing a moral example for male readers; see "Multilingualism, Romance, and Language Pedagogy; or, Why Were So Many Sentimental Romances Printed as Polyglot Texts?," in *Tudor Translation*, ed. Fred Schurink (New York: Palgrave Macmillan, 2011), 27–28.

79. Phillips, "Schoolmasters, Seduction, and Slavery," 144.

80. John Florio, *Florio His firste Fruites: which yeelde familiar speech, merie Proverbes, wittie Sentences, and golden sayings* (London: Thomas Dawson for Thomas Woodcocke, 1578), sig. A1v.

81. Rubright, "Incorporating Kate," 478; on Quickly's mobile and ironic approach to the English language, see Tudeau-Clayton, *Shakespeare's Englishes*, 63–64, 67–69.

82. William Shakespeare, *A Most pleasaunt and excellent conceited Comedie, of Syr John Falstaffe, and the merrie Wives of Windsor* (London: T[homas] C[reede] for Arthur Johnson, 1602), sig. B3r. Barbara Traister analyzes Caius's position within the play's English setting in "A French Physician in an English Community," in Gajowski and Rackin, *New Critical Essays*, 121–29; Ostovich comments on the suggestion of "live-in sexual service" between Quickly and Caius in the quarto, but without mentioning any "priuities"; see "Bucking Tradition," 100.

83. See Kastan, ed., 3.3.92, where the Hostess's identity as "Mistress Quickly" is clear. On the array of names and speech prefixes designating this character, see James Mardock's remarks in Rosemary Gaby et al., "To Nell and Back: Revisiting Mistress Quickly," *Renaissance Drama* 47, no. 2 (2019): 212–23.

84. Frances E. Dolan, "Time, Gender, and the Mystery of English Wine," in *Gendered Temporalities in the Early Modern World*, ed. Merry E. Wiesner-Hanks (Amsterdam: Amsterdam University Press, 2018), 20.

85. Dolan, "Time, Gender," 21.

86. Barbara Sebek, "'Wine and Sugar of the Best and the Fairest': Canary, the Canaries, and the Global in Windsor," in *Culinary Shakespeare: Staging Food and Drink in Early Modern England*, ed. David B. Goldstein and Amy L. Tigner (Pittsburgh: Duquesne University Press, 2016), 53.

87. Magnusson, "Language," 253–54.

88. In this way, my method, here and across the following chapters, draws on the approach employed by Rubright, "Incorporating Kate," e.g., 470, as well as Traub, *Thinking Sex*, e.g., 4.

89. John Florio, *A Worlde of Wordes, Or Most copious, and exact Dictionarie in Italian and English* (London: Arnold Hatfield for Edw. Blount, 1598), sig. 2P3v; Randle Cotgrave, *A Dictionarie of the French and English Tongues* (London: Adam Islip, 1611), sig. 4A4v.

90. *Oxford English Dictionary*, online ed., s.v. "riesling."

91. Parker, *Shakespeare from the Margins*, 126. Meanwhile, Magnusson reads Mistress Quickly's "go-between" status as evoking "a linguistic culture in transit between orality and literacy"; see "Language," 251.

92. Williams proposes that this moment "also foregrounds the connections between conquest and courtship dramatized in *Henry V*"; see *French Fetish*, 214.

93. Falstaff represents an oppositional force in my reading, but Tudeau-Clayton classes Falstaff alongside Mistress Quickly as a figure of verbal extravagancy; see *Shakespeare's Englishes*, 73–74.

94. For Williams, Falstaff "attempts to disrupt the wives' specifically Anglophone political and linguistic identities by construing them as always, already adulterated by the French" (*French Fetish*, 222). For Landreth, Falstaff turns Mistress Ford's honesty "into a Latin that he imagines to be necessarily sexual; and only then does he propose to enjoy that sexuality, to English her" ("Once More," 427–28). Parker reads Falstaff's translation alongside the Latin lesson: "*Construing* or *construction* . . . appear, then, in the sense of interpreting or translating—out of Latin or honesty—into English" (*Shakespeare from the Margins*, 119).

95. Melchiori offers a conflated textual solution, which I follow; the folio text reads "He hath studied her will; and translated her will: out of honesty, into English" (sig. D3r), while the quarto reads "He hath studied her well, out of honestie, / Into English" (sig. B2r).

96. Santos, "Hosting Language," 61.

97. See Greene, *Unrequited Conquests*, 1–33.

98. Parker, *Shakespeare from the Margins*, 124.

99. Williams, *French Fetish*, 221

100. Williams, *French Fetish*, 223.

101. The word "Pible," rather than "Bible," surfaces in Caius's speech, and this orthography/pronunciation resembles Evans's tendency to substitute "p" for "b" (2.3.7). Meanwhile, by saying "absence" for "absent" (2.2.79), it seems Quickly adopts Evans's turns of phrase also; see Melchiori, ed., 195n, 182n.

102. Archer, *Citizen Shakespeare*, 56.

103. Santos, "Hosting Language," 67.

104. Tudeau-Clayton, *Shakespeare's Englishes*, 57–58, 69–71; Parker, *Shakespeare from the Margins*, 135.

105. Reading the moment as invoking England's wine trade is Sebek, "Wine and Sugar," 51.

106. Archer supposes the offstage Germans are in fact Evans and Caius in disguise, and links the scene to courtly German visitors to Elizabethan England; see *Citizen Shakespeare*, 57. In Santos's account, which most accords with my view, "Whether Evans and Caius physically disguise themselves as Germans or fabricate the idea of a German presence behind the scenes, the play's immigrants make calculated use of another alien identity in order to undo the Host's treatment of the strangers, which

remains predictably consistent in his interaction with the offstage Germans"; see "Hosting Language," 68.

107. Landreth, "Once More," 432. On the theater as a "one-large-room schoolhouse," see Robert N. Watson, "Shakespeare's New Words," 360.

108. Parker, *Shakespeare from the Margins*, 126.

109. Jean E. Howard comments on the transgressive nature of Falstaff's disguise in "Crossdressing, the Theatre, and Gender Struggle in Early Modern England," *Shakespeare Quarterly* 39, no. 4 (1988): 423–24. On the gendered implications of theatrical crossdressing, see Stephen Orgel, *Impersonations: The Performance of Gender in Shakespeare's England* (Cambridge, UK: Cambridge University Press, 1996).

110. Ben Jonson, *Every Man Out of His Humour*, ed. Randall Martin, in *The Cambridge Edition of the Works of Ben Jonson*, ed. David Bevington, Martin Butler, and Ian Donaldson, 7 vols. (Cambridge, UK: Cambridge University Press, 2012), 1:249–428; 2.3.167. Korda reads Evans's observation against the play's discourse of female discretion in English households; see *Domestic Economies*, 94–95.

111. Noting the connection to *Midsummer* is Parker, *Shakespeare from the Margins*, 136; on the pedagogical subtexts of this moment in *Midsummer*, see Enterline, *Shakespeare's Schoolroom*, 1–8. Helgerson reads Falstaff's transformation as representing both transgressive witchcraft and its containment (*Adulterous Alliances*, 67–71).

112. On this "old tale" and its position within a broader spatial discourse of forests, see Zucker, *Places of Wit*, 40–41.

113. John M. Steadman, "Falstaff as Actaeon: A Dramatic Emblem," *Shakespeare Quarterly* 14 no. 3 (1963): 231–44.

114. Wall, *Staging Domesticity*, 123; reading Falstaff as "a stolen stag" is Zucker, *Places of Wit*, 39.

115. See, e.g., Williams, *French Fetish*, 225; Landreth, "Once More," 446; Wall, *Staging Domesticity*, 124.

116. As critics have noticed, Evans's language during the majority of this scene appears in the quarto and folio texts without its characteristic accent, possibly suggesting, as Pittenger puts it, how the "monarchy transforms all differences into uniformity" ("Dispatch Quickly," 402). Zucker argues that Evans is integrated into the Windsor society, while Caius is not (*Places of Wit*, 44–46). In any case, Falstaff can still recognize Evans's foreign-sounding voice and links him with transformation.

117. Pittenger, "Dispatch Quickly," 391. In similarly English terms, Wall views this "faux fairy queen" guise as amplifying Quickly's role as "Shakespeare's most notorious housekeeper"; see *Staging Domesticity*, 116. Helgerson reads Quickly as a figure for Elizabeth (*Adulterous Alliances*, 72–73); Korda blends these domestic and monarchical aspects in her interpretation (*Domestic Economies*, 102–10); Kolkovich views the servant woman as exhibiting "tribute to Queen Elizabeth" in the quarto text, while in the folio, she "steps into Elizabeth's role and rules Windsor Castle" ("Pageantry, Queens, and Housewives," 348).

118. Zucker, *Places of Wit*, 23.

119. Appiah, *Cosmopolitanism*, 98.

120. Peter Holland, "*The Merry Wives of Windsor*: The Performance of Community," *Shakespeare Bulletin* 23, no. 2 (2005): 5–18; particularly regarding the figure of Caius, see Traister, "French Physician," 126–28.

121. Roland Greene, *Five Words: Critical Semantics in the Age of Shakespeare and Cervantes* (Chicago: University of Chicago Press, 2013); Patricia Parker, *Shakespearean Intersections: Language, Contexts, Critical Keywords* (Philadelphia: University of Pennsylvania Press, 2018).

CHAPTER 2

1. Thomas Kyd, *The Spanish Tragedy*, ed. Clara Calvo and Jesús Tronch (London: Arden Shakespeare, 2013), 4.4.9, s.d. 2, 1–2. Unless otherwise noted, all subsequent quotations from Kyd's play will be taken from this edition and cited parenthetically in the text by act, scene, and line.

2. Lukas Erne, *Beyond "The Spanish Tragedy": A Study of the Works of Thomas Kyd* (Manchester, UK: Manchester University Press, 2001), 65.

3. S. F. Johnson, "*The Spanish Tragedy*, or Babylon Revisited," in *Essays on Shakespeare and Elizabethan Drama in Honor of Hardin Craig*, ed. Richard Holsey (London: Routledge, 1963), 23–36; Frank Ardolino, "'Now Shall I See the Fall of Babylon': *The Spanish Tragedy* as a Reformation Play of Daniel," *Renaissance and Reformation* 14, no. 1 (1990): 49–55.

4. See J. R. Mulryne, "Nationality and Language in Thomas Kyd's *The Spanish Tragedy*," in *Travel and Drama in Shakespeare's Time*, ed. Jean-Pierre Maquerlot and Michèle Villems (Cambridge, UK: Cambridge University Press, 1996), 87–105; and Janette Dillon, *Language and Stage in Medieval and Renaissance England* (Cambridge, UK: Cambridge University Press, 1998), 162–87.

5. On the ways *The Spanish Tragedy*'s polyglossia contributed productively to a broader culture of real and represented confusion, rather than expressing hostility toward foreignness, see William N. West, "'But This Will Be a Mere Confusion': Real and Represented Confusions on the Elizabethan Stage," *Theater Journal* 60, no. 2 (2008): 217–33.

6. Carla Mazzio, *The Inarticulate Renaissance: Language Trouble in an Age of Eloquence* (Philadelphia: University of Pennsylvania Press, 2009), 97.

7. In her unpublished dissertation, Kathryn Vomero Santos offers a fascinating reading of Kyd's tragedy grounded in early modern discourses of learned translation, which asserts along the same lines that Hieronimo's polyglot spectacle "prohibits communication among his performers as well as with their multiple audiences on stage and in the theater"; see "Staging Translation in Early Modern English Drama" (PhD diss., New York University, 2013), 35.

8. Mazzio, *Inarticulate Renaissance*, 95, 104.

9. See Eugene Hill, "Senecan and Vergilian Perspectives in *The Spanish Tragedy*," *English Literary Renaissance* 15, no. 2 (1985): 143–65, esp. 144, though I focus on contemporary and vernacular elements, rather than classical, as Hill does. In this way, I complement Eric Griffin's focus on ethnicity and empire in the play, which from a Spanish-specific perspective challenges much of the national and Protestant-focused work of earlier studies; see *English Renaissance Drama and the Specter of Spain: Ethnopoetics and Empire* (Philadelphia: University of Pennsylvania Press, 2012), 67–96. On complications to the linear pattern of translation presupposed by *translatio imperii*, see A. E. B. Coldiron, *Printers Without Borders: Translation and Textuality in the Renaissance* (Cambridge, UK: Cambridge University Press, 2015), 20–30.

10. Marianne Montgomery, *Europe's Languages on England's Stages, 1590–1620*

(Farnham, UK: Ashgate, 2012), 82–83. On the stage as a similarly efficacious place for lessons in Dutch and its "jumbled" relation to English, see Marjorie Rubright, *Doppelgänger Dilemmas: Anglo-Dutch Relations in Early Modern English Literature and Culture* (Philadelphia: University of Pennsylvania Press, 2014), 89–109.

11. Jason Lawrence, *Who the Devil Taught Thee So Much Italian? Italian Language Learning and Literary Imitation in Early Modern England* (Manchester, UK: Manchester University Press, 2005), 5–6, 19–29. On the advantages of foreign language training among London's gentry, courtiers, and emerging middle classes, see Vivian Salmon, "The Study of Foreign Languages in Seventeenth Century England," in *Language and Society in Early Modern England: Selected Essays, 1981–1984* (Amsterdam: John Benjamins, 1996), 173–76.

12. Roger Ascham, *The Scholemaster. Or plaine and perfite way of teachyng children, to understand, write, and speake, the Latin tong* (London: John Daye, 1570), sig. L1v, H1r.

13. More generally on Ascham's technique for Latin, including its precedents, see William E. Miller, "Double Translation in English Humanistic Education," *Studies in the Renaissance* 10 (1963): 163–74, and Jeff Dolven, *Scenes of Instruction in Renaissance Romance* (Chicago: University of Chicago Press, 2007), 41–44. On the bodily, emotionally fraught dimensions of this practice as expressed in *A Midsummer Night's Dream*, see Lynn Enterline, *Shakespeare's Schoolroom: Rhetoric, Discipline, Emotion* (Philadelphia: University of Pennsylvania Press, 2012), 1–8.

14. Though it used increasingly sophisticated printing techniques, this effort built on existing traditions. For medieval precedents in the instruction of French, see both Douglas A. Kibbee, *For to Speke French Trewely: The French Language in England, 1000–1600: Its Status, Description, and Instruction* (Amsterdam: John Benjamins, 1991), 1–93; and Kathleen Lambley, *The Teaching and Cultivation of the French Language in England during Tudor and Stuart Times* (Manchester, UK: Manchester University Press, 1920), 3–57. I should note that while I am highlighting the cosmopolitan potential of the *Alvearie*'s translingual substance, Margaret Tudeau-Clayton emphasizes how the dictionary presses for "a stable system bound to and guaranteed by the centre of power"; see *Shakespeare's Englishes: Against English* (Cambridge, UK: Cambridge University Press, 2020), 89.

15. George Koppelman and Daniel Wechsler, *Shakespeare's Beehive: An Annotated Elizabethan Dictionary Comes to Light* (New York: Axletree, 2014). Responding skeptically to this claim are Michael Witmore and Heather Wolfe, "Buzz or Honey? Shakespeare's Beehive Raises Questions," *Collation* (blog), April 21, 2014; and Adam G. Hooks, "Shakespeare's Beehive 2.0," *Anchora* (blog), March 2016.

16. See Margaret Ascham's dedication to Cecil in Ascham, *Scholemaster*, sig. ☞2r–☞2v; and Baret's Latin dedication to Cecil in John Baret, *An Alvearie or Triple Dictionarie, in Englishe, Latin, and French* (London: Henry Denham, 1574), sig. *2r (missigned *3r) –*3r. On Baret's "yong beginners," see James Sledd, "Baret's *Alvearie*, an Elizabethan Reference Book," *Studies in Philology* 43, no. 2 (1946), 151; as well as DeWitt T. Starnes, *Renaissance Dictionaries: English-Latin and Latin-English* (Austin: University of Texas Press, 1954), 184.

17. John Gallagher, *Learning Languages in Early Modern England* (Oxford, UK: Oxford University Press, 2019), 41.

18. Starnes, *Renaissance Dictionaries*, 186–88.

19. On various early modern discourses of imitation, see G. W. Pigman III, "Versions of Imitation in the Renaissance," *Renaissance Quarterly* 33, no. 1 (1980): 1–32.

20. On "gathering and framing," see Mary Thomas Crane, *Framing Authority: Sayings, Self, and Society in Sixteenth-Century England* (Princeton, NJ: Princeton University Press, 1993); on the "relationship between lexicography and different kinds of topographical writing and collection," see John Considine, *Dictionaries in Early Modern Europe: Lexicography and the Making of Heritage* (Cambridge, UK: Cambridge University Press, 2008), 11.

21. John Baret, *An Alvearie or Quadruple Dictionarie, containing foure sundrie tongues: namelie, English, Latine, Greeke, and French* (London: Henry Denham, 1580), sig. *4v, University of Chicago PA2364.B3.

22. Baret, *Alvearie or Quadruple Dictionarie*, sig. 2C3v, 4I2r, Columbia University KENT PA2364 .B35 1580g. On discipline in early modern education, see Enterline, *Shakespeare's Schoolroom*, 33–61. On the word *phrontisteru[m]*, see *Oxford English Dictionary*, online ed., s.v. "phrontistery," which entered the English language in 1623.

23. A reproduction appears in Koppelman and Wechsler, *Shakespeare's Beehive*, 221.

24. Claudius Hollyband, *The French Schoolemaister, wherein is most plainlie shewed, the true and most perfect way of pronouncinge of the Frenche tongue, without any helpe of Maister or teacher* (London: William How for Abraham Veale, 1573), sig. A2r–A4r. Also commenting on Hollyband's publications and double translation methods are Montgomery, *Europe's Languages*, 6–11; and Nina Levine, *Practicing the City: Early Modern London on Stage* (New York: Fordham University Press, 2016), 89–98. On Hollyband's life more broadly, see Mark Eccles, "Claudius Hollyband and the Earliest French-English Dictionaries," *Studies in Philology* 83, no. 1 (1986): 51–61; and Laurent Berec, *Claude de Sainliens: Un Huguenot Bourbonnais au Temps de Shakespeare* (Paris: Orizons, 2012).

25. William Thomas, *Principal Rules of the Italian Grammer, with a Dictionarie for the better understandynge of Boccace, Petrarcha, and Dante* (Londini [London]: in aedibus H. Wykes, 1567), University of Chicago PC1109.T452 c.1; a title page inscription reads, "Robert Sackevill oweth [owneth] this booke." On the importance of Italian for Thomas's English language advocacy, see Cathy Shrank, *Writing the Nation in Reformation England, 1530–1580* (Oxford, UK: Oxford University Press, 2006), 116–24; on Thomas more broadly, see E. R. Adair, "William Thomas: A Forgotten Clerk of the Privy Council," in *Tudor Studies*, ed. R. W. Seton-Watson (London: Longmans, 1924), 133–60.

26. In fact, Oxford would become a thriving center for vernacular language studies over the next decades; see Lawrence, *Who the Devil*, 9–10; as well as Lambley, *The Teaching and Cultivation of the French Language*, 198–210. On the prominence of French at English universities during the late medieval period, though, see Lambley, *Teaching and Cultivation*, 6, 15–16; Kibbee, *Speke French Trewely*, 74–75.

27. Claudius Hollyband, *The Frenche Littelton. A Most Easie, Perfect, and Absolute way to learne the frenche tongue* (London: Thomas Vautroullier, 1566 [1576]), sig. *2r. On the date of this book, which has been a point of confusion among scholars since it appears to read "1566," see Alfred W. Pollard, "Claudius Hollyband and his *French Schoolmaster* and *French Littelton*," *The Library*, 3rd ser., 6, no. 21 (1915): 77–93,

reprinted with the permission of The Bibliographical Society (Nendeln, Liechtenstein: Kraus Reprint, 1966).

28. On the long afterlife of Hollyband's texts, see Gallagher, *Learning Languages*, 77–78.

29. Richard Halpern, *The Poetics of Primitive Accumulation: English Renaissance Culture and the Genealogy of Capital* (Ithaca, NY: Cornell University Press, 1991), 19–60; Jenny C. Mann, *Outlaw Rhetoric: Figuring Vernacular Eloquence in Shakespeare's England* (Ithaca, NY: Cornell University Press, 2012); Enterline, *Shakespeare's Schoolroom*, 33–61. More broadly on education in Renaissance England, see Dolven, *Scenes of Instruction*, 15–64.

30. On the relative paucity of guides to the Spanish language in early modern England, see Gustav Ungerer, *Anglo-Spanish Relations in Tudor Literature* (Bern: Francke, 1956), 169; and Edmund Valentine Campos, "Imperial Lexicography and the Anglo-Spanish War," in *Remapping the Mediterranean World in Early Modern English Writings*, ed. Goran V. Stanivukovic (New York: Palgrave, 2007), 77. On the way an octolingual ballad printed on vellum and paper expresses these tensions, see Coldiron, *Printers Without Borders*, 199–254. More generally on Anglo-Spanish relations, see Barbara Fuchs, *The Poetics of Piracy: Emulating Spain in English Literature* (Philadelphia: University of Pennsylvania Press, 2013); Griffin, *Specter of Spain*; and Hill, "Senecan and Vergilian Perspectives," 152–57.

31. John Thorius, trans., *The Spanish Grammer: With certeine Rules teaching both the Spanish and French tongues*, by Antonio del Corro (London: John Wolfe, 1590), Bodleian Library 4° C 71(1) Art.

32. On Wolfe's Italian printing, see Harry R. Hoppe, "John Wolfe, Printer and Publisher, 1579–1601," *The Library*, 4th ser., 14, no. 3 (1933): 241–88, esp. 243; Clifford Chalmers Huffman, *Elizabethan Impressions: John Wolfe and His Press* (New York: AMS, 1988), 1–47; Michael Wyatt, *The Italian Encounter with Tudor England: A Cultural Politics of Translation* (Cambridge, UK: Cambridge University Press, 2005), 185–99, 262–64; and Lawrence, *Who the Devil*, 187–201. See also the bibliographical account of Wolfe's Italian imprints in Denis B. Woodfield, *Surreptitious Printing in England, 1550–1640* (New York: Bibliographical Society of America, 1973).

33. Something like this technique can be found in Baret's and Hollyband's books and also appears in Wolfe's trilingual edition of Baldassare Castiglione's *The Courtier*; see Coldiron, *Printers Without Borders*, 160–98. Also commenting on this typographic strategy is Steven K. Galbraith, "'English' Black-Letter Type and Spenser's *Shepheardes Calendar*," *Spenser Studies* 23 (2008): 13–40; and Rubright, *Doppelgänger Dilemmas*, 110–61. Addressing language and typeface in Noël de Berlaimont's *Colloquia et Dictionariolum*, which I will discuss more in chapter 4, is Susan E. Phillips, "Schoolmasters, Seduction, and Slavery: Polyglot Dictionaries in Pre-Modern England," *Medievalia et Humanistica*, n.s., 34 (2008): 138–42. For an account that groups the national significance of black-letter type with a sense of cultural nostalgia, see Zachary Lesser, "Typographic Nostalgia: Play-Reading, Popularity, and the Meanings of Black Letter," in *The Book of the Play: Playwrights, Stationers, and Readers in Early Modern England*, ed. Marta Straznicky (Amherst: University of Massachusetts Press, 2006), 99–126. On how handwriting anticipated and accompanied these typographic developments, see Jonathan Goldberg, *Writing Matter: From the Hands of the English Renaissance* (Stanford, CA: Stanford University Press, 1990), 13–55.

34. András Kiséry, *"Hamlet"'s Moment: Drama and Political Knowledge in Early Modern England* (Oxford, UK: Oxford University Press, 2016), 244–48.

35. Caroline B. Bourland, "Gabriel Harvey and the Modern Languages," *Huntington Library Quarterly* 4, no. 1 (1940): 94. On the disbinding of early modern *Sammelbände*, see Jeffrey Todd Knight, *Bound to Read: Compilations, Collections, and the Making of Renaissance Literature* (Philadelphia: University of Pennsylvania Press, 2013), esp. 21–53.

36. See lot no. 971 in *Bibliotheca Heberiana: Catalogue of the Library of the Late Richard Heber, Esq.*, vol. 6 (London: W. Nicol, 1835), 73. Evidence suggests that the "Comoediae" mentioned by Harvey on the Lentulo title page refers to Terence, *Le Comedie di Terentio Volgari* (Vinegia [Venice]: Aldus, 1546), Houghton Library *EC.2623 Zz546t, which features fore-edge markings corresponding to those in the other volumes (excepting the *Italian Grammar*, which has gilted leaves obscuring any markings).

37. Virginia F. Stern, *Gabriel Harvey: His Life, Marginalia, and Library* (Oxford, UK: Clarendon, 1979), 156–58. See also Claudius Hollyband, *The Pretie and wittie Historie of Arnalt & Lucenda: With certen Rules and Dialogues set foorth for the learner of th'Italian tong* (London: Thomas Purfoote, 1575), British Library C.60.a.1(2); and John Florio, *Florio His firste Fruites: which yeelde familiar speech, merie Proverbes, wittie Sentences, and golden sayings* (London: Thomas Dawson for Thomas Woodcocke, 1578), Houghton Library *EC H2623 Zz578f; the latter features Harvey's inscription, "Now to the 4. books of Guazzo, the sweetest & daintiest of Italian Dialogues. Then to Eliots French Dialogues: as fine as those Italian, & more pleasant" (sig. 2E1v).

38. On the vibrant language-learning practices of university students nonetheless, see Gallagher, *Learning Languages*, 19–23.

39. On *The Images of the Old Testament*'s place within a "radiant pattern" of multilingual *figure* publications issued in Lyon, see Coldiron, *Printers Without Borders*, 112–19.

40. Bourland, "Gabriel Harvey," 88.

41. Warren Boutcher, "'A French Dexterity, & an Italian Confidence': New Documents on John Florio, Learned Strangers and Protestant Humanist Study of Modern Languages in Renaissance England from c. 1547 to c. 1625," *Reformation* 2, no. 1 (1997): 51–52; Joyce Boro, "Multilingualism, Romance, and Language Pedagogy; or, Why Were So Many Sentimental Romances Printed as Polyglot Texts?" in *Tudor Translation*, ed. Fred Schurink (New York: Palgrave Macmillan, 2011), 24–25.

42. See Lisa Jardine and Anthony Grafton, "'Studied for Action': How Gabriel Harvey Read His Livy," *Past and Present* 129 (November 1990): 30–78. On Harvey's complementary interest in jests and wordplay, see Chris Stamatakis, "'With Diligent Studie, but Sportingly': How Gabriel Harvey Read His Castiglione," *Journal of the Northern Renaissance* 5, published online November 9, 2013.

43. While it occurs across several of Harvey's language manuals, it might be misleading to call this a language-learning motto, for it occurs in other contexts; I thank Matthew Symonds for this point. For instance, the phrase appears in Princeton University's copy of Thomas Tusser, *Five Hundred Pointes of Good Husbandrie* (London: Henrie Denham, 1580), sig. C3r, V3r (where Harvey mentions Ascham and Mulcaster); the item is RHT 16th-99a. Inscriptions in this book appear in English, Greek, Italian, Latin, and Spanish.

44. Lodovico Dolce, *Medea tragedia di M. Lodovico Dolce* (Venetia [Venice]: Domenico Farri, 1566), sig. A1v, Folger Shakespeare Library PQ4621 .D3 M4 1566a Cage.

45. Euripides, *Hecuba, & Iphigenia in Aulide Euripidis tragoediae,* trans. Desiderius Erasmus (Venetiis [Venice]: in aedibus Aldi, 1507), fol. 7r–7v, Houghton Library *E.C.H263.ZZ507e. See also Stern, *Gabriel Harvey,* 173–74. Wolfe was Harvey's publisher during the 1590s; on their relationship, see Huffman, *Elizabethan Impressions,* 49–67, and Hoppe, "John Wolfe," 267–69.

46. On further connotations of "sweet" and its affective dimensions, see Jeffrey Masten, *Queer Philologies: Sex, Language, and Affect in Shakespeare's Time* (Philadelphia: University of Pennsylvania Press, 2016), 69–82.

47. Stern, *Gabriel Harvey,* 157. Harvey makes specific mention of Thomas in his annotations in Florio, *Firste Fruites,* sig. A3r, Houghton Library *EC H2623 Zz578f.

48. Harvey's copies of Pierre du Ploiche, *A treatise in Englishe and Frenche, right necesarie, and profitable for all young Children* (London: Jhon Kingston for Gerard Dewes), sig. H3r, Huntington Library RB 53922; and Richard Perceval, *Bibliotheca Hispanica. Containing a Grammar; with a Dictionarie in Spanish, English, and Latine; gathered out of divers good Authors: very profitable for the studious of the Spanish toong* (London: John Jackson for Richard Watkins, 1591), sig. F3r, Huntington Library RB 56972. My translation.

49. Stefano Guazzo, *La Civil Conversatione* (Venetia [Venice]: Gratioso Perchacino, 1581), sig. ††6r, British Library C.60.a.1(1).

50. Enterline, *Shakespeare's Schoolroom,* 9–32; Mann, *Outlaw Rhetoric,* 1–28.

51. Montgomery, *Europe's Languages,* 15.

52. The quoted phrase is in Mazzio, *Inarticulate Renaissance,* 95.

53. Richard Mulcaster, *The First Part of the Elementarie which Entreateth Chefelie of the right writing of our English tung* (London: Thomas Vautroullier, 1582), sig. K4v; for a reading of Mulcaster's *Elementarie* as an imperializing text, see Goldberg, *Writing Matter,* 27–41.

54. Tudeau-Clayton, *Shakespeare's Englishes,* 193.

55. See Mulcaster's commendatory verse in Baret, *Alvearie or Triple Dictionarie,* sig. *4v; a longer version appears in the 1580 edition (sig. A4v). See also Claudius Hollyband, *Campo di Fior or else The Flourie Field of Foure Languages* (London: Thomas Vautroullier, 1583), sig. *3v. On the printer Thomas Vautrollier, see William LeFanu, "Thomas Vautrollier, Printer and Bookseller," *Proceedings of the Huguenot Society of London* 20 (1959): 12–25.

56. This multilingual theater in Latin and English offered the earliest known instance of a commercial boys' acting company; see Erne, *Beyond "The Spanish Tragedy,"* 2. According to Enterline, "The theater's ubiquitous presence in schoolroom practice may have gone relatively unexamined in part because of a long-standing, anachronistic distinction between rhetoric and drama"; see *Shakespeare's Schoolroom,* 41.

57. Jeffrey Masten, "Playwrighting: Authorship and Collaboration," in *A New History of Early English Drama,* ed. John D. Cox and David Scott Kastan (New York: Columbia University Press, 1997), 376–77.

58. This is my own count, based on Calvo and Tronch's edition and using the 1602 additions. Montgomery counts only two Spanish words (*Europe's Languages,* 77); to these, I add Hieronimo's "corregidor" (3.13.58), a word John Minsheu defines

as "*a corrector, an amender. Also an officer in Spaine, the chiefe Iusticer or gouernor of a towne*" in *A Dictionarie in Spanish and English* (London: Edm. Bollifant, 1599), sig. G6r. Of course, the boundaries of English were subject to much debate at this time.

59. Mazzio, *Inarticulate Renaissance*, 136.

60. Dillon, *Language and Stage*, 162–87; see also Richard Foster Jones, *The Triumph of the English Language: A Survey of Opinions Concerning the Vernacular from the Introduction of Printing to the Restoration* (Stanford, CA: Stanford University Press, 1953); and the influential account in Benedict Anderson, *Imagined Communities: Reflections on the Origin and Spread of Nationalism* (London: Verso, 1983), 37–46.

61. Dillon, *Language and Stage*, 164.

62. This is according to my survey of all surviving quarto editions, omitting proper nouns, stage directions, and epistles among characters; exceptions include Pedringano's "Signor" (2.1.41), which appears in roman, and 3 Citizen's "*eiectione firmae*" (3.13.62), which appears in a mix of roman, italic, and black letter. A type shortage might explain the mixing-in of black letter with italic and roman in Q6.

63. Montgomery, *Europe's Languages*, 83, 17. See this point about typography and performance made compellingly in Claire M. L. Bourne, *Typographies of Performance in Early Modern England* (Oxford, UK: Oxford University Press, 2020); see also Rubright, *Doppelgänger Dilemmas*, 113.

64. Dillon, *Language and Stage*, 165. English translations of foreign words in Kyd's play are supplied from Calvo and Tronch's edition, unless otherwise noted.

65. John Minsheu, *Pleasant and Delightfull Dialogues in Spanish and English, profitable to the learner, and not unpleasant to any other Reader* (London: Edm. Bollifant, 1599), sig. I4v. Saint Martin refers properly to a type of white wine.

66. Arthur Freeman, *Thomas Kyd: Facts and Problems* (Oxford, UK: Clarendon, 1967), 68.

67. Freeman, *Thomas Kyd*, 68.

68. As Jonathan Goldberg notes on many occasions, italic hands were associated with literariness, universities, and prestige; see *Writing Matter*, 1–2, 8–9, 50–55.

69. See Enterline, *Shakespeare's Schoolroom*, 33–61, as well as Dolven, *Scenes of Instruction*, 30–32. On the accompanying oral, conversational use of sententious quotations and proverbs taken out of plays, see András Kiséry, "'Flowers for English Speaking': Play Extracts and Conversation," in *Rethinking Theatrical Documents in Shakespeare's England*, ed. Tiffany Stern (London: Arden Shakespeare, 2020), 155–74.

70. See James Sanforde, trans., *The Garden of Pleasure: Contayninge most pleasante Tales, worthy deeds and witty sayings of noble Princes & learned Philosophers, Moralized. No lesse delectable, than profitable*, by Lodovico Guicciardini (London: Henry Bynneman, 1573), sig. H2v; as well as George Puttenham, *The Arte of English Poesie. Contrived into three Bookes: The first of Poets and Poesie, the second of Proportion, the third of Ornament* (London: Richard Field, 1589), sig. 2I3v.

71. Mazzio, *Inarticulate Renaissance*, 113.

72. William Shakespeare, *Hamlet*, ed. Ann Thompson and Neil Taylor (London: Arden Shakespeare, 2006), 3.2.99. According to Erne, who attributes an earlier version of *Hamlet* to Kyd, "Kyd's contribution to the dramatic architecture of Shakespeare's *Hamlet* was substantial"; see *Beyond "The Spanish Tragedy,"* 6.

73. Hieronimo first laments his son's murder with "My grief no heart, my

thoughts no tongue can tell" (3.2.67), and after his polyglot playlet, he asserts that his "tongue is tuned to tell his latest tale" (4.4.84) before biting it out (4.4.187 s.d.). On potential class discrepancies between Hieronimo's "tell what to speak" and Balthazar's "tell how to speak," see James R. Siemon, "Sporting Kyd," *English Literary Renaissance* 24, no. 3 (1994): 558–59.

74. Lynette M. F. Bosch, *Art, Liturgy, and Legend in Renaissance Toledo: The Mendoza and the Iglesia Primada* (University Park: Pennsylvania State University Press, 2000), 32–37; a very substantive study of the Escuela is Juan Francisco Rivera Recio, *La Iglesia de Toledo en el Siglo XII [i.e. doce] (1086–1208)* (Toledo, Spain: Disputatión Provincial, 1976).

75. Bosch, *Art, Liturgy, and Legend*, 36.

76. On the Jerome subtext, see Frank Ardolino, "Hieronimo as Saint Jerome in *The Spanish Tragedy*," *Etudes Anglaises* 36, no. 4 (1983): 435–37.

77. Bourland, "Gabriel Harvey," 96.

78. Richard Carew, trans., *The Examination of mens Wits. In whicch, by discouering the varietie of natures, is shewed for what profession each one is apt, and how far he shall profit therein*, by Juan Huarte (London: Adam Islip for Richard Watkins, 1594), sig. H4v.

79. William Phiston, trans., *The Most Pleasaunt and delectable Historie of Lazarillo de Tormes, a Spanyard: and of his Marvellous Fortunes and Adversities. The second part*, by Diego Hurtado de Mendoza (London: T[homas] C[reede] for John Oxenbridge, 1596), sig. I4v.

80. Caroline B. Bourland, "*The Spanish Schoole-master* and the Polyglot Derivatives of Noël de Berlaimont's *Vocabulare*," *Revue Hispanique* 81, no. 1 (1933): 293–94, 317–18.

81. Juliet Fleming, "The French Garden: An Introduction to Women's French," *English Literary History* 56, no. 1 (1989): 19–51.

82. Fleming, "French Garden," 46; recognizing two female readers of Erondelle is Boro, "Multilingualism, Romance," 20–21. Gallagher notes that while French was deemed appropriate for women, female conversation generally was "freighted with sexual and moral suspicion," a topic I will return to in chapter 5; see *Learning Languages*, 118.

83. Richard Mulcaster, *Positions wherin those Primitive Circumstances be Examined, which are Necessarie for the Training up of children, either for skill in their booke, or health in their bodie* (London: Thomas Vautrollier for Thomas Chare [Chard], 1581), sig. X4r. Chamberleine's inscribed books are: Claudius Hollyband, *The French Schoole-maister* (London: William Howe for Abraham Veale, 1582), Columbia University Plimpton 448 1582 Sa2; and Robert Sherwood, *The French Tutour* (London: [H. Lownes] for Robert Young, 1625), University of Chicago PC2109.S58.

84. Anston Bosman, "Renaissance Intertheater and the Staging of Nobody," *English Literary History* 71, no. 3 (2004): 562–64.

85. See Michael Hattaway, *Elizabethan Popular Theatre: Plays in Performance* (London: Routledge, 1982), 110; and Gordon Braden, *Renaissance Tragedy and the Senecan Tradition* (New Haven, CT: Yale University Press, 1985), 215.

86. Mazzio, *Inarticulate Renaissance*, 102.

87. Halpern, *Poetics of Primitive Accumulation*, 47.

88. Christopher Crosbie, *Revenge Tragedy and Classical Philosophy on the Early Modern Stage* (Edinburgh: Edinburgh University Press, 2018), 41–87.

89. John Florio, *Florios Second Frutes, To be gathered of twelve Trees, of divers but delightsome tastes to the tongues of Italian and Englishmen* (London: for Thomas Woodcock, 1591), sig. A3r.

90. Crosbie, *Revenge Tragedy*, 73. According to Crosbie, "revenge functions as a subset of the vegetative capacity" (76); similarly, noticing a "framework of cultivation and fruition" in revenge tragedy is Lisa Hopkins, "What's Hercules to Hamlet? The Emblematic Garden in *The Spanish Tragedy* and *Hamlet*," *Hamlet Studies* 21, no. 1–2 (1999): 123.

91. On the importance of the arbor as "synecdoche for the playhouse," see Vin Nardizzi, *Wooden Os: Shakespeare's Theatres and England's Trees* (Toronto: University of Toronto Press, 2013), 84–111, esp. 87.

92. Crosbie, *Revenge Tragedy*, 77–79; likewise, Nardizzi suggests that "Isabella displaces vengeance onto the garden's fertility and then onto her body" (*Wooden Os*, 86).

93. On the ways dramatic "plots" and illustrations could come together in the space of the book, and for the role of the illustrated *Spanish Tragedy* quartos within those dynamics, see Bourne, *Typographies of Performance*, 185–228, esp. 206–7.

94. On the multinational costumes in Hieronimo's play, see Mazzio, *Inarticulate Renaissance*, 102.

95. *Oxford English Dictionary*, online ed., s.v. "confusion," 4. All subsequent references to the *OED* in the main text will appear parenthetically.

96. On these dominant critical interpretations, see Johnson, "*Spanish Tragedy*"; Ardolino, "Now Shall I See"; Mulryne, "Nationality and Language," 88; Geoffrey Aggeler, "The Eschatological Crux in *The Spanish Tragedy*," *Journal of English and Germanic Philology* 86, no. 3 (1987): 319–31. For a recent interpretation rooted in the Acts of the Apostles, see Griffin, *Specter of Spain*, 91–92.

97. Thomas McAlindon, *English Renaissance Tragedy* (Vancouver: University of British Columbia Press, 1986), 55.

98. Watson, "Shakespeare's New Words," 360.

99. Tiffany Stern, "Watching as Reading: The Audience and the Written Text in Shakespeare's Playhouse," in *How to Do Things with Shakespeare: New Approaches, New Essays*, ed. Laurie Maguire (Malden, MA: Blackwell, 2008), 138. See also the range of essays in Stern's recent edited collection of essays unpacking the relationships between print and performance, *Rethinking Theatrical Documents in Shakespeare's England* (London: Arden Shakespeare, 2020).

100. Stern, "Watching as Reading," 140–41.

101. Thomas Kyd, *The Spanish Tragedie: Containing the lamentable end of Don Horatio, and Bel-Imperia: with the pittiful death of olde Hieronimo* (London: W. W. for T. Pavier, 1602), title page. On dramatic title pages as presenting performances familiar to the reader, see also Jeffrey Masten, *Textual Intercourse: Collaboration, Authorship, and Sexualities in Renaissance Drama* (Cambridge, UK: Cambridge University Press, 1997), 113–21.

102. On the play's date, see Erne, *Beyond "The Spanish Tragedy,"* 58.

103. See W. W. Greg, *A Bibliography of the English Printed Drama to the Restoration*, 4 vols. (London: Bibliographical Society at Oxford University Press, 1939–1959), 1.187–91; and Alan B. Farmer and Zachary Lesser, eds., *DEEP: Database of Early English Playbooks*, 2007, which lists ten editions, tied with *Richard II* for third

below *Mucedorus* (sixteen) and *Henry IV Part 1* (eleven). Using different criteria (reprints for professional public performance within a twenty-five-year period), Peter W. M. Blayney ranks *The Spanish Tragedy* as third, with seven editions, on par with *Henry IV Part 1* but below *Doctor Faustus*'s eight editions; see Blayney, "The Publication of Playbooks," in Cox and Kastan, *New History of Early English Drama*, 388.

104. Roslyn L. Knutson, "*Henslowe's Diary* and the Economics of Play Revision, 1592–1603," *Theater Research International* 10, no. 1 (1985): 9. The play seems to have remained in theater repertories until 1614.

105. Erne, *Beyond "The Spanish Tragedy,"* 127–35.

106. Thomas Middleton, *The Roaring Girle. Or Moll Cut-Purse* (London: [Nicholas Okes] for Thomas Archer, 1611), sig. A3r, quoted by Stern, who adds, "his approach must reflect the theater's attitude"; see "Watching as Reading," 139.

107. Sarah Wall-Randell, "What Is a Staged Book? Books as 'Actors' in the Early Modern English Theatre," in Stern, *Rethinking Theatrical Documents*, 128–51. On stage props and the effects they could have across performances, see Andrew Sofer, *The Stage Life of Props* (Ann Arbor: University of Michigan Press, 2003).

108. For the epistemological consequences of these possibilities, which I will discuss in more depth, see Margreta de Grazia, "Soliloquies and Wages in the Era of Emergent Consciousness," *Textual Practice* 9, no. 1 (1995): 67–92.

109. Ben Jonson, *Every Man in His Humour (Q)*, ed. David Bevington, in *The Cambridge Edition of the Works of Ben Jonson*, eds. David Bevington, Martin Butler, and Ian Donaldson, 7 vols. (Cambridge, UK: Cambridge University Press, 2012), 1:111–227, 1.3.101–4; all subsequent references will be cited parenthetically. This edition represents the 1601 quarto text. On the "Englishing" of the Italianate names in this play for publication in Jonson's dramatic folio—arguably a kind of "translation" in its own way—see *Every Man in His Humour (F)*, ed. David Bevington, in *Cambridge Edition*, 4:621–22.

110. Stern, "Watching as Reading," 145.

111. Calvo and Tronch, eds., 240n. On the circulation and recirculation of "Go by, Hieronimo," see William N. West, "Intertheatricality," in *Early Modern Theatricality*, ed. Henry S. Turner (Oxford, UK: Oxford University Press, 2013), 162–66; on the dynamic of stage characters quoting *sententiae* within a culture of viral quotations, see Kiséry, "Flowers for English Speaking," 160. Jonson also received payments for "his adicians in geronymo," though it is doubtful these are the additions that survive today; see Erne, *Beyond "The Spanish Tragedy,"* 119–22.

112. Wall-Randell, "Staged Book," 133. The first known performance of *Every Man in His Humor* was in 1598; at this time, the most "new" edition of Kyd's play was Q3 (1594).

113. According to Hill, the "playlet is an enacted pun on translation in different senses and different media. The real 'passing' involved is the *translatio imperii*—to England, to English" ("Senecan and Vergilian Perspectives," 163). Offering further intriguing possibilities beyond the scope of my discussion are two editions of *The Tragedye of Solyman and Perseda* (1592?, 1599), which accompanied Kyd's play on the book market.

114. Ardolino, "Now Shall I See," 54.

115. Thomas Kyd, *The Spanish Tragedie, Containing the lamentable end of Don Horatio, and Bel-imperia: with the pittiful death of olde Hieronimo* (London: Edward

Allde for Edward White, 1592), sig. K3r. For stage directions and paratextual elements, all following citations will refer to this Q1 text, referring parenthetically in the main text by signature.

116. Dolven, *Scenes of Instruction*, 7; my emphasis in early modern titles only, with specific reference to Thomas's *Principal Rules*, Hollyband's *French Littelton*, and the extended title page remarks for a grammar appended to Minsheu's *Pleasant and Delightfull Dialogues*.

117. de Grazia, "Soliloquies and Wages," 73–81.

118. Scott McMillin, "The Book of Seneca in *The Spanish Tragedy*," *Studies in English Literature 1500–1900* 14, no. 2 (1974): 201–8.

119. Mazzio, *Inarticulate Renaissance*, 129–30. Lodovico Dolce, whose translations of classical drama were owned and annotated by Harvey, also translated Seneca into Italian.

120. On "arguments" and "abstracts" in early modern drama, see Tiffany Stern, *Documents of Performance in Early Modern England* (Cambridge, UK: Cambridge University Press, 2009), 63–80.

121. Montgomery, *Europe's Languages*, 86; see also Johnson, "*Spanish Tragedy*," 24.

122. I use "publisher" here in the sense of "making public" and "every public reader"; see *OED*, s.v. "publish," I.2a.

Chapter 3

1. Philip Sidney, *The Poems of Sir Philip Sidney*, ed. William A. Ringler Jr. (Oxford, UK: Clarendon, 1962), 172. As other analyses suggest, this alliterative line may also gesture to a poorly rendered link between sound and meter.

2. The latter quotation is included in the extended title of William Thomas, *Principal Rules of the Italian Grammer, with a Dictionarie for the better understandyng of Boccace, Petrarcha, and Dante* (London: Thomas Berthelet, 1550). This bilingual dictionary was the first of its kind in England and was owned by figures including Robert Sackville, discussed in the previous chapter, and, as it appears—as I will discuss subsequently—Mary Sidney Herbert.

3. The word "denisend" is a textual variant, appearing in the authoritative 1598 text edited by Mary Sidney Herbert. Readings in other editions include "deuised wit" and "wit disguised," which sustain a sense of alteration or artifice even if they obscure explicit foreign connotations.

4. On the denizen in early modern England, see Jeffrey Masten, "More or Less: Editing the Collaborative," *Shakespeare Studies* 29 (2001): 120–21; and Alan Stewart, "'Euery Soyle to Mee is Naturall': Figuring Denization in William Haughton's *English-men for My Money*," *Renaissance Drama*, n.s., 35 (2006): 55–81. On the early modern alien in England more broadly, see James Shapiro, *Shakespeare and the Jews*, 1997, 20th anniversary ed. with a new preface by the author (New York: Columbia University Press, 2016), chap. 6.

5. Sidney echoes this stance in his *Apologie for Poetrie*, describing the English language's eloquence as "one time with so farre fette words, that may seeme Monsters: but must seeme straungers to any poore English man. Another tyme, with coursing of a Letter, as if they were bound to followe the method of a Dictionary"; see *An Apologie for Poetrie* (London: [James Roberts] for Henry Olney, 1595), sig. K4r. On Sidney's position within a reformation ideology of "plainness" eschewing

foreign qualities or verbal "extravagancy," see Margaret Tudeau-Clayton, *Shakespeare's Englishes: Against English* (Cambridge, UK: Cambridge University Press, 2020), 175.

6. For this epithet for Philip Sidney, see John Harington, trans., *Orlando Furioso in English Heroical Verse*, by Ludovico Ariosto (London: Richard Field, 1591), sig. L4v.

7. Mary Sidney Herbert, "Even Now That Care," in *The Collected Works of Mary Sidney Herbert, Countess of Pembroke*, ed. Michael Brennan, Margaret P. Hannay, and Noel J. Kinnamon, 2 vols. (Oxford, UK: Clarendon, 1998), 1:92–104, lines 29–30. This authoritative edition of Sidney Herbert's works will hereafter be referred to as *CW*. Along with "Even Now That Care," "The Triumph of Death" (1:255–82), *A Discourse of Life and Death* (1:208–54), and *The Tragedy of Antony* (1:139–207) will be cited parenthetically in the main text by line number, while references to Sidney Herbert's other works and any editorial remarks from *CW* will be cited in the endnotes by volume, page, and, as applicable, line. I will refer to the poet and playwright as Mary Sidney Herbert, Sidney Herbert, the Countess of Pembroke, or the countess (her title at the time *The Tragedy of Antony* was first published).

8. See Tina Krontiris, *Oppositional Voices: Women as Writers and Translators in the English Renaissance* (London: Routledge, 1992), 64–77; Elaine V. Beilin, *Redeeming Eve: Women Writers of the English Renaissance* (Princeton, NJ: Princeton University Press, 1987), 121–50; Mary Ellen Lamb, *Gender and Authorship in the Sidney Circle* (Madison: University of Wisconsin Press, 1990), 115–41; and Danielle Clarke, *The Politics of Early Modern Women's Writing* (Harlow, UK: Longman, 2001), 80–118; as well as Paulina Kewes, "'A Fit Memorial for the Times to Come . . .': Admonition and Topical Allusion in Mary Sidney's *Antonius* and Samuel Daniel's *Cleopatra*," *Review of English Studies*, n.s., 63, no. 259 (2011): 243–64. Urging critics to hold Garnier's original text in focus is Richard Hillman, "De-centring the Countess's Circle: Mary Sidney Herbert and Cleopatra," *Renaissance and Reformation* 28, no. 1 (2004): 61–79; see also Howard B. Norland, *Neoclassical Tragedy in Elizabethan England* (Newark: University of Delaware Press, 2009), 204–11. There is a considerable range of opinion regarding the proper way to refer to Sidney Herbert's closet drama; I will refer to the work as "*The Tragedy of Antony*" in keeping with the 1595 octavo second edition, though modernizing the spelling.

9. Margaret P. Hannay, *Philip's Phoenix: Mary Sidney, Countess of Pembroke* (Oxford, UK: Oxford University Press, 1990), 106–42; Victor Skretkowicz, "Mary Sidney Herbert's *Antonius*, English Philhellenism and the Protestant Cause," *Women's Writing* 6, no. 1 (1999): 7–25. See also Edward Wilson-Lee, "Women's Weapons: Country House Diplomacy in the Countess of Pembroke's French Translations," in *The Culture of Translation in Early Modern England and France, 1500–1660*, ed. Tania Demetriou and Rowan Tomlinson (Basingstoke: Palgrave Macmillan, 2015), 128–44.

10. John Donne, "Upon the Translation of the Psalmes by Sir Philip Sydney, and the Countesse of Pembroke His Sister," in *The Divine Poems*, ed. Helen Gardner (Oxford, UK: Clarendon, 1952), 33–35, lines 50–55.

11. On the relationship between *The Tragedy of Antony* and the comparatively freer translation of Garnier's *Cornélie* undertaken by Thomas Kyd, see: Karen Raber, *Dramatic Difference: Gender, Class, and Genre in the Early Modern Closet Drama* (Newark: University of Delaware Press, 2001), 70–77; Lukas Erne, *Beyond "The Spanish*

Tragedy": A Study of the Works of Thomas Kyd (Manchester, UK: Manchester University Press, 2001), 203–16; and Norland, *Neoclassical Tragedy*, 218–33.

12. John Florio, trans., *The Essayes Or Morall, Politike and Millitarie Discourses of Lo: Michaell de Montaigne*, by Michel de Montaigne (London: Val. Sims for Edward Blount, 1603), sig. A2r. For critical perspectives on Florio's gendered terms, see Mary Ellen Lamb, "The Cooke Sisters: Attitudes toward Learned Women in the Renaissance," in *Silent but for the Word: Tudor Women as Patrons, Translators, and Writers of Religious Works*, ed. Margaret P. Hannay and Margaret Patterson (Kent, OH: Kent State University Press, 1985), 115–17; as well as Raber's discussion of Sidney Herbert in *Dramatic Difference*, 65–77. I will examine Florio's position in this debate in greater depth in chapter 5.

13. Jonathan Goldberg, "The Countess of Pembroke's Literal Translation," in *Subject and Object in Renaissance Culture*, ed. Margreta de Grazia, Maureen Quilligan, and Peter Stallybrass (Cambridge, UK: Cambridge University Press, 1996), 326.

14. *Oxford English Dictionary*, s.v. "translation," II.10. All subsequent references to the *OED* in the main text will appear parenthetically.

15. See Hebrews 11:5 in the Latin Vulgate, as well as *The Holy Bible, Containing The Old and New Testaments*, ed. Josiah Forshall and Frederic Madden, 4 vols. (Oxford, UK: Oxford University Press, 1850), 4:498.

16. See, for example, *The new Testament in Englishe after the greeke translation annexed wyth the translation of Erasmus in Latin* (Londini: in officina Thomae Gaultier pro J. C[awood], 1550), sig. 2D4v. The Geneva Bible, which would have been more familiar to Sidney Herbert for its Calvinist significance, offers "taken away" instead, with printed marginalia pointing also to "Enochs and Elias taking vp"; see *The Bible and Holy Scriptures Conteyned in the Old and Newe Testament* (Geneva: Rouland Hall, 1560), sig. 3D1r–3D1v; all successive citations to this text will refer to it as the Geneva Bible. However, both the Bishop's Bible of 1568 and the King James Bible of 1611 would use "translated" in this verse; see both *The holie Bible conteyning the olde Testament and the newe* (London: Richarde Jugge, 1568), sig. R4v (sustained in the 1572 revision); and *The Holy Bible, conteyning the Old Testament, and the New* (London: Robert Barker, 1611), hereafter cited as the King James Bible, sig. X5r. John Milton's use appears in *A Maske Presented At Ludlow Castle, 1634* (London: [Augustine Mathewes] for Humphrey Robinson, 1637), sig. C1r.

17. John Ludham, trans., *A speciall Treatise of Gods Providence, and of comforts against all kinds of crosses & calamities to be fetched from the same*, by Andreas Hyperius ([London]: John Wolfe, [1588]), sig. 2I2r.

18. Peter Allibond, trans., *The Golden Chayne of Salvation*, by Hermann Rennecher (London: Valentine Simmes for Thomas Man, 1604), sig. R7r. Clarifying that such transport could point to heaven or hell, another sermon noted that the "soule of the vngodly is translated immediatlie after death to paine"; see Robert Rollock, *Lectures upon the First and Second Epistles of Paul to the Thessalonians* (Edinburgh: Robert Charteris, [1606]), sig. O8v.

19. This, of course, was in addition to the term's current and more common meanings, such as substitution of one thing for another (*OED*, "change," I.1a) and "to give and receive reciprocally" (I.2a), which often crop up in the mercantile contexts examined in the next chapter.

20. See also the reading "change" in the King James Bible, sig. 2Z5r.

21. William Shakespeare, *The Tempest*, ed. Virginia Mason Vaughan and Alden T. Vaughan (London: Arden Shakespeare, 2011), 1.2.401. "Sea-change," "a change wrought by the sea . . . an alteration or metamorphosis, a radical change," is original to Shakespeare; see *OED*.

22. John Baret, *An Alvearie or Triple Dictionarie, in Englishe, Latin, and French* (London: Henry Denham, 1574), sig. M3v; John Florio, *A Worlde of Wordes, Or Most copious, and exact Dictionarie in Italian and English* (London: Arnold Hatfield for Edw. Blount, 1598), sig. V4v.

23. William Shakespeare, *A Midsummer Night's Dream*, ed. Sukanta Chaudhuri (London: Arden Shakespeare, 2017), 3.1.110, 114–15.

24. John Minsheu, *A Dictionarie in Spanish and English* (London: Edm. Bollifant, 1599), sig. C1r.

25. Edmund Spenser, *The Mutabilitie Cantos*, ed. Sheldon P. Zitner (London: Nelson, 1968), 6.1.3–5.

26. Thomas Hawkins, trans., *The Holy Court. Or The Christian Institution of Men of Quality. With Examples of those who in Court have flourished in Sanctity*, by Nicholas Caussin (Paris [Saint-Omer]: [English College Press], 1626), sig. V4v–X1r.

27. Thomas Stocker, trans., *Divers Sermons of Master John Calvin, concerning the Divinitie, Humanitie, and Nativitie of our Lorde Jesus Christe*, by John Calvin (London: [Thomas Dawson] for George Byshop, 1581), sig. Z2r.

28. Thomas Wilson, *A Christian Dictionary, Opening the signification of the chiefe wordes dispersed generally through Holie Scriptures of the Old and New Testament, tending to increase Christian knowledge* (London: W[illiam] Jaggard, 1612), sig. 2I6r.

29. Commonplace book, Danby family of Yorkshire, approximately 1570–1625, Huntington Library mssHM 60413, fol. 74r.

30. John Dee, *General and Rare Memorials pertayning to the Perfect Arte of Navigation* (London: John Daye, 1577), sig. G3v; quoted in Alan B. Farmer, "Cosmopolitanism and Foreign Books in Early Modern England," *Shakespeare Studies* 35 (2007): 61–62. My discussion of "cosmopolite" follows Farmer's useful account; on the overlapping religious and linguistic dimensions of "stranger" that shade into this subject, see Tudeau-Clayton, *Shakespeare's Englishes*, 153–62.

31. Thomas Adams, *The Divells Banket. Described in foure Sermons* (London: Thomas Snodham for Ralph Mab, 1614), sig. Y3v.

32. John Vicars, *A Prospective Glasse to Looke Into Heauen, or The Caelestiall Canaan described* (London: W. Stansby for John Smethwicke, 1618), sig. E3r.

33. Richard Field issued two Thomas Preston publications, *Apologia Cardinalis Bellarimini pro iure principum* (Cosmopoli, 1611) and *Rogeri Widdringtoni Catholici Angli Responsio apologetica* (Cosmopoli, 1612); Thomas Creede printed William Welwood's *De domino maris* with a Cosmopoli imprint in 1615. The "Cosmopoli" edition of Pietro Aretino's *Ragionamenti*, which I will discuss more in chapter 5, appeared in 1660.

34. On this document, which is Petyt MS 538.43.14 at the Inner Temple Library, London, see Mary Sidney Herbert, "*The Triumph of Death*: A Critical Edition in Modern Spelling of the Countess of Pembroke's Translation of Petrarch's *Trionfo della Morte*," ed. Gavin Alexander, *Sidney Journal* 17, no. 1 (1999): 2–18; as well as *CW* 1:264–65. Parenthetical citations to the poem as it appears in *CW* will be made in the main text by part and by line number. On the possibility that Sidney Herbert

was responsible for more *Trionfi* translations featuring representations of Cleopatra, see Hannay, *Philip's Phoenix*, 107; and *The Triumph of Death and Other Unpublished and Uncollected Poems*, ed. Gary F. Waller (Salzburg: Institut für Englische Sprache und Literatur, 1977), 18.

35. *Triumph of Death*, ed. Waller, 17.

36. Here, Sidney Herbert's Laura assumes a less passive and more eloquent character than the representation in Thomas Morley's earlier English rendering; see *CW* 1:265–66, 1:269–70.

37. Andrew S. Keener, "A 1562 Petrarchan Italian-English Dictionary Inscribed by 'Maria Sidney,'" *Sidney Journal* 36, no. 1 (2018): 41–52.

38. Keener, "Petrarchan Italian-English Dictionary," 43–45.

39. That "Maria sidney" appears below rather than above these Italian lines (along with pen trials) could suggest an autograph rather than a commonplace book–style attribution or ascription; for this point I am indebted to Heather Wolfe. I have not been able to ascertain which edition of Petrarch the annotator was using.

40. While "pertain" connotes regard, concern, or relation today, in Renaissance England the word could also signal belonging or possession (*OED*, "pertain," 1b).

41. For these thoughts, I am indebted to Jeffrey Masten and Heather Wolfe, who also helped me to reflect on the variability of handwriting within a person's own lifetime due to age, mood, writing speed, etc.

42. Jason Lawrence, *Who the Devil Taught Thee So Much Italian? Italian Language Learning and Literary Imitation in Early Modern England* (Manchester, UK: Manchester University Press, 2005), 14, 34.

43. Historical Manuscripts Commission, *Report on the Manuscripts of Lord De L'Isle and Dudley Preserved at Penshurst Place*, 6 vols. (London: HMSO, 1925–66), 1:381. The *Concetti* volume survives at Penshurst today; see Germaine Warkentin, Joseph L. Black, and William R. Bowen, eds., *The Library of the Sidneys of Penshurst Place Circa 1665* (Toronto: University of Toronto Press, 2013), 15.

44. Andrew Strycharski, "Some Verses of Henry and Mary Dudley Sidney and Prince Edward's 'Little School,'" *American Notes & Queries* 24, no. 4 (2011): 253; according to Beilin, the Countess of Pembroke's "literary apprenticeship may owe more to her humanist parents than to her brother"; see *Redeeming Eve*, 123.

45. Keener, "Petrarchan Italian-English Dictionary," 47.

46. Keener, "Petrarchan Italian-English Dictionary," 47.

47. On the use of "marigold" to refer to Mary Sidney Herbert, see Hannay, *Philip's Phoenix*, 114–15. However, on account of two names inscribed on the title page, "Edwardus" and "Jaffri Sponer," it is important to keep in mind the words of Joseph L. Black: "Other ownership marks . . . indicate that [printed books] did not remain long in the family after the deaths of Henry and Mary [Dudley Sidney] in 1586"; see "The Sidneys and Their Books," in *The Ashgate Research Companion to the Sidneys, 1500–1700*, ed. Margaret P. Hannay, Mary Ellen Lamb, and Michael G. Brennan, 2 vols. (Burlington, VT: Ashgate, 2015), 2:4. By 1598, John Florio's much more robust Italian-English dictionary was available in any case.

48. *CW* 1:3, 1:255. This figure also might have been a domestic servant; see John Gallagher, *Learning Languages in Early Modern England* (Oxford, UK: Oxford University Press, 2019), 19.

49. Margaret P. Hannay, "'Your Vertuous and Learned Aunt': The Countess of

Pembroke as a Mentor to Mary Wroth," in *Reading Mary Wroth: Representing Alternatives in Early Modern England*, ed. Naomi J. Miller and Gary F. Waller (Knoxville: University of Tennessee Press, 1991), 15–34.

50. The Clarendon editors use the 1599 Penshurst manuscript as copy-text; on the whereabouts of these manuscripts, see *CW* 1:47–49. On the extensive reworking of the Psalms as a conservative form of pious practice, rather than indecisive "tinkering" or stylistic improvement, see Danielle Clarke, "The Countess of Pembroke and the Practice of Piety," *Literature Compass* 9, no. 3 (2012): 252–61. On the Psalm translations as a political project, see Margaret P. Hannay, "'Doo What Men May Sing': Mary Sidney and the Tradition of Admonitory Dedication," in Hannay and Patterson, *Silent but for the Word*, 163–64.

51. Beilin, *Redeeming Eve*, 145. This encouragement also included princely council on Anglo-Spanish relations; see Jaime Goodrich, *Faithful Translators: Authorship, Gender, and Religion in Early Modern England* (Evanston, IL: Northwestern University Press, 2014), 113–28.

52. See *CW* 1:45–47. See also Margaret P. Hannay, "Re-revealing the Psalms: Mary Sidney, Countess of Pembroke, and Her Early Modern Readers," in *Psalms in the Early Modern World*, ed. Lynda Phyllis Austern, Kari Boyd McBride, and David L. Orvis (Burlington, VT: Ashgate, 2011), 226–27.

53. Sidney Herbert, "*Triumph of Death*," ed. Alexander, 2–3.

54. Thomas Moffett, *The Silkewormes, and their Flies: Lively described in verse* (London: V[alentine] S[immes] for Nicholas Ling, 1599), sig. A3r.

55. See Anne Lake Prescott, "The Countess of Pembroke's Ruins of Rome," *Sidney Journal* 23, no. 1–2 (2005): 1–17; Beilin, *Redeeming Eve*, 148. Meanwhile, finding "a highly appropriate impression of urgency" in Psalm 57 is Gary F. Waller, *Mary Sidney, Countess of Pembroke: A Critical Study of Her Writings and Literary Milieu* (Salzburg: Institut für Anglistik and Amerikanistik, 1979), 193.

56. *CW* 2:104, lines 51–52.

57. On this trope and on the accompanying clothing metaphors at work here, see Hannay, "Re-revealing the Psalms," 222–26; as well as Goodrich, *Faithful Translators*, 119–20. Furthermore, for some readers of the Psalms, "change" could have resonated with connotations of music or sound in keeping with David's celebrated method of divine praise; see *OED*, "change," I.9a.

58. Waller, *Mary Sidney*, 116; see also Anne Lake Prescott, "Mary Sidney's *Antonius* and the Ambiguities of French History," *Yearbook of English Studies* 38, no. 1 (2008): 231. On Mary Sidney Herbert's "ruinish" poetic vocabulary in the Psalm translations, see Prescott, "Countess of Pembroke's Ruins," 3–10. The specifics of Sidney Herbert's role as patron of poetry and drama have been much debated; see Mary Ellen Lamb, "The Myth of the Countess of Pembroke: The Dramatic Circle," *Yearbook of English Studies* 11 (1981): 194–202; and "The Countess of Pembroke's Patronage," *English Literary Renaissance* 12, no. 2 (1982): 162–79.

59. Edmund Spenser, *Complaints. Containing sundrie small Poemes of the Worlds Vanitie* (London: for William Ponsonbie, 1591), sig. A3v.

60. Spenser, *Mutabilitie Cantos*, 7.56.2–3.

61. Lamb, *Gender and Authorship*, 127–32; as well as Waller, *Mary Sidney*, 133–36.

62. On particular techniques used by the Countess of Pembroke in carrying out this translation, as well as points of comparison with Edward Aggas's earlier English

version, see Diane Bornstein, "The Style of the Countess of Pembroke's Translation of Philippe de Mornay's *Discourse de la vie et de la mort*," in Hannay and Patterson, *Silent but for the Word*, 126–48.

63. Beilin, *Redeeming Eve*, 128; on elements of transnational diplomacy in this double volume, see Wilson-Lee, "Women's Weapons," 128–44. Though there are parallels between the two works, Sidney Herbert's rendering of *Marc Antoine* seems to endorse a more secular, Stoic perspective than Mornay's treatise—already present in Garnier's text of course—in which suicide offers a welcome refuge from the world's unavoidable mutability (even if Cleopatra's death is deferred); see Hillman, "De-centring the Countess's Circle," 71–75; Skretkowicz, "Mary Sidney Herbert's *Antonius*," 10; and *CW* 1:143.

64. The 1595 octavo edition features only the tragedy and reads instead: "*The Tragedie of Antonie. Doone into English by the Countesse of Pembroke*." On the "out-of-into" formulation as it accompanied translations in early modern England, see Kathryn Vomero Santos, "Hosting Language: Immigration and Translation in *The Merry Wives of Windsor*," in *Shakespeare and Immigration*, ed. Ruben Espinosa and David Ruiter (Farnham, UK: Ashgate, 2014), 61–64.

65. Beilin, *Redeeming Eve*, 131. Putting this in more mild terms is Raber, who finds "Antony pondering the extent to which his identity and destiny have been shaped by Cleopatra's influence"; see *Dramatic Difference*, 60.

66. Christopher Marlowe, *Edward the Second*, ed. Charles R. Forker (Manchester, UK: Manchester University Press, 1994), 1.1.50, 54.

67. Krontiris, *Oppositional Voices*, 72.

68. *CW*, 1:142.

69. Robert Garnier, *Les Tragedies de Robert Garnier Conseiller du Roy* (Paris: Mamert Patisson for Robert Estienne, 1585), sig. F12v–G1r; here and hereafter, English translations from this edition are all my own. This is recognized as the edition Mary Sidney Herbert consulted (see *CW* 1:147); all other references to Garnier's text will be to this edition and will appear parenthetically in the discussion. On Garnier's dramatization of civil war, see Gillian Jondorf, *Robert Garnier and the Themes of Political Tragedy in the Sixteenth Century* (Cambridge, UK: Cambridge University Press, 1969), 76–99.

70. There has been much comment on Mary Sidney Herbert's particularly free treatments of Garnier's chorus, but see especially Coburn Freer, "Mary Sidney: Countess of Pembroke," in *Women Writers of the Renaissance and Reformation*, ed. Katharina Wilson (Athens: University of Georgia Press, 1987), 486–89; as well as Coburn Freer, *The Poetics of Jacobean Drama* (Baltimore: Johns Hopkins University Press, 1981), 206–8. Waller supposes that the experimental treatment of the chorus anticipates Sidney Herbert's English renderings of the Psalms and quantitative verse experimentation more generally; see *Mary Sidney*, 118–28.

71. Kewes, "A Fit Memorial for the Times," 248. Kewes is concerned with an allegorical reading of Garnier's Caesar as a Machiavellian Philip II figure; this is most evident in act 4.

72. Raber, *Dramatic Difference*, 64.

73. Skretkowicz, "Mary Sidney Herbert's *Antonius*," 15–17. The translator mentions Plutarch in "The Argument" preceding the play and seems indebted to North's English rendering in the text proper; see *CW*, 1:153, 150.

74. On representations of Cleopatra throughout the early modern period, see Mary Morrison, "Some Aspects of the Treatment of the Theme of Antony and Cleopatra in the Tragedies of the Sixteenth Century," *Journal of European Studies* 4, no. 2 (1974): 113–25.

75. *CW*, 1:146; see also Skretkowicz, "Mary Sidney Herbert's *Antonius*," 15–16.

76. Kewes, "A Fit Memorial for the Times," 250. Queen Elizabeth also received praise from Mary Sidney Herbert both as the just Astraea and as a divinely empowered King David figure; see Beilin, *Redeeming Eve*, 139–44. However, for an analysis emphasizing Sidney Herbert's more critical views of Elizabeth, see Danielle Clarke, "The Politics of Translation and Gender in the Countess of Pembroke's *Antonie*," *Translation and Literature* 6, no. 2 (1997): 149–66. For the point about Philip II as monoglot, I am indebted to Emily Wood.

77. Lamb, *Gender and Authorship*, 132. Similarly, Waller remarks on Cleopatra's "unfaltering allegiance"; see *Mary Sidney*, 113.

78. On the gendered significance of Cleopatra's assumption of blame, see Raber, *Dramatic Difference*, 55–65.

79. For this point, I am grateful to Amanda Zoch.

80. Liz Oakley-Brown, *Ovid and the Cultural Politics of Translation in Early Modern England* (Burlington, VT: Ashgate, 2006), 61.

81. In Golding's Ovid, the mother's attempt to tear the branches down results in bloodshed: "The daughter that was rent / Cride spare vs mother spare I pray, for in the shape of tree / The bodies and the flesh of vs your daughters wounded bee"; see Ovid, *The xv Bookes of P. Ovidius Naso, entytuled Metamorphosis*, trans. Arthur Golding (London: Willyam Seres, 1567), sig. D4v.

82. On the ways Sidney Herbert's poetic commemoration of her brother functions strikingly as a kind of embalming, see Whitney Sperrazza, "Mary Sidney's Postmortem Poetics," *Shakespeare Studies* 49 (2021): 175–80.

83. Claudius Hollyband, *A Dictionarie French and English: Published for the benefite of the studious in that language* (London: T[homas O[rwin] for Thomas Woodock, 1593), sig. 2H4v; see also the entry for *tradurre*, which includes "*to bring, to turne, to conuert*," in Florio, *Worlde of Wordes*, sig. 2N3v.

84. Beilin, *Redeeming Eve*, 133, and Clarke, *Early Modern Women's Writing*, 89. Beilin is not convinced by Krontiris's claim that the countess's translation "purifies [Cleopatra] by purging her love from political motives" (*Oppositional Voices*, 69–70), and contrasts the Egyptian queen with the more divine and sanctified figure of Laura in "The Triumph of Death." Viewing both women as Stoic "models of negation" is Lamb, *Gender and Authorship*, 141. The Clarendon editors state that even if Cleopatra and Laura display opposite tendencies, "both women are eloquent and both die nobly" (*CW*, 1:267).

85. On the use of similar "coupling" language in the countess's elegy for Philip Sidney, see Hillman, "De-centring the Countess's Circle," 65–66.

86. *CW*, 1:151; Hollyband's lexicon defines *vomir* as "*to parbreake, to vomit, to spue*" (*Dictionarie*, sig. 2I8r).

87. With varying degrees of connection to Mary Sidney Herbert, these works include Thomas Kyd's *Cornelia*, Samuel Daniel's *Cleopatra*, Samuel Brandon's *Virtuous Octavia*, William Shakespeare's *Antony and Cleopatra*, and Elizabeth Cary's *Tragedy of Mariam*.

CHAPTER 4

1. Anthony uses "outlandish" to describe the foreign traders; see William Haughton, *Englishmen for My Money*, in *Three Renaissance Usury Plays*, ed. Lloyd Edward Kermode (Manchester, UK: Manchester University Press, 2009), 165–274, 2.3.317. Unless noted otherwise, all citations of Haughton's play will refer to this edition and will appear parenthetically by act, scene, and line. Like other recent studies of Haughton's play, this chapter will use "foreigner," "alien," and "stranger" indiscriminately, though these words could point in different directions in early modern England. On "stranger," see Jeffrey Masten, "More or Less: Editing the Collaborative," *Shakespeare Studies* 29 (2001): 117–21; on "alien" or "stranger" pertaining to discourse about Jewish people, see James Shapiro, *Shakespeare and the Jews*, 1997, 20th anniversary ed. with a new preface by the author (New York: Columbia University Press, 2016), 180–89.

2. On this technique, see Andrew Fleck, "'Ick verstaw you niet': Performing Foreign Tongues on the Early Modern English Stage," *Medieval & Renaissance Drama in England* 20 (2007): 209–10. Offering a helpful correction to the assumption of monolingualism in London playhouses, however, is Marjorie Rubright, "Incorporating Kate: the Myth of Monolingualism in Shakespeare's *Henry the Fifth*," in *The Oxford Handbook of Shakespeare and Embodiment: Gender, Sexuality, and Race*, ed. Valerie Traub (Oxford, UK: Oxford University Press, 2016), 468–90.

3. Emma Smith, "'So Much English by the Mother': Gender, Foreigners, and the Mother Tongue in William Haughton's *Englishmen for My Money*," *Medieval & Renaissance Drama in England* 13 (2001): 171.

4. Here, I am concerned mainly with connotations of the market and exchange. On the poetic "figure of exchange" expressed in both sonnet 20 ("Master Mistress," also known as "The Exchange") and in Ben Jonson's *Epicene*, a play I will discuss in the next chapter, see Jenny C. Mann, *Outlaw Rhetoric: Figuring Vernacular Eloquence in Shakespeare's England* (Ithaca, NY: Cornell University Press, 2012), 146–70.

5. Nina Levine, *Practicing the City: Early Modern London on Stage* (New York: Fordham University Press, 2016), 79–108. While Levine focuses principally on Claudius Hollyband's French-English manuals, which in many cases draw on the multilingual text of the *Colloquia et Dictionariolum* I discuss in this chapter, her emphasis remains on the educational context, while I am addressing the economic tropes of interchangeability governing these immensely popular *multiple*-language publications and their various evident uses.

6. According to *Englishmen for My Money*'s most recent editor, "the play's criticism has fallen into two camps, discussing money-mercantile issues or the question of identity as revealed through linguistic tropes and practices" (Kermode, ed., 45). Kermode also recognizes Haughton's comedy as a "usury play" (42–47); for a similar generic claim about the play, see Haughton, *Englishmen for My Money*, ed. Albert Croll Baugh (PhD diss., University of Pennsylvania, 1917), 41–42. On the Royal Exchange and the emerging capitalist market as a backdrop for the play, see Jean E. Howard, *Theater of a City: The Places of London Comedy, 1598–1642* (Philadelphia: University of Pennsylvania Press, 2007), 38–49; and Crystal Bartolovich, "London's the Thing: Alienation, the Market, and *Englishmen for My Money*," *Huntington Library Quarterly* 71, no. 1 (2008): 137–56.

7. On Pisaro as "crypto-Jew," see Edmund Valentine Campos, "Jews, Spaniards,

and Portingales: Ambiguous Identities of Portuguese *Marranos* in Elizabethan England," *English Literary History* 69, no. 3 (2002): 599–616; on the complexity of denization in relation to the play, see Alan Stewart, "'Euery Soyle to Mee is Naturall': Figuring Denization in William Haughton's *English-men for My Money*," *Renaissance Drama*, n.s., 35 (2006): 55–81; on the play's treatment of the "mother tongue," see Smith, "So Much English," 165–81; on foreign language as disease, see Diane Cady, "Linguistic Dis-Ease: Foreign Language as Sexual Disease in Early Modern England," in *Sins of the Flesh: Responding to Sexual Disease in Early Modern Europe*, ed. Kevin Siena (Toronto: Centre for Reformation and Renaissance Studies, 2005), 176–80. On attitudes toward non-English aliens in the comedy, see Lloyd Edward Kermode, *Aliens and Englishness in Elizabethan Drama* (Cambridge, UK: Cambridge University Press, 2009), 121–33; Janette Dillon, *Language and Stage in Medieval and Renaissance England* (Cambridge, UK: Cambridge University Press, 1998), 173–74; and A. J. Hoenselaars, *Images of Englishmen and Foreigners in the Drama of Shakespeare and His Contemporaries: A Study of Stage Characters and National Identity in English Renaissance Drama, 1558–1642* (Rutherford, NJ: Fairleigh Dickinson University Press, 1992), 53–58. In her interlingually focused analysis, Margaret Tudeau-Clayton perceives *Englishmen for My Money* as "blatantly xenophobic" and locates it as a foil to the more inclusive linguistic landscape of *The Merry Wives of Windsor* (considered in the first chapter of my own analysis); see *Shakespeare's Englishes: Against English* (Cambridge, UK: Cambridge University Press, 2020), 9, 66–69.

8. Scott Oldenburg, *Alien Albion: Literature and Immigration in Early Modern England* (Toronto: University of Toronto Press, 2014), 128; and Marjorie Rubright, *Doppelgänger Dilemmas: Anglo-Dutch Relations in Early Modern English Literature and Culture* (Philadelphia: University of Pennsylvania Press, 2014), 125. See also Kathryn Vomero Santos's analysis of the play's hospitality and hostility to foreigners in "Staging Translation in Early Modern English Drama" (PhD diss., New York University, 2013), 169–91.

9. Kelly J. Stage, *Producing Early Modern London: A Comedy of Urban Space, 1598–1616* (Lincoln: University of Nebraska Press, 2018), 40.

10. On the development of typographical conventions underpinning the delivery of speech in both these genres, see Claire M. L. Bourne, *Typographies of Performance in Early Modern England* (Oxford, UK: Oxford University Press, 2020), 32–76.

11. Susan E. Phillips, "Schoolmasters, Seduction, and Slavery: Polyglot Dictionaries in Pre-Modern England," *Medievalia et Humanistica*, n.s., 34 (2008): 130; see also Werner Hüllen, *English Dictionaries 800–1700: The Topical Tradition* (Oxford, UK: Clarendon), 106–18. See also my consideration of the *Colloquia* in chapter 1.

12. The qualities of portability, format, and mise-en-page among polyglot conversation manuals, based on a recent survey of extant European-language editions issued between 1480 and 1715, are considered in John Gallagher, *Learning Languages in Early Modern England* (Oxford, UK: Oxford University Press, 2019), 73–75, 88–93.

13. A. E. B. Coldiron, *Printers Without Borders: Translation and Textuality in the Renaissance* (Cambridge, UK: Cambridge University Press, 2015), 26; 20–30.

14. Gallagher, *Learning Languages*, 135–44, esp. 136.

15. My translation. This phrase appears on the title page of the following extant six-, seven-, and eight-language editions: Antwerp 1586, Liège 1591, Padua 1592,

Lyon 1593, Liège 1595, Liège 1597, Delft 1598, Liège 1600, Liège 1604, Venice 1606, Geneva 1608, Liège 1610, Delft 1613, Vlissingen 1613, The Hague 1613, Antwerp 1616, Amsterdam 1622, Amsterdam 1623, Venice 1627, Antwerp 1630, Middleborough 1631, Delft 1631.

16. Gallagher, *Learning Languages*, 71.

17. Phillips, "Schoolmasters, Seduction, and Slavery," 140–42. On the portrayal of English people and language among representations of foreign fashions, see Tudeau-Clayton, *Shakespeare's Englishes*, 93–131.

18. There are, however, subtle distinctions among the figures in terms of their hair, hats, cuffs, cloak length, etc. My thoughts on these engravings are indebted to my conversation with Marjorie Rubright.

19. See the entry for "Mercury" in Thomas Blount, *Glossographia: or a Dictionary, Interpreting all such Hard Words, Whether Hebrew, Greek, Latin, Italian, Spanish, French, Teutonick, Belgick, British or Saxon; as are now used in our refined English Tongue* (London: Tho. Newcomb for Humphrey Moseley, 1656), sig. 2B5r. The Janus head here, showing the armored "Mars Pacifier" opposite the Mercury, could also recall the language manual *Janua Linguarum*, and the standing figures in the illustration seem to enact the book's potential; see Nigel Stoughton, "Mars and Mercury at Market: An Engraved Title-Page for Noel van Barlement *Dictionariolum et Colloquia*, 1662," *Book Collector* 67, no. 4 (2018): 873–74.

20. On the discourse of collaborative association within Vaughan's engraving, see Jeffrey Masten, *Textual Intercourse: Collaboration, Authorship, and Sexualities in Renaissance Drama* (Cambridge, UK: Cambridge University Press, 1997), 28–31; on the early modern discourse of friendship more broadly, see Laurie Shannon, *Sovereign Amity: Figures of Friendship in Shakespearean Contexts* (Chicago: University of Chicago Press, 2002).

21. Noël de Berlaimont, *Colloquia et Dictionariolum Octo Linguarum* (Delphis [Delft]: ex officina Brunonis Schinkelii, 1598), sig. A7r; also noting the discourses of trading and friendship, or sociability, are Hüllen, *English Dictionaries*, 113; and Gallagher, *Learning Languages*, 136. The imperfect spelling of this edition's English text is a reminder of both the period's orthographic instability and the difficulty of publishing a work of compressed translation; I quote from it because it was issued the year of *Englishmen for My Money*'s first performance and because it is the first "complete" edition. Though I quote this book in English throughout this chapter, it should be remembered that the text appeared in up to eight languages.

22. See Jeffrey Masten, *Queer Philologies: Sex, Language, and Affect in Shakespeare's Time* (Philadelphia: University of Pennsylvania Press, 2016), 99–105.

23. Coldiron, *Printers Without Borders*, 160–98; Rubright, *Doppelgänger Dilemmas*, 110–61; Steven K. Galbraith, "'English' Black-Letter Type and Spenser's *Shepheardes Calender*," *Spenser Studies* 23 (2008): 13–40. Observing the *Colloquia*'s typeface use in particular is Phillips, "Schoolmasters, Seduction, and Slavery," 140.

24. Coldiron, *Printers Without Borders*, 27.

25. Hüllen, *English Dictionaries*, 108–11.

26. Rubright, *Doppelgänger Dilemmas*, 143, 111–37; also remarking on the contingencies of typeface is Coldiron, *Printers Without Borders*, 49. The case of black letter is particularly complex. On the nostalgic applications of black letter, see Zachary Lesser, "Typographic Nostalgia: Play-Reading, Popularity, and the Meanings

of Black Letter," in *The Book of the Play: Playwrights, Stationers, and Readers in Early Modern England*, ed. Marta Straznicky (Amherst: University of Massachusetts Press, 2006), 99–126; on a sense of vulnerability, "the gothic," or "the medieval" attached to black letter, rather than connoting the commoner's type, see Adrian Weiss, "Casting Compositors, Foul Cases, and Skeletons: Printing in Middleton's Age," in *Thomas Middleton and Early Modern Textual Culture: A Companion to the Collected Works*, ed. Gary Taylor and John Lavagnino (Oxford, UK: Oxford University Press, 2008), 195–225.

27. Coldiron, *Printers Without Borders*, 177. *Colloquia* editions do not have catchword patterns as intricate as what one finds in Wolfe's *Courtier*, but the resulting mise-en-page still challenges the linguistic separateness of each column.

28. Gallagher, *Learning Languages*, 83–85. On comparable learning methods for Latin language used during the period, see András Kiséry, "'Flowers for English Speaking': Play Extracts and Conversation," in *Rethinking Theatrical Documents in Shakespeare's England*, ed. Tiffany Stern (London: Arden Shakespeare, 2020), 162–66.

29. Markings accompanying Delves's signature on the title page match those in the book's blank leaves. The oblong format of this book makes it difficult to observe any difference between or among watermarks, but a distinction in paper texture can be observed between the leaves A1–2D8 and six leaves (and pastedowns) preceding and following the letterpress leaves. A binder's leaf of a third texture seems to have been added later.

30. On the importance of converting currency and other units of measure to polyglot conversation manuals more broadly, see Gallagher, *Learning Languages*, 146. For this part of my discussion I am also indebted to Casey Caldwell.

31. On Claudius Hollyband's widely known French-English manuals, see Levine, *Practicing the City*, 89–98.

32. John Minsheu, *Ductor in Linguas, the Guide into Tongues* (Londini [London]: [William Stansby and Eliot's Court Press] for John Browne, 1617), sig. A4r.

33. Edmund Valentine Campos, "Imperial Lexicography and the Anglo-Spanish War," in *Remapping the Mediterranean World in Early Modern English Writings*, ed. Goran V. Stanivukovic (New York: Palgrave, 2007), 91.

34. Quoted in Stephen Greenblatt, *Learning to Curse: Essays in Early Modern Culture* (London: Routledge, 1990), 22–23.

35. John Considine, *Dictionaries in Early Modern Europe: Lexicography and the Making of Heritage* (Cambridge, UK: Cambridge University Press, 2008).

36. Franklin B. Williams Jr., "Scholarly Publication in Shakespeare's Day: A Leading Case," in *Joseph Quincy Adams Memorial Studies*, ed. J. G. MacManaway et al. (Washington, DC: Folger Shakespeare Library, 1948), 755–73.

37. Jason Lawrence, *Who the Devil Taught Thee So Much Italian? Italian Language Learning and Literary Imitation in Early Modern England* (Manchester, UK: Manchester University Press, 2005), 177–79.

38. Giovanni Torriano, *Vocabolario Italiano & Inglese, a Dictionary Italian & English* (London: T. Warren for Jo. Martin, Ja. Allestry, and Tho. Dicas, 1659), sig. b1v.

39. Gallagher, *Learning Languages*, 66–67.

40. A notable exception is Levine, *Performing the City*, 100.

41. Richard Halpern, *The Poetics of Primitive Accumulation: English Renaissance*

Culture and the Genealogy of Capital (Ithaca, NY: Cornell University Press, 1991), 19–60; Tudeau-Clayton, *Shakespeare's Englishes*, 181–92. Baugh conjectures that "if Haughton was a university man at all he probably received his university training at Oxford" (17).

42. See Karen Newman, *Fashioning Femininity and English Renaissance Drama* (Chicago: University of Chicago Press, 1991), 131–43; and Cady, "Linguistic Dis-Ease," 161–64. On the cosmopolitan contours of this "city talk," see chapter 5.

43. William Shakespeare, *The Taming of the Shrew*, ed. Barbara Hodgdon (London: Arden Shakespeare, 2010), 3.1.20. For this point, I am indebted to Deanne Williams; on the instruction scenes in *Taming*, see Lynn Enterline, *Shakespeare's Schoolroom: Rhetoric, Discipline, Emotion* (Philadelphia: University of Pennsylvania Press, 2012), 95–119.

44. On the play's title as "a literal description of an attempted homogenizing of audience experience," see Bartolovich, "London's the Thing," 155. However, on the complexities of the title for a play focused on a half-English, half-Portuguese family, see Howard, *Theater of a City*, 41; as well as Oldenburg, *Alien Albion*, 133. For the ways the title's second half ("A Woman Will Have Her Will") expresses xenophobic and gendered attitudes, see Cady, "Linguistic Dis-Ease," 180. Interestingly, the play's second and third printed editions shear away "*Englishmen for My Money*," presenting the comedy solely as "*A Woman Will Have Her Will*."

45. While Baugh wonders on metrical grounds if "conversions" should read as "conversations" (220), and Kermode picks up on a "pseudo-religious devotion to their Englishmen" (171n), my own analysis emphasizes the printed word's connotations of language and translation; see my epigraph, Randle Cotgrave's definition of *tourner*, which includes "*conuert*," and which appeared in *A Dictionarie of the French and English Tongues* (London: Adam Islip, 1611), sig. 4H5v. In any case, "conversations" would have sexual connotations for early audiences; see Jeffrey Masten, *Queer Philologies*, 83–86.

46. See Levine, *Practicing the City*, 84–98; Santos, "Staging Translation," 175–76; and Emma Smith, "So Much English," 173. As Cady illustrates with recourse to both Haughton's play and the comedy *Jack Drum's Entertainment*, these instructors were also seen to pose moral problems to the English body politic; see "Linguistic Dis-Ease," 173–76.

47. Kermode alters the early quartos' "Language" to "languages," but the singular reading suggests the mixture commonly associated not only with foreign tongues but with the English language itself. I take Campos's point, however, that "the representation of the Frenchman, Dutchman, and Italian can obscure the curious racialization of Pisaro and his daughters" ("Jews, Spaniards, and Portingales," 611); see also Howard, *Theater of a City*, 48.

48. Smith, "So Much English," 172. In act 3, Heigham threatens Alvaro with "Signiore me no Signiores, nor cassa me no cassas, but get you hence, or you are like to taste of the bastinado" (3.2.47–48). On links between violence and foreign language in early modern England, see John Gallagher, "The Italian London of John North: Cultural Contact and Linguistic Encounter in Early Modern England," *Renaissance Quarterly* 70, no. 1 (2017): 118–22.

49. See Hoenselaars, *Englishmen and Foreigners*, 58; Bartolovich, "London's the Thing," 151–52 (Bartolovich's emphasis); and Cady, "Linguistic Dis-Ease," 177.

50. Levine, *Practicing the City*, 99–106; Rubright, *Doppelgänger Dilemmas*, 98; Oldenburg, *Alien Albion*, 129–30; see also Kermode, ed., 127.

51. The letter in which Petit mentions *Titus Andronicus* is Lambeth Palace Library MS 654 fol. 253a. On Horatio Busino and his contemporary, the Swiss humanist Thomas Platter, see Busino and Platter, *The Journals of Two Travellers in Elizabethan and Early Stuart England*, ed. Peter Razzell (London: Caliban, 1995). De Witt's drawing survives in a copy made by his friend Arendt van Buchell; today it is University of Utrecht MS 842 f. 132r.

52. Stage, *Producing Early Modern London*, 56.

53. Levine, *Practicing the City*, 102.

54. To emphasize the typography early readers saw, I cite here and through the remainder of this exchange from the Q1 text, *English-men For my Money: Or, A pleasant Comedy, called, A Woman will have her Will* (London: W. White, 1616), sig. D4v–D5r. Find the passage in Kermode, ed., 2.3.79–81.

55. Claudius Hollyband, *A Dictionarie French and English: Published for the benefite of the studious in that language* (London: T[homas] O[rwin] for Thomas Woodcock, 1593). sig. V7r. Later, Cotgrave's French-English dictionary would define "Maistre mousche" as "*(The name of a cunning Iugler; hence also) a craftie fellow, subtill companion, slye mate*" (*Dictionarie*, sig. 3H6v).

56. Santos, "Staging Translation," 189–90.

57. Rubright, *Doppelgänger Dilemmas*, 126; see also Smith, "So Much English," 172.

58. On the similarity of Dutch and English, see the contemporary discussion in Richard Verstegan, *A Restitution of Decayed Intelligence: In antiquities. Concerning the most noble and renowmed English nation* (Antwerp: Robert Bruney, 1605), sig. 2B3v–2B4r; as well as Rubright, *Doppelgänger Dilemmas*.

59. See, for instance: John Baret, *An Alvearie or Triple Dictionarie, in Englishe, Latin, and French* (London: Henry Denham, 1574), sig. L5r; John Florio, *A Worlde of Wordes, Or Most copious, and exact Dictionarie in Italian and English* (London: Arnold Hatfield for Edw. Blount, 1598), sig. 2N3v.

60. Kermode, *Aliens and Englishness*, 132–33; and Emma Smith, "So Much English," 171. Howard notes that "*Englishmen for My Money* comes closer to acknowledging the complicated status of certain Jews" than *The Merchant of Venice*; see *Theater of a City*, 45.

61. Hoenselaars, *Englishmen and Foreigners*, 57; Levine, *Practicing the City*, 101–2.

62. Howard, *Theater of a City*, 47. On the limitations of Frisco's foreign language skills, see Santos, "Staging Translation," 186–90, though I take the clown's knowledge of the strangers' tongues to be more capacious and fluid.

63. Stage, *Producing Early Modern London*, 67.

64. Phillips, "Schoolmasters, Seduction, and Slavery," 129.

65. Richard Verstegan, in his discussion of Germanic surnames, mentions both "*Higham* for the situation of his ham or home vpon *high-grownd*" and lists "*Waldgraue*" among names of those "to haue borne office in the tyme of our English-Saxon anceters," later specifying "waldgraue, who had the rule or ouerseeing of the wald or forest" (sig. 2O1v, 2S3r). The antiquarian William Camden, meantime, included in his dictionary of English surnames "WALD, a Wood" and "GRAVE, A

ditch or trench or rather a wood"; see *Remaines, concerning Britaine: But especially England, and the Inhabitants thereof* (London: John Legatt for Simon Waterson, 1614), sig. Q4v, Q3r.

66. See both "frisk" and "frisco" in the *OED*, as well as the remarks in Stage, *Producing Early Modern London*, 268n9. All subsequent uses of the *OED* in the main text will appear parenthetically. Users of Claudius Hollyband's 1593 French-English dictionary could find "*turning, friskes or gamboles*" listed after the headword "Virement"; the subsequent entry reads "Virevoter, *to turne about*"; see *Dictionarie*, sig. 2I6r, 2I6v.

67. See Thomas Dekker, *The Shoemaker's Holiday*, ed. R. L. Smallwood and Stanley Wells, The Revels Plays (Manchester, UK: Manchester University Press, 1979; repr., 1999), 20.63–64; William Shakespeare, *The Winter's Tale*, ed. John Pitcher (London: Arden Shakespeare, 2010), 1.2.67.

68. Stage, *Producing Early Modern London*, 61.

69. See the *OED*, "sinister," as designating the left-hand side (II.9) but also signaling "intent to deceive or mislead" (I.1a) and "Astray from the correct course" (I.5b).

70. Daniel Vitkus, *Turning Turk: English Theater and the Multicultural Mediterranean, 1570–1630* (New York: Palgrave Macmillan, 2003); Jonathan Burton, *Traffic and Turning: Islam and English Drama, 1579–1624* (Newark: University of Delaware Press, 2005).

71. See William Shakespeare, *Othello*, ed. E. A. J. Honigmann, with a new introduction by Ayanna Thompson (London: Arden Shakespeare, 2016), 2.3.166; and William Shakespeare, *Much Ado About Nothing*, ed. Claire McEachern (London: Arden Shakespeare, 2016), 2.319–20. On the various typographical "turnings" in Benedick's words here, see Masten, *Queer Philologies*, 255n27; on the metaphor of the banquet or feast in relation to foreign word uses in Shakespeare's plays, see Mylène Lacroix, "Shakespeare au 'Banquet' des Langues Étrang(èr)es," *Actes des Congrès de la Société Française Shakespeare* 31 (2014): 1–17.

72. John Florio, trans., *The Essayes Or Morall, Politike and Millitarie Discourses of Lo: Michaell de Montaigne*, by Michel de Montaigne (London: Val. Sims for Edward Blount, 1603), sig. A2r.

73. See Stage's discussion in *Producing Early Modern London*, 46.

74. Stage, *Producing Early Modern London*, 61.

75. William Shakespeare, *A Midsummer Night's Dream*, ed. Sukanta Chaudhuri (London: Arden Shakespeare, 2017), 3.1.114–15; Ben Jonson, *Every Man Out of His Humour*, ed. Randall Martin, in *The Cambridge Edition of the Works of Ben Jonson*, ed. David Bevington, Martin Butler, and Ian Donaldson, 7 vols. (Cambridge, UK: Cambridge University Press, 2012), 1:249–428, 2.3.167. See also my discussion of *Epicene*'s metaphorical translations in the next chapter.

76. Santos offers an alternative reading focused on the scene's articulations of anxiety, but which is equally interested in linguistic relationships between the categories of foreign and native; see "Staging Translation," 177–78.

77. Cady, "Linguistic Dis-Ease," 179. On the collaborative social implications of these marriages and their offspring, see Oldenburg, *Alien Albion*, 134–37.

78. On the implications of this trope, see Wendy Wall, *The Imprint of Gender: Authorship and Publication in the English Renaissance* (Ithaca, NY: Cornell Universi-

ty Press, 1993), 181–82. On associations of printing and parenting, particularly in relation to drama, see Douglas A. Brooks, "Inky Kin: Reading in the Age of Gutenberg Paternity," in *The Book of the Play: Playwrights, Stationers, and Readers in Early Modern England*, ed. Marta Straznicky (Amherst: University of Massachusetts Press, 2006), 203–28.

79. Kermode, *Aliens and Englishness*, 128.

80. On the broader picture of female same-sex desire in early modern contexts, see Valerie Traub, *The Renaissance of Lesbianism in Early Modern England* (Cambridge, UK: Cambridge University Press, 2002).

81. William Shakespeare, *The Merchant of Venice*, ed. John Drakakis (London: Arden Shakespeare, 2010), 5.1.305.

82. While the label "city comedy" has been associated with the play for several decades, the narrower impression of the play as the "first London comedy" has been strengthened recently by Jean E. Howard (*Theater of a City*, 49) and Kelly J. Stage (*Producing Early Modern London*, 38–55). Meanwhile, the most recent editorial treatment of the play includes it among other "usury plays" (Kermode, ed., 42–47).

83. Baugh, ed., 32.

Chapter 5

1. Ben Jonson, *Epicene, or The Silent Woman*, ed. David Bevington, in *The Cambridge Edition of the Works of Ben Jonson*, ed. David Bevington, Martin Butler, and Ian Donaldson, 7 vol. (Cambridge, UK: Cambridge University Press, 2012), 3:373–516; 5.1.9–10. Unless otherwise noted, all subsequent quotations from the play will be taken from this edition and will be cited parenthetically in the text by act, scene, and line.

2. For reasons I will discuss in more depth, I have italicized the text from the Cambridge edition. For this passage's appearance in the Jonson Folio, see *Epicoene, or the Silent Woman*, in *The Workes of Benjamin Jonson* (London: Will[iam] Stansby, 1616), sig. 3D1r. Subsequent references to the Jonson folio will appear parenthetically in the text by signature.

3. Claire M. L. Bourne, *Typographies of Performance in Early Modern England* (Oxford, UK: Oxford University Press, 2020), 102.

4. Latin could appear in italic too, but this analysis highlights its vernacular valences. On the associations between foreign languages and typeface variation, see Steven K. Galbraith, "'English' Black-Letter Type and Spenser's *Shepheardes Calender*," *Spenser Studies* 23 (2008): 13–40; A. E. B. Coldiron, *Printers Without Borders: Translation and Textuality in the Renaissance* (Cambridge, UK: Cambridge University Press, 2015), 160–98; and Marjorie Rubright, *Doppelgänger Dilemmas: Anglo-Dutch Relations in Early Modern English Literature and Culture* (Philadelphia: University of Pennsylvania Press, 2014), 110–61; see also my discussion in the previous chapter.

5. Tina Krontiris, *Oppositional Voices: Women as Writers and Translators in the English Renaissance* (London: Routledge, 1992), 10. On women's authorship in the English Renaissance, see also Barbara K. Lewalski, *Writing Women in Jacobean England* (Cambridge, MA: Harvard University Press, 1993); and Danielle Clarke, *The Politics of Early Modern Women's Writing* (Harlow, UK: Longman, 2001).

6. John Florio, trans., *The Essayes Or Morall, Politike and Millitarie Discourses of Lo: Michaell de Montaigne*, by Michel de Montaigne (London: Val. Sims for Edward

Blount, 1603), sig. A2r. A quarto copy of Ben Jonson's *Volpone* (London: Thomas Thorppe, 1607) is extant with the inscription "To his louing Father, & worthy Freind / Mr. John Florio: The ayde of his Muses. / Ben Jonson seales this testemony / of Freindship, & Loue" (British Library C.12.e.17).

7. Patricia Parker, *Literary Fat Ladies: Rhetoric, Gender, Property* (London: Methuen, 1987), 107. Other scholars recognize this phenomenon as well; see Valerie Traub, *Thinking Sex with the Early Moderns* (Philadelphia: University of Pennsylvania Press, 2016), 180–83; Michael Wyatt, *The Italian Encounter with Tudor England: A Cultural Politics of Translation* (Cambridge, UK: Cambridge University Press, 2005), 251–54; and John Gallagher, *Learning Languages in Early Modern England* (Oxford, UK: Oxford University Press, 2019), 115–25.

8. Jonathan Goldberg, *Desiring Women Writing: English Renaissance Examples* (Stanford, CA: Stanford University Press, 1997), 75–90. On women's involvement in Renaissance rhetoric and translation, see Jaime Goodrich, *Faithful Translators: Authorship, Gender, and Religion in Early Modern England* (Evanston, IL: Northwestern University Press, 2014), 1–8; and Micheline White, "Renaissance Englishwomen and Religious Translations: The Case of Anne Lock's *Of the Markes of the Children of God* (1590)," *English Literary Renaissance* 29, no. 3 (1999): 376–80.

9. Lawrence Venuti, *The Translator's Invisibility: A History of Translation* (London: Routledge, 1995).

10. John Florio, *A Worlde of Wordes, Or Most copious, and exact Dictionarie in Italian and English* (London: Arnold Hatfield for Edw. Blount, 1598), sig. 2B5v.

11. Marjorie Rubright, "Becoming Scattered: The Case of Iphis's Trans*version and the Archipelogic of John Florio's *Worlde of Wordes*," in *Ovidian Transversions: "Iphis and Ianthe," 1300–1650*, ed. Valerie Traub, Patricia Badir, and Peggy McCracken (Edinburgh: Edinburgh University Press, 2019), 121–29.

12. On this definition, see Wyatt, *Italian Encounter*, 1–2. This investigation has also benefited from the advanced search functions of *Lexicons of Early Modern English*, which identifies nine appearances of "translate" in *A Worlde of Wordes* and 233 results more broadly in printed lexicons issued before 1800. See Ian Lancashire, ed., *Lexicons of Early Modern English (LEME)* (Toronto: University of Toronto Press and University of Toronto Libraries, 2021); online, accessed January 29, 2024.

13. William Shakespeare, *The Taming of the Shrew*, ed. Barbara Hodgdon (London: Arden Shakespeare, 2010), 3.1.20; see also the discussion about gender and language tutors in *Englishmen for My Money* in the previous chapter.

14. Margaret Tudeau-Clayton, *Shakespeare's Englishes: Against English* (Cambridge, UK: Cambridge University Press, 2020); for this discussion, which largely accords with my own here, see esp. 192–99.

15. Richard Mulcaster, *The First Part of the Elementarie which Entreateth Chefelie of the right writing of our English tung* (London: Thomas Vautroullier, 1582), sig. V2v.

16. Richard Carew, "The Excellencie of the English tongue," in *Remaines, concerning Britaine: But especially England, and the Inhabitants thereof*, ed. William Camden (London: John Legatt for Simon Waterson, 1614), sig. F4v.

17. George Puttenham, *The Arte of English Poesie. Contrived into three Bookes: The first of Poets and Poesie, the second of Proportion, the third of Ornament* (London: Richard Field, 1589), sig. 2E4r.

18. Richard Verstegan, *A Restitution of Decayed Intelligence: In antiquities.*

Concerning the most noble and renowmed English nation (Antwerp: Robert Bruney, 1605), sig. 2C2v.

19. Tudeau-Clayton, *Shakespeare's Englishes*, 127–28.

20. Carla Mazzio, *The Inarticulate Renaissance: Language Trouble in an Age of Eloquence* (Philadelphia: University of Pennsylvania Press, 2009), 183–98.

21. Erin Ellerbeck, "The Female Tongue as Translator in Thomas Tomkis's *Lingua, or The Combat of the Tongue and the Five Senses for Superiority*," *Renaissance and Reformation* 32, no. 1 (2009): 30.

22. Ellerbeck, "Female Tongue as Translator," 37.

23. [Thomas Tomkis], *Lingua: Or The Combat of the Tongue, And the five Senses for Superiority* (London: G. Eld for Simon Waterson, 1607), sig. A3r–A3v.

24. Mazzio, *Inarticulate Renaissance*, 189. The passage also clearly demonstrates the oft-coinciding nature of vernacular and classical languages, such as seen in chapter 2.

25. On etymologies of "confusion" pointing to the pouring-together of languages, rather than total incomprehension, see both chapter 2 and Jeffrey Masten's discussion of breeding genres in *Queer Philologies: Sex, Language, and Affect in Shakespeare's Time* (Philadelphia: University of Pennsylvania Press, 2016), 191–210. See also the *Oxford English Dictionary*, online ed., s.v. "confusion," 7a.

26. On the "pendent" relation between "tongue" and "language" in the period, see Roland Greene, *Five Words: Critical Semantics in the Age of Shakespeare and Cervantes* (Chicago: University of Chicago Press, 2013), 46–73.

27. Douglas Bruster, "'In a Woman's Key': Women's Speech and Women's Language in Renaissance Drama," *Exemplaria* 4, no. 2 (1992): 250. On the broader premodern discourses at hand here, see Peter Stallybrass, "Patriarchal Territories: The Body Enclosed," in *Rewriting the Renaissance: The Discourses of Sexual Difference in Early Modern Europe*, ed. Margaret W. Ferguson, Maureen Quilligan, and Nancy J. Vickers (Chicago: University of Chicago Press, 1986), 123–42; as well as Carissa Harris, *Obscene Pedagogies: Transgressive Talk and Sexual Education in Late Medieval Britain* (Ithaca, NY: Cornell University Press, 2018).

28. On the term "gallimaufry," see Masten, *Queer Philologies*, 196–97; on the term's relation to English dress, see Tudeau-Clayton, *Shakespeare's Englishes*, 22–32.

29. On the discourses of prostitution and language in early modern England, see Stephen Spiess, "Shakespeare's Whore: Language, Prostitution, and Knowledge in Early Modern England" (PhD diss., University of Michigan, 2013).

30. John Addington Symonds, *Renaissance in Italy: Italian Literature*, 2 vols. (London: Smith, Elder, 1881), 2:178–79. On *Il Marescalco*'s first performances and printings, see Richard Andrews, *Scripts and Scenarios: The Performance of Comedy in Renaissance Italy* (Cambridge, UK: Cambridge University Press, 1993), 74–77, 272.

31. Oscar James Campbell, "The Relation of *Epicoene* to Aretino's *Il Marescalco*," *PMLA* 46, no. 3 (1931): 752–62. On the means by which Aretino's play conditions Jonson's imitations in *Epicene*, see Donald A. Beecher, "Aretino's Minimalist Art Goes to England," in *Pietro Aretino Nel Cinquecentenario della Nascita*, 2 vols. (Rome: Salerno, 1995), 2:775–85.

32. There is a nurse known as "Balia" in *Il Marescalco*, though her character functions differently from the Collegiates in *Epicene*; see Louise George Clubb, *Italian Drama in Shakespeare's Time* (New Haven, CT: Yale University Press, 1989),

8–12. Campbell could not account for Morose's aversion to noise, but Daniel C. Boughner uncovered a connection to Niccolò Machiavelli's play *Clizia* in "*Clizia* and *Epicoene*," *Philological Quarterly* 19 (1940): 89–91.

33. Clubb, *Italian Drama*, 1–26. Clubb lists *Epicene* among a number of Italian comedies that were "translated or adapted in England" (49) but does not investigate it in any greater depth. For my thoughts here, I am grateful to Susanne Wofford for further considerations of the theatergram in her conference paper, "Wit and Doltishness in Shakespeare and Lope: A Comment on a European Comic Tradition" (Shakespeare Association of America, 2018).

34. For examples of the scholarship advancing beyond "source studies," see Jonathan Goldberg, "Speculations: *Macbeth* and Source," in *Shakespeare Reproduced: The Text in History and Ideology*, ed. Jean E. Howard and Marion F. O'Connor (New York: Methuen, 1987), 242–64; Robert S. Miola, "Seven Types of Intertextuality," in *Shakespeare, Italy, and Intertextuality*, ed. Michele Marrapodi (Manchester, UK: Manchester University Press, 2004), 19–20.

35. Karen Newman, *Fashioning Femininity and English Renaissance Drama* (Chicago: University of Chicago Press, 1991), 129–43; I should acknowledge that Newman's recent scholarship is deeply invested in transnational methodologies. Regarding the established concept of "city talk" in *Epicene*, see also the analysis of English female academies in Rebecca Merrens, "'Ignoring the Men': Female Speech and Male Anxiety in Cavendish's *The Female Academy* and Jonson's *Epicoene*," *In-between* 9, no. 1 (2000): 243–60; for a parallel account focusing on staged social tension and the participation of women in the spectacle, see Jean E. Howard, *The Stage and Social Struggle in Early Modern England* (New York: Routledge, 1994), 93–128.

36. See Jean E. Howard, *Theater of a City: The Places of London Comedy, 1598–1642* (Philadelphia: University of Pennsylvania Press, 2007), 162–208, although Howard offers some recognition for the foreign and the cosmopolitan; Heather C. Easterling, *Parsing the City: Jonson, Middleton, Dekker, and City Comedy's London as Language* (New York: Routledge, 2007), 47–81; Adam Zucker, *The Places of Wit in Early Modern English Comedy* (Cambridge, UK: Cambridge University Press, 2011), 62; Kelly J. Stage, *Producing Early Modern London: A Comedy of Urban Space, 1598–1616* (Lincoln: University of Nebraska Press, 2018), 164–84; and Isaac Hui, *Volpone's Bastards: Theorising Jonson's City Comedy* (Edinburgh: Edinburgh University Press, 2018), 80–87. One notable, interesting exception pointing to Ottoman subtexts in the play is Corinne Zeman, "Sultanic Drag in Ben Jonson's *Epicene*," *Shakespeare Studies* 47 (2019): 134–40.

37. Ian Frederick Moulton, *Before Pornography: Erotic Writing in Early Modern England* (Oxford, UK: Oxford University Press, 2000), 211–19; James Grantham Turner, *Schooling Sex: Libertine Literature and Erotic Education in Italy, France, and England, 1534–1685* (Oxford, UK: Oxford University Press, 2003), 62–63.

38. Ben Jonson, *Epicene, or The Silent Woman*, ed. Richard Dutton (Manchester, UK: Manchester University Press, 2003), 299–309, 43. Dutton includes excerpts from Jonson's classical sources in the appendixes but omits any passages from *Il Marescalco*. His introduction offers only a paragraph on Aretino's play, misspells the title, and confuses the edition Jonson could have consulted with a Latin folio of Libanius published in Paris in 1606.

39. Bevington, ed., 381, 506–16. To be sure, "classical or vernacular" is not a

zero-sum game when it comes to Jonson; for an account tracing elements in *Epicene* to Erasmian and classical traditions *through* Aretino, see Christopher Cairns, "Aretino's Comedies and the Italian 'Erasmian' Connection in Shakespeare and Jonson," in *Theatre of the English and Italian Renaissance*, ed. J. R. Mulryne and Margaret Shewring (New York: St. Martin's, 1991), 113–37.

40. Michele De Filippis, "The Literary Riddle in Italy to the End of the Sixteenth Century," *University of California Publications in Modern Philology* 34, no. 1 (1948), 12.

41. De Filippis refers briefly to "Pietro Aretino, *Ragionamenti*, Giornata III"; see "Literary Riddle," 6n17.

42. Humfrey Gifford, *A Posie of Gilloflowers, eche differing from other in colour and odour, yet all sweete* (London: [Thomas Dawson] for John Perin, 1580), sig. *2v.

43. *The Riddles of Heraclitus and Democritus* (London: Arn. Hatfield for John Norton, 1598), sig. *4r.

44. For the publication history of the two portions of the *Ragionamenti*'s first editions, see the notes in Pietro Aretino, *Sei Giornate: Ragionamento della Nanna e della Antonia (1534), Dialogo nel quale la Nanna insegna a la Pippa (1536), Scrittori d'Italia n. 245*, ed. Giovanni Aquilecchia (Bari, Italy: Gius. Laterza and Figli, 1969), 359–417.

45. On premodern connections between education, language, and gender and sexuality, see Harris, *Obscene Pedagogies*, as well as Joseph Gamble, "Practicing Sex," *Journal for Early Modern Cultural Studies* 19, no. 1 (2019): 85–116. With the midwife, wetnurse, mother, and daughter, this constitutes an interesting variation on the gossips' feast, as in texts such as the *Gospelles of Dystaues* (French and English) and the *Quinze Joyes de Mariage* (also French and English); on this point, I am grateful to Susan E. Phillips. On premodern gossip more broadly, see Susan E. Phillips, *Transforming Talk: The Problem with Gossip in Late Medieval England* (University Park: Pennsylvania State University Press, 2007), esp. 147–202.

46. Pietro Aretino, *La Seconda Parte de Ragionamenti di M. Pietro Aretino* (Bengodi [London]: [John Wolfe], 1584), sig. A6v. This constitutes the second part of this edition and features a separate half title, a new register, and new pagination; for simplicity's sake I will cite it as a separate publication. For an English translation of the *Ragionamenti*, see Pietro Aretino, *Dialogues*, ed. and trans. Raymond Rosenthal (New York: Stein and Day, 1971), 166. Further citations of the Italian text and the English translation will be made together parenthetically in the text, using Rosenthal's translation.

47. See David O. Frantz, *Festum Voluptatis: A Study of Renaissance Erotica* (Columbus: Ohio State University Press, 1989); and also Moulton, *Before Pornography*; on late medieval treatments of womens' debates and erudition, see Phillips, *Transforming Talk*, 172–74, 176–202.

48. Frantz, *Festum Voluptatis*, 106–9.

49. Andrews, *Scripts and Scenarios*, 76; hailing the *Ragionamenti* as "a kind of crossgendered autobiography" is Moulton, *Before Pornography*, 135.

50. On Wolfe's Italian printing, see Harry R. Hoppe, "John Wolfe, Printer and Publisher, 1579–1601," *The Library*, 4th ser., 14, no. 3 (1933): 241–88, esp. 243; Clifford Chalmers Huffman, *Elizabethan Impressions: John Wolfe and His Press* (New York: AMS, 1988), 1–47; Wyatt, *Italian Encounter*, 185–99, 262–64; and Jason Lawrence,

Who the Devil Taught Thee So Much Italian? Italian Language Learning and Literary Imitation in Early Modern England (Manchester, UK: Manchester University Press, 2005), 187–201. See also the bibliographical account of Denis B. Woodfield, *Surreptitious Printing in England, 1550–1640* (New York: Bibliographical Society of America, 1973); and the focus on Wolfe's editorial work in Sonia Massai, "John Wolfe and the Impact of Exemplary Go-Betweens on Early Modern Print Culture," in *Renaissance Go-Betweens: Cultural Exchange in Early Modern Europe*, ed. Andreas Höfele and Werner Von Koppenfels (Berlin: Walter de Gruyter, 2005), 104–18.

51. Kate De Rycker, "The Italian Job: John Wolfe, Giacomo Castelvetro and the Printing of Pietro Aretino," in *Specialist Markets in the Early Modern Book World*, ed. Richard Kirwan and Sophie Mullins (Leiden: Brill, 2015), 241–57.

52. Roger Ascham, *The Scholemaster. Or plaine and perfite way of teachyng children, to understand, write, and speake, the Latin tong* (London: John Daye, 1570), sig. I2v. On Ascham's moralistic critiques of Italy, see Wyatt, *Italian Encounter*, 159–63; and Moulton, *Before Pornography*, 113–18.

53. Richard Harvey, *A Theologicall Discourse of the Lamb of God and His Enemies: Contayning a briefe Commentarie of Christian faith and felicitie, together with a detection of old and new Barbarisme, now commonly called Martinisme* (London: John Windet for W[illiam] [Ponsonby], 1590), sig. N4v.

54. John Eliot, *Ortho-epia Gallica. Eliots Fruits for the French: Enterlaced with a double new Invention, which teacheth to speake truly, speedily and volubly the French-tongue* (London: [Richard Field for] John Wolfe, 1593), sig. D2v. Wolfe printed this book; in Huffman's view, "Wolfe enjoyed pointing to his own audacity" (*Elizabethan Impressions*, 165n19). On the pedagogical rivalry between Eliot and Florio, see Frances A. Yates, *John Florio: The Life of an Italian in Shakespeare's England* (Cambridge, UK: Cambridge University Press, 1934), 139–73.

55. On the "pictures," as they were known, see Moulton, *Before Pornography*, 121–27, and Frantz, *Festum Voluptatis*, 46–60. See also Stephen Orgel, *Imagining Shakespeare: A History of Texts and Visions* (New York: Palgrave Macmillan, 2003), 112–43; as well as the recent contextualization and discussion of Kate De Rycker in "Staging the Imagined City: Aretino in Rome and London," *Renaissance Studies* 37, no. 2 (2023): 14–24. For an extensive study with a reproduction of the images and their corresponding texts, see Bette Talvacchia, *Taking Positions: On the Erotic in Renaissance Culture* (Princeton, NJ: Princeton University Press, 1999).

56. Field's "Cosmopoli" publications are both by Thomas Preston: *Apologia Cardinalis Bellarimini pro iure principum* (Cosmopoli, 1611), and *Rogeri Widdringtoni Catholici Angli Responsio apologetica* (Cosmopoli, 1612). On the connections between this Cosmopoli edition and Wolfe's, see De Rycker, "Italian Job," 253–54.

57. Frantz, *Festum Voluptatis*, 142–44; see also Huffman, *Elizabethan Impressions*, 11.

58. Thomas Nashe, *The Unfortunate Traveller*, in *The Works of Thomas Nashe*, ed. Ronald B. McKerrow, 5 vols. (London: A. H. Bullen, 1904-1908), 2:264.

59. Thomas Nashe, *Nashes Lenten Stuffe*, in *The Works*, ed. McKerrow, 3:152; see also Frantz, *Festum Voluptatis*, 186–207.

60. David C. McPherson, "Aretino and the Harvey-Nashe Quarrel," *PMLA* 84, no. 6 (1969): 1551–58, esp. 1553.

61. Florio, *Worlde of Wordes*, Houghton Library STC 11098 (B), sig. b4v.

62. On this copious quality of Florio's dictionary, amplified by the inclusion of Aretino, see David O. Frantz, "Florio's Use of Contemporary Italian Literature in *A Worlde of Wordes*," *Dictionaries* 1 (1979): 47–56; and Wyatt, *Italian Encounter*, 231–37.

63. John Florio, *Florio His firste Fruites: which yeelde familiar speech, merie Proverbes, wittie Sentences, and golden sayings* (London: Thomas Dawson for Thomas Woodcocke, 1578), sig. M2r–S1v, S4v–T3r.

64. Lynda E. Boose, "The 1599 Bishops' Ban, Elizabethan Pornography, and the Sexualization of the Jacobean Stage," in *Enclosure Acts: Sexuality, Property, and Culture in Early Modern England*, ed. Richard Burt and John Michael Archer (Ithaca, NY: Cornell University Press, 1994), 185–200, esp. 195, 197. On this Bishops' Ban's focus on Italianate material, see Andrew S. Keener, "Robert Tofte's *Of Mariage and Wiuing* and the Bishops' Ban of 1599," *Studies in Philology* 110, no. 3 (2013): 506–32.

65. Mentioning this copy are Neil Rhodes, *Elizabethan Grotesque* (London: Routledge, 1980), 134, 185n9; and Moulton, *Before Pornography*, 146, 239n106. Woodfield offers 1597 as the edition's date, but it may have appeared anytime between 1592 and 1598 (*Surreptitious Printing*, 23). This volume is not included in David McPherson, "Ben Jonson's Library and Marginalia: An Annotated Catalogue," *Studies in Philology* 71, no. 5 (1974): 1–106.

66. Yates, *John Florio*, 277–83. In his copy of Euripides, Gabriel Harvey inscribed "Quattro comedie del divino Aretino. Cioè, Il Marescalco, o pedante, La Cortegiana, La Talanta, Lo Hipocrito. Habeo, et legi"; see Euripides, *Hecuba, & Iphigenia in Aulide Euripidis tragoediae*, trans. Desiderius Erasmus (Venetiis [Venice]: in aedibus Aldi, 1507), fol. 7r, Houghton Library *E.C.H263.ZZ507e. Florio evidently had access to a copy of the *Quattro Comedie* volume, too; "Le quatro comedie dell'Aretino" appears on the list of sources used to compile *A Worlde of Wordes* (sig. b4v). A 1535 edition of Aretino's comedies appears in a catalog of books in the Bodleian Library, suggesting that editions other than Wolfe's were available in England; see Thomas Bodley, *Catalogus Librorum Bibliothecae Publicae Quam Vir Ornatissimus Thomas Bodlaeus Eques Auratus in Academia Oxoniensi nuper instituit* (Oxoniae [Oxford]: apud Josephum Barnesium, 1605), sig. 2O1r. Wolfe's edition was included in this catalog's second edition of 1620. William Drummond owned Wolfe's edition, but Jonson did not meet him until after *Epicene*'s first performance. On these and other imprints, see John Leon Lievsay, *The Englishman's Italian Books, 1550–1700* (Philadelphia: University of Pennsylvania Press, 1969); as well as Lawence, *Who the Devil*, 189–90.

67. Frantz, *Festum Voluptatis*, 61; see also Virginia Cox, *The Renaissance Dialogue: Literary Dialogue in its Social and Political Contexts, Castiglione to Galileo* (Cambridge, UK: Cambridge University Press, 1992), 18, 32, 73–74.

68. Anston Bosman, "Renaissance Intertheater and the Staging of Nobody," *English Literary History* 71, no. 3 (2004): 559–85.

69. Howard, *Theater of a City*, 205; for a discussion about the longer trajectory of this tradition extending to Margaret Cavendish, see Merrens, "Ignoring the Men."

70. Campbell, "Relation of *Epicoene*," 756. This scene occurs in Aretino, *Il Marescalco*, in *Quattro Comedie del Divino Pietro Aretino* ([London]: [John Wolfe], 1588), sig. C5r, C6v.

71. On "convey" and its position among the period's translation keywords, including "theft," see Patricia Parker, *Shakespeare from the Margins: Language, Culture, Context* (Chicago: University of Chicago Press, 1996), 124–39.

72. See *OED*, s.v. "publish," I.3a.

73. See the recognition of the form's Italian heritage in *Epicene*, ed. Dutton, 152n; Bevington (415n) argues against this word's Italian connotation. On the tradition of translating Italian madrigals into English, see Joshua Scodel, "Non-Dramatic Verse: Lyric," in *The Oxford History of Literary Translation in English*, vol. 2, *1550–1600*, ed. Gordon Braden, Robert Cummings, and Stuart Gillespie (Oxford, UK: Oxford University Press, 2010), 240–41.

74. Zucker, *Places of Wit*, 5. The scene also resonates with Aretino's pompous characterization of the Pedante in *Il Marescalco*; on this character, see Andrews, *Scripts and Scenarios*, 76.

75. On late medieval women's gossip, see Phillips, *Transforming Talk*, 165–67.

76. The Collegiates resist Mistress Otter's induction into the group, however; see Stage, *Producing Early Modern London*, 172–74.

77. De Rycker, "Staging the Imagined City," 6.

78. Daw and La Foole join in this conversation, but their presence helps contribute to their effeminate character, rather than evincing masculine infiltration; meanwhile, as Bevington's editorial note for this scene suggests, Truewit and Clerimont "*stand aside, observing*."

79. Aretino's *Ragionamenti* preceded the *Puttana Errante*, a more explicitly erotic set of dialogues that deepens the association between femaleness and waywardnesss, but books with this title were often attributed to Aretino; see Moulton, *Before Pornography*, 150.

80. Seeing in these puns and names a persistent fear of castration is Hui, *Volpone's Bastards*, 82.

81. Find a discussion of concoctions and cosmetic tips for attracting men in Aretino, *Ragionamenti*, sig. G6v (and the translation in Rosenthal, 218). On early modern receipts, see Wendy Wall, *Recipes for Thought: Knowledge and Taste in the Early Modern English Kitchen* (Philadelphia: University of Pennsylvania Press, 2016), 3–4.

82. Richard Helgerson, *Self-Crowned Laureates: Spenser, Jonson, Milton, and the Literary System* (Berkeley: University of California Press, 1983), 101–84; on "dissimulative" imitation, see G. W. Pigman III, "Versions of Imitation in the Renaissance," *Renaissance Quarterly* 33, no. 1 (1980): 1–32, esp. 10–11.

83. Joseph Loewenstein, *Ben Jonson and Possessive Authorship* (Cambridge, UK: Cambridge University Press, 2002), 2; for studies of Jonson's folio, see Peter Stallybrass and Allon White, *The Politics and Poetics of Transgression* (London: Methuen, 1986), 27–79; and the essays in Jennifer Brady and W. H. Herendeen, eds., *Ben Jonson's 1616 Folio* (Newark: University of Delaware Press, 1991). Especially considering contemporary collections of dramatic works printed in octavo (e.g., Robert Garnier) and folio (e.g., Jacob Ayrer), I agree with Jeffrey Masten's view that at this time "the folio continued to be a site of contestation, a busy and often discursively chaotic authorial construction site"; see *Textual Intercourse: Collaboration, Authorship, and Sexualities in Renaissance Drama* (Cambridge, UK: Cambridge University Press, 1997), 120.

84. Stallybrass, "Patriarchal Territories," 123–42.

85. Howard, *Stage and Social Struggle*, 109; a more straightforward reading of these lines against the play's background of city noise is Stage, *Producing Early Modern London*, 181.

86. Ben Jonson, *The English Grammar*, in *The Workes of Benjamin Jonson. The second Volume* (London: [John Beale, James Dawson, Bernard Alsop, and Thomas Fawcet] for Richard Meighen [and Thomas Walkley], 1640), sig. E1r. Situating Jonson's grammar in a longer history of efforts to order and rule the English vernacular is Raashi Rastogi, "Unruly Grammar: Linking Vernacular English to Changing Models of Early Modern Pedagogy and Power Politics," *English Literary Renaissance* 48, no. 1 (2018): 98–120, esp. 107–11.

87. The epigraph for *Epicene*, found in Horace's defense of satire in *Satires* 1.4.69–70, is "*Ut sis tu similis Caeli, Byrrhique latronum, / Non ego sim Capri, neque Sulci. Cur metuas me?*" (Though you may be like highwaymen, Coelus and Byrrhus, I am not like Caprius or Sulcius. Why should you fear me?); see Bevington, ed., 385n. The defensive tone of this epigraph is fitting for the position Jonson takes up in regard to *Epicene*'s theatergrammatical intertexts.

88. On contemporary attention to classical intertexts in editions of Jonson's works surviving today at the Huntington Library, including the copy mentioned here, see Jane Rickard, "Seventeenth-Century Readers of Jonson's 1616 *Works*," in *Ben Jonson and Posterity: Reception, Reputation, Legacy*, ed. Martin Butler and Jane Rickard (Cambridge, UK: Cambridge University Press, 2020), 85–104, esp. 102–3. Isaac Hui's modern-day examination of Jonsonian translation also emphasizes the poet's classical, rather than contemporary, tendencies; see "Translation in Ben Jonson: Towards a Definition of Imitation," *Ben Jonson Journal* 20, no. 2 (2013): 223–40.

89. Parker, *Literary Fat Ladies*, 123, 119.

90. On the invocation of metamorphoses and "trans*versions" in Florio's writing about translation, particularly through the Ovidian figure of Iphis, who changes from female to male, see Rubright, "Becoming Scattered," 124–33. Wyatt perceives a similarly gendered trajectory in Florio's lexicographic career; see *Italian Encounter*, 251–54. For a reading that alternatively perceives the play's conclusion as a proliferation of castrations, see Hui, *Volpone's Bastards*, 86–87.

91. Bosman, "Renaissance Intertheater," 564.

Coda

1. John Florio, *A Worlde of Wordes, Or Most copious, and exact Dictionarie in Italian and English* (London: Arnold Hatfield for Edw. Blount, 1598), sig. A4r.

2. Michael Wyatt, *The Italian Encounter with Tudor England: A Cultural Politics of Translation* (Cambridge, UK: Cambridge University Press, 2005), 211–12.

3. John Gallagher, "'Ungratefull Tuscans': Teaching Italian in Early Modern England," *Italianist* 36, no. 3 (2016): 393–94. I am grateful to John Gallagher for his conversation about this book.

4. Gallagher, "Ungrateful Tuscans," 394.

5. My bidirectional thinking about language-learning books and playtexts accords with that of Claire M. L. Bourne, who writes, "To be clear, the designs produced by these processes do not—nor were they necessarily meant to—record actual past performances or provide scores for future performances. Instead, they materialize in textual form what the title pages of early modern playbooks so often promised readers: that the printed text *is* the play *as* it has been (or is being) played"; see *Typographies of Performance in Early Modern England* (Oxford, UK: Oxford University Press, 2020), 10.

6. While the surviving documents I have researched do bear witness to the phenomena I have been examining, Jeffrey Todd Knight gives the indispensable reminder that "Renaissance books in today's libraries are fundamentally divorced from their earliest readerly contexts"; see *Bound to Read: Compilations, Collections, and the Making of Renaissance Literature* (Philadelphia: University of Pennsylvania Press, 2013), 13.

7. Jacques Derrida, *Monolingualism of the Other; or, The Prosthesis of Origin*, trans. Patrick Mensah (Stanford, CA: Stanford University Press, 1998), 5.

8. Walter Jackson Bate, *Samuel Johnson* (New York: Harcourt Brace Jovanovich, 1975), 240.

9. It was a catalog of knowledge, however, that could not escape its own literariness; see Robin Valenza, "How Literature Becomes Knowledge: A Case Study," *English Literary History* 76, no. 1 (2009): 215–45. On the development of the index, see Dennis Duncan, *Index, A History of the: A Bookish Adventure from Medieval Manuscripts to the Digital Age* (New York: W. W. Norton, 2022).

10. Michael Bundock, *The Fortunes of Francis Barber: The True Story of the Jamaican Slave Who Became Samuel Johnson's Heir* (New Haven, CT: Yale University Press, 2015), 45–53.

11. Bundock, *Fortunes of Francis Barber*, 68.

12. Samuel Johnson, *Mr. Johnson's Preface to his Edition of Shakespear's Plays* (London: for J. and R. Tonson et al., 1765), sig. A4r.

Bibliography

A Note on Primary Sources

My bibliography of early modern primary sources reflects both the overlapping nature of print and manuscript and this book's focus on translation. In "Primary Print Sources" I include early modern materials I discuss mainly for their textual content (usually, first editions only). Among these, translated works are listed by the translator's name first, with the original or prior author second. The next section, "Primary Manuscript Sources," includes both manuscript sources *and* printed books which are considered in my analyses mainly for their unique material-textual features, such as marginalia. These items I list by library shelf mark, along with brief identificatory information (e.g., author, title, date, etc.).

Primary Print Sources

Adams, Thomas. *The Divells Banket. Described in foure Sermons.* London: Thomas Snodham for Ralph Mab, 1614. STC 110.5.

Allibond, Peter, trans. *The Golden Chayne of Salvation.* By Hermann Rennecher. London: Valentine Simmes for Thomas Man, 1604. STC 20889.

Aretino, Pietro. *Capricciosi & Piacevoli Ragionamenti di M. Pietro Aretino.* Cosmopoli, 1660.

———. *La Prima . . . Seconda Parte de Ragionamenti di M. Pietro Aretino.* Bengodi [London]: [John Wolfe], 1584. STC 19911.5.

———. *Quattro Comedie del Divino Pietro Aretino.* [London]: [John Wolfe], 1588. STC 19911.

Ascham, Roger. *The Scholemaster. Or plaine and perfite way of teachyng children, to understand, write, and speake, the Latin tong.* London: John Daye, 1570. STC 832.

Baret, John. *An Alvearie or Triple Dictionarie, in Englishe, Latin, and French.* London: Henry Denham, 1574. STC 1410.

———. *An Alvearie or Quadruple Dictionarie, containing foure sundrie tongues: namelie, English, Latine, Greeke, and French.* London: Henry Denham, 1580. STC 1411.

Berlaimont, Noël de. *Colloquia et Dictionariolum Octo Linguarum.* Delphis [Delft]: ex officina Brunonis Schinkelii, 1598.

———. *Colloquia et Dictionariolum octo Linguarum*. Amstelodami [Amsterdam]: apud Everardum Cloppenburgium, 1631.

———. *Dictionariolum et Colloquia Octo Linguarum*. Antuerpiae [Antwerp]: apud Henricum Aertsens, 1662.

The Bible and Holy Scriptures Conteyned in the Old and Newe Testament. Geneva: Rouland Hall, 1560. STC 2093.

Bibliotheca Heberiana: Catalogue of the Library of the Late Richard Heber, Esq. Vol. 6. London: W. Nicol, 1835.

Blount, Thomas. *Glossographia: or a Dictionary, Interpreting all such Hard Words, Whether Hebrew, Greek, Latin, Italian, Spanish, French, Teutonick, Belgick, British or Saxon; as are now used in our refined English Tongue*. London: Tho. Newcomb for Humphrey Moseley, 1656. Wing B3334.

Bodley, Thomas. *Catalogus Librorum Bibliothecae Publicae Quam Vir Ornatissimus Thomas Bodlaeus Eques Auratus in Academia Oxoniensi nuper instituit*. Oxoniae [Oxford]: apud Josephum Barnesium, 1605. STC 14449.

Brathwait, Richard. *The English Gentleman: Containing Sundry excellent Rules or exquisite Observations, tending to Direction of every Gentleman, of selecter ranke and qualitie*. London: John Haviland for Robert Bostock, 1630. STC 3563.

Bryskett, Lodowick. *A Discourse of Civill Life: Containing the Ethike part of Morall Philosophie*. London: [R. Field] for William Aspley, 1606. STC 3959.

Camden, William. "The Languages." In *Remaines, concerning Britaine: But especially England, and the Inhabitants thereof*, edited by William Camden, sig. D2r–F2v. London: John Legatt for Simon Waterson, 1614. STC 4522.

———, ed. *Remaines, concerning Britaine: But especially England, and the Inhabitants thereof*. London: John Legatt for Simon Waterson, 1614. STC 4522.

Carew, Richard, trans. *The Examination of mens Wits. In whicch, by discouering the varietie of natures, is shewed for what profession each one is apt, and how far he shall profit therein*. By Juan Huarte. London: Adam Islip for Richard Watkins, 1594. STC 13890.

———. "The Excellencie of the English tongue." In *Remaines, concerning Britaine: But especially England, and the Inhabitants thereof*, edited by William Camden, sig. F2v–G2v. London: John Legatt for Simon Waterson, 1614. STC 4522.

Cotgrave, Randle. *A Dictionarie of the French and English Tongues*. London: Adam Islip, 1611. STC 5830.

Dee, John. *General and Rare Memorials pertayning to the Perfect Arte of Navigation*. London: John Daye, 1577. STC 6459.

Eliot, John. *Ortho-epia Gallica. Eliots Fruits for the French: Enterlaced with a double new Invention, which teacheth to speake truly, speedily and volubly the French-tongue*. London: [Richard Field for] John Wolfe, 1593. STC 7574.

Florio, John, trans. *The Essayes Or Morall, Politike and Millitarie Discourses of Lo: Michaell de Montaigne*. By Michel de Montaigne. London: Val. Sims for Edward Blount, 1603. STC 18041.

———. *Florio His firste Fruites: which yeelde familiar speech, merie Proverbes, wittie Sentences, and golden sayings*. London: Thomas Dawson for Thomas Woodcocke, 1578. STC 11096.

———. *Florios Second Frutes, To be gathered of twelve Trees, of divers but delightsome tastes to the tongues of Italians and Englishmen*. London: for Thomas Woodcock, 1591. STC 11097.

———. *A Worlde of Wordes, Or Most copious, and exact Dictionarie in Italian and English*. London: Arnold Hatfield for Edw. Blount, 1598. STC 11098.

Garnier, Robert. *Les Tragedies de Robert Garnier Conseiller du Roy*. Paris: Mamert Patisson for Robert Estienne, 1585.

Gifford, Humfrey. *A Posie of Gilloflowers, eche differing from other in colour and odour, yet all sweete*. London: [Thomas Dawson] for John Perin, 1580. STC 11872.

Golding, Arthur, trans. *The xv Bookes of P. Ovidius Naso, entytuled Metamorphosis*. By Ovid. London: Willyam Seres, 1567. STC 18956.

Harington, John, trans. *Orlando Furioso in English Heroical Verse*. By Ludovico Ariosto. London: Richard Field, 1591. STC 746.

Hart, John. *An Orthographie, conteyning the due order and reason, howe to write or paint thimage of mannes voice, most like to the life or nature*. London: [Henry Denham?] for William Seres, 1569. STC 12890.

Harvey, Richard. *A Theologicall Discourse of the Lamb of God and His Enemies: Contayning a briefe Commentarie of Christian faith and felicitie, together with a detection of old and new Barbarisme, now commonly called Martinisme*. London: John Windet for W[illiam] [Ponsonby], 1590. STC 12915.

Haughton, William. *English-men For my Money: Or, A pleasant Comedy, called, A Woman will have her Will*. London: W. White, 1616. STC 12931.

Hawkins, Thomas, trans. *The Holy Court. Or The Christian Institution of Men of Quality. With Examples of those who in Court have flourished in Sanctity*. By Nicholas Caussin. Paris [Saint-Omer]: [English College Press], 1626. STC 4872.

The holie Bible conteyning the olde Testament and the newe. London: Richarde Jugge, 1568. STC 2099.

The Holy Bible, conteyning the Old Testament, and the New. London: Robert Barker, 1611. STC 2217.

Hollyband, Claudius. *Campo di Fior or else The Flourie Field of Foure Languages*. London: Thomas Vautroullier, 1583. STC 6735.

———. *A Dictionarie French and English: Published for the benefite of the studious in that language*. London: T[homas] O[rwin] for Thomas Woodcock, 1593. STC 6737.

———. *The Frenche Littelton. A Most Easie, Perfect, and Absolute way to learne the frenche tongue*. London: Thomas Vautroullier, 1566 [1576]. STC 6738.

———. *The French Schoolemaister, wherein is most plainlie shewed, the true and most perfect way of pronouncinge of the Frenche tongue, without any helpe of Maister or teacher*. London: William How for Abraham Veale, 1573. STC 6748.

Howell, James. *Lexicon Tetraglotton, an English-French-Italian-Spanish Dictionary*. London: J[ohn] G[rismond] for Samuel Thomson, 1660. Wing H3088.

———. *A New English Grammar, Prescribing as certain Rules as the Language will bear, for Forreners to learn English*. London: for T. Williams, H. Brome, and H. Marsh, 1662. Wing H3095.

Johnson, Samuel. *Mr. Johnson's Preface to his Edition of Shakespear's Plays*. London: for J. and R. Tonson et al., 1765.

Jonson, Ben. *The English Grammar*. In *The Workes of Benjamin Jonson: The second Volume*, sig. D4r–L2v of 3rd registered section. London: [John Beale, James

Dawson, Bernard Alsop and Thomas Fawcet] for Richard Meighen [and Thomas Walkley], 1640 [1641]. STC 14754.

———. *The Workes of Benjamin Jonson*. London: Will[iam] Stansby, 1616. STC 14751.

Kyd, Thomas. *The Spanish Tragedie, Containing the lamentable end of Don Horatio, and Bel-imperia: with the pittiful death of olde Hieronimo*. London: Edward Allde for Edward White, 1592. STC 15086.

———. *The Spanish Tragedie: Containing the lamentable end of Don Horatio, and Bel-imperia: with the pittifull death of olde Hieronimo*. London: W. W[hite] for T. Pavier, 1602. STC 15089.

Ludham, John, trans. *A speciall Treatise of Gods Providence, and of comforts against all kinds of crosses & calamities to be fetched from the same*. By Andreas Hyperius. [London]: John Wolfe, [1588]. STC 11760.

Middleton, Thomas. *The Roaring Girle. Or Moll Cut-Purse*. London: [Nicholas Okes] for Thomas Archer, 1611. STC 17908.

Milton, John. *A Maske Presented At Ludlow Castle, 1634*. London: [Augustine Mathewes] for Humphrey Robinson, 1637. STC 17937.

Minsheu, John. *A Dictionarie in Spanish and English*. London: Edm. Bollifant, 1599. STC 19620.

———. *Ductor in Linguas, The Guide into Tongues*. Londini [London]: [William Stansby and Eliot's Court Press] for John Browne, 1617. STC 17944.

———. *Pleasant and Delightfull Dialogues in Spanish and English, profitable to the learner, and not unpleasant to any other Reader*. London: Edm. Bollifant, 1599. STC 19622.

Moffett, Thomas. *The Silkewormes, and their Flies: Lively described in verse*. London: V[alentine] S[immes] for Nicholas Ling, 1599. STC 17994.

Mulcaster, Richard. *The First Part of the Elementarie which Entreateth Chefelie of the right writing of our English tung*. London: Thomas Vautroullier, 1582. STC 18250.

———. *Positions wherin those Primitive Circumstances be Examined, which are Necessarie for the Training up of children, either for skill in their booke, or health in their bodie*. London: Thomas Vautrollier for Thomas Chare [Chard], 1581. STC 18253.

The new Testament in Englishe after the greeke translation annexed wyth the translation of Erasmus in Latin. Londini [London]: in officina Thomae Gualtier pro J. C[awood], 1550. STC 2821.

Perceval, Richard. *Bibliotheca Hispanica. Containing a Grammar; with a Dictionarie in Spanish, English, and Latine; gathered out of divers good Authors: very profitable for the studious of the Spanish toong*. London: John Jackson for Richard Watkins, 1591. STC 19619.

Phiston, William, trans. *The Most Pleasaunt and delectable Historie of Lazarillo de Tormes, a Spanyard: and of his Marvellous Fortunes and Adversities. The second part*. By Diego Hurtado de Mendoza. London: T[homas] C[reede] for John Oxenbridge, 1596. STC 15340.

Puttenham, George. *The Arte of English Poesie. Contrived into three Bookes: The first of Poets and Poesie, the second of Proportion, the third of Ornament*. London: Richard Field, 1589. STC 20519.

The Riddles of Heraclitus and Democritus. London: Arn. Hatfield for John Norton, 1598. STC 13174.

Rollock, Robert. *Lectures upon the First and Second Epistles of Paul to the Thessalonians*. Edinburgh: Robert Charteris, [1606]. STC 21281.

Sanforde, James, trans. *The Garden of Pleasure: Contayninge most pleasante Tales, worthy deeds and witty sayings of noble Princes & learned Philosophers, Moralized. No lesse delectable, than profitable*. By Lodovico Guicciardini. London: Henry Bynneman, 1573. STC 12464.

Shakespeare, William. *A Most pleasaunt and excellent conceited Comedie, of Syr John Falstaffe, and the merrie Wives of Windsor*. London: T[homas] C[reede] for Arthur Johnson, 1602. STC 22299.

———. *Mr. William Shakespeares Comedies, Histories, and Tragedies*. London: Isaac Jaggard, and Ed. Blount, 1623. STC 22273.

Sidney, Philip. *An Apologie for Poetrie*. London: [James Roberts] for Henry Olney, 1595. STC 22534.

Sidney Herbert, Mary, trans. *The Tragedie of Antonie. Doone into English by the Countesse of Pembroke*. By Robert Garnier. London: for William Ponsonby, 1595. STC 11623.

Spenser, Edmund. *Complaints: Containing sundrie small Poemes of the Worlds Vanitie*. London: for William Ponsonbie, 1591. STC 23078.

Stepney, William. *The Spanish Schoole-master. Containing Seven Dialogues, according to every day in the weeke, and what is necessarie everie day to be done, wherein is also most plainly shewed the true and perfect pronunciation of the Spanish tongue, toward the furtherance of all those which are desirous to learne the said tongue within this our Realme of England*. London: R. Field for John Harison, 1591. STC 23256.

Stocker, Thomas, trans. *Divers Sermons of Master John Calvin, concerning the Divinitie, Humanitie, and Nativitie of our Lorde Jesus Christe*. By John Calvin. London: [Thomas Dawson] for George Byshop, 1581. STC 4437.

Thomas, William. *Principal Rules of the Italian Grammer, with a Dictionarie for the better understandyng of Boccace, Petrarcha, and Dante*. London: Thomas Berthelet, 1550. STC 24020.

Thorius, John, trans. *The Spanish Grammer: With certeine Rules teaching both the Spanish and French tongues*. By Antonio del Corro. London: John Wolfe, 1590. STC 5790.

[Tomkis, Thomas]. *Lingua: Or The Combat of the Tongue, And the five Senses for Superiority*. London: G. Eld for Simon Waterson, 1607. STC 24104.

Torriano, Giovanni. *Vocabolario Italiano & Inglese, a Dictionary Italian & English*. London: T. Warren for Jo. Martin, Ja. Allestry, and Tho. Dicas, 1659. Wing F1368.

Verstegan, Richard. *A Restitution of Decayed Intelligence: In antiquities. Concerning the most noble and renowmed English nation*. Antwerp: Robert Bruney, 1605. STC 21361.

Vicars, John. *A Prospectiue Glasse to Looke Into Heauen, or The Caelestiall Canaan described*. London: W. Stansby for John Smethwicke, 1618. STC 24698.

Wilson, Thomas. *A Christian Dictionarie, Opening the signification of the chiefe wordes dispersed generally through Holie Scriptures of the Old and New Testament, tending to increase Christian knowledge*. London: W[illiam] Jaggard, 1612. STC 25786.

Primary Manuscript Sources

Biblioteca Nazionale Marciana Rari 0139. Shakespeare, *Comedies, Histories, & Tragedies*, 1632, annotated copy.

Bodleian Library Douce A.642. Aretino, *Ragionamenti*, 1597[?], Ben Jonson copy.

British Library C.12.e.17. Jonson, *Volpone*, 1607, John Florio copy.

British Library C.57.d.5. Kyd, *The Spanish Tragedie*, 1602, annotated copy.

British Library C.60.a.1(1). Guazzo, *Civil Conversatione*, 1581, Gabriel Harvey copy.

British Library C.60.a.1(2). Hollyband, *Arnalt & Lucenda*, 1575, Gabriel Harvey copy.

Cambridge University Library Peterborough G.6.40. Thomas, *Principal Rules*, 1562, John Florio copy[?].

Columbia University B85 Ar3. Aretino, *Ragionamenti*, 1584, annotated copy.

Columbia University KENT PA2364 .B35 1580g. Baret, *An Alvearie*, 1580, annotated copy.

Columbia University Plimpton 448 1582 Sa2. Hollyband, *French Schoole-maister*, 1582, Anne Chamberleine copy.

Folger Shakespeare Library PQ4621 .D3 M4 1566a Cage. Dolce, *Medea tragedia*, 1566, Gabriel Harvey copy.

Folger Shakespeare Library STC 1431.86. Berlaimont, *Colloquia*, 1616, Henry Delves copy.

Folger Shakespeare Library STC 12721 copy 2. Hall, *The union of the two noble and illustrate famelies*, 1548, Henry Sidney and Mary Dudley Sidney copy.

Houghton Library *EC.2623.Zz546t. Terence, *Le Comedie*, 1546, Gabriel Harvey copy.

Houghton Library EC.H2623.Zz507e. Euripides, *Hecuba et Iphigenia*, 1507, Gabriel Harvey copy.

Houghton Library EC.H2623.Zz578f. Florio, *Firste Fruites*, 1578. Gabriel Harvey copy.

Houghton Library STC 11098 (B). Florio, *Worlde of Wordes*, 1599, annotated copy.

Houghton Library STC 24021. Thomas, *Principal Rules*, 1562, Mary Sidney Herbert copy.

Huntington Library mssHM 60413. Commonplace book, Danby family of Yorkshire, approximately 1570–1625.

Huntington Library RB 53880. Thorius, *Spanish Grammer*, 1590, Gabriel Harvey copy.

Huntington Library RB 53922. Du Ploiche, *Treatise in Englishe and Frenche*, 1578, Gabriel Harvey copy.

Huntington Library RB 56972. Perceval, *Bibliotheca Hispanica*, 1591, Gabriel Harvey copy.

Huntington Library RB 60231. Eliot, *Ortho-epia Gallica*, 1593, Gabriel Harvey copy.

Huntington Library RB 62184. Grantham, *An Italian Grammer*, 1575, Gabriel Harvey copy.

Inner Temple Library Petyt MS 538.43.14. Mary Sidney Herbert, "Triumph of Death," 1601, nonauthorial manuscript copy.

Lambeth Palace Library MS 654 fol. 253a. Jacques Petit, letter mentioning a performance of *Titus Andronicus*, January 1596.

Österreichische Nationalbibliothek 19.V.22. Marlowe, *Edward the Second*, 1622, annotated copy.

Princeton University RHT 16th-99a. Tusser, *Five Hundred Pointes*, 1580, Gabriel Harvey copy.

University of Chicago PA2364.B3. Baret, *An Alvearie*, 1580, annotated copy.

University of Chicago PC2109.S58. Sherwood, *French Tutour*, 1625, Anne Chamberleine copy.

University of Chicago PC1109.T452 c.1. Thomas, *Principal Rules*, 1567, Robert Sackville copy.

University of Illinois Baldwin 0706. Berlaimont, *Colloquia*, 1623, annotated copy.

University of Utrecht MS 842 f. 132r. Arnoldus Buchelius, after Johannes de Witt, sketch of the Swan Theatre, ca. 1596.

Modern Editions

Aretino, Pietro. *Dialogues*. Edited and translated by Raymond Rosenthal. New York: Stein and Day, 1971.

———. *Sei Giornate: Ragionamento della Nanna e della Antonia (1534), Dialogo nel quale la Nanna insegna a la Pippa (1536), Scrittori d'Italia n. 245*. Edited by Giovanni Aquilecchia. Bari, Italy: Gius. Laterza and Figli, 1969.

Berlaimont, Noël de. *Colloquia et Dictionariolum Septem Linguarum*. Edited by R. W. R. Verdeyen. 3 vols. Vereeninging Derantwerpsche Bibliophilen, Uitgave Nr. 39, 40, 42. Antwerp: Nederlandsche Boekhandel, 1925–1935.

Busino, Horatio, and Thomas Platter. *The Journals of Two Travellers in Elizabethan and Early Stuart England*. Edited by Peter Razzell. London: Caliban, 1995.

Dekker, Thomas. *The Shoemaker's Holiday*. Edited by R. L. Smallwood and Stanley Wells. The Revels Plays. Manchester, UK: Manchester University Press, 1979; repr., 1999.

Donne, John. *The Divine Poems*. Edited by Helen Gardner. Oxford, UK: Clarendon, 1952.

Haughton, William. *Englishmen for My Money*. In *Three Renaissance Usury Plays*, edited by Lloyd Edward Kermode, 165–274. Manchester, UK: Manchester University Press, 2009.

———. *Englishmen for My Money; or A Woman Will Have Her Will*. Edited by Albert Croll Baugh. PhD diss., University of Pennsylvania, 1917.

The Holy Bible, Containing the Old and New Testaments. Edited by Josiah Forshall and Frederic Madden. 4 vols. Oxford, UK: Oxford University Press, 1850.

Jonson, Ben. *The Cambridge Edition of the Works of Ben Jonson*. Edited by David Bevington, Martin Butler, and Ian Donaldson. 7 vols. Cambridge, UK: Cambridge University Press, 2012.

———. *Epicene, or The Silent Woman*. Edited by Richard Dutton. Manchester, UK: Manchester University Press, 2003.

Kyd, Thomas. *The Spanish Tragedy*. Edited by Clara Calvo and Jesús Tronch. London: Arden Shakespeare, 2013.

Marlowe, Christopher. *Edward the Second*. Edited by Charles R. Forker. Manchester, UK: Manchester University Press, 1994.

Nashe, Thomas. *The Works of Thomas Nashe*. Edited by Ronald B. McKerrow. 5 vols. London: A. H. Bullen, 1904-1908.

Shakespeare, William. *Hamlet*. Edited by Ann Thompson and Neil Taylor. London: Arden Shakespeare, 2006.

———. *King Henry IV: Part 1*. Edited by David Scott Kastan. London: Arden Shakespeare, 2002.

———. *The Merchant of Venice*. Edited by John Drakakis. London: Arden Shakespeare, 2010.

———. *The Merry Wives of Windsor*. Edited by Giorgio Melchiori. London: Arden Shakespeare, 2000.

———. *A Midsummer Night's Dream*. Edited by Sukanta Chaudhuri. London: Arden Shakespeare, 2017.

———. *Much Ado About Nothing*. Edited by Claire McEachern. London: Arden Shakespeare, 2016.

———. *Othello*. Edited by E. A. J. Honigmann, with a new introduction by Ayanna Thompson. London: Arden Shakespeare, 2016.

———. *The Taming of the Shrew*. Edited by Barbara Hodgdon. London: Arden Shakespeare, 2010.

———. *The Tempest*. Edited by Virginia Mason Vaughan and Alden T. Vaughan. London: Arden Shakespeare, 1999.

———. *The Winter's Tale*. Edited by John Pitcher. London: Arden Shakespeare, 2010.

Sidney Herbert, Mary. *The Collected Works of Mary Sidney Herbert, Countess of Pembroke*. Edited by Michael Brennan, Margaret P. Hannay, and Noel J. Kinnamon. 2 vols. Oxford, UK: Clarendon, 1998.

———. "*The Triumph of Death*: A Critical Edition in Modern Spelling of the Countess of Pembroke's Translation of Petrarch's *Trionfo della Morte*." Edited by Gavin Alexander. *Sidney Journal* 17, no. 1 (1999): 2–18.

———. *The Triumph of Death and Other Unpublished and Uncollected Poems*. Edited by Gary F. Waller. Salzburg: Institut für Englische Sprache und Literatur, 1977.

Sidney, Philip. *The Poems of Sir Philip Sidney*. Edited by William A. Ringler Jr. Oxford, UK: Clarendon, 1962.

Spenser, Edmund. *The Mutabilitie Cantos*. Edited by Sheldon P. Zitner. London: Nelson, 1968.

Secondary Sources

Adair, E. R. "William Thomas: A Forgotten Clerk of the Privy Council." In *Tudor Studies*, edited by R. W. Seton-Watson, 133–60. London: Longmans, 1924.

Aggeler, Geoffrey. "The Eschatological Crux in *The Spanish Tragedy*." *Journal of English and Germanic Philology* 86, no. 3 (1987): 319–31.

Akhimie, Patricia, and Bernadette Andrea, eds. *Travel and Travail: Early Modern Women, English Drama, and the Wider World*. Lincoln: University of Nebraska Press, 2019.

Anderson, Amanda. *The Way We Argue Now: A Study in the Cultures of Theory*. Princeton, NJ: Princeton University Press, 2006.

Anderson, Benedict. *Imagined Communities: Reflections on the Origin and Spread of Nationalism*. London: Verso, 1991.

Andrews, Richard. *Scripts and Scenarios: The Performance of Comedy in Renaissance Italy*. Cambridge, UK: Cambridge University Press, 1993.

Appiah, Kwame Anthony. *Cosmopolitanism: Ethics in a World of Strangers*. New York: W. W. Norton, 2006.

Archer, John Michael. *Citizen Shakespeare: Freemen and Aliens in the Language of the Plays*. New York: Palgrave Macmillan, 2005.

Ardolino, Frank. "Hieronimo as Saint Jerome in *The Spanish Tragedy*." *Etudes Anglaises* 36, no. 4 (1983): 435–37.

———. "'Now Shall I See the Fall of Babylon': *The Spanish Tragedy* as a Reformation Play of Daniel." *Renaissance and Reformation* 14, no. 1 (1990): 49–55.

Bartolovich, Crystal. "London's the Thing: Alienation, the Market, and *Englishmen for My Money*." *Huntington Library Quarterly* 71, no. 1 (2008): 137–56.

Bate, Walter Jackson. *Samuel Johnson*. New York: Harcourt Brace Jovanovich, 1975.

Beecher, Donald A. "Aretino's Minimalist Art Goes to England." In *Pietro Aretino Nel Cinquecentenario della Nascita*, 2 vols., 2:775–85. Rome: Salerno, 1995.

Beilin, Elaine V. *Redeeming Eve: Women Writers of the English Renaissance*. Princeton, NJ: Princeton University Press, 1987.

Berec, Laurent. *Claude de Sainliens: Un Huguenot Borbonnais au Temps de Shakespeare*. Paris: Orizons, 2012.

Best, Stephen, and Sharon Marcus. "Surface Reading: An Introduction." *Representations* 108, no. 1 (2009): 1–21.

Bhabha, Homi K. "The Vernacular Cosmopolitan." In *Voices of the Crossing: The Impact of Britain on Writers from Asia, the Caribbean, and Africa*, edited by Ferdinand Dennis and Naseem Khan, 133–42. London: Serpent's Tail, 2000.

Billings, Timothy. "Two New Sources for Shakespeare's Bawdy French in *Henry V*." *Notes & Queries* 52, no. 2 (2005): 202–4.

Black, Joseph L. "The Sidneys and Their Books." In *The Ashgate Research Companion to the Sidneys, 1500–1700*, edited by Margaret P. Hannay, Mary Ellen Lamb, and Michael G. Brennan, 2 vols., 2:3–20. Burlington, VT: Ashgate, 2015.

Blank, Paula. *Broken English: Dialects and the Politics of Language in Renaissance Writings*. London: Routledge, 1996.

Blayney, Peter W. M. "The Publication of Playbooks." In *A New History of Early English Drama*, edited by John D. Cox and David Scott Kastan, 383–422. New York: Columbia University Press, 1997.

Boose, Lynda E. "The 1599 Bishops' Ban, Elizabethan Pornography, and the Sexualization of the Jacobean Stage." In *Enclosure Acts: Sexuality, Property, and Culture in Early Modern England*, edited by Richard Burt and John Michael Archer, 185–200. Ithaca, NY: Cornell University Press, 1994.

Bornstein, Diane. "The Style of the Countess of Pembroke's Translation of Philippe de Mornay's *Discourse de la vie et de la mort*." In *Silent but for the Word: Tudor Women as Patrons, Translators, and Writers of Religious Works*, edited by Margaret P. Hannay and Margaret Patterson, 126–48. Kent, OH: Kent State University Press, 1985.

Boro, Joyce. "Multilingualism, Romance, and Language Pedagogy; or, Why Were So Many Sentimental Romances Printed as Polyglot Texts?" In *Tudor Translation*, edited by Fred Schurink, 18–38. New York: Palgrave Macmillan, 2011.

Bosch, Lynette M. F. *Art, Liturgy, and Legend in Renaissance Toledo: The Mendoza and the Iglesia Primada*. University Park: Pennsylvania State University Press, 2000.

Bosman, Anston. "British Drama as a Polysystem: Visualizing Multilingualism and Mobility." *Shakespeare Studies* 48 (2020): 48–56.

———. "Renaissance Intertheater and the Staging of Nobody." *English Literary History* 71, no. 3 (2004): 559–85.

Boughner, Daniel C. "*Clizia* and *Epicoene*." *Philological Quarterly* 19 (1940): 89–91.

Bourland, Caroline B. "Gabriel Harvey and the Modern Languages." *Huntington Library Quarterly* 4, no. 1 (1940): 85–106.

———. "*The Spanish Schoole-master* and the Polyglot Derivatives of Noël de Berlaimont's *Vocabulare*." *Revue Hispanique* 81, no. 1 (1933): 283–318.

Bourne, Claire M. L. *Typographies of Performance in Early Modern England*. Oxford, UK: Oxford University Press, 2020.

Boutcher, Warren, "'A French Dexterity, & an Italian Confidence': New Documents on John Florio, Learned Strangers and Protestant Humanist Study of Modern Languages in Renaissance England from c. 1547 to c. 1625." *Reformation* 2, no. 1 (1997): 39–109.

Braden, Gordon. *Renaissance Tragedy and the Senecan Tradition*. New Haven, CT: Yale University Press, 1985.

Brady, Jennifer, and W. H. Herendeen, eds. *Ben Jonson's 1616 Folio*. Newark: University of Delaware Press, 1991.

Brayman Hackel, Heidi. *Reading Material in Early Modern England: Print, Gender, and Literacy*. Cambridge, UK: Cambridge University Press, 2005.

Breckenridge, Carol A., Sheldon Pollock, Homi K. Bhabha, and Dipesh Chakrabarty, eds. *Cosmopolitanism*. Durham, NC: Duke University Press, 2002.

Brennan, Timothy. *At Home in the World: Cosmopolitanism, Now*. Cambridge, MA: Harvard University Press, 1997.

Brooks, Douglas A. "Inky Kin: Reading in the Age of Gutenberg Paternity." In *The Book of the Play: Playwrights, Stationers, and Readers in Early Modern England*, edited by Marta Straznicky, 203–28. Amherst: University of Massachusetts Press, 2006.

Bruster, Douglas. "'In a Woman's Key': Women's Speech and Women's Language in Renaissance Drama." *Exemplaria* 4, no. 2 (1992): 235–66.

Bundock, Michael. *The Fortunes of Francis Barber: The True Story of the Jamaican Slave Who Became Samuel Johnson's Heir*. New Haven, CT: Yale University Press, 2015.

Burton, Jonathan. *Traffic and Turning: Islam and English Drama, 1579–1624*. Newark: University of Delaware Press, 2005.

Cady, Diane. "Linguistic Dis-Ease" Foreign Languages as Sexual Disease in Early Modern England." In *Sins of the Flesh: Responding to Sexual Disease in Early Modern Europe*, edited by Kevin Siena, 159–86. Toronto: Centre for Reformation and Renaissance Studies, 2005.

Cairns, Christopher. "Aretino's Comedies and the Italian 'Erasmian' Connection in Shakespeare and Jonson." In *Theatre of the English and Italian Renaissance*, edited by J. R. Mulryne and Margaret Shewring, 113–37. New York: St. Martin's, 1991.

Campbell, Oscar James. "The Relation of *Epicoene* to Aretino's *Il Marescalco*." *PMLA* 46, no. 3 (1931): 752–62.

Campos, Edmund Valentine. "Imperial Lexicography and the Anglo-Spanish War." In *Remapping the Mediterranean World in Early Modern English Writings*, edited by Goran V. Stanivukovic, 75–95. New York: Palgrave, 2007.

———. "Jews, Spaniards, and Portingales: Ambiguous Identities of Portuguese *Marranos* in Elizabethan England." *English Literary History* 69, no. 3 (2002): 599–616.

Carlson, Marvin. *Speaking in Tongues: Language Play in the Theatre*. Ann Arbor: University of Michigan Press, 2006.

Cheah, Pheng, and Bruce Robbins, eds. *Cosmopolitics: Thinking and Feeling Beyond the Nation*. Minneapolis: University of Minnesota Press, 1998.

Clarke, Danielle. "The Countess of Pembroke and the Practice of Piety." *Literature Compass* 9, no. 3 (2012): 252–61.

———. *The Politics of Early Modern Women's Writing*. Harlow, UK: Longman, 2001.

———. "The Politics of Translation and Gender in the Countess of Pembroke's *Antonie*." *Translation and Literature* 6, no. 2 (1997): 149–66.

Clegg, Cyndia Susan. *Shakespeare's Reading Audiences: Early Modern Books and Audience Interpretation*. Cambridge, UK: Cambridge University Press, 2017.

Clubb, Louise George. *Italian Drama in Shakespeare's England*. New Haven, CT: Yale University Press, 1989.

Coldiron, A. E. B. *Printers Without Borders: Translation and Textuality in the Renaissance*. Cambridge, UK: Cambridge University Press, 2015.

Considine, John. *Dictionaries in Early Modern Europe: Lexicography and the Making of Heritage*. Cambridge, UK: Cambridge University Press, 2008.

———. *Sixteenth-Century English Dictionaries*. Oxford, UK: Oxford University Press, 2022.

———. *Small Dictionaries and Curiosity: Lexicography and Fieldwork in Post-Medieval Europe*. Oxford, UK: Oxford University Press, 2017.

Cox, Virginia. *The Renaissance Dialogue: Literary Dialogue in its Social and Political Contexts, Castiglione to Galileo*. Cambridge, UK: Cambridge University Press, 1992.

Crane, Mary Thomas. *Framing Authority: Sayings, Self, and Society in Sixteenth-Century England*. Princeton, NJ: Princeton University Press, 1993.

Crosbie, Christopher. *Revenge Tragedy and Classical Philosophy on the Early Modern Stage*. Edinburgh: Edinburgh University Press, 2018.

De Filippis, Michele. "The Literary Riddle in Italy to the End of the Sixteenth Century." *University of California Publications in Modern Philology* 34, no. 1 (1948): 1–173.

de Grazia, Margreta. "Soliloquies and Wages in the Era of Emergent Consciousness." *Textual Practice* 9, no. 1 (1995): 67–92.

de Grazia, Margreta, Maureen Quilligan, and Peter Stallybrass, eds. *Subject and Object in Renaissance Culture*. Cambridge, UK: Cambridge University Press, 1996.

Derrida, Jacques. *Monolingualism of the Other; or, The Prosthesis of Origin*, trans. Patrick Mensah. Stanford, CA: Stanford University Press, 1998.

———. "On Cosmopolitanism." In *On Cosmopolitanism and Forgiveness*, trans. Mark Dooley and Michael Hughes, 3–24. London: Routledge, 2001.

De Rycker, Kate. "The Italian Job: John Wolfe, Giacomo Castelvetro and the Printing of Pietro Aretino." In *Specialist Markets in the Early Modern Book World*, edited by Richard Kirwan and Sophie Mullins, 241–57. Leiden: Brill, 2015.

———. "Staging the Imagined City: Aretino in Rome and London." *Renaissance Studies* 37, no. 2 (2023): 268–91.

Dillon, Janette. *Language and Stage in Medieval and Renaissance England.* Cambridge, UK: Cambridge University Press, 1998.

Dolan, Frances E. "Time, Gender, and the Mystery of English Wine." In *Gendered Temporalities in the Early Modern World,* edited by Merry E. Wiesner-Hanks, 19–46. Amsterdam: Amsterdam University Press, 2018.

Dolven, Jeff. *Scenes of Instruction in Renaissance Romance.* Chicago: University of Chicago Press, 2007.

Duncan, Dennis. *Index, A History of the: A Bookish Adventure from Medieval Manuscripts to the Digital Age.* New York: W. W. Norton, 2022.

Easterling, Heather C. *Parsing the City: Jonson, Middleton, Dekker, and City Comedy's London as Language.* New York: Routledge, 2007.

Eccles, Mark. "Claudius Hollyband and the Earliest French-English Dictionaries." *Studies in Philology* 83, no. 1 (1986): 51–61.

Ellerbeck, Erin. "The Female Tongue as Translator in Thomas Tomkis's *Lingua: or The Combat of the Tongue and the Five Senses for Superiority.*" *Renaissance and Reformation* 32, no. 1 (2009): 27–45.

Enterline, Lynn. *Shakespeare's Schoolroom: Rhetoric, Discipline, Emotion.* Philadelphia: University of Pennsylvania Press, 2012.

Erickson, Peter. "The Order of the Garter, the Cult of Elizabeth, and Class-Gender Tension in *The Merry Wives of Windsor.*" In *Shakespeare Reproduced: The Text in History and Ideology,* edited by Jean E. Howard and Marion F. O'Connor, 116–40. New York: Methuen, 1987.

Erne, Lukas. *Beyond "The Spanish Tragedy": A Study of the Works of Thomas Kyd.* Manchester, UK: Manchester University Press, 2001.

———. *Shakespeare and the Book Trade.* Cambridge, UK: Cambridge University Press, 2013.

Evans, Kasey. *Colonial Virtue: The Mobility of Temperance in Renaissance England.* Toronto: University of Toronto Press, 2012.

Farmer, Alan B. "Cosmopolitanism and Foreign Books in Early Modern England." *Shakespeare Studies* 35 (2007): 58–65.

Farmer, Alan B., and Zachary Lesser, eds. *DEEP: Database of Early English Playbooks.* Created 2007.

Fleck, Andrew. "'Ick verstaw you niet': Performing Foreign Tongues on the Early Modern English Stage." *Medieval & Renaissance Drama in England* 20 (2007): 204–21.

Fleming, Juliet. "The French Garden: An Introduction to Women's French." *English Literary History* 56, no. 1 (1989): 19–51.

Frantz, David O. *Festum Voluptatis: A Study of Renaissance Erotica.* Columbus: Ohio State University Press, 1989.

———. "Florio's Use of Contemporary Italian Literature in *A Worlde of Wordes.*" *Dictionaries* 1 (1979): 47–56.

Freeman, Arthur. *Thomas Kyd: Facts and Problems.* Oxford, UK: Clarendon, 1967.

Freer, Coburn. "Mary Sidney: Countess of Pembroke." In *Women Writers of the Renaissance and Reformation,* edited by Katharina Wilson, 481–521. Athens: University of Georgia Press, 1987.

———. *The Poetics of Jacobean Drama.* Baltimore: Johns Hopkins University Press, 1981.

Fuchs, Barbara. *The Poetics of Piracy: Emulating Spain in English Literature*. Philadelphia: University of Pennsylvania Press, 2013.

Gaby, Rosemary, Alice Leonard, James Mardock, and Helen Ostovich. "To Nell and Back: Revisiting Mistress Quickly." *Renaissance Drama* 47, no. 2 (2019): 201–37.

Gajowski, Evelyn, and Phyllis Rackin, eds. *"The Merry Wives of Windsor": New Critical Essays*. London: Routledge, 2015.

Galbraith, Steven K. "'English' Black-Letter Type and Spenser's *Shepheardes Calendar*." *Spenser Studies* 23, no. 1 (2008): 13–40.

Gallagher, John. "The Italian London of John North: Cultural Contact and Linguistic Encounter in Early Modern England." *Renaissance Quarterly* 70, no.1 (2017): 88–131.

———. *Learning Languages in Early Modern England*. Oxford, UK: Oxford University Press, 2019.

———. "'Ungratefull Tuscans': Teaching Italian in Early Modern England." *Italianist* 36, no. 3 (2016): 392–413.

Gamble, Joseph. "Practicing Sex." *Journal for Early Modern Cultural Studies* 19, no. 1 (2019): 85–116.

Games, Alison. *The Web of Empire: English Cosmopolitans in an Age of Empire*. Oxford, UK: Oxford University Press, 2008.

Goldberg, Jonathan. "The Countess of Pembroke's Literal Translation." In *Subject and Object in Renaissance Culture*, edited by Margreta de Grazia, Maureen Quilligan, and Peter Stallybrass, 321–36. Cambridge, UK: Cambridge University Press, 1996.

———. *Desiring Women Writing: English Renaissance Examples*. Stanford, CA: Stanford University Press, 1997.

———. "Speculations: *Macbeth* and Source." In *Shakespeare Reproduced: The Text in History and Ideology*, edited by Jean E. Howard and Marion F. O'Connor, 242–64. New York: Methuen, 1987.

———. *Writing Matter: From the Hands of the English Renaissance*. Stanford, CA: Stanford University Press, 1990.

Goodrich, Jaime. *Faithful Translators: Authorship, Gender, and Religion in Early Modern England*. Evanston, IL: Northwestern University Press, 2014.

Greenblatt, Stephen. *Learning to Curse: Essays in Early Modern Culture*. London: Routledge, 1990.

Greene, Roland. *Five Words: Critical Semantics in the Age of Shakespeare and Cervantes*. Chicago: University of Chicago Press, 2013.

———. *Unrequited Conquests: Love and Empire in the Colonial Americas*. Chicago: University of Chicago Press, 1999.

Greg, W. W. *A Bibliography of the English Printed Drama to the Restoration*. 4 vols. London: Bibliographical Society at Oxford University Press, 1939–1959.

———. *The Shakespeare First Folio: Its Bibliographic and Textual History*. Oxford, UK: Oxford University Press, 1955.

Griffin, Eric. *English Renaissance Drama and the Specter of Spain: Ethnopoetics and Empire*. Philadelphia: University of Pennsylvania Press, 2012.

Hadfield, Andrew. *Literature, Politics, and National Identity: Reformation to Renaissance*. Cambridge, UK: Cambridge University Press, 1994.

Halpern, Richard. *The Poetics of Primitive Accumulation: English Renaissance Culture and the Genealogy of Capital*. Ithaca, NY: Cornell University Press, 1991.

Hannay, Margaret P. "'Doo What Men May Sing': Mary Sidney and the Tradition of Admonitory Dedication." In *Silent but for the Word: Tudor Women as Patrons, Translators, and Writers of Religious Works*, edited by Margaret P. Hannay and Margaret Patterson, 149–65. Kent, OH: Kent State University Press, 1985.

———. *Philip's Phoenix: Mary Sidney, Countess of Pembroke*. Oxford, UK: Oxford University Press, 1990.

———. "Re-revealing the Psalms: Mary Sidney, Countess of Pembroke, and Her Early Modern Readers." In *Psalms in the Early Modern World*, edited by Lynda Phillis Austern, Kari Boyd McBride, and David L. Orvis, 19–36. Burlington, VT: Ashgate, 2011.

———. "'Your Vertuous and Learned Aunt': The Countess of Pembroke as a Mentor to Mary Wroth." In *Reading Mary Wroth: Representing Alternatives in Early Modern England*, edited by Naomi J. Miller and Gary F. Waller, 15–34. Knoxville: University of Tennessee Press, 1991.

Harris, Carissa. *Obscene Pedagogies: Transgressive Talk and Sexual Education in Late Medieval Britain*. Ithaca, NY: Cornell University Press, 2018.

Hattaway, Michael. *Elizabethan Popular Theatre: Plays in Performance*. London: Routledge, 1982.

Helgerson, Richard. *Adulterous Alliances: Home, State, and History in Early Modern European Drama and Painting*. Chicago: University of Chicago Press, 2000.

———. *Forms of Nationhood: The Elizabethan Writing of England*. Chicago: University of Chicago Press, 1992.

———. "Language Lessons: Linguistic Colonialism, Linguistic Postcolonialism, and the Early Modern English Nation." *Yale Journal of Criticism* 11, no. 1 (1998): 289–99.

———. *Self-Crowned Laureates: Spenser, Jonson, Milton, and the Literary System*. Berkeley: University of California Press, 1983.

Hendricks, Margo. "Race: A Renaissance Category?" In *A New Companion to English Renaissance Literature and Culture*, edited by Michael Hattaway, 2 vols., 1:535–44. Malden: Blackwell, 2010.

Henke, Robert, and Eric Nicholson, eds. *Transnational Exchange in Early Modern Theatre*. Aldershot, UK: Ashgate, 2008.

Hill, Eugene. "Senecan and Virgilian Perspectives in *The Spanish Tragedy*." *English Literary Renaissance* 15, no. 2 (1985): 143–65.

Hillman, Richard. "De-centring the Countess's Circle: Mary Sidney Herbert and Cleopatra." *Renaissance and Reformation* 28, no. 1 (2004): 61–79.

Historical Manuscripts Commission. *Report on the Manuscripts of Lord De L'Isle and Dudley Preserved at Penshurst Place*. 6 vols. London: HMSO, 1925–1966.

Hoenselaars, A. J. *Images of Englishmen and Foreigners in the Drama of Shakespeare and His Contemporaries: A Study of Stage Characters and National Identity in English Renaissance Drama, 1558–1642*. Rutherford, NJ: Fairleigh Dickinson University Press, 1992.

Höfele, Andreas, and Werner von Koppenfels, eds. *Renaissance Go-Betweens: Cultural Exchange in Early Modern Europe*. Berlin: Walter de Gruyter, 2005.

Holland, Peter. "*The Merry Wives of Windsor*: The Performance of Community." *Shakespeare Bulletin* 23, no. 2 (2005): 5–18.

Hooks, Adam G. *Selling Shakespeare: Biography, Bibliography, and the Book Trade*. Cambridge, UK: Cambridge University Press, 2016.

———. "Shakespeare's Beehive 2.0." *Anchora* (blog), March 2016.

Hopkins, Lisa. "What's Hercules to Hamlet? The Emblematic Garden in *The Spanish Tragedy* and *Hamlet*." *Hamlet Studies* 21, no. 1–2 (1999): 114–43.

Hoppe, Harry R. "John Wolfe, Printer and Publisher, 1579–1601." *The Library*, 4th ser., 14, no. 3 (1933): 241–88.

Howard, Jean E. "Crossdressing, the Theatre, and Gender Struggle in Early Modern England." *Shakespeare Quarterly* 39, no. 4 (1988): 418–40.

———. *The Stage and Social Struggle in Early Modern England*. New York: Routledge, 1994.

———. *Theater of a City: The Places of London Comedy, 1598–1642*. Philadelphia: University of Pennsylvania Press, 2007.

Huffman, Clifford Chalmers. *Elizabethan Impressions: John Wolfe and His Press*. New York: AMS, 1988.

Hui, Isaac. "Translation in Ben Jonson: Towards a Definition of Imitation." *Ben Jonson Journal* 20, no. 2 (2013): 223–40.

———. *Volpone's Bastards: Theorising Jonson's City Comedy*. Edinburgh: Edinburgh University Press, 2018.

Hüllen, Werner. *English Dictionaries 800–1700: The Topical Tradition*. Oxford, UK: Clarendon, 1999.

Jardine, Lisa, and Anthony Grafton. "'Studied for Action': How Gabriel Harvey Read His Livy." *Past and Present* 129 (November 1990): 30–78.

Johnson, S. F. "*The Spanish Tragedy*, or Babylon Revisited." In *Essays on Shakespeare and Elizabethan Drama in Honor of Hardin Craig*, edited by Richard Holsey, 23–36. London: Routledge, 1963.

Jondorf, Gillian. *Robert Garnier and the Themes of Political Tragedy in the Sixteenth Century*. Cambridge, UK: Cambridge University Press, 1969.

Jones, Richard Foster. *The Triumph of the English Language: A Survey of Opinions Concerning the Vernacular from the Introduction of Printing to the Restoration*. Stanford, CA: Stanford University Press, 1953.

Katritzky, M. A., and Pavel Drábek, eds. *Transnational Connections in Early Modern Theatre*. Manchester, UK: Manchester University Press, 2020.

Keener, Andrew S. "A 1562 Petrarchan Italian-English Dictionary Inscribed by 'Maria Sidney.'" *Sidney Journal* 36, no. 1 (2018): 41–52.

———. "Robert Tofte's *Of Mariage and Wiuing* and the Bishops' Ban of 1599." *Studies in Philology* 110, no. 3 (2013): 506–32.

———. "Windsor's World of Words: Multilingualism in *The Merry Wives of Windsor*." *English Literary Renaissance* 51, no. 3 (2021): 409–41.

Kermode, Lloyd Edward. *Aliens and Englishness in Elizabethan Drama*. Cambridge, UK: Cambridge University Press, 2009.

Kewes, Paulina. "'A Fit Memorial for the Times to Come . . .': Admonition and Topical Allusion in Mary Sidney's *Antonius* and Samuel Daniel's *Cleopatra*." *Review of English Studies*, n.s., 63, no. 259 (2011): 243–64.

Kibbee, Douglas A. *For to Speke French Trewely: The French Language in England,*

1000–1600: Its Status, Description, and Instruction. Amsterdam: John Benjamins, 1991.

Kiséry, András. "'Flowers for English Speaking': Play Extracts and Conversation." In *Rethinking Theatrical Documents in Shakespeare's England*, edited by Tiffany Stern, 155–74. London: Arden Shakespeare, 2020.

———. *"Hamlet"'s Moment: Drama and Political Knowledge in Early Modern England*. Oxford, UK: Oxford University Press, 2016.

Knight, Jeffrey Todd. *Bound to Read: Compilations, Collections, and the Making of Renaissance Literature*. Philadelphia: University of Pennsylvania Press, 2013.

Knutson, Roslyn L. "*Henslowe's Diary* and the Economics of Play Revision, 1592–1603." *Theater Research International* 10, no. 1 (1985): 1–18.

Kolkovich, Elizabeth Zeman. "Pageantry, Queens, and Housewives in the Two Texts of *The Merry Wives of Windsor*." *Shakespeare Quarterly* 63, no. 3 (2012): 328–54.

Koppelman, George, and Daniel Wechsler. *Shakespeare's Beehive: An Annotated Elizabethan Dictionary Comes to Light*. New York: Axletree, 2014.

Korda, Natasha. *Shakespeare's Domestic Economies: Gender and Property in Early Modern England*. Philadelphia: University of Pennsylvania Press, 2002.

Krontiris, Tina. *Oppositional Voices: Women as Writers and Translators in the English Renaissance*. London: Routledge, 1992.

Lacroix, Mylène. "Shakespeare au 'Banquet' des Langues Étrang(èr)es." *Actes des Congrès de la Société Française Shakespeare* 31 (2014): 1–17.

Lamb, Mary Ellen. "The Cooke Sisters: Attitudes toward Learned Women in the Renaissance." In *Silent but for the Word: Tudor Women as Patrons, Translators, and Writers of Religious Works*, edited by Margaret P. Hannay and Margaret Patterson, 107–25. Kent, OH: Kent State University Press, 1985.

———. "The Countess of Pembroke's Patronage." *English Literary Renaissance* 12, no. 2 (1982): 162–79.

———. *Gender and Authorship in the Sidney Circle*. Madison: University of Wisconsin Press, 1990.

———. "The Myth of the Countess of Pembroke: The Dramatic Circle." *Yearbook of English Studies* 11 (1981): 194–202.

Lambley, Kathleen. *The Teaching and Cultivation of the French Language in England during Tudor and Stuart Times*. Manchester, UK: Manchester University Press, 1920.

Lancashire, Ian, ed. *Lexicons of Early Modern English*. Toronto: University of Toronto Press and University of Toronto Libraries, 2021.

Landreth, David. "Once More into the Preech: The Merry Wives' English Pedagogy." *Shakespeare Quarterly* 55, no. 4 (2004): 420–49.

Lawrence, Jason. *Who the Devil Taught Thee So Much Italian? Italian Language Learning and Imitation in Early Modern England*. Manchester, UK: Manchester University Press, 2005.

LeFanu, William R. "Thomas Vautrollier, Printer and Bookseller." *Proceedings of the Huguenot Society of London* 20 (1959): 12–25.

Lesser, Zachary. "Typographic Nostalgia: Play-Reading, Popularity, and the Meanings of Black Letter." In *The Book of the Play: Playwrights, Stationers, and*

Readers in Early Modern England, edited by Marta Straznicky, 99–126. Amherst: University of Massachusetts Press, 2006.

Lever, J. W. "Shakespeare's French Fruits." *Shakespeare Survey* 6 (1953): 79–90.

Levine, Nina. *Practicing the City: Early Modern London on Stage*. New York: Fordham University Press, 2016.

Lewalski, Barbara K. *Writing Women in Jacobean England*. Cambridge, MA: Harvard University Press, 1993.

Lievsay, John Leon. *The Englishman's Italian Books, 1550–1700*. Philadelphia: University of Pennsylvania Press, 1969.

Loewenstein, Joseph. *Ben Jonson and Possessive Authorship*. Cambridge, UK: Cambridge University Press, 2002.

Magnusson, Lynne. "Language." In *The Oxford Handbook of Shakespeare*, edited by Arthur F. Kinney, 239–57. Oxford, UK: Oxford University Press, 2012.

Mann, Jenny C. *Outlaw Rhetoric: Figuring Vernacular Eloquence in Shakespeare's England*. Ithaca, NY: Cornell University Press, 2012.

Marcus, Leah S. *Unediting the Renaissance: Shakespeare, Marlowe, Milton*. London: Routledge, 1996.

Massai, Sonia. "John Wolfe and the Impact of Exemplary Go-Betweens on Early Modern Print Culture." In *Renaissance Go-Betweens: Cultural Exchange in Early Modern Europe*, edited by Andreas Höfele and Werner Von Koppenfels, 104–18. Berlin: Walter de Gruyter, 2005.

Masten, Jeffrey. "*More* or Less: Editing the Collaborative." *Shakespeare Studies* 29 (2001): 109–31.

———. "Playwrighting: Authorship and Collaboration." In *A New History of Early English Drama*, edited by John D. Cox and David Scott Kastan, 357–82. New York: Columbia University Press, 1997.

———. *Queer Philologies: Sex, Language, and Affect in Shakespeare's Time*. Philadelphia: University of Pennsylvania Press, 2016.

———. *Textual Intercourse: Collaboration, Authorship, and Sexualities in Renaissance Drama*. Cambridge, UK: Cambridge University Press, 1997.

Mazzio, Carla. *The Inarticulate Renaissance: Language Trouble in an Age of Eloquence*. Philadelphia: University of Pennsylvania Press, 2009.

McAlindon, Thomas. *English Renaissance Tragedy*. Vancouver: University of British Columbia Press, 1986.

McEachern, Claire. *The Poetics of English Nationhood, 1590–1612*. Cambridge, UK: Cambridge University Press, 1996.

McMillin, Scott. "The Book of Seneca in *The Spanish Tragedy*." *Studies in English Literature, 1500–1900* 14, no. 2 (1974): 201–8.

McPherson, David. "Aretino and the Harvey-Nashe Quarrel." *PMLA* 84, no. 6 (1969): 155–58.

———. "Ben Jonson's Library and Marginalia: An Annotated Catalogue." *Studies in Philology* 71, no. 5 (1974): 1–106.

Merrens, Rebecca. "'Ignoring the Men': Female Speech and Male Anxiety in Cavendish's *The Female Academy* and Jonson's *Epicoene*." *In-between* 9, no. 1 (2000): 243–60.

Miller, William E. "Double Translation in English Humanistic Education." *Studies in the Renaissance* 10 (1963): 163–74.

Miola, Robert S. "Seven Types of Intertextuality." In *Shakespeare, Italy, and Intertextuality*, edited by Michele Marrapodi, 13–25. Manchester, UK: Manchester University Press, 2004.

Montgomery, Marianne. *Europe's Languages on England's Stages, 1590–1620*. Farnham, UK: Ashgate, 2012.

Morrison, Mary. "Some Aspects of the Treatment of the Theme of Antony and Cleopatra in the Tragedies of the Sixteenth Century." *Journal of European Studies* 4, no. 2 (1974): 113–25.

Moulton, Ian Frederick. *Before Pornography: Erotic Writing in Early Modern England*. Oxford, UK: Oxford University Press, 2000.

Mullaney, Steven. *The Place of the Stage: License, Play, and Power in Renaissance England*. Ann Arbor: University of Michigan Press, 1995.

Mulryne, J. R. "Nationality and Language in Thomas Kyd's *The Spanish Tragedy*." In *Travel and Drama in Shakespeare's Time*, edited by Jean-Pierre Maquerlot and Michèle Villems, 87–105. Cambridge, UK: Cambridge University Press, 1996.

Nardizzi, Vin. *Wooden Os: Shakespeare's Theatres and England's Trees*. Toronto: University of Toronto Press, 2013.

Ndiaye, Noémie. *Scripts of Blackness: Early Modern Performance and Culture and the Making of Race*. Philadelphia: University of Pennsylvania Press, 2022.

Newman, Karen. *Cultural Capitals: Early Modern London and Paris*. Princeton, NJ: Princeton University Press, 2007.

———. *Fashioning Femininity and English Renaissance Drama*. Chicago: University of Chicago Press, 1991.

Ng, Su Fang. "Speaking Transnationally: Early Modern European Linguistic Exchanges with Islamic Southeast Asia." *Genre* 48, no. 2 (2015): 289–313.

Norland, Howard B. *Neoclassical Tragedy in Elizabethan England*. Newark: University of Delaware Press, 2009.

Nussbaum, Martha C. *The Cosmopolitan Tradition: A Noble but Flawed Ideal*. Cambridge, MA: Belknap, 2019.

———. "Patriotism and Cosmopolitanism." In *For Love of Country?* Boston: Beacon, 1996.

Oakley-Brown, Liz. *Ovid and the Cultural Politics of Translation in Early Modern England*. Burlington, VT: Ashgate, 2006.

Oldenburg, Scott. *Alien Albion: Literature and Immigration in Early Modern England*. Toronto: University of Toronto Press, 2014.

Orgel, Stephen. *Imagining Shakespeare: A History of Texts and Visions*. New York: Palgrave Macmillan, 2003.

———. *Impersonations: The Performance of Gender in Shakespeare's England*. Cambridge, UK: Cambridge University Press, 1996.

Ostovich, Helen. "Bucking Tradition in *The Merry Wives of Windsor*, 1602: Not a Bad Quarto, Really." In *"The Merry Wives of Windsor": New Critical Essays*, edited by Evelyn Gajowski and Phyllis Rackin, 96–106. London: Routledge, 2015.

Oxford Dictionary of National Biography. Oxford, UK: Oxford University Press, 2004. Online edition.

Oxford English Dictionary. Oxford, UK: Oxford University Press, 2023. Online edition.

Parker, Patricia. *Literary Fat Ladies: Rhetoric, Gender, Property*. London: Methuen, 1987.

———. *Shakespearean Intersections: Language, Contexts, Critical Keywords*. Philadelphia: University of Pennsylvania Press, 2018.

———. *Shakespeare from the Margins: Language, Culture, Context*. Chicago: University of Chicago Press, 1996.

Phillips, Susan E. "Schoolmasters, Seduction, and Slavery: Polyglot Dictionaries in Pre-Modern England." *Medievalia et Humanistica*, n.s., 34 (2008): 129–58.

———. *Transforming Talk: The Problem with Gossip in Late Medieval England*. University Park: Pennsylvania State University Press, 2007.

Pigman, G. W., III. "Versions of Imitation in the Renaissance." *Renaissance Quarterly* 33, no. 1 (1980): 1–32.

Pittenger, Elizabeth. "Dispatch Quickly: The Mechanical Reproduction of Pages." *Shakespeare Quarterly* 42, no. 4 (1991): 389–408.

Pollard, Alfred W. "Claudius Hollyband and his *French Schoolmaster* and *French Littelton*." *The Library*, 3rd ser., 6, no. 21 (1915): 77–93. Reprinted with the permission of The Bibliographical Society. Nendeln, Liechtenstein: Kraus Reprint, 1966.

———, ed. *A Short-Title Catalogue of Books Printed in England, Scotland, & Ireland and of English Books Printed Abroad, 1475–1640*. 2nd ed. Revised and enlarged by W. A. Jackson and F. S. Ferguson, and completed by Katharine F. Pantzer. London: Bibliographical Society, 1976–1991.

Pollock, Sheldon. "Cosmopolitanism and Vernacular in History." *Public Culture* 12, no. 3 (2000): 591–625.

———. "The Cosmopolitan Vernacular." *Journal of Asian Studies* 57, no. 1 (1998): 6–37.

———. "India in the Vernacular Millennium: Literary Culture and Polity, 1000–1500." *Daedalus* 127, no. 3 (1998): 41–74.

———. *The Language of the Gods in the World of Men: Sanskrit, Culture, and Power in Premodern India*. Berkeley: University of California Press, 2006.

Porter, Joseph A. "More Echoes from Eliot's *Ortho-epia Gallica*, in *King Lear* and *Henry V*." *Shakespeare Quarterly* 37, no. 4 (1986): 486–88.

Prescott, Anne Lake. "The Countess of Pembroke's Ruins of Rome." *Sidney Journal* 23, no. 1–2 (2005): 1–17.

———. "Mary Sidney's *Antonius* and the Ambiguities of French History." *Yearbook of English Studies* 38, no.1 (2008): 216–33.

Raber, Karen. *Dramatic Difference: Gender, Class, and Genre in the Early Modern Closet Drama*. Newark: University of Delaware Press, 2001.

Ramachandran, Ayesha. *The Worldmakers: Global Imagining in Early Modern Europe*. Chicago: University of Chicago Press, 2015.

Rancière, Jacques. *The Emancipated Spectator*. Translated by Gregory Elliott. London: Verso, 2011.

———. *The Ignorant Schoolmaster: Five Lessons in Intellectual Emancipation*. Translated by Kristin Ross. Stanford, CA: Stanford University Press, 1991.

Rastogi, Raashi. "Unruly Grammar: Linking Vernacular English to Changing Models of Early Modern Pedagogy and Power Politics." *English Literary Renaissance* 48, no. 1 (2018): 98–120.

Rhodes, Neil. *Elizabethan Grotesque*. London: Routledge, 1980.

Rickard, Jane. "Seventeenth-Century Readers of Jonson's 1616 *Works*." In *Ben Jonson and Posterity: Reception, Reputation, Legacy*, edited by Martin Butler and Jane Rickard, 85–104. Cambridge, UK: Cambridge University Press, 2020.

Rivera Recio, Juan Francisco. *La Iglesia de Toledo en el Siglo XII [i.e. doce] (1086–1208).* Toledo, Spain: Disputatión Provincial, 1976.

Roberts, Jeanne Addison. *Shakespeare's English Comedy: "The Merry Wives of Windsor" in Context.* Lincoln: University of Nebraska Press, 1979.

Robbins, Bruce, and Paulo Lemos Horta, eds. *Cosmopolitanisms.* New York: New York University Press, 2017.

Rubright, Marjorie. "Becoming Scattered: The Case of Iphis's Trans*version and the Archipelogic of John Florio's *Worlde of Wordes.*" In *Ovidian Transversions: "Iphis and Ianthe," 1300–1650*, edited by Valerie Traub, Patricia Badir, and Peggy McCracken, 118–49. Edinburgh: Edinburgh University Press, 2019.

———. *Doppelgänger Dilemmas: Anglo-Dutch Relations in Early Modern English Literature and Culture.* Philadelphia: University of Pennsylvania Press, 2014.

———. "Incorporating Kate: The Myth of Monolingualism in Shakespeare's *Henry the Fifth.*" In *The Oxford Handbook of Shakespeare and Embodiment: Gender, Sexuality, and Race*, edited by Valerie Traub, 468–90. Oxford, UK: Oxford University Press, 2016.

Salmon, Vivian. *Language and Society in Early Modern England: Selected Essays, 1981–1984.* Amsterdam: John Benjamins, 1996.

Santos, Kathryn Vomero. "Hosting Language: Immigration and Translation in *The Merry Wives of Windsor.*" In *Shakespeare and Immigration*, edited by Ruben Espinosa and David Ruiter, 59–72. Farnham, UK: Ashgate, 2014.

———. "Staging Translation in Early Modern England." PhD diss., New York University, 2013.

Scodel, Joshua. "Non-Dramatic Verse." In *The Oxford History of Literary Translation in English*, vol. 2, *1550–1660*, edited by Gordon Braden, Robert Cummings, and Stuart Gillespie, 212–47. Oxford, UK: Oxford University Press, 2010.

Sebek, Barbara. "'Wine and Sugar of the Best and the Fairest': Canary, the Canaries, and the Global in Windsor." In *Culinary Shakespeare: Staging Food and Drink in Early Modern England*, edited by David B. Goldstein and Amy L. Tigner, 41–56. Pittsburgh: Duquesne University Press, 2016.

Shaheen, Naseeb. "Shakespeare's Knowledge of Italian." *Shakespeare Survey* 47 (1994): 161–69.

Shannon, Laurie. *Sovereign Amity: Figures of Friendship in Shakespearean Contexts.* Chicago: University of Chicago Press, 2002.

Shapiro, James. *Shakespeare and the Jews.* 1997. 20th anniversary ed. with a new preface by the author. New York: Columbia University Press, 2016.

Shapiro, Michael. *Children of the Revels: The Boy Companies of Shakespeare's Time and Their Plays.* New York: Columbia University Press, 1977.

Sherman, William H. *Used Books: Marking Readers in Renaissance England.* Philadelphia: University of Pennsylvania Press, 2008.

Shrank, Cathy. *Writing the Nation in Reformation England, 1530–1580.* Oxford, UK: Oxford University Press, 2006.

Siemon, James R. "Sporting Kyd." *English Literary Renaissance* 24, no. 3 (1994): 553–82.

Singh, Jyotsna G., ed. *A Companion to the Global Renaissance: English Literature and Culture in the Era of Expansion.* London: Wiley-Blackwell, 2013.

Skretkowicz, Victor. "Mary Sidney Herbert's *Antonius*, English Philhellenism and the Protestant Cause." *Women's Writing* 6, no. 1 (1999): 7–25.

Sledd, James. "Baret's *Alvearie*, an Elizabethan Reference Book." *Studies in Philology* 43, no. 2 (1946): 147–63.

Smith, Emma. "'So Much English by the Mother': Gender, Foreigners, and the Mother Tongue in William Haughton's *Englishmen for My Money*." *Medieval & Renaissance Drama in England* 13 (2001): 165–81.

Sofer, Andrew. *The Stage Life of Props*. Ann Arbor: University of Michigan Press, 2003.

Sperrazza, Whitney. "Mary Sidney's Postmortem Poetics." *Shakespeare Studies* 49 (2021): 175–80.

Spiess, Stephen. "Shakespeare's Whore: Language, Prostitution, and Knowledge in Early Modern England." PhD diss., University of Michigan, 2013.

Stage, Kelly J. *Producing Early Modern London: A Comedy of Urban Space, 1598–1616*. Lincoln: University of Nebraska Press, 2018.

Stallybrass, Peter. "Patriarchal Territories: The Body Enclosed." In *Rewriting the Renaissance: The Discourses of Sexual Difference in Early Modern Europe*, edited by Margaret W. Ferguson, Maureen Quilligan, and Nancy J. Vickers, 123–42. Chicago: University of Chicago Press, 1986.

Stallybrass, Peter, and Allon White. *The Politics and Poetics of Transgression*. London: Methuen, 1986.

Stamatakis, Chris. "'With Diligent Studie, but Sportingly': How Gabriel Harvey Read His Castiglione." *Journal of the Northern Renaissance* 5. Published online November 9, 2013.

Starnes, DeWitt T. *Renaissance Dictionaries: English-Latin and Latin-English*. Austin: University of Texas Press, 1954.

Steadman, John M. "Falstaff as Actaeon: A Dramatic Emblem." *Shakespeare Quarterly* 14, no. 3 (1963): 231–44.

Stern, Tiffany. *Documents of Performance in Early Modern England*. Cambridge, UK: Cambridge University Press, 2009.

———, ed. *Rethinking Theatrical Documents in Shakespeare's England*. London: Arden Shakespeare, 2020.

———. "Watching as Reading: The Audience and the Written Text in Shakespeare's Playhouse." In *How to Do Things with Shakespeare: New Approaches, New Essays*, edited by Laurie Maguire, 136–59. Malden, MA: Blackwell, 2008.

Stern, Virginia F. *Gabriel Harvey: His Life, Marginalia, and Library*. Oxford, UK: Clarendon, 1979.

Stewart, Alan. "'Euery Soyle to Mee is Naturall': Figuring Denization in William Haughton's *English-men for My Money*." *Renaissance Drama*, n.s., 35 (2006): 55–81.

Stoughton, Nigel. "Mars and Mercury at Market: An Engraved Title-Page for Noel van Barlement, *Dictionariolum et colloquia*, 1662." *Book Collector* 67, no. 4 (2018): 873–74.

Strycharski, Andrew. "Some Verses of Henry and Mary Dudley Sidney and Prince Edward's 'Little School.'" *American Notes & Queries* 24, no. 4 (2011): 249–54.

Symonds, John Addington. *Renaissance in Italy: Italian Literature*. 2 vols. London: Smith, Elder, 1881.

Talvacchia, Bette. *Taking Positions: On the Erotic in Renaissance Culture*. Princeton, NJ: Princeton University Press, 1999.

Traister, Barbara. "A French Physician in an English Community." In *"The Merry Wives of Windsor": New Critical Essays*, edited by Evelyn Gajowski and Phyllis Rackin, 121–29. London: Routledge, 2015.

Traub, Valerie. *The Renaissance of Lesbianism in Early Modern England*. Cambridge, UK: Cambridge University Press, 2002.

———. *Thinking Sex with the Early Moderns*. Philadelphia: University of Pennsylvania Press, 2016.

Tudeau-Clayton, Margaret. *Shakespeare's Englishes: Against English*. Cambridge, UK: Cambridge University Press, 2020.

Turner, James Grantham. *Schooling Sex: Libertine Literature and Erotic Education in Italy, France, and England, 1534–1685*. Oxford, UK: Oxford University Press, 2003.

Ungerer, Gustav. *Anglo-Spanish Relations in Tudor Literature*. Bern: Francke, 1956.

Valenza, Robin. "How Literature Becomes Knowledge: A Case Study." *English Literary History* 76, no. 1 (2009): 215–45.

Venuti, Lawrence. *The Translator's Invisibility: A History of Translation*. London: Routledge, 1995.

Vitkus, Daniel. *Turning Turk: English Theater and the Multicultural Mediterranean, 1570–1630*. New York: Palgrave Macmillan, 2003.

Wall, Wendy. *The Imprint of Gender: Authorship and Publication in the English Renaissance*. Ithaca, NY: Cornell University Press, 1993.

———. *Recipes for Thought: Knowledge and Taste in the Early Modern English Kitchen*. Philadelphia: University of Pennsylvania Press, 2016.

———. *Staging Domesticity: Household Work and English Identity in Early Modern Drama*. Cambridge, UK: Cambridge University Press, 2002.

Waller, Gary F. *Mary Sidney, Countess of Pembroke: A Critical Study of Her Writings and Literary Milieu*. Salzburg: Institut für Anglistik and Amerikanistik, 1979.

Wall-Randell, Sarah. "What Is a Staged Book? Books as 'Actors' in the Early Modern English Theatre." In *Rethinking Theatrical Documents in Shakespeare's England*, edited by Tiffany Stern, 128–51. London: Arden Shakespeare, 2020.

Warkentin, Germaine, Joseph L. Black, and William R. Bowen, eds. *The Library of the Sidneys of Penshurst Place Circa 1665*. Toronto: University of Toronto Press, 2013.

Watson, Robert N. "Shakespeare's New Words." *Shakespeare Survey* 65 (2012): 358–77.

Weiss, Adrian. "Casting Compositors, Foul Cases, and Skeletons: Printing in Middleton's Age." In *Thomas Middleton and Early Modern Textual Culture: A Companion to the Collected Works*, edited by Gary Taylor and John Lavagnino, 195–225. Oxford, UK: Oxford University Press, 2008.

Werner, Winter Jade. *Missionary Cosmopolitanism in Nineteenth-Century British Literature*. Columbus: Ohio State University Press, 2020.

West, William N. "'But This Will Be a Mere Confusion': Real and Represented Confusions on the Elizabethan Stage." *Theater Journal* 60, no. 2 (2008): 217–33.

———. "Intertheatricality." In *Early Modern Theatricality*, edited by Henry S. Turner, 151–72. Oxford, UK: Oxford University Press, 2013.

White, Micheline. "Renaissance Englishwomen and Religious Translation: The Case of Anne Lock's *Of the Markes of the Children of God* (1590)." *English Literary Renaissance* 29, no. 3 (1999): 375–400.

Williams, Deanne. *The French Fetish from Chaucer to Shakespeare.* Cambridge, UK: Cambridge University Press, 2004.

Williams, Franklin B., Jr. "Scholarly Publication in Shakespeare's Day: A Leading Case." In *Joseph Quincy Adams Memorial Studies,* edited by James G. MacManaway, Giles E. Dawson, and Edwin E. Willoughby, 755–73. Washington, DC: Folger Shakespeare Library, 1948.

Wilson-Lee, Edward. "Women's Weapons: Country House Diplomacy in the Countess of Pembroke's French Translations." In *The Culture of Translation in Early Modern England and France, 1500–1660,* edited by Tania Demetriou and Rowan Tomlinson, 128–44. Basingstoke: Palgrave Macmillan, 2015.

Wing, Donald, ed., with John J. Morrison and Carolyn W. Nelson. *Short-Title Catalogue of Books Printed in England, Scotland, Ireland, Wales, and British America, and of English Books Printed in Other Countries, 1641–1700.* 2nd ed. New York: Modern Language Association of America, 1992–98.

Witmore, Michael, and Heather Wolfe. "Buzz or Honey? Shakespeare's Beehive Raises Questions." *Collation* (blog), April 21, 2014.

Woodfield, Denis B. *Surreptitious Printing in England, 1550–1640.* New York: Bibliographical Society of America, 1973.

Wyatt, Michael. *The Italian Encounter with Tudor England: A Cultural Politics of Translation.* Cambridge, UK: Cambridge University Press, 2005.

Yates, Frances A. *John Florio: The Life of an Italian in Shakespeare's England.* Cambridge, UK: Cambridge University Press, 1934.

Yates, Julian. *Error, Misuse, Failure: Object Lessons from the English Renaissance.* Minneapolis: University of Minnesota Press, 2003.

Zeman, Corrine. "Sultanic Drag in Ben Jonson's *Epicene.*" *Shakespeare Studies* 47 (2019): 134–40.

Zucker, Adam. *The Places of Wit in Early Modern English Comedy.* Cambridge, UK: Cambridge University Press, 2001.

Index

Page numbers in italics refer to figures

Actaeon myth, 30, 31
Adams, Thomas, 76, 77
Allde, Edward, 170n29
Anderson, Amanda, 12, 172n47
Anderson, Benedict, 8
Andrews, Richard, 146, 210n74
Appiah, Kwame Anthony, *Cosmopolitanism*, 32; cosmopolitan as anti-Semitic or xenophobic slur, 11; and partial cosmopolitanism, 11, 171n44
Archer, John Michael, 27, 173n58, 176n106
Aretino, Pietro, 48, 209n62; Bishop's Ban, 151, 209n64; engravings depicting sexual positions, 147; *Il Marescalco*, 34, 140–42, 154, 210n70, 210n74; *Quattro comedie*, 48, 147, 151, 209n66; theatergrammatical adaptations of female speech, 151
Aretino, Pietro, *Ragionamenti*, 7, 34, 141, *152*, 153, 207n44, 210n79, 210n81; academic and erotic tradition of Italian riddling, 142; Aretino's linking of riddles to himself, 146, 154; "Cosmopoli" edition, 1660, 76, 148, *150*, 191n33; cosmopolitan position in vernaculars of Europe, 148; and gossips' feast, 207n45; imitations of in prose, satire, and drama, 148; as Italian source for Jonson's *Epicene*, 135, 140, 153–60, 205n31, 206–7nn38–39, 209n65; reader underlining and glossing in Italian and English, 147–48, *149*; second part of, 207n46; theatrical format, 153; Wolfe's Italian-language edition of, 147–48; women's erotic rhymes and riddles in context of lessons, 143–46
Ariosto, Ludovico, *Suppositi*, 48
Aristotle, 55, 138
ars moriendi, 71, 80, 91–92, 96
Ascham, Roger, 40, 43, 47, 147, 161, 182n43, 208n52; and "double translation," 38, 39, 45, 55; language instructor for Queen Elizabeth, 39, 93; on need for translation in language learning, 42, 179n13; *The Scholemaster*, 1570, 32, 36, 38, 39, 42, 132, 179n16

Barber, Francis (born Quashey), 165
Baret, John, *Alvearie*, 183n55; annotated copy of Koppelman and Wechsler, 39, 42, 163; association of translation with "gathering and framing," 42; bilingual translation exercises for and by students, 39–42, 44, 50, 51, 54, 67, 179n14, 179n16, 181n33; "change" as translation or mutation and as inconstancy, 74; dictionary in English, French, Greek, and Latin, 33, 39, 58; discourse of bees and beehives and beehive frontispiece, 40, *41*, 59; inscriptions and additions to dictionary by users, 42, 163
Baugh, Albert Croll, 130, 200n41, 200n45

Beilin, Elaine V., 83, 87–88, 96, 192n44, 195n84
Berlaimont, Noël de, *Colloquia et Dictionariolum*, 34, 163, 174n69, 174nn72–73; "A Dinner of Ten Persons" dialogue, 18; Antwerp edition of 1616, and inscribed words on bound-in blank leaves, 110–11, *111*; catchwords, 109, 199n27; common elements with tavern scene in *Henry IV Part I*, 18, 20, 24; "compressed translation," 102–3, 174n70, 198n21; dialogues featuring mercantile exchange, 106–7; dialogues in eight languages, 18, 20, 23, 32, 102, 174n72, 198n21; and discourse of exchange and interchangeability represented in *Englishmen for My Money*, 100–101, 118; frontispiece of 1662 portraying same-sex interchangeability, *104*, 105–6, 108, 119, 125, 126, 198n18; frontispieces portraying eight figures, from 1631 and 1662, 103, *104*, 105–6, 120–21; hostess and lodger dialogue, 20, 22, 25, 26, 30, 31; and male homosociality as site for cosmopolitan exchange, 105–6, *106*; and *Merry Wives*, 17, 18; mise-en-page, 18, *19*, 102, 107–9, 129, 174n70, 197n12, 199n27; printing techniques, 109, *110*; "Proposes of merchandise" dialogue, 107, 124; publication history and features, 18, 102; readers' inscriptions of monetary conversions, 111–12, *112*; representation of Janus-Mercury-Mars on frontispiece of 1662 edition, 24, *24*, 105, 198n19; *The Spanish Schoole-master* (Stepney version), 18, 174n73; specified as useful to merchants, 7, 103, 197n15; typographical illustration of foreign languages, 107–9, 120; Venice and Bologna editions, and typography, 108
Best, Stephen, 6
Bevington, David, 141–42, 210n73, 210n78
Bhabha, Homi K., "cosmopolitan vernaculars," 8, 9–10, 11
black-letter type, 44–45, 108–9, 181n33, 184n62, 198n26, 203n4
Blayney, Peter W. M., 187n103
Blount, Edward, 170n29
Boccaccio, Giovanni, *Decameron*, 147
Boose, Lynda, 151
border crossing: and cosmopolitan vernaculars, 3, 9, 23, 28, 76, 78, 105, 157; and early modern English theater, 5, 57–58, 70–71, 96–97, 122, 128, 169n22; use of citizenship terms for, 13, 70
Boro, Joyce, 47, 175n78
Bosman, Anston: and multilingualism of English plays, 10; "Renaissance intertheater," 3, 5, 57–58, 153, 160
Bourland, Caroline B., 45, 47
Bourne, Claire M. L., and relation between early modern book design and dramaturgy, 7–8, 133, 170n26, 184n63, 186n93, 197n10, 211n5
Boutcher, Warren, 47
Brandon, Samuel, 195n87
Brathwait, Richard, *The English Gentleman (1630)*, frontispiece, 105, *106*
Breckenridge, Carol A., 11
Brennan, Timothy, 10
Brooks, Douglas A., 203n78
Bryskett, Lodowick, 14
Bullokar, William, *Bref Grammar for English*, 17
Burton, Jonathan, 123
Busino, Horatio, 117–18

Cady, Diane, 115, 200n44, 200n46
Calhoun, Joshua, 170n26
Calvin, John, 75; Calvinism, 190n16
Camden, William: dictionary of English surnames, 201n65; on linguistic mingling in English language, 12–13, 34
Campbell, Oscar, 140–41, 206n32
Campos, Edmund Valentine, 113, 200n47
Carew, Richard (trans.), *The Examination of Men's Wits*, 56, 136

Cary, Elizabeth, 195n87
Castelvetro, Giacomo, 34, 147, 153
Castiglione, Baldassare, *The Courier*, 181n33
catchwords, 109, 199n27
Caussin, Nicholas, 75
Cawdrey, Robert, *A Table Alphabeticall*, 17
Cecil, William, 40
Chakrabarty, Dipesh, 11
Chamberleine, Anne, annotations in French-language books, 57, 185n83
"change," and discourse of translation: association with inconstancy in bilingual dictionaries and theological discourse, 74–76; association with "translate" or "mutate" in bilingual dictionaries, 74; in Book of Job, 1560 Geneva Bible, 73, 74, 90, 91, 96; connotations of in gendered contexts, 74–75; current meanings, 190n19; as divine transport to life after death, 73–76; in First Letter to the Corinthians, Geneva Bible, 69, 73, 91; in Letter to the Hebrews, Enoch's "translation" from earthly realm to heaven, 72–73, 74, 91
Cheah, Pheng, 10
Cheke, John, 47
city comedy, 134, 134, 140, 141, 160; inadequacy as subgeneric term, 131, 135; multilingual and foreign elements, 164; view of *Englishmen for My Money* as, 34, 100, 101, 130–31, 203n82
"city talk," 34, 115, 141, 160, 200n42, 206n35
Clarke, Danielle, 96, 193n50, 195n76
Clegg, Cyndia Susan, 7
Cleopatra (character), 34, 88, 89, 91, 92–98, 192n34, 194n63, 194n65, 195n74, 195nn77–78, 195n84, 195n87
closet drama: as enacting a theatrical drama in one's own mind, 8, 87, 163; Sidney Herbert's *Tragedy of Antony* as, 7–8, 33, 70–71, 72, 86, 97, 163
Clubb, Louise George: Mistress Quickly, 168n10; transnationally circulating "theatergrams," 5–6, 141, 206n33
Coldiron, A. E. B.: and catchwords, 109; and "catenary" and "radiant" texts, 103; and "compressed translation," 102–3, 174n70; *Images of the Old Testament*, 182n39; and *translatio imperii*, 178n9; typography, 181n30, 181n33, 198n26
Colet, John, 1
Company of Turkey Merchants, London, 114
Concetti di Girolamo Garimberto, 79
"confusion," as mingling of multiple languages, 37, 58, 61–62, 137, 178n5, 205n25
Considine, John, 3, 168n11, 180n20
Contarino, Luigi, 47
copia, 43, 58, 59, 61, 115, 135, 140
Corro, Antonio del, 115; *Reglas Gramaticales para Aprender la Lengua Española y Francesa*, 44
"cosmofeminine," 11
cosmopolitanisms: "city talk," 34, 115, 141, 160, 200n42, 206n35; linguistic, in early modern England, 12; London as a space for, 170n22; "minoritarian cosmopolitanisms," 11; modern critical narratives, 10–11; "new cosmopolitanisms," 11; partial cosmopolitanism, 11; studies emphasizing Greco-Kantian genealogy and modern applications, 11. *See also* Appiah, Kwame Anthony, *Cosmopolitanism*
cosmopolitan vernaculars, early modern Europe, 14; accessibility to socially elite and literate women, 57; anthropomorphized in terms of citizenship, naturalization, and denization, 12, 13, 136; and border crossing, 3, 9, 23, 28, 78, 105, 157; circulation between language-learning publications and playhouses, 3–8, 9, 12, 16–17, 35, 151, 153, 163; and classical languages, 138–39, 205n24; and development of England as imperial power, 4, 9, 35, 164; in domains of

education, religion, economics, and sex, 9; mercantile-themed, theatrical expression of, 34, 99–102, 114, 119, 128, 130–31; and schoolroom practices, 3–4, 9, 39–40, 45, 50, 163–64. *See also* vernacular education
"cosmopolite": Dee's progressive view of, 75–76; Protestant contempt for as worldly sinfulness, 76
Cosmopolitics (Cheah, Pheng, and Bruce Robbins), 10–11
Cotgrave, Randle, French-English lexicon, 23, 25, 99, 200n45, 201n55
Crane, Mary Thomas, 180n20
Creede, Thomas, 191n30
Crosbie, Christopher, 58–59, 186n90
cross-dressing as translation: Haughton's *Englishmen for My Money*, 127; Jonson's *Epicene*, 34, 159; *The Merry Wives of Windsor*, 29–30, 159, 177n109, 177n111

Daniel, Samuel, 84, 98, 113, 195n87
Davies, John, 84, 147
Dee, John, on "cosmopolites," 12, 75–76, 77
De Filippis, Michele, 142
de Grazia, Margreta, 12, 187n108; interpretation of *Hamlet*'s Q1, 66
Dekker, Thomas, 130; *The Shoemaker's Holiday*, 32, 65, 122
Delamothe, George, *French Alphabeth*, 170n29
Delves, Henry, Second Baron of Cheshire, 110–11, 112, 199n29
denization, linguistic, 12–13, 136, 163
"denizen," foreigner made English by royal patent, 13, 70, 188nn3–4
Denny, Edward, 84
Derrida, Jacques: on mixed nature of English language, 13, 163; on modern cosmopolitan projects, 11
De Villalobos, Francisco, 56–57
dictionaries: and European Enlightenment, 165; and meanings of "change," 74–76; and vernacular language study and dramatic reading, 48, 50, 183n47; words and phrases from in theatrical productions, 22–23. *See also* language-learning publications, multilingual
Dillon, Janette, 51, 52
discipline in early modern education, 42, 180n22
Dolan, Frances E., 22
Dolce, Lodovico: *Medea*, 47; *Thieste*, 47, 188n119
Dolven, Jeff, 66
Donne, John, on Sidney Herbert and Philip Sidney as "translated translators," 69, 71, 83, 86, 91
double-translation language learning, 38, 39, 45, 164
Drummond, William, 209n66
du Ploiche, Pierre, *Treatise in Englishe and Frenche*, 47, 48
Dutch and English, similarity of, 120, 201n58
Dutton, Richard, Revels edition of *Epicene*, 141, 142, 206n38

education. *See* vernacular education
Eliot, John: bilingual language manuals, 17; *Ortho-epia Gallica*, 47, 147; pedagogical rivalry between Eliot and Florio, 208n54
Elizabeth, Queen: appeal to, 173n58; Ascham as language instructor for, 39; language skills, 57, 93; Mistress Quickly, 31, 177n117; Sidney Herbert's views of, 84, 195n76
Ellerbeck, Ellen, and Tomkis's *Lingua*, 137–38
"Englishing," as translation, 26, 133, 159, 187n109
English language, early modern: transnational and transatlantic scope of, 5; use of "foreigner," "alien," and "stranger," 173n62, 191n30, 196n1; vernacular, 168n12. *See also* "change," and discourse of translation; cosmopolitan vernaculars, early modern Europe
Enoch, in Letter to the Hebrews,

"translation" from earthly realm to heaven, 72–73, 74
Enterline, Lynn, 3, 43, 183n56
Erasmus: Latin translations of Euripides's *Hecuba* and *Iphigenia*, 47; rhetorical *copia*, 43
Erne, Lukas, 37, 184n72
Erondelle, Pierre, *The French Garden*, 8, 57, 185n82
Escuela de Traductores Toledanos, Toledo, 55

Farmer, Alan B., 191n30
Field, Richard, 17, 148, 174n66, 191n33
First Folio, Shakepeare, 6, 170n29
First Letter to the Corinthians, and "change," Geneva Bible, 69, 73, 91
Fleming, Juliet, 57
Florio, John, 4, 5, 61, 68, 71, 97, 114, 115, 124, 144, 166, 192n47, 204n6, 209n62; advocate for Aretino, 151; bilingual language manuals, 17, 47, 163; definitions of "change," 74; definitions of *tradurre*, 135–36, 154, 159, 195n83, 195n83, 204n12; English translation of Montaigne's *Essais*, 134–35, 140, 161; *Firste Fruites*, 21, 48, 53, 59, 148, 183n47; gendered treatment of translation, 123, 134, 135, 141, 190n12, 211n90; inscriptions on personal copy of Thomas's *Principale Rules*, 161–62, *162*; key to language in *Ragionamenti's* dialogues, 148; pedagogical rivalry between Eliot and Florio, 208n54; and *Quattro Comedie*, 209n66; *Second Fruites*, 59; *A Worlde of Wordes* (Italian-English lexicon), 8, 23, 27, 74, 148, 151, 161, 164–65, 166, 170n29, 195n83, 209n66
foreign languages: association with violence, 117, 200n48; in city comedies, 164; cosmopolitan mixing of with English in *The Merry Wives of Windsor*, 14, 16–17, 173n63; as social and conversational practice, 162; study of, 179n11; typographical illustrations of in dramatic publications, 51, 54, 118, 119–20, 132–33, 151, 153, 158, 168n7, 184n62, 203n2, 203n4; typographical illustrations of in language-learning publications, 82, 108–9, 163. *See also* cosmopolitan vernaculars, early modern Europe; language-learning publications, multilingual
Franco, Niccolò, tradition of "cock-riddles," 146
Frantz, David, 153
French vernacular, women's study of, 57, 185n82

Galen, 55
Gallagher, John, 3, 4, 174n70; drinking rituals in language-learning manuals, 175n77; on female conversation, 185n82; and foreign language as social and conversational practice, 110, 162; on Hollyband's texts, 181n28; language-learning practices, 182n38; and language manuals directed toward merchants, 103; on notion of monoglot nation, 173n59; polyglot conversation manuals, 197n12, 199n30; on prefatory spaces in language-learning manuals, 40; violence and foreign language in early modern England, 200n48
Garnier, Robert: *Cornélie*, 51; *Marc Antoine*, 33, 89, 90–93, 95–98, 194n63, 194n71
Gascoigne, George, *Jocasta*, 48
Geneva Bible: and "change," 73, 74, 90, 91, 96; I Corinthians 15:52, 69; and "taken away," 190n16
Gifford, Humfrey, *A Posie of Gilloflowers*, 142–43
Giraldi Cinzio, Giambattista, 14
Goldberg, Jonathan, 71–72, 134, 184n68, 206n34
Golding, Arthur: and Baret's *Alvearie*, 40; translation of Ovid's *Metamorphoses*, 30, 95, 195n81
Grantham, Henry, *An Italian Grammer*, 45, *46*, *49*

Greene, Roland, and "critical semantics," 33, 205n26
Greene's Groatsworth of Wit, 158
Griffin, Eric, 178n9
Grotius, Hugo, 171n45
Guazzo, Stefano, *Civil Conversatione*, 48
Guicciardini, Lodovico, *L'Hore di Ricreatione*, 53
Guilpin, Edward, 151

Hall, Edward, *The union of the two noble and illustrate famelies of Lancastre & Yorke*, inscriptions of Henry and Mary Dudley Sidney, 80, *81*
Halpern, Richard, 43, 58
Hannay, Margaret P., 71, 192n47, 193n57
Harington, John, 84
Hart, John, 13
Harvey, Gabriel: annotations in Aldine copy of Euripedes's plays, 48; annotations in copy of Scipione Lentulo, *An Italian Grammer*, trans. Henry Grantham, 1575, 45, *46*, 47, *49*, 182n36; annotations in Dolce's translations of classical drama, 188n119; annotations in *Sammelband* in English, Italian, Latin, and Spanish, 47–48, 182n43; continuously growing technique of language learning, 47; inscription in copy of Euripides, 209n66; inscription in copy of Florio, 182n37; Italian grammar bound with vernacular playbooks, 7, 33, 38, 67, 183n45; pamphlet exchange with Thomas Nashe, 148; project in vernacular-language learning and dramatic reading, 45; and role of dictionaries in vernacular language-learning practice, 48, 183n47; and wordplay, 182n42
Harvey, Richard, *A Theologicall Discourse of the Lamb of God and His Enemies*, 147, 148
Haughton, William, *Englishmen for My Money*, 5, 7, 196n1, 199n41, 204n13; and bringings, turnings, and conversions (translations), 122–25; critical view of as anti-alien or nationalist, 101, 196nn6–7; critical view of as "city" or "London" comedy and "usury play," 34, 100, 101, 130, 131, 160, 196n6, 203n82; homosocial friendship between foreign and native, and interchangeability, 101, 125–26, 129; linguistic challenges and failures of Englishmen as well as foreigners, 117, 118–19; linguistic commentary and language experimentation, 121–22, 127–28; metatheatrical meaning of disguises and "turning," 123–25; as new subgenre of cosmopolitan comedy of European languages, 130; notion of women's "city talk," 115; "stage language" or patois, 120; and status of Jews, 101, 120, 196n1, 196n7, 200n47, 201n60; theatrical expression of cosmopolitan vernaculars in mercantile-themed language manuals, 34, 99–102, 114, 119, 128, 130–31, 164; title, 116, 200n44; transition from education to romance, sex and reproduction, and money, 115–16, 128; translation, as practice of disguise (cross dressing) and religious transport to afterlife, 127; translational mode of interchangeability, 100–101, 115, 118, 120–26, 127, 131, 200n45; typographical illustration of foreign languages, 119–20
Heffernan, Megan, 170n26
Helgerson, Richard, 172n57; and Falstaff's transformation, 177n111; *Forms of Nationhood*, 163; on Jonson, 157; and Mistress Quickly, 177n117; on Prince Hal's tavern behavior as language lesson, 18
hendiadyses, 50
Herne the Hunter, 30
Hill, Eugene, 38, 187n113
Hoenselaars, A. J., 121
Hollyband, Claudius, 180n24, 181n28, 181n33; bilingual language manuals

and dictionaries, 17, 47, 50, 61, 67, 96, 118, 162, 163, 180n24, 196n5; *Campo di Fior*, 51; emphasis on understanding, 65; *The Frenche Littelton*, 43–44, 45, 180n27, 188n116; French-English dictionary, 195n86, 196n5, 199n31, 202n66; *The French Schoolemaister*, 42, 43, 57, 185n83; Italian dialogues, 48; and multilingual text of the *Colloquia*, 196n5; and techniques for classical-language learning applied to vernacular instruction, 43–44, 65; two-column presentation facilitating translation, 43–44
Hooks, Adam G., 170n26, 173n66
Hopkins, Lisa, 186n90
Horace, *Satires*, 211n87
Howard, Jean E., 121, 153, 157–58, 177n109, 196n6, 200n44, 201n60, 203n82, 206nn35–36
Howell, James, *Lexicon Tetraglotton*, 14, *15*
Huarte, Juan, *Examen de Ingenios*, 56
Hui, Isaac, 210n80, 211n88, 211n90
Huise, John, *A Perfect Survey of the English Tongue*, 44
Huntington Library, 211n88; and Harvey's *Sammelband*, 45, *46*, 47–48, *49*; language-learning publications annotated by Harvey, 47
Hyperius, Andreas, 73

The Images of the Old Testament, 47
indexing, development of, 212n9
"inkhorn terms," 14
Italian *mezzana* archtype, 3, 31
Italian riddles: academic and erotic, 142; in Aretino's dialogues, 143–46; availability in early modern England, 142–43, 146–48; "cock-riddles," 144; in Jonson's *Epicene*, 132–33, 142, 145, 154, 160. *See also* Aretino, Pietro
italic handwriting, 53, 78, 80, 82, *82*, 161, *162*, 184n68
italic type: indicating foreign words and phrases in dramatic publications, 118, 119–20, 132–33, 151, 153, 158, 168n7, 184n62, 203n2, 203n4; indicating foreign words and phrases in language-learning publications, 51, 54, 108–9, 163; indicating sententious value, 89

Janua Linguarum, 198n19
Jews and Judaism, 13, 120, 143; "alien" or "stranger" pertaining to discourse about, 188n4, 196n1; anti-Semitism, 11; "crypto-Jews," 101, 196n7; representation of, 201n60
Job, Book of, and "change," 1560 Geneva Bible, 73, 74, 90, 91, 96
Johnson, Samuel: editing of Shakespeare's works, 164, 165; *English Dictionary*, 164–66
Jones, Richard Foster, 16
Jonson, Ben, 5, 14, 66, 130, 163, 166, 211n86, 211n88; *The Alchemist*, 65; conflicted efforts to balance high and low, 157; contributions to *The Spanish Tragedy*, 187n111; *English Grammar* (1640), 32, 158; *Every Man in His Humour*, 64–65, 187n109, 187n112; *Every Man Out of His Humour*, 29, 126, 177n110; position between classical anglophone tradition and cosmopolitan vernaculars, 134–35, 157, 206n39; *Ragionamenti* (Aretino), Jonson's copy of, 7, 34, 151, *152*; self-styled "laureate dramatist," 157; *Volpone*, 32, 204n6; and William Camden, 34–35; *The Workes of Benjamin Jonson*, 8, 157, *158*, 158–59, 211n87
Jonson, Ben, *Epicene, or The Silent Woman*, 7, 34, 132–60, 164, 203n2, 206n35, 209n66; Aretino's *Ragionamenti* as Italian source for, 135, 140, 205n31, 206–7nn38–39; and "Cosmopoli," 148, *150*, 160; designation as "city comedy," 134, 140, 141, 160; "hermaphroditical authority" of Collegiate women, 153–56, 164, 210n76; inclusion of book of verses and

madrigals, 154–55; "Italian riddle," 132–33, 142, 145, 154, 160; Jonson's signature and motto on London edition of *Ragionamenti*, 151, *152*; opposition of masculine classical discourse and sexualized vernacular of Collegiates, 158–59, 164; poetic "figure of exchange" in, 196n4; references suggesting wider world and colonialism, 156, 164; and theatergrams of Aretino's *Il Marescalco*, 140–42, 151, 154, 160, 205n32; translation from female to male, 34, 159; translation of theatergrammatical elements of Aretino's dialogues, and propagation of women's speech, 34, 132–35, 140–42, 151, 153, 155–57, 159–60, 211n87; typographical marginal note, 133; vernacular linguistic cosmopolitanism, and misogyny, 135, 157–58

Keener, Andrew S., "Windsor's World of Words," 173n63
Kennett, John, 161
Kermode, Lloyd, 120, 129, 196n6, 200n45, 200n47
Kewes, Paulina, 194n71
King James Bible, 190n16, 190n20
Kiséry, András, 7, 45, 184n69, 187n111
Knight, Jeffrey Todd, 6, 212n6
Kolkovich, Elizabeth Zeman, 173n58, 177n117
Koppelman, George, 39, 42
Korda, Natasha, 177n110, 177n117
Krontiris, Tina, 133, 195n84
Kyd, Thomas, 5, 195n87; bilingual education and performance at Merchant Taylors' School under Mulcaster, 50–51, 55; and Shakespeare's *Hamlet*, 184n72; translation of Tasso's *Padre di Famiglia* and Garnier's *Cornélie*, 51
Kyd, Thomas, *Spanish Tragedy*, 178n7; among most in-demand printed plays of era, 63–64, 186n103; annotations in British Library copy, 53, *53*; Bel-imperia, and French language, 57; cosmopolitan vernaculars and linguistic instruction, 38, 164; critical view of multiple languages as incomprehensible or nationalist or xenophobic elements, 37, 178n5; discourse of cultivation, gardening, and profitability, 58–61, 186n90; discourse of fruit and bodily violence, 59–61, 186n92; Hieronimo's early devotion to "fruitless poetry," 54–55, 59, 61; Hieronimo's emphasis on ability of "tongues" to tell, 55, 184n73; Horatio's death in the garden, on title page, 59, *60*; instructional origins, 50–58; Italian phrases structured as proverbs in language manuals, 53–54; as language lessons for audience members, 38, 50, 66, 68; non-English words in early printed editions, 51, 183n58; performances in England and Continental Europe in various languages, 64; as possible "staged book" in Jonson's *Every Man in His Humour*, 64–65; printed editions as context for performance or circulation within the playhouse, 63–68, 184n63; theatrical expression of multiple vernaculars in dictionaries, grammars, and dialogues, 33, 38, 52, 66, 67–68; typography of early quartos, 51–52, 184n62
Kyd, Thomas, *Spanish Tragedy*, playlet within play (*Soliman and Perseda*): association of Hieronimo's Senecan playbook and his playlet, 66; in both English and "sundry" languages, 36–37, 58; "confusion" as mingling of multiple languages, 37, 61–62, 178n5; Hieronimo's linking of schoolroom and playhouse, 54–55; Hieronimo's reference to Toledo, 55; and language lessons for readers or playgoers, 50, 66–68; paratextual device translating the multiple languages into English in early quarto editions, 37, 65–68; as surrogate for deceased Horatio, 59

Lamb, Mary Ellen, 93
Landreth, David, 28, 167n2, 176n94
language instructors, foreign, in London, 116–17, 200n46
language-learning publications, multilingual: annotated in foreign languages, 7, 162–63; association of French vernacular with women and femininity, 57, 185n82; bridge from Latin schoolroom to vernacular drama, 3–4, 39–40, 44–45, 50, 54–55, 65–68, 123, 163 (*See also* Kyd, Thomas, *Spanish Tragedy*); double-translation method, 38, 39, 45, 164; foreign words and phrases in italics, 51, 54, 89, 108–9, 163; and instructional modes of translation, 38; mercantile-themed, and theatrical expression of cosmopolitan vernaculars, 34, 99–102, 114, 119, 128, 130–31, 164; and *Merry Wives*, 16–17, 22; multilingual manuals, grammars, and dictionaries for vernacular languages, 3, 17, 47, 67, 166; qualities of portability, format, and mise-en-page, 102, 197n12; shared features with printed drama, 3–8, 45; translation dialogues in terms of seduction, 21; visual assistance through typography, 44–45, 107–8, 181n33
Latin pedagogy, 39, 44, 179n13, 199n28
Lawrence, Jason, 79
Lentulo, Scipione, *Italicae Grammatices Praecepta ac Ratio*, 45, *46*, *49*, 182
Levine, Nina, 101, 117, 118, 121, 196n5
lexicons and indices, known in early modern era as "treasuries," 48
Lilly, William, 1
Lyon, France, publications in, 182n39, 197–98n15

Machiavelli, Niccolò, 147; *Mandragola* and *Clitia*, 48, 206n32; Machiavellianism, 51, 194n71
Magnusson, Lynne, on multilingualism of *Merry Wives*, 16, 17, 23, 176n91
manières de langage, 21
Mann, Jenny, and "vernacular eloquence," 43, 50
Marcus, Leah S., 16, 167n1
Marcus, Sharon, 6
Markham, Gervase, 147
Marlowe, Christopher, *Edward II*, 3, 88
Marot, Clément, 142
Marston, John, 151
Masten, Jeffrey, 12, 168n8, 172n50, 183n46, 186n101, 188n4, 192n41, 196n1, 198n20, 200n45, 202n71, 205n25, 208n28, 210n83
Mazzio, Carla, 4, 54, 169n16, 186n93; on *Spanish Tragedy* characterized by "linguistic incoherence," 37, 58; on Tomkis's *Lingua*, 137
McAlindon, Thomas, 62
Melchiori, Giorgio, 168n7, 174n68, 176n95, 176n101
Merchant Taylors' School, multilingual education and theatrical performances, 50–51, 55, 183n56
"messenger" character of Mistress Quickly, 2, 24–25; based on Italian *mezzana* archtype, 3, 31
Middleton, Thomas, 130, 187n106; *Roaring Girl* playbook, 64
Milton, John, 73
"minoritarian cosmopolitanisms," 11
Minsheu, John, 115, 183n58; association of "change" with inconstancy, 74; *Ductor in Linguas*, 113–14, 128; and emphasis on understanding, 65–66; Spanish-English dialogues, 52, 55–56, 65–66
Moffett, Thomas, 84
Montgomery, Marianne, 16, 38, 50, 51–52
Morley, Thomas, 192n36
Mornay, Philippe de, *Discours de la Vie et de la Mort*, 70, 87, 91, 194n63
Moulton, Ian, 207n47, 207n49, 208n52, 208n55
Mucedorus, 64, 186n103
Mulcaster, Richard: commendatory verse in Baret's *Alvearie*, 183n55; *Elementarie*, 59, 183n53;

"enfranchisement" (word-borrowing), 136; progressive view of English borrowing from vernacular languages, 50–51, 58, 59, 62, 67; recommendation of language instruction for women, 57, 93

Nardizzi, Vin, 186nn91–92
Nash, Thomas, *The Unfortunate Traveller*, praise for Aretino, 148
Nebrija, Antonio de, first European vernacular grammar, 10
"new cosmopolitanisms," 11
Newman, Karen, 115, 141, 206n35
Nussbaum, Martha C., 10, 11

Oakley-Brown, Liz, 94
oeconomia (household management), 59
Oldenburg, Scott, 101, 117, 173n62, 200n44, 202n77
Ostovich, Helen, 175n82
Ottoman subtexts, 206n36
Ovid, *Metamorphoses*, 30, 40, 94–96, *158*, 159, 195n81, 211n90
Oxford, as community of polyglot scholars and lexicographers, 44, 115, 180n26
Oxford English Dictionary (*OED*), 23–24, 61, 62, 73, 91, 93, 126, 186n95, 188n122, 190n14, 190n19, 191n21, 192n40, 193n57, 202n66, 202n69, 210n72

Parker, Patricia: and critical keywords, 33, 209n71; and *Epicene*'s "disposition," 159; and Falstaff's translation, 176n94, 177n111; and Florio's gendered language, 134; and gendered wordplay in *Merry Wives*, 1, 17, 26, 29
partial cosmopolitanism, 11
Perceval, Richard, *Bibliotheca Hispanica*, 47, 48, 52
performance and print, intersections of, 7–8, 63–68, 162–63
Petit, Jacques, 117
Petrarch: *Il Canzoniere*, 70; "Trionfo della Morte," Sidney Herbert's translation of, 70, 76–78, *79*, 84, 87, 91, 97
Philip II, King of Spain, 93
Phillips, Susan E., 207n47; on the *Colloquia*, 102, 105, 121; on premodern women's gossip, 207n45, 210n75; "Schoolmasters, Seduction, and Slavery," 18, 20, 175n78
Phiston, William (trans), *Lazarillo de Tormes*, 56
Pigman, G. W., III, 180n19
Pittenger, Elizabeth, 1, 177n116
Plutarch, 194n73; *Lives*, 92
Pollock, Sheldon, 11, 12; and adoption of Sanskrit literature's cosmopolitan aesthetic by regional South Asian courts, 8–9; "philologization" involving grammars and dictionaries, 171n32; and "vernaculars of necessity," 9
Ponsonby [Ponsonbie], William, 86
Pratt, Aaron T., 170n26
propagation, and translation: Florio's gendered treatment of, 123, 134, 135, 141; and women's speech in Jonson's *Epicene*, 34, 132–35, 140–42, 151, 153, 155–57, 159–60
prostitution, 134, 139, 146, 205n29
Ptholomaeus, Claudius, 142
Ptolemy, 55
Puttenham, George, *Arte of English Poesie*, 53, 137

Quilligan, Maureen, 12

Raber, Karen, 91, 194n65
Rancière, Jacques, 4
Rennecher, Hermann, 73
Riccard, Andrea, 114
Riddles of Heraclitus and Democritus, 142, 143
Robbins, Bruce, 10
Roberts, Jeanne Addison, 167n1
Rollock, Robert, 190n18
Roman type, 151, 184n62; as registering normatively as English against italic or black-letter type, 118, 120, 133; as

signaling a particular language, 44, 108, 109, 168n7
Rosenthal, Raymond, and Aretino's *Dialogues*, 144–47
Rubright, Marjorie, 198n18; on Dutch and English, 174n70, 179n10; on *Englishmen for My Money*, 101, 117, 119; on *Henry V*, 168n7; "Incorporating Kate," 175n88; on John Florio's approach to gender, 135, 211n90; and "presumptive monolingualism," 16, 196n2; "typographical relativism," 108

Sackville, Richard, 42
Sackville, Robert, 42–43, 161, 180n25, 188n2
Sackville, Thomas, *Gorboduc*, 42
Saint Martin (wine), 52, 184n65
Salmon, Vivian, 179n11
Sammelbände, 6, 7, 45, 47, 182n35
Sansovino, Francesco, 48
Santos, Kathryn Vomero: on Haughton's *Englishmen for My Money*, 197n8, 201n62, 202n76; on Kyd's *Spanish Tragedy*, 178n7, 202n76; on the "out-of-into" language associated with translation, 26, 194n64; on the treatment of immigrant characters in *Merry Wives*, 17, 27, 173n62, 176n106
schoolroom-to-playhouse model, 3–4, 39–40, 44–45, 50, 54–55, 65–68, 123, 163. *See also* vernacular education
Sebek, Barbara, 22–23, 176n105
secretary handwriting, 2, 42, 80, 82, *82*, 161
Shakespeare, William: *Antony and Cleopatra*, 98, 195n87; First Folio, 6, 170n29; *Hamlet*, 54, 58, 66, 67; *Henry IV Part I*, printed editions, 64, 187n103; *Henry IV Part I*, tavern scene, 18, 20, 22, 24, 175n77; *Henry V*, 21, 65, 136, 168n7, 176n92; *The Merchant of Venice*, 129; *A Midsummer Night's Dream*, and transformation of Bottom, 29, 31, 74, 95, 124, 126, 159; *Much Ado About Nothing*, 123, 202n71; *Othello*, 123, 126; *The Rape of Lucrece*, 174n66; Second Folio, *2*, 2–3, 167n6; *The Taming of the Shrew*, 115, 136, 200n43; *The Tempest*, coercive learning of Caliban, 10; *The Tempest*, "sea-change," 191n21; *Titus Andronicus*, 117, 201n51; and use of multilingual language manuals, 17–18, 20; *Venus and Adonis*, 174n66; *The Winter's Tale*, 122. *See also* Shakespeare, William, *The Merry Wives of Windsor*
Shakespeare, William, *The Merry Wives of Windsor*, 167nn1-3, 172–73nn57–58, 174n68; cosmopolitan mixing of foreign languages and English, 16–17, 173n63; critical tendencies toward "anglocentric bias," 16, 173n59; and cross-dressing as translation, 29–30, 159, 177n109, 177n111; as "English comedy," 14, 32, 164; Falstaff's appeal to seductions in classical mythology, 30; Falstaff's connections between sexual coercion and colonial conquests, 26, 164; Falstaff's translation of women's intentions for his own sexual desires, 25–26; Falstaff's use of translation undermined by counter-translations of multilingual women characters, 14, 16, 17, 27, 28–31; and "immigrant" characters, 17, 27–28, 173n62, 176n106; links to notions of translation and seduction in foreign-language manuals and dictionaries, 17, 22; marginal annotations, Second Folio, *2*, 2–3; Mistress Page, 167n2; Mistress Quickly (*See* Shakespeare, William, *The Merry Wives of Windsor*, Mistress Quickly); multiple senses of "conveyance," 28–29; and power of translation, 31; prioritization of folio text above 1602 quarto, 16, 173n58; seductive translations, 25–32; translinguistic ability of the Host of the Garter, 27–28;

transposition of foreign vernaculars onto stage and back into print, 14, 16–17

Shakespeare, William, *The Merry Wives of Windsor*, Mistress Quickly, 14, 16, 175n81; boundary-crossing and mixing of languages, 1–3; and Continental wines, 22–23; critical claims of malapropisms, 1, 23; as a "free-lance mezzana," 168n10; as linguistic "go-between," 2, 17, 22, 176n91; linking of with messenger-god in the 1662 *Colloquia*, 24; and links between language learning, translation, and reproductive and erotic vocabularies, 1; and links to chambermaid-hostess (Joan) in the *Colloquia*, 22, 25, 31, 175n83; multilingualism bridging national and linguistic communities, 22, 23, 24, 31; as "Queen of Fairies," 31, 177n117; Venice Second Folio, designation as German woman in marginal annotations, *2*, 2–3, 21, 31; words and phrases of polyglot dictionaries, 22–24

Shapiro, James, 188n4, 196n1

Sherman, William H., 6

Sherwood, Robert, *French Tutour*, 57

Short Introduction of Grammar (William Lilly and John Colet), 1

Sidney, Henry, and Mary Dudley Sidney's inscriptions in Edward Hall, *The union of the two noble and illustrate famelies of Lancastre & Yorke*, 80, *81*

Sidney, Mary Dudley (mother of Countess of Pembroke), 78, 79–80, *81*

Sidney, Philip: *Apologie for Poetry*, 70, 188n5; *Astrophil and Stella*, 69–70, 78, 98, 188n1; collaborator on the Sidney Psalms, 80, 83; "Dictionaries methode" surfacing in drama, 118; elegy for 195n85; "English Petrarch," 70, 80; named "translated . . . translator" by John Donne alongside sister Mary Sidney Herbert, 69, 71, 83, 91; and Spenser's *Ruins of Time*, 86

Sidney Herbert, Mary, Countess of Pembroke, 5, 57, *85*, 188n3, 189n7, 193n58, 193–94nn62–63, 194n73, 195n76, 195n82, 195n87; and annotated Italian-English dictionary with lines from Petrarch's "Trionfo della Morte," 7, 33, 78–79, *79*, *82*, 82–83, 98, 161, 192n34, 192n36, 192nn39–41, 192n44, 192nn47–48; collaborator on the Sidney Psalms, 80, 83; the Countess of Pembroke holding a book of "Davids Psalmes," engraved by Simon van de Passe, 84, *85*; "denizen" Psalms of King David, 13, 70, 85, 86; "Dictionaries method," 76, 78; discourse of translation and change from contemporary sermons on death of the righteous, 77; elegy for Philip Sidney, 195n85; named "translated . . . translator" by John Donne alongside brother Philip Sidney, 69, 71, 83, 91; thematic concern with transcendence of worldliness, 77–78, 84; translation as both worldly practice and heavenly passage, 84, 86; translation of Mornay's *Un Discours de la Vie et de la Mort*, 70, 87, 91, 98; translation of Petrarch's "Trionfo della Morte," 7, 33, 70, 76–78, 79, 83, 192n36; translations of Psalms, 13, 33, 70, 80, 83–86, 91, 193nn50–51, 193nn57–58

Sidney Herbert, Mary, Countess of Pembroke, *The Tragedy of Antony*, 7, 33, 86–92, 189n8, 189n11; change, and worldly threat of domination by foreign powers and inevitability of death, 90–91; chorus, and comfort of death over the mutability and suffering of the world, 89, 90–92; Cleopatra's multilingual facility and skill as translator, 34, 92–93; Cleopatra's resistance to change, 93–94; as "closet drama," 7–8, 33, 70–71, 72, 86, 87, 97, 163; critical views of as women-centered version of *ars moriendi*, 71, 92, 97; first publication

with translation of Mornay's *Discours de la Vie et de la Mort*, 87; influence on further translations of "Antony and Cleopatra" genre, 97–98; inseparability of linguistic and religious translation, 70, 71, 72, 98; and Ovid's *Metamorphoses*, 94–96; reflection on death as devotional and cosmopolitan, 72; resolution in sanctified change or translation to divine afterlife, 86, 87, 90–92, 94–97, 126, 164; theme of humanity's inconstancy, 86, 87–89; themes of change, mutability, and alteration, 88–89; as translation of Robert Garnier play, 57, 70–71, 98, 194nn69–70; use of European cosmopolitan vernaculars, 71
Siemon, James, 167n6
Skretkowicz, Victor, 71, 92
Smith, Emma, 100
Sofer, Andrew, 187n107
Spark, John, 161
Spenser, Edmund, 76, 148; *Mutability Cantos*, 75, 86, 91; *Ruines of Time*, 86
Sperrazza, Whitney, 195n82
Stage, Kelly J., 101, 118, 124, 203n82, 210n85
"staged books," 64
Stallybrass, Peter, 12, 157, 205n27
Stanier, James, 114
Stepney, William, *The Spanish Schoole-master*, 18, 174n73
Stern, Tiffany, 63, 65, 186n99, 187n106, 188n120
Stern, Virginia F., 47
Sternhold, Thomas, translation of Solomon's proverbs, 80
Stigliani, Tommaso, 142
Symonds, John Addington, and origins of *Epicene*, 140
Symonds, Matthew, 182n43

Tasso, Torquato, 48; *Padre di Famiglia*, 51
Terence, comedies of, 47
theater, early modern English: border-crossing tendencies, 5, 6, 8, 57–58, 70–71, 76, 96–97, 122, 128, 169n22; costume plots, 29; discourse of translation as propagation, 134; discourse on ethnic "turning," 123; gendered costuming practices and gender politics, 123; interplay between print and performance, 8, 63–68; and language dialogues, 8; language-learning publications as bridge from Latin schoolroom to vernacular drama, 3–4, 39–40, 44–45, 50, 54–55, 65–68, 123, 163; and "staged books," 64; theatrical expression of cosmopolitan vernaculars in mercantile-themed language manuals, 34, 99–102, 114, 119, 128, 130–31, 164; transnational approaches of studies of, 5
theatergrammatical elements, 6, 141; of Aretino's dialogues in Jonson's *Epicene*, 34, 140–42, 151, 153, 155–57, 159–60
Thomas, William, *Principal Rules of the Italian Grammer*, 42, 48, 164–65, 188n2, 183n47; emphasis on understanding, 65, 70; inscriptions in Sidney family copy of, 78–79, *79*, *82*, 82–83, 188n2, 192n39–41
Thorius, John, *Spanish Grammer*, 50, 67, 115; copy owned by Gabriel Harvey, 47; first London-published manual, 44–45; guide to words in *The Spanish Tragedy*, 52
Toledo: and Escuela de Traductores Toledanos, 55–56; linguistic preeminence, 55–57
Tomkis, Thomas, *Lingua: Or The Combat of the Tongue, And the five Senses for Superiority*, 34, 135; and male rejection of propagation or transmission of multilingual skills to female speaker, 137–40; translation, and linguistic multiplicity, 137–40
Torriano, Giovanni, *Vocabolario Italiano & Inglese*, 114
Traister, Barbara, 175n82
translatio imperii, 178n9, 187n113
translation, early modern England, 4; as

ascendance or reception into heaven or afterlife, 72–76, 86, 87, 90–92, 94–98, 127, 190n18; and "change," 72–76, 90–91, 96; drama of, 32–35; and linguistic multiplicity, 136–40; modes of, 32–33; and propagation (*See* propagation, and translation); translational mode of instruction, 38–45, 66; translational mode of interchangeability, 100–101, 115, 118, 120–26, 127, 131, 200n45. *See also* Jonson, Ben, *Epicene, or The Silent Woman*; Shakespeare, William, *The Merry Wives of Windsor*; Sidney Herbert, Mary, Countess of Pembroke, *The Tragedy of Antony*

transubstantiation, doctrine of, Protestant scorn for, 75

Traub, Valerie, 12, 175n88, 203n80

Tudeau-Clayton, Margaret, 4, 51, 136, 169n17, 174n68, 175n81, 176n93, 179n14, 189n5, 191n30, 197n7, 198n17, 205n28

"turnings," 122–25

typography, 201n54, 202n71, 203n4; and performance, 184n63, 197n10; typographical illustration of foreign languages in multilingual language-learning and dramatic publications, 33, 44–45, 51–52, 107–8, 119–20, 181n33; "typographical relativism," 108–9

van de Passe, Simon, engraving of the Countess of Pembroke holding a book of "Davids Psalmes," 84, *85*

Vaughan, Robert, engraving of "ACQVAINTANCE," 105, *106*

Vautrollier, Thomas, 17

Venice Second Folio, *2*, 2–3, 6, 31

Venuti, Lawrence, and "translator's invisibility," 134

vernacular education: and dictionaries, 48, 50; language instructors in London, 116–17, 200n46; language-learning publications as bridge from Latin schoolroom to vernacular drama, 3–4, 39–40, 44–45, 50, 54–55, 65–68, 123, 163; multilingual education and performance at Merchant Taylors' School, 50–51, 55; multilingual language-learning books produced in classroom setting, 39–40; Toledo's linguistic preeminence, 55–57. *See also* language-learning publications, multilingual

"vernacular eloquence," 43, 50

Verstegan, Richard, *A Restitution of Decayed Intelligence in Antiquities*, 124, 137, 139, 201n65

Vicars, John, *A Prospective Glasse to Looke Into Heaven*, 76, 77

Vitkus, Daniel, 123

Wade, Mara, 167n6

Wall, Wendy, 30, 177n117, 202n78

Waller, Gary F., 76–77, 86, 193n55

Wall-Randell, Sarah, and "staged books," 64

Watson, Robert N., theater as "one-large-room schoolhouse," 63

Webster, John, *Duchess of Malfi*, 118

Wechsler, Daniel, 39

Werner, Sarah, 170n26

Werner, Winter Jade, 172n47

West, William N., 178n5

Whitly, John, 161

Whitly, Samuel, 161

Williams, Deanne, 16, 176n92, 176n94., 200n43

Williams, William, 114

Wilson, Thomas, *Christian Dictionary*, 75

Wofford, Susanne, 206n33

Wolfe, Heather, 167n6, 179n15, 192n39, 192n41

Wolfe, John, 34, 48, 156, 181nn32–33, 183n45, 207n50, 208n54, 208n56, 209n66; *The Book of the Courtier*, 109, 199n27; Italian-language books, 44; Italian-language editions of Aretino's *Ragionamenti*, 147–48, 151, 153; multilingual typography, 44, 181n33

women, early modern England: academy for, early modern association with frivolity and promiscuity, 153; and "city talk," 115, 160, 206n35; erotic rhymes and riddles in Aretino's dialogues, 143–46; and French language study, 57, 185n82; language instruction for, 57, 93; and notion of women's writing, 71, 97, 203n5, 204n8; and propagation of women's speech, 34, 132–35, 140–42, 151, 153, 155–57, 159–60; regulation of, and efforts to civilize, 157–59; transnational tradition of gossip, 155–56. *See also* Shakespeare, William, *The Merry Wives of Windsor*

Woodrington, Robert, 161

"world of words," 27, 28, 97, 114, 166

Wroth, Mary, 78, 83

Yates, Frances A., 151, 208n54

Yates, Julian, 12, 168–69n15

Zeno, Apostolo, 167n6

Zucker, Adam, 31, 154, 172n57, 177n112, 177n114, 177n116